The Emancipation of Europe's Muslims

PRINCETON STUDIES IN MUSLIM POLITICS

Series Editors: Dale F. Eickelman and Augustus Richard Norton

A list of titles in this series can be found at the back of the book.

The Emancipation of Europe's Muslims

THE STATE'S ROLE IN MINORITY INTEGRATION

Jonathan Laurence

PRINCETON UNIVERSITY PRESS

PRINCETON AND OXFORD

Copyright © 2012 by Princeton University Press
Published by Princeton University Press, 41 William Street, Princeton, New Jersey 08540
In the United Kingdom: Princeton University Press, 6 Oxford Street, Woodstock,
Oxfordshire OX20 1TW

All Rights Reserved

ISBN: 978-0-691-14421-4 (cloth)
ISBN: 978-0-691-14422-1 (pbk)

Library of Congress Control Number: 2011931886

British Library Cataloging-in-Publication Data is available

This book has been composed in Palatino

Printed on acid-free paper ∞

press.princeton.edu

Printed in the United States of America

10   9   8   7   6   5   4   3   2   1

To my family

Contents

Illustrations

Tables

Abbreviations

AAE	*Amicale des algériens en Europe* (Fraternal organization of Algerians in Europe)
AIVD	*Algemene Inlichtingen- en Veiligheidsdienst* (Dutch General Intelligence and Security Service)
AKF	al-Khoei Foundation
AKP	*Adalet ve Kalkınma Partisi* (Turkish Justice and Development Party)
AQIM	Al Qaeda in the Maghreb
ATCMF	*Amicale des Travailleurs et Commerçants Marocains en France* (Fraternal organization of Moroccan workers and merchants in France)
CSU	Christlich-Soziale Union (Christian Social Union in Bavaria)
BMF	British Muslim Forum
BMI	*Bundesministerium des Innern* (German Federal Ministry of the Interior)
CII	*Consiglio Islamico d'Italia* (Italian Islamic Council)
CCME	*Le Conseil de la communauté marocaine à l'étranger* (Council for the Moroccan Community Abroad)
CFCM	*Conseil français du culte musulman* (French Council of the Muslim Faith)
CGI	Contact Groep Islam (Dutch Contact Group with Islam)
CGIL	*Confederazione Generale Italiana del Lavoro* (Italian General Confederation of Labour)
CGT	*Confédération Générale du Travail* (French General Labor Confederation)
CICI	*Centro Islamico Culturale d'Italia* (Italian Islamic Cultural Centre)
CIE	Council on Islamic Education
CIMG	*Communauté islamique de Millî Görüş* (French Islamic Community of the National Vision)
CLG	Department for Community and Local Government
CMO	*Contactorgaan Moslims en Overheid* (Dutch Contact Organ of Muslims and Government)
CORIF	*Conseil d'Orientation et de Réflexion sur l'Islam en France* (The Council of Reflection on Islam in France)
COREIS	*Comunità Religiosa Islamica* (Italian Islamic Religious Community)

CRCM	*Conseil Régional du Culte Musulman* (Regional Councils for the Muslim Faith)
CRIF	*Conseil représentatif des institutions juives de France* (Representative Council of French Jewish Institutions)
Comintern	Communist International
DİB	*Diyanet İşleri Başkanliği* (Turkish directorate for religious affairs)
DIK	*Deutsche Islam Konferenz* (German Islam Conference)
DİTİB	*Diyanet İşleri Türk İslam Birliği* (Turkish-Islamic Union for Religious Affairs)
EAD	Euro-Arab Dialogue
ECFR	European Council for Fatwa and Research
EEC	European Economic Community
EI	Embassy Islam
ELCO	*Enseignement des langues et cultures d'origine* (Teaching of languages and cultures of origin)
EMB	*L'Exécutif des musulmans de Belgique* (Muslims' Executive Council of Belgium)
EMF	*Étudiants musulmans de France* (Muslim Students of France)
EU	European Union
FEERI	*Federación Española de Entidades Religiosas Islámicas* (Spanish Federation of Islamic Religious Entities)
FEMYSO	Forum of European Muslim Youth and Student Organisations
FHII	*La Fondation Hassan II pour les Marocains Résidant à l'étranger* (Hassan II Foundation for Moroccans living abroad)
FIOE	Federation of Islamic Organizations in Europe
FION	*Federatie van Islamitische Organisaties Nederland* (Federation of Islamic Organizations in the Netherlands)
FNMF	*Fédération nationale des musulmans de France* (National Federation of French Muslims)
FOSIS	Federation of Student Islamic Societies in the UK and Ireland
GDP	Gross domestic product
GICM	*Groupe islamique combatant marocain* (Moroccan Islamic Combatant Group)
GMI	*Giovani Musulmani d'Italia* (Young Muslims of Italy)
GMP	*Grande Mosquée de Paris* (Great Mosque of Paris)
GSPC	*Groupe salafiste de combat et predication* (Salafist Group for Preaching and Combat)
ICC	Islamic Cultural Center

ICE	Islamic Council of Europe
ICMG	Islamic Community of *Millî Görüş* (National Vision)
IESH	*Institut Européen des Sciences de l'Homme* (European Institute for Human Sciences)
IGD	*Islamische Gemeinschaft Deutschland* (Islamic Community of Germany)
IGMG	*Islamische Gemeinschaft Millî Görüş* (Islamic Community of the National Vision)
IIFSO	International Islamic Federation of Student Organzations
IMA	*Institut du monde arabe* (Institute for the Arab World)
ISB	Islamic Society of Britain
IYO	Islamic youth organization
JI	*Jama'at-i Islami* (Islamic Community)
JMF	*Jeunes musulmans de France* (Young Muslims of France)
LICEP	*Ligue internationalle cojépienne* (International COJEP league)
MAB	Muslim Association of Britain
MB	Muslim Brotherhood (*Ikhwan al-Muslimin*)
MCB	Muslim Council of Britain
MEMRI	Middle East Media Research Institute
MG	*Millî Görüş* (National Vision)
MG-J	*Millî Görüş Jugendabteilung* (Youth Divisino)
MG-Y	Millî Görüş Youth
MGIT	*Millî Görüş Italia Teskilati* (Italian Organization of the National Vision)
MGNN	*Milli Görüş* of the North Netherlands
MJD	*Muslimische Jugend Deutschland* (Muslim Youth of Germany)
MINAB	Mosques and Imams National Advisory Board
MRA	Ministry of Religious Affairs
MRE	*Marocains résidents à l'étranger* (Moroccans living abroad)
MSA	Muslim student associations
MSP	Movement of the Society for Peace
MWL	Muslim World League (*Rabitat al Alam al Islami*)
NGO	Non-governmental organization
OIC	Organisation of the Islamic Conference
OPEC	Organization of the Petroleum Exporting Countries
PI	Political Islam
PLO	Palestine Liberation Organization
RMF	*Rassemblement des musulmans de France* (Gathering of French Muslims)
UCIDE	*Unión de Comunidades Islámicas de España* (Union of Islamic Communities in Spain)

UCOII	*Unione delle Comunità e Organizzazioni Islamiche in Italia* (Union of Islamic Communities and Organizations in Italy)
UJM	*Union des jeunes musulmans* (Union of Young Muslims)
UKIM	United Kingdom Islamic Mission
UOIF	*Union des Organisations Islamiques de France* (Union of Islamic Organizations of France)
YMUK	Young Muslims United Kingdom
ZMD	*Zentralrat der Muslime in Deutschland* (Central Council of Muslims in Germany)
WAMY	World Assembly of Muslim Youth

Preface

THE TITLE OF THIS BOOK might seem to reflect wishful thinking by the author: it appears at a moment of rising criticism of Islamic religious practices, as European governments of left and right renounce past "excesses" of religious toleration toward Islam. As the type is being set, the French government was following up a "grand debate on national identity" with a ban on burkas and a supplementary debate on secularism and Islam. German discussions of a federal banker's book on how Muslims are "dumbing down" the country threatened to re-open the German question. The Dutch Kingdom was busy reevaluating its centuries-long tradition of religious toleration. Italian officials debated whether or not to place a moratorium on mosque construction following Switzerland's minaret ban. Given the succession of official restrictions on the outward expression of Muslim piety, and the fact that public opinion has grown increasingly skeptical of Muslims' integration, perhaps the ambiance is not best described as "emancipatory." In early 2011, a former presidential advisor in France even called on fellow Muslims to start wearing a "green star."

An American correspondent writing seventy years ago observed that in early-twentieth-century Europe, "emancipation and democratic ideals are so closely related, they are bound to share the same fate." The decline of emancipation, he wrote, "preceded or was followed closely by the decline of democracy and liberalism."[1] However, it would be inappropriate to interpret contemporary restrictions on Islamic religious practices as a prefiguration of mass denaturalization or deportation. Today's nativist voices ask for cultural sacrifices and adaptation as a condition of national membership and as such are actually echoing the policy agenda of European governments toward Muslim communities in the past twenty years. No retrogression of emancipation is conceivable, however, without the coming to term of emancipation in the first place—and this is still under way.

The fitting analogy for the uneven entry of Muslims into contemporary European politics is therefore neither 1791 nor 1938, but rather a handful of nation-building moments in between. This book's use of the term "emancipation" reflects neither activism nor optimism, but instead the cold-eyed pragmatism of governing techniques born of the nineteenth century and periodically revived to integrate groups into the social, economic, and political life of the nation. Emancipation should be understood here as the initiation—not the end state—of a formal process in which a group enters the democratic order. The application of the rule of law and equal rights and obligations to the group as *citizens* is expected to lead over time to political, civil, and legal equality. The experience of other religious minorities—notably, nineteenth-century Jews, Protestants, and Catholics—suggests that the recent anti-Islam backlash is a natural counterpart to the historic process of Muslim integration into European politics and society that began only a couple of decades ago.

The timeline of events related to Muslims' emancipation has been remarkably compressed. When I began fieldwork in the late 1990s in Germany, France, and Italy to examine the role of religious communities in immigrant integration, my object of study—state-mosque relations—had yet to come into formal existence. To be sure, the cities I visited already bore ample traces common to immigration societies across the Western world. Predominantly "ethnic" neighborhoods—and their houses of worship—took the place of upwardly mobile working classes. Public housing and social welfare budgets came under strain from a surge of new users. There was also cautious ethnic mixing at the edges, unavoidable in cuisine, popular music, and youth culture. The riders on urban mass transit systems formed a more visibly diverse crowd toward the ends of the line. Many-hued groups of schoolchildren out for field trips could be seen happily navigating city sidewalks, one another's wrists loosely tied together for safety—a walking metaphor for the next generation's pluralist future. But the material shortages of religious infrastructure in Europe, and the politicization of Islam in North Africa and the Middle East, led to a spillover of Islamic practices into the public sphere—e.g., the classic examples of headscarves worn in schools, lambs slaughtered in bathtubs, and prayer mats laid on the sidewalk—that led to tensions and a growing gap of perceptions between the new minority and their European host societies.

European governments were not prepared for this: at the time, the religious practices of Muslims were still filed under the category of foreign affairs. In the early years of this project, my search for official interlocutors brought me mostly to the offices of immigration authorities and diplomats—not parliaments and interior ministries. Islam remained basically unknown as a domestic political issue to politicians and administrators alike. Islamic community structures in European cities reflected—and reinforced —this state of affairs. My first meetings with religious leaders took place either in consular annexes or what appeared to be foreign political parties' constituency offices. Local and national authorities did not yet have the quality of institutional contacts with Islamic communities that they enjoyed with other religious groups. Islam's "foreignness" became a self-fulfilling prophecy.

This book highlights the largely untold narrative of a process of "domesticating" Islam that began in the mid-1990s and accelerated in the aftermath of Islam-inspired terrorist events in Europe and the United States in the early 2000s. A new political consensus—and administrative praxis—took hold before my eyes, reflecting the spreading pragmatic recognition of Muslims' irreversible presence in Europe. The decade from the mid-1990s to the mid-2000s was a period of major growth in state-Islam relations: Gone were the ad hoc responses, the interministerial working groups, and in came corporatist-style institution building and the establishment of "state-mosque" relations. A nineteenth-century flavor pervades recent policymaking toward Muslim communities, from governments' insistence on screening foreign clergy to the administrative oversight and imposition of a hierarchy on religious associations. But the intersection of Islamic communities' evolution in Europe together with recent political and religious developments in their countries of origin and the broader Muslim-majority world—from Islamist movements to the most recent wave of democratization—also roots this story unmistakably in the late twentieth and early twenty-first centuries.

Completion of this book leaves me indebted to many who generously gave of their time and knowledge. I am particularly grateful to Stanley Hoffmann and Peter A. Hall of Harvard University for their early and persistent encouragement and guidance. Several communities helped shape this project, and my time getting acquainted with the material was enriched by the hospitality of the following institutions and individuals. In Berlin, Ruud Koopmans of the Wissenschaftszentrum Berlin, and Paul Statham, now of the University of Bristol, got me on my feet and remained close friends and colleagues. The Minda de Gunzburg Center for European Studies was a crossroads of European scholars and American researchers, many of whom left an imprint on this work. I am especially grateful to Yoshiko Herrera, of the University of Wisconson–Madison for her constructive criticism at a key moment in this book's development. My current and former colleagues at the Center on the US and Europe of the Brookings Institution—Justin Vaïsse, Andrew Moffatt, Amanda Kefalas, Jeremy Shapiro, Phil Gordon, Dan Benjamin, and Fiona Hill—provided a friendly and invigorating niche. The faculty and students at Boston College have welcomed me into a collegial, supportive, and stimulating intellectual home.

For their incisive critiques at different stages, I thank Noah Dauber, Ines Michalowski, Rahsaan Maxwell, Michael Jones-Correa, Jytte Klausen, Sheri Berman, Carolyn Warner, Hugh Roberts, Romain Garbaye, Peter Mandaville, Ray Koslowski, Sidney Tarrow, Nick Ziegler, José Pedro Zúquete, Andrew Gould, and an anonymous reviewer. I also learned a great deal from fellow participants in the Bellagio Dialogue on Immigration, the Transatlantic Dialogue on Islam, and from my co-organizers of conferences on religion and political integration at Sciences Po, Woodrow Wilson Center, the Transatlantic Academy, and the Friedrich Ebert Stiftung.

The various stages of researching and writing behind this book were steeped in the hospitality and academic camaraderie of the following individuals and their colleagues: Stephen Szabo of the Transatlantic Academy; Martin Schain of NYU's Center for European Studies; Peter D. Hall of the Hauser Center at Harvard Kennedy School; Ariane Chebel d'Appollonia and Francis Vérillaud of Sciences Po; Abby Collins and Anna Popiel of the Minda de Gunzburg Center for European Studies; Konstanza Prinzessin zu Löwenstein and Jütta Höhne of the Wissenschaftszentrum Berlin. The support of these institutions made possible stretches of writing and a cumulative thirty months of fieldwork between the fall of 1998 and the winter of 2011 in France, Germany, and Italy, in addition to shorter stints of 1–2 weeks in the Netherlands, Belgium, Ireland, United Kingdom, Morocco, and Turkey. I gratefully acknowledge the research and/or travel support from the above-named institutions in addition to the Deustcher Akademischer Austauschdienst, the Clough Center for Constitutional Democracy at Boston College, and the Office of the Dean of the College of Arts and Sciences at Boston College.

Studying political institutions at their moment of development is challenging and thrilling. In order to help slow these moving targets to an observable speed, I benefited from the patient advice of academics and local experts who provided introductions to politicians, civil servants, and religious community leaders, who in turn took time from negotiating with each other to explain their positions to an outsider. I wish to recognize the contribution to this book of all my interview respondents in hundreds of conversations during those twelve years. Many of these became regular discussion partners, and I am deeply indebted to them, although I cannot cite them all here by name. I would also like to acknowledge the advice and generosity of those who helped orient me during fieldwork—alas, this list is nowhere near exhaustive: Mounir Azzaoui, Alon Bar, Alain Boyer, Khédidjia Bourcart, Federica Caciagli, Sebastiano Cardi, Robin Doeswijk, Jean-Marc Dreyfus, Abdelhak Eddouk, Hakim Elghissassi, Claire de Galembert, Bertrand Gaume, Azzedine Gaci, Bernard Godard, Jean-Pierre Guardiola, Barbara John, Ian Johnson, Riva Kastoryano, Merve Kavakci, Didier Leschi, Zouhair Louassini, Giancarlo Loquenzi, Gregory Maniatis, Raffaello Mattarazzo, Frédéric Martel, Anna Nardini, Veysel Özcan, Alessandro Orsini, Cem Özdemir, Yahya Pallavicini, Dimitiri Papadimitriou, Diana Pinto, Abdinasser Rezkallah, Cecilia Rinaldini, Nathalie Serfaty, Vianney Sévaistre, Levent Soysal, Riem Spielhaus, Fabrizio Spinetti, Jean Tillie, Allen Tobias, Patrick Weil.

For their dedicated assistance with research and manuscript preparation at Boston College, my heartfelt recognition goes to Rebecca Clark, John Delea, Alex Harris, Stephanie Keller, Andrew Lim, Chris Maroshegyi, Kerem Oge, Iulia Padeanu, Jennifer Unter, Michael Weston-Murphy, and Krista Yacovone.

For sharing permission to reprint their photographs or images, I wish to thank Bernard Godard, Yahya Pallavicini, the Ministero dell'Interno, Fotografie Katy Otto/Deutsche Islam Konferenz, Islamische Gemeinschaft *Millî Görüş*, Saudi Aramco World/PADIA, and Pew Research Center's Forum on Religion & Public Life.

Finally, I owe so much—not least, a phone call—to the friends who have enriched recent years with conversation and kindness: Adèle, Adelheid, Alessandra, Alex, Allegra, Altinaï, Antje, Béatrice, Bella, Benjamina, Bernd, Cecilia, Cem, Christophe, Dodi, Elie, Erika, Flori, Emanuele, Emma, Federica, Frank, Fabrice, Fabio, Hartmut, Hubert, Ilana, Ines, Jacob, Jamie, Jean-Marc, Jean-Pierre, Jeremy, Jessica, Julia, Justin, Karin, Laura, Léa, Leland, Lew, Lucila, Lynne, Maple, Marie-Pierre, Marion, Martino, Nathalie, Noah, Michael, Paul, Peter, Régis, Roger, Pia, Raffaello, Rahsaan, Richard, Riem, Ruud, Semjon, Sergey, Shilpa, Stephan, Sylvie, Tarek, Thomas, Thorsten, Veysel, Wei-Li, Will, Zouhair, Züli and others.

This book is dedicated to my family—to my parents, my sister and her family, and in particular to my wife and daughters. Their love and candor enabled me to complete what often felt like a daunting project, and have given meaning to all the spaces in between.

The Emancipation of Europe's Muslims

CHAPTER ONE

A Leap in the Dark

MUSLIMS AND THE STATE IN
TWENTY-FIRST-CENTURY EUROPE

JUST OVER 1 PERCENT of the world's 1.5 billion Muslims reside in Western Europe, yet this immigrant-origin minority has had a disproportionate impact on religion and politics in its new and former homelands. The Muslim population ballooned in just fifty years from some tens of thousands to 16 or 17 million—approximately one out of every twenty-five Western Europeans—in 2010. During the formative decades of this settlement (1960–1990), Europeans permitted foreign governments and NGOs from the Islamic world to have a free hand in shaping Muslims' religious and political life. But persistent integration difficulties and sporadic terrorism persuaded European governments that their laissez-faire approach had far-reaching unintended consequences on host societies' way of life. Between 1990 and 2010, authorities across Europe belatedly acknowledged that the once-temporary labor migrants—and now, their children and grandchildren—are part of the permanent demographic and political landscape. Their earlier hesitation incurred costs, however, and their newfound sense of ownership is plagued by ambivalence. With projections showing continued demographic growth before leveling off at 25–30 million people (or 7–8%) in 2030, Western European governments have no choice but to look upon their Muslim minorities today as angels imprisoned in a block of marble: a community of new and future citizens whose contours are still being sculpted.[1]

As European Muslims have become more numerous and visible in public life in the past decade, national governments have expended time, effort, and resources on pursuing policies that would encourage the integration of these immigrant-origin populations. The consolidating instinct of the nation-state has been in full resurgence, as governments across Europe conspicuously pursue the preservation of national identity, social cohesion, and "guiding culture." Measures have ranged from religious restrictions—such as banning burkas, minarets, or headscarves—to civic impositions, like mandatory language and integration courses and citizenship tests. In the realm of state-mosque relations,

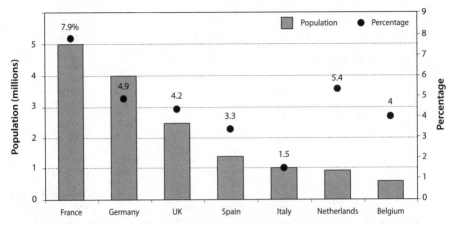

Figure 1.1. Largest Muslim Minorities in Western Europe. Note: These seven countries account for more than 90 percent of the approximately 16.3 million Muslims in Western Europe. Sources: Casa Arabe 2009; Haug et al. 2009; Kerba 2009; Laurence and Vaisse 2006; European Muslim Network 2007; European Parliament 2007.

European governments have encouraged the development of national forms of Islam by way of formal councils and consultative bodies. If there was ever a mythical postwar era of "multiculturalism" in which host societies sent mixed signals to new arrivals about the cultural expectations of national citizenship, a new and more demanding phase has replaced it.

For host societies like Britain, France, Germany, Italy, the Netherlands and Spain, Islam in Europe is no longer just a matter of ginger diplomacy with former colonies or current trading partners: the integration of Muslims has become a nation-building challenge of historical significance. This religious minority is novel for its sheer scale and swift pace of migratory settlement: Muslims now make up 4–8 percent of their national populations—and several times that proportion in some cities (see figures 1.1, 1.2, and 1.3). Foreign governments and transnational nongovernmental organizations (NGOs) continue to compete for influence over the Islamic diaspora, but Muslims' permanent settlement in Europe now places this competition squarely within domestic politics.

In important respects, European countries have been here before: in the past two hundred years, Jews, Catholics, Protestants, working classes, women, and other ethnic minority or migrant groups once absent from the body politic gradually acquired full citizenship and in many cases were granted "group" access to representative institutions. Not all groups

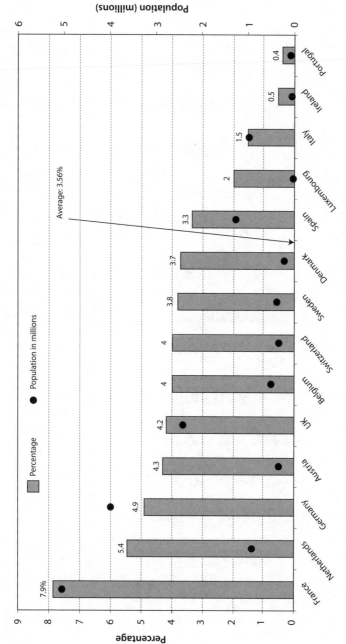

Figure 1.2. Muslims as a Percentage of Western European Population. Sources: Casa Arabe 2009; Haug et al. 2009; Kerba 2009; Laurence and Vaisse 2006; European Muslim Network 2007; European Parliament 2007.

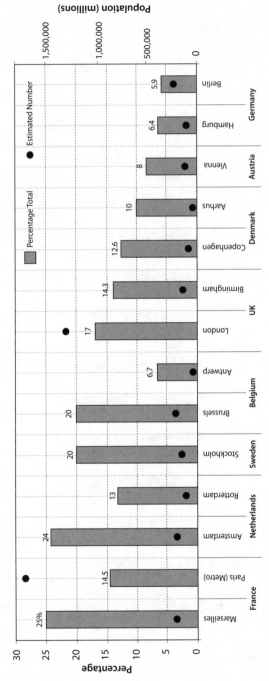

Figure 1.3. Muslims as a Percentage of Population in Selected Western European Cities. Source: "Muslim Population in European Cities (a compilation of statistical sources)", http://islamineurope.blogspot.com/2007/11/muslim-population-in-european-cities.html.

(or host societies) made the transition without difficulty, and in different contexts those challenges also produced radicalism, persistent integration problems, or political violence. Integration never depended purely on individual equality before the law. In the words of a nineteenth-century historian, "The real touchstone for success . . . was its collective emancipation."[2]

The institutional responses during these earlier moments of "emancipation" left behind an architecture of state-society relations and consultative mechanisms which governments today have restored to facilitate the integration of Muslim communities. European nation-states now face an added challenge in comparison with the past: the persistence of foreign interests that keep a hand in European Muslim life. Today, the interaction of religion policies in Europe and the Muslim world has geopolitical resonance.

During the half-century since the first guestworkers arrived, official and nongovernmental religious organizations originating in the Islamic world supplied funding and personnel in support of rival political-religious tendencies in European mosques and cultural centers. Diasporas play a decisive role for the main countries of emigration—Algeria, Morocco, Pakistan, and Turkey—some of which are still in an intermediate phase of political and economic development. For them, Europe is home to 50–85 percent of their nationals living abroad: roughly four million Turks, three million Algerians, three million Moroccans, and two million Pakistanis.[3] These European residents remain a reservoir of support or opposition for homeland regimes, including the remittances and investments that make up a significant portion of homeland GDP as well as extremist elements that plot political violence at home. Europe's Muslims have also been the target of extensive missionary work by transnational Islamist movements—based in Saudi Arabia, Egypt, Libya, Pakistan, but also in Europe—who aim to strengthen their own religious hegemony within the international *ummah*. Viewed from the capitals of the Islamic world, the Muslim diaspora vacillates between the role of budding vanguard or potential rearguard.

The crucial years of 1989–1990 provided an early glimpse of a newly politicized minority—during the first headscarf affair, the Rushdie Affair, the first Iraq war—and national governments in Europe soon afterward began to take "ownership" of their Muslim communities. In particular, they initiated the process of bringing Islamic leadership into state-church institutions to mitigate the religion's "foreignness" and to gain regulatory oversight over mosques and prayer rooms. After leaving them outside domestic institutions, public authorities across Europe have come to encourage Muslims to embrace national citizenship and to pursue the institutional adaptation of Islamic organizations.

Nonetheless, Muslims' long-term integration into European politics and society is a work in progress. Across the region, a lively debate rages over Islam's compatibility—and Muslims' ability and willingness—to accept the rule of law and the separation of religion from the public sphere. The populist right wing's growing share in several major immigration countries reflects mounting anxiety about the threat posed to national identity and national security by a permanent and growing Islamic minority. Several major fault lines of international conflict of the last forty years lie in the Middle East, which has amplified the significance of Muslims' political and religious orientations in Europe as an issue of domestic and international interest.

Many Muslims living in these countries, in turn, feel stigmatized by growing antagonism toward their religious background—negative feelings about Muslims reached 35–60 percent in a recent European study—and so they experience an increasingly scrutinized existence.[4] A flurry of restrictive legislation marked the first decade of this century: governments passed laws to prohibit mainstream religious symbols such as minarets and headscarves, as well as less widespread cultural practices associated with the Islamic world like burkas, polygamy, and forced marriages. Official and informal opposition to mosque construction is increasingly commonplace, as is the conditioning of naturalization on "moderate" religious practice.

The repressive measures that have put Muslim communities on the defensive, in fact, belie a broader trend toward greater religious freedom and institutional representation for Islam in Europe over the last twenty years. The gestures of restriction and toleration are complementary and part of a unified process. European Muslims are experiencing the throes of a distilled and abbreviated era of emancipation: a dual movement of expanding religious liberty *and* increasing control exerted over religion.[5] Every religious community that has joined the national fabric accepted certain restrictions on its freedoms and autonomy at the moment of recognition: from the use of local clergy who preach in the local language, to abandoning distinctive dress in the public sphere.[6] As Muslims are transitioning from a majority-immigrant to majority-citizen group, European states have begun the effort to relieve what they consider excessive pressures of foreign political or religious influences.

This dual movement is most visible in the officially encouraged "privatization" of religious practices—the nineteenth-century injunction, for example, to "be a man in the street and a Jew at home . . . a brother to your countrymen and a servant to your king"[7]—that other religious communities have also experienced during the modern era. The variegated experience of post-Emancipation Jewish minorities in

Europe also illustrates the dangers of unresolved tension between individual and collective rights. This is reflected in the preoccupation that communities must effectively sacrifice their distinctiveness and collective identity in the name of legal and political equality, compounded by the sinking fear that they may never entirely escape suspicion and persecution. With the contemporary restrictions of visible Islamic symbols, host societies trace the outer limits for practices which they consider beyond the pale. But there is much more *within the pale* that is now treated as routine. Until 1990, European Muslims existed in a pre-emancipatory state: adult migrants (and sometimes their native-born children) enjoyed highly circumscribed political rights, subject to limits on freedom of assembly and association, to voting, holding public office, and public employment.[8] The basic rights and freedoms granted to religious communities, too, were largely out of reach in the absence of citizenship. Between 1990 and 2010, European governments implemented new policies, raising standards and expectations for the integration of newcomers, but they have made citizenship more accessible and increased both individual *and* collective equality before the law for those who were already there.

Today, national interior ministries across Europe help oversee and coordinate the routinization and banalization of Islamic religious practices in Europe (what one French Muslim leader has called "the right to indifference," in opposition to "the right to be different"): the financing and construction of mosques; the civic integration of imams; the appointment of Muslim chaplains in prisons, the army, and hospitals; the design of religious curriculum in publicly funded schools; and the celebration of major holidays and religious events—from lamb slaughter for Eid al-Adha to the pilgrimage to Mecca. There are now thousands of Islamic houses of worship—2,100 in France, 2,600 in Germany, 1,200 in the UK, 661 in Italy, 450 in Spain, 432 in the Netherlands[9]—and thousands of imams who preach and lead prayer in these mosques. Muslim schoolchildren are increasingly free to choose an Islamic education class at school or to attend a publicly subsidized Islamic school, and Islamic theology chairs in public universities—to train religion teachers as well as prayer leaders—are gradually being endowed. These developments are not yet on a par with other religious communities, but they are the rights and privileges—from the controversial to the mundane—that make up the business of state-mosque relations.

Contemporary Islam Councils are the culmination of a search for "moderate" yet legitimate interlocutors who can negotiate a representative bargain with the state in exchange for a monopoly on a set of narrowly defined religious issues. Together, these policies aimed to ensure that both public claims and private practices associated with the group are accorded similar rights—and are subject to similar restrictions—as any other recognized group under national law.

However difficult and unique the contemporary difficulties with Islamic groups could appear, the challenges today's governments face and the strategies they have adopted echo earlier institutional interactions with "new" groups of citizens. European states have pursued a twofold strategy of incorporation toward Muslims in the early twenty-first century—full citizenship followed by institutional organization—similar to what they did for nineteenth-century emancipated Jews and for the newly enfranchised working classes in the early twentieth century. First, governments have sought to establish the bases for participation in state and society as equal citizens, irrespective of affiliations an individual may privately hold. Second, they endeavored to bind the group's associations to the state through formal relations and corporatist institution-building. The political philosopher Wendy Brown has observed the paradoxical nature of this sort of recognition: it "redraws the very configurations and effects of power" from which the individuals were apparently being freed.[10]

UNINTENDED CONSEQUENCES

European countries have rich and complex pasts with the Islamic world, including cultural, intellectual, and commercial exchange, but also more than a millennium of reciprocal conquest and colonization. The historic settlement of a permanent Muslim minority in Western Europe, however, took place in a period of relative peace and prosperity between the mid-twentieth-century retraction of European empires and the end of the Cold War. With the exception of the relatively small number who sought refuge from persecution in their countries of origin, today's European Muslim populations are the result of voluntary economic migration and its aftermath.

Western European economies stimulated by the Marshall Plan were in full expansion in the 1960s, and governments secured foreign manual labor in a series of bilateral accords as Europeans looked to states with which they had former colonial ties or earlier diplomatic alliances as natural sources of manpower: for the United Kingdom this was Pakistan and India; for France, it was Algeria, Morocco, and Tunisia; for Germany, it was Turkey. The predominantly Muslim Mediterranean basin and South Asian subcontinent provided most of the temporary workers who satisfied the growing domestic and international demand for mass manufactured goods: from automobiles and pharmaceuticals, to textiles and household appliances. In the 1960s and early 1970s, the "Muslims of Europe" were a single male group.

The worker rotation schemes in place functioned as planned for a decade: men came and went, and remittances were sent to the old country, where homes were built and families were supported. The workers lived in dormitories, and socialized or prayed with one another in clubs sponsored by their countries of origin. Despite the arrival of hundreds of thousands of refugees from Algeria (Harkis), Iran, or Turkey (Kurds), for example, the predominant host society policies were consistent with a straightforward "guestworker" arrangement, and the Muslim presence did not raise domestic political antennae. The expectation of *temporary* migration meant that governments avoided the question of Muslims' status in European societies and treated Islam as the religion of foreigners. Every European government, whether it overtly embraced "multiculturalism" or not, accepted foreign funds and allowed outside authorities—from Morocco and Turkey to Saudi Arabia and Libya and beyond—to exert influence on the religious practices of their local Muslim population.

But an unplanned if unsurprising development took place in the late 1960s and early 1970s when the economy soured, first due to a small recession and then major stagnation following the oil shock of 1973. Europeans raised the immigration drawbridge and foreign workers could no longer rotate in and out at will. They stayed, and with the aid of high court rulings across Europe in the mid-1970s, began to bring over spouses, children, fiancées, and other family members. Within a decade, the relatively self-contained and low-maintenance male population was transformed into a more dynamic and unwieldy minority of men, women, children, and extended families.

The precise number of immigrant-origin individuals of Muslim background living in Western Europe today is elusive, but national estimates total approximately 16–17 million (see figure 1.4 for geographic distribution).[11] Muslims' natural population growth helped slow demographic decline in Europe, but it also raised policy questions that a temporary male laborer population never had: from social welfare, education, and health care, to cultural and religious adaptation to the host society. Instead of continuing to build "bridges to the homeland," European governments realized they would have to get more involved if they wanted to influence the design of durable edifices that others were constructing on their territory.[12]

The Swiss novelist Max Frisch's remark that Europeans were startled to find that they had "called for guestworkers, and human beings came instead" took on special meaning in several significant policy areas in the 1990s.[13] The unexpected settlement of an Islamic-origin minority

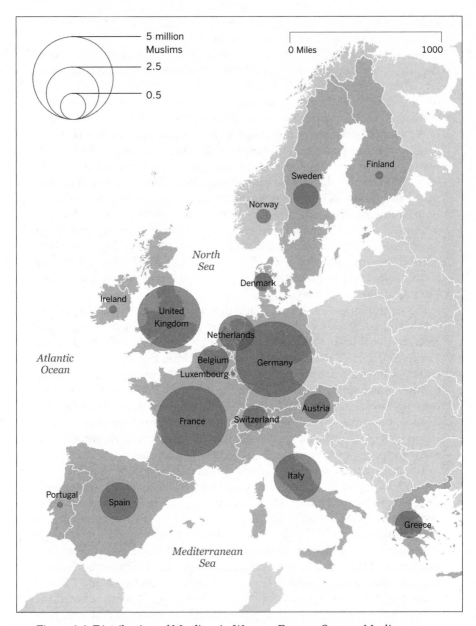

Figure 1.4. Distribution of Muslims in Western Europe. Source: *Muslim Networks and Movements in Western Europe*, Pew Research Center's Forum on Religion & Public Life, © 2010, Pew Research Center. http://pewforum.org/.

has raised a set of fundamental questions dear to concerned observers and political scientists alike, and which this book attempts to tackle: How do democratic governments cope with the emergence of new religious communities? How are new groups of citizens incorporated? What is the appropriate relationship between religious diasporas and their countries of origin or with international religious movements? How are challenging or threatening ideologies from abroad reconciled with the domestic rule of law? And finally, what is the relationship between governments' policies and groups' integration outcomes?

It may seem at times that the political and social integration of Muslims in Europe has already failed spectacularly. This century's first decade brought a succession of grim news, from bombings in Britain and Spain to assassination in the Netherlands, from French riots to German unemployment, prompting observers to declare a grave crisis of previous models of immigrant integration.[14] Second- and third-generation immigrants experience disproportionately high unemployment, widespread social discrimination, and feeble political representation in local and national institutions. The French scholar Gilles Kepel commented that Europe faces an urgent choice: "either we train our Muslims to become global citizens, who live in a democratic, pluralist society, or on the contrary, the Islamists win, and take over those Muslim European constituencies. Then we're in serious trouble."[15] This captures the *raison d'état* that inspires current policies toward Islam but misstates the relevant policy arena: European governments want to fashion *national* citizens who are *less* globally interlinked. To use an analogy from the first era of modern state-building, today's states attempt to make Frenchmen, Germans, or Italians out of Muslims—as previous generations undertook the state-building process of turning "peasants into Frenchmen," Jews into "*Israélites*," or Christians into "good citizens."

Between 1990 and 2010, governments across Western Europe actively sought to facilitate this alchemy by integrating Islam into state-church relations: a progressive reclaiming, domestication, and national orientation has taken place. During those twenty years, organized Islam in Europe progressed from being unregulated, unrecognized, and underfunded to coming under state oversight and receiving its associated benefits and restrictions.

The Establishment of Islam Councils

The most striking illustration of a Europe-wide move toward the "domestication" of Islam—and the summit of the process of institutional recognition—came with the development of national consultations with prayer spaces and civil society organizations. Between 1990 and 2010, national interior ministries established local and national "Islam Councils"—from the French Council for the Muslim Religion, the Spanish Islamic Commission, the Belgian Muslim Executive, the Italian Islamic Consultation, to the German Islam Conference—comprising the religious leadership of foreign governments, NGOs, and prominent Muslim citizens active in their territories (see table 1.1). The creation of these councils guarantees equal access to religious freedoms at the same time that they exert control by placing the state in the familiar role of broker and guarantor of religious freedoms.

The parallel development of Islam Councils in these countries was the result of key policy actors finding similar solutions to similar problems. European governments have created local and national councils to resolve practical issues of religious freedom and infrastructure—imams, chaplains, mosques, education, halal food, etc.—for their Muslim citizens and residents. But the essence of state-mosque relations is a twofold struggle on a higher plane: first, to free European Muslims from direct foreign government oversight. And second, to induce the "moderation" of the religious organizations linked to transnational Islamist movements. Governments' goal is to diminish the foreign ties of Islamic prayer spaces and leadership, and to attract the participation of "moderate" political-religious movements within state-mosque relations. To understand the ambition of these councils, one needs to take into account not only the evolution of religion policy in Muslim-majority states between the moment of modern state formation and the departure of emigrants in diaspora, but also the ways in which Islamic movements have been transformed upon contact with the institutional parallelism they have encountered across Europe. European governments are not just reconciling Islam with the western democratic state; they are tampering with a fragile equilibrium in the respective host countries and entire Islamic world, intentionally or not.

Government ministries involved in this consultation process do not presume the existence of some essential "Muslim" waiting to be whitewashed into a mythical "citizen." But regardless of Muslims' diversity of national origin, piety, and religious affiliation, governments in Europe have nonetheless come to see "their" Muslims as a community, a collectivity, and the object of public policymaking. Religion was not the first or only trait that governments took on: outreach programs in favor of naturalization, linguistic integration, civic knowledge, and political participation have all had their day. But religion policy in particular allows European governments to gradually take "ownership" of their Muslim populations because it grants them unique influence over organizations and leadership within this hard-to-reach minority. European

TABLE 1.1
Islam Councils in Western Europe

Name	Date founded
Islamische Glaubensgemeinschaft in Österreich (IGGiÖ, Austria)	1979
Islamiska Samarbetsrådets (IS, Sweden)	1990
Comisión Islámica de España (CIE, Spain)	1992
Exécutif des musulmans de Belgique (EMB, Belgium)	1994
Conseil français du culte musulman (CFCM, France)	2003
Contactorgaan Moslims en Overheid (CMO, Netherlands)	2004
Consulta per l'Islam in Italia (CII, Italy)	2005
Deutsche Islam Konferenz (DIK, Germany)	2006
Mosques and Imams National Advisory Board (MINAB, United Kingdom)	2006

states exercise an unusual amount of regulatory control over state-church issues from the controversial to the mundane: entry/residence visas for clergy and diplomatic religious counselors, tax breaks and nonprofit status for religious organizations, construction permits for prayer space, the licensing of slaughterhouses. Administrators are not engaged in the special accommodation of Muslims; they are incorporating Islam into pre-existing state-church institutions. European governments are trying to create the institutional conditions for the emergence of an Italian or German Islam, e.g., rather than just tolerating Islam "in" Italy or Germany.

Councils are also often pointed to as a way to deny oxygen to religious extremists who allege a general Western hostility to Islam. State-mosque relations reinforce religious freedom and create a shared sense of belonging by reaching out to respected religious leaders in Europe and ensuring that Muslims can fully practice their faith in European contexts. By bringing Islam in, these governments hoped to diminish the risks of the exposure of Europe's Muslims to the globalized marketplace of religious ideas, poor socioeconomic integration, local religious tensions, and the shortcomings of Europeans' other integration policies. This layered agenda was, I argue, expressed in policies that grant religious rights to Muslims while affirming the state's oversight authority and the rule of law.

While important milestones in the "citizen-ization" of Europe's Muslim population and the "naturalization" of Islam have been achieved, the situation remains in flux. The status and role granted within the Councils to a select group of mosques and other religious organizations—i.e., those who represent Muslim positions on everyday "religious questions"— remain among the most contentious and pressing issues in European politics today. In a debate rife with speculation and extrapolation, state-mosque relations are happily grounded in concrete facts and measurable relationships and institutional behavior. This permits the evaluation of the growing track record of Islamic organizations' most sustained encounter with democratic institutions outside the Muslim-majority world. Do Islamic groups adapt to Western institutions or not? How have governments attempted to shepherd this process? This book examines the constructive and interventionist side of Europeans' Islam policies: the organization of Islamic groups for state-mosque relations.[16]

The Islam Councils were created to bring state-mosque relations out of the embassies and Foreign Affairs ministries, and into domestic political institutions. Broadly speaking, consultations have also succeeded in bringing the groups indirectly associated with political Islam in Europe (e.g., Muslim Brotherhood, Millî Görüş, Jam'aat-i Islami) to accept the conditions of participation and join in council elections. The councils establish participants' citizenship bona fides, encourage the reconciliation of religious observance with the rule of law and the institutionalized expression of dissent, and meet the demand of Islamic religious associations for recognition and interest representation. The councils provide a channel of communication between religious groups and the state, which is necessary to establish a framework for Muslims' religious equality in European countries, but they have also proven useful in times of crisis or cultural tensions. These institutions may be destined for obscurity—just like the nineteenth-century Israelite consistories or the trade union–oriented Labor Councils before them—but they serve an important purpose at the time. The creation of Islam Councils marks a breakthrough as significant and peremptory as a common European currency or the laying of a mosque cornerstone in a city center. From this moment on, Islam is an integral part of the political landscape (figures 1.5, 1.6, and 1.7 show Islam Councils at work in France, Germany, and Italy).

THE ARGUMENT IN BRIEF: FROM OUTSOURCING TO INCORPORATION

Despite their historical, institutional and cultural differences, the seven European countries with the largest Muslim minorities—Belgium, France, Germany, Italy, Netherlands, Spain, and the United Kingdom—

Figure 1.5. Election of the Bureau exécutif of the *Conseil français du culte musulman*, 2003. Source: © Bernard Godard.

have followed remarkably similar pathways to managing their relations with Islam and they display parallel policy developments. The specific mechanisms differ according to the institutional and political features of each country, but state-mosque relations in all of them share broad characteristics: a first stage (1960–1990) when European governments

Figure 1.6. Meeting of the *Deutsche Islam Konferenz*, 2010. Source: © Fotografie Katy Otto / Deutsche Islam Konferenz.

Figure 1.7. Meeting of the *Consulta per l'Islam italiano*, 2006. Source: © Yahya Pallavicini.

outsourced the management of Islam. And then, a second stage (1990–2010) during which European countries pursued the *incorporation* of religious NGOs, Embassy Islam, and other Muslim notables by way of the creation of an Islam Council.

The second stage repeats the patterns of relationship that the emancipation and eventual "citizen-ization" of the Jewish communities of these countries took following the Napoleonic example. It also resembles in many of its central mechanisms the neo-corporatist strategies more familiar from the political-economic realm. Governments have treated the challenge of Islam not primarily as a problem of human rights but as a subtle task of administration: to build a framework for state-society relations that would isolate religious affairs from the social, economic, and political bases of Muslims' integration. How to provide Muslim chaplains to prisons and the army, where to bury the Muslim dead, or how and where to construct mosques and train imams were the issues that drove the response of the European states to Islamic communities. This book stresses the omnipresent needs of democratic states for advice about such issues and for the search for "moderate" and "representative" interlocutors to provide that advice: the result is a portrait of state-society relations that aims to bring the discussion back to its fundamentals.

Any consideration of how different European governments have attempted to institutionalize Islam must first recognize the underlying goals of a government that initiates this process. Why would a state accommodate the practical requirements of religious communities? Although some stentorian voices will always warn that religious accommodation is the equivalent of political capitulation, it paradoxically has actually been the painful method through which the modern state has asserted itself: first, by changing the nature of individuals' relationship to organized religion; and second, by explicitly requiring religious communities to subjugate religious law to the national constitutional order. Here, accommodation is a mechanism for securing a community's respect for state authority. It is an act that enables and legitimates a collective subnational—or supranational—identity, certainly, but it is also a process of political control.

There is no perfect historical analogy for the settlement of millions of Muslims and the development of complex layers of religious organizations. But the emergence of Muslims as a permanent segment of national society has evoked familiar questions about the relationship between religious faith, political ideologies, and loyalty that European states have encountered before: How to persuade civil-society organizations to operate within the framework of domestic laws? How to reduce the influence of potentially seditious ideologies? How to create a unified interlocutor to channel community demands? Similar or even greater challenges to their authority and political legitimacy confronted European nation-states in the relatively recent past: Catholic, Protestant, and Jewish minorities in the period of nation-formation, and the newly enfranchised working classes after the industrial revolution and during the consolidation of the modern state.

In earlier centuries, statesmen had objected in different national contexts to the collective emancipation of the Catholics, Protestant or Jews or, later, the working classes, on the grounds that the trans-border fealty of these communities threatened national political unity. Their presumed sympathies with foreign powers—e.g., Jewish Britons for the Ottoman Empire, French Protestants for the German states, German Catholics for Rome, Italian workers for Moscow—endangered and slowed these groups' equality before the law. Although the scale of Jewish migration from Central and Eastern to Western Europe never approached the magnitude of arrivals from the Muslim world, the percentage of Jews in some Western European cities did approximate the proportion of Muslims in urban areas today.[17] Political Catholicism, furthermore, was viewed by governments as a mortal danger to nascent liberal states in the nineteenth century – sometimes leading to the prohibition of specific religious orders.[18] The millions of working-class voters who flirted with international revolutionary movements in the early decades of the twentieth century were similarly perceived as a threat to constitutional orders in Western Europe, leading to restrictions on the political activities of trade unions and political parties.[19]

There is ample precedent for the struggle of twenty-first-century politicians in contemporary Europe to disentangle Islamic organizations from their international linkages and root them in domestic institutional contexts. Democratizing countries in Europe responded to political tensions related to social class and religion—and parliaments' inadequacy at resolving them—in the form of top-down negotiation with economic and religious interest groups, respectively, —over the heads of "the people's" elected representatives and "modify[ing] in fact the sovereignty of parliament."[20] Extra-parliamentary consultation has a long pedigree, beginning with nineteenth- and early twentieth-century profession-based and religious corporatism through postwar race-oriented, agricultural, and trade union–oriented neo-corporatism. By institutionalizing Islam today, states convey their interest in reforming religion or in transforming how citizens relate to their religion. Olivier Roy writes that this implies a "westernization" of religious belonging "in a theological sense, i.e. its dogmatic content" and "in forms of religiosity: the relationship of the faithful to a universal liturgy."[21]

Scholars currently argue either that there are big differences between the Islam policies of European countries or that the countries are converging toward international norms. I distinguish my approach from that of path dependency enthusiasts, post-nationalists, and the disciples of convergence theory by placing the nation-state back at the center of discussions of religious politics. This framework is rooted in my empirical finding that European policy responses to Muslim communities have not been dictated by "inherited" institutional traits,[22] nor by post-national forces such as supra-national regulation or shared values,[23] nor by cross-national convergence toward more inclusive citizenship rights.[24] Across a striking range of countries, Islam Councils are the instrument through which Islamic organizations and the state now cooperate on a broad and substantive range of issues, including appointing chaplains in prisons and the armies, the civic education of imams, mosque construction, faculty chairs, religion teacher training as well as symbolic roles like sitting on public broadcasting or overseeing halal slaughter rituals.

The richest data in this book come from the French, German, British, and Italian cases for which I was able to conduct extensive fieldwork and interviews; but a conscientious effort was made to include the Netherlands, Belgium, and Spain—where I spent shorter periods of time— and other European cases as often as possible. The cross-national parallels in state-mosque relations that I observe across these countries owe nothing to a unified or coordinated approach, but are rather a case of similar solutions being pursued in the face of similar challenges— a concept that an Italian politician once referred to as "convergenze parallele"—for their own separate, national reasons. A broad, uncoordinated effort of institution-building is under way. The parallel development of Islam Councils shows that governments do not simply reproduce existing policy regimes, like trains barreling down pre-set tracks to different destinations. The primary sources of public policy are self-interest and realism, that motivate states to change: we are witnessing the assertion of national sovereignty, with a modicum of cross-border learning. The trend toward the active integration of Muslim communities across Europe today is that governments have treated relations with Islamic representatives in similar terms across divergent national contexts. These developments have not entailed a loss of national sovereignty; indeed, they reflect a shared affirmation of the nation-state's supremacy.

One might counter this argument with the alternative hypothesis that the creation of some sort of Islamic interlocutor is an almost inevitable response to terror attacks, which would privilege another explanation, namely: 9/11, 3/11, and 7/7. The violence committed by Islamic extremists—including longtime European residents and citizens—on three days in the early years of the twenty-first century has had an undeniable impact on the development of state-mosque relations, and had major consequences for perceptions and treatment of the religious community in state and society. But while terrorism focused the minds of officials and has served as a catalyst for the overtures to Muslim communities, the process of state-building that would encompass the new Muslim minority had already been under way for a decade before September 2001.

Islam Councils in European countries differ from one another in two important dimensions: the ambit of their working agenda and the ideological breadth of their participants. In some cases, councils are intended to "represent" only the mosque-going public, and the working agenda is strictly limited to state-church affairs (France). In others, the councils cover issues that affect all Muslims regardless of formal religious observance, such as religion in public schools (Germany and Italy), and the working groups are more likely include topics like social values and gender relations. Since these are institutions with unique internal voting mechanisms, the way governments designed electoral systems determines the proportion of seats ultimately assigned to representatives of Embassy Islam, religious NGOs, or other Muslim notables. In particular, the invitation to Islamist groups to participate has sometimes been linked to their acceptance of a "values charter." There is also variation in the councils' respective bureaucratic efficiency and religious governance at the local or national levels, but they share striking institutional commonalities—and have remained relatively stable through internal leadership alternation and successive left- and right-leaning national governments.

Governments have altered their approaches to Muslim communities over a fifty-year period, as a function of domestic politics, international relations, and exogenous shocks (including terrorism), and Islamic religious actors have responded to these policy shifts by adapting to national political opportunity structures. State-mosque relations have shaped the nature of Muslim leaders' political participation and the extent of Islam's integration in their respective national settings. Countries that successfully pursued *incorporation* have elicited moderate political participation from Political-Islam groups, and Embassy Islam actors have adapted their diaspora outreach to fit the new domestic contexts of Islam in Europe. Both categories of religious leaders have adjusted the style and content of their religious activities to fit the new institutional contexts of national Islam Councils.

In a broader theoretical context regarding the survival of the nation-state, this book presents evidence that the state is alive and well in the age of globalization. Islam-related conflict in the public sphere is often portrayed as evidence of weak or defensive states overrun by transnational religious movements. But the European Muslim experience is marked by robust state responses, in line with Stephen Krasner's view that "globalization and state activity have moved in tandem."[25] Just because Islam remains a transnational phenomenon does not mean that is intractable to the Western democratic state's purposes.

In the sustained effort to integrate Muslim leaders and mosques into local and national state-Islam institutions, the contemporary European nation-state appears not as a "weathervane" being spun around by shifting gales, nor as a neutral broker among competing interests, but rather as an interested actor that structures the incorporation of new interests.[26] Two decades of increasingly assertive policies toward organized Islam in Europe, between 1990 and 2010, militate against the image of states meekly acquiescing to the unplanned settlement of an adversarial religious minority. This book contributes to the growing evidence that states remain important actors despite the ascendance of market ideals and transnational forces.[27]

The development of state-mosque relations has already borne some fruit. Many practical accommodations are now in place that reconcile Islamic practices with the European *Rechtstaat*. The nascent Islam Councils have been forged and tested by crises—headscarf and burka bans, homegrown terrorism, blasphemy controversies, national identity debates—and survived. Whether they will arrive at a stable equilibrium and enter historical posterity is a test of the relevance and strength of the national state to filter the transnational forces exerted on its citizens in a globalized world. For now, it is unfinished work, and even the adaptation of transnational networks to domestic contexts can sometimes have ambiguous effects.

One significant irony of the new integration-minded approach is the degree to which Europeans' state activism has inspired countries in the Muslim-majority world to revitalize ties with their emigrant diasporas in Europe. In the last ten years, southern Mediterranean governments have institutionalized outreach to their national communities living abroad, mirroring the inroads that Western European governments have tried to make within these same population groups. Contrary to earlier expectations from the social science literature that political, economic, and religious links between successive generations of migrants and erstwhile sending states tend to diminish over time, there has been an unexpected resurgence of governmental activity for citizens abroad—including expanded access to elections, investment opportunities, and religion services.[28] Former sending countries have brought to life a growing thicket of emigrant-oriented bureaucracies, where hundreds of officials are charged with the para-diplomatic duties of maintaining political, economic, and religious ties with their respective communities of origin residing in Europe.

Even though Islam Councils have been established, it would be misleading to assume that a new era of domestic normalcy is completely under way. Homeland governments in North Africa, Turkey, and outside actors in the broader Middle East are still a highly influential force on Islam in Europe. This trend is at tension with the spirit of rhetorical consensus: the fostering of a "German" Islam, "French" Islam, "Italian" or "British" Islam, etc. The mosques and Islamic leadership sanctioned by Islam Councils are still overwhelmingly foreign-run and foreign-staffed. Regular meetings of European ministers with officials in the Islamic world—from Ankara to Islamabad, and Rabat to Cairo—have led, in particular, to the sustained practice of importing imams and funding for mosque construction.[29] At the same time that European ministers declared Islam to be an integral part of their respective national fabrics, they have continued to extend and renew foreign influence over their Muslim minorities—often for compelling pragmatic reasons but to the detriment of their institution-building efforts.

THE STRUCTURE OF THE BOOK

The body of chapters between the introduction and conclusion is divided into thirds. Chapters 2 and 3 introduce the main Islamic "actors" in Europe—including foreign envoys and transnational dissident networks—and describe how they got there and how European Islam policies at the time of their arrival influenced their position within Muslim communities. Chapters 4 and 5 treat the theoretical bases of creating consultative councils and offer an empirical profile of how European countries arrived at parallel policy responses with the creation of Islam Councils. Chapters 6 and 7 evaluate the performance of the Islam Councils, how they have influenced the political behavior of religious organizations, and where they fit into the broader question of Muslim integration into European politics and society.

Chapter 2. European Outsourcing and Embassy Islam: *L'islam, c'est moi*. European governments refrained from active intervention during the initial phase of state-mosque relations (1960–1990), during which they tolerated—and formalized—foreign embassies' free reign over the development of Islamic religious infrastructure. In this first period, Europe conceded minority rights to Muslim labor migrants in exchange for foreign governments' guarantees of economic stability (e.g., trade and oil supply) and European political influence in the greater Middle East. The Embassy Islam networks exported imams, built mosques, and established domestically registered federations in Europe to extend the reach of the official homeland religion. European governments allowed this for practical reasons—the foreign sponsors had the experience and resources to provide religious infrastructure for Muslims—and in part to avoid a less desirable alternative: the imams who represented Islamist opposition in their home countries might import a revolutionary or violent form of the religion to Europe. There were clear electoral and geopolitical disincentives—from potential instability in North Africa, Turkey, and the Middle East, to insurgent right-wing parties at home—against engaging this new Muslim minority as if it were to be a permanent segment of national society.

Scholars have made much of German-speaking countries' use of the term *Gastarbeiter* (guestworker) to contrast the immigrant integration experience there compared to, say, that of Britain or France, where citizenship was granted more casually—what Brubaker called the "genealogical" versus "geographic" boundaries of European nations.[30] A little understood fact of Muslims' settlement—and the lag in Europeans' policymaking with regard to integrating them—is that they were broadly viewed as "guestworkers" in nearly every host society. Even in self-described immigration societies like Britain and France, governments hoped that the newcomers would return home. They actively pursued expulsion policies and return migration incentives that prevented a view of the immigrant community as a permanent presence from taking hold well into the 1980s. This coincided with an expansion in sending states' exportation of official religion in furtherance of their ties with diaspora populations, on whose cash remittances they depended and whose Islamic activism they feared.

Chapter 3. A Politicized Minority: *The Qur'ân is our constitution.* The third chapter addresses the growth of Political Islam and transnational religious NGOs in Western Europe. While the European receiving states were granting a de facto monopoly of religious representation to the diplomatic envoys of immigrants' sending states, competing networks of well-organized activists with a more conservative, politicized view of Islam also flourished on the margins of religious community life.[31] Political-Islam federations also provided prayer spaces, imams, lecturers, and social activities and established what may best be described as an Islamist subculture. Although such organizations may represent a relatively small membership base in terms of the local Muslim population (usually only 2–4 percent), they often control a sizable proportion of the registered Muslim religious associations and prayer spaces— sometimes as many as one out of three—where mosque-going Muslims congregate to socialize and pray.

Many of these federations' leaders share indirect descent from the Muslim Brotherhood and dissident religious–political movements in Algeria, Egypt, Morocco, Syria, Tunisia, Turkey, and elsewhere. They are the putative heirs of divisive figures of international Islamism like Yusuf al-Qaradawi and Necmettin Erbakan, and of the brotherhood movements that in the broader Middle East have portrayed Islam as an "all-inclusive system of religion, world and state."[32] Their success has reinforced fears that they will encourage native-born European Muslim generations to disregard the rule of law in favor of a higher calling: "*al-Qur'ân dusturna*" (the Qur'ân is our constitution). Islamist spokesmen objected to images of the Prophet Mohammad in British novels, Italian frescoes, and Danish caricatures, or in operas in Geneva and Berlin. They encourage "modesty" among young women, and push for their right to wear headscarves and skip physical education class. To some observers, they are pursuing the creeping Islamization of Europe.

Chapter 4. Citizens, Groups, and the State. The fourth chapter places European governments' relationships with contemporary Muslim communities into historical and theoretical context, by reviewing earlier encounters with new categories of citizens and state-building challenges. For the past two centuries, the religion bureaus of interior ministries across Europe have asserted state authority by structuring and mediating the activities of religious organizations. Against the view that the accommodation of religious communities is the equivalent of "capitulation," this chapter shows that formal recognition has been the method through which the modern state has historically asserted its authority over new citizen groups. The view that Islam is inherently incompatible with, or otherwise presents an unprecedented challenge to, state authority in western democracies is critically examined. The chapter brings together summaries of literature on intermediary associations and the recognition of trade unions, with the establishment of representative bodies for Jewish and other religious communities. These historical examples demonstrate that the granting of political rights and equal citizenship—of the franchise and the right to hold office—were earlier supplemented with corporatist or public law status: extra-parliamentary representation. These cases yield insights into the institutional architecture of contemporary State-Islam consultations.

Seen in this light, the efforts to assert state sovereignty over transnational Islam look very similar to earlier moves to create centralized interlocutors for religious and even socioeconomic affairs. The corporatist methodology for interest management and mediation is a three-step process: setting preconditions for participation, selecting participants from available leadership, and defining the working agenda and electoral method. This process signals the state's goals of integration in each step, echoing the reasoning that invited syndicalists, trade unions, Jews, and other religious communities into the state apparatus. Governments aim to change the nature of individuals' relationship to organized religion and/or political groups by institutionally rooting it in a *national* context and requiring the subjugation of religious law—or revolutionary ardor—to the constitutional order.

Chapter 5. The Domestication of State-Mosque Relations. The fifth chapter discusses the creation of Islam Councils in response to a series of integration-related alarm bells that sounded at the end of the Cold War. Nineteen eighty-nine was a watershed year that initiated a second phase of state-mosque relations, after which governments sought to reassert state sovereignty over transnational Muslim networks. There were several confrontational events involving Islam in the international arena that year. First, the Ayatollah Khomenei pronounced an unfavorable fatwa against the Indian-British author Salman Rushdie for his allegedly blasphemous novel *The Satanic Verses*; then, three headscarf-wearing girls were expelled from a junior high school outside Paris; and finally, that same year, Soviet troops withdrew from Afghanistan.[33] The post-Communist void in central Asia would soon reveal to Europe the extent of Saudi (and later, Turkish) institutional and financial deployment and proselytizing outside of the Muslim-majority world. These events pointed all eyes toward the European territory itself, where Islamic organizations had begun to expand. The events of 1988–9 reverberated within Muslim communities across the continent, and opened local governments' eyes to the reality of transnational memberships among the minority populations. Soon thereafter, the allied war to drive Iraq out of Kuwait provoked further ripples across Muslim populations—where there was some expression of sympathy for President Hussein and lack of understanding for the Saudi alliance with the U.S.-led coalition.

Between 1990 and 2010, each country under examination experienced this process somewhat differently, but the similarities of the challenges and institutional responses far outnumber the distinctions. This period has seen the reassertion of nation-state sovereignty over the informal influence of international religious NGOs and foreign embassies. This phase of Muslim incorporation has been about undoing the power arrangement of the 1970s and 1980s that had privileged Saudi Arabia and other Muslim "sending" states in the practice of Islam in Europe—in addition to reining in the unregulated associations of transnational "political" Islam active on national territory. During this second phase of state-mosque relations, Interior Ministries initiated consultations with a broader swath of Muslim representatives, expanding their contacts with Muslims well beyond the "official" Islams of the homeland. This required delicate negotiations in which authorities felt a need to tread lightly, and comprised not just diplomatic representatives (who remained crucial) but also civil society organizations—including international NGOs affiliated with Political Islam.

Chapter 6. Imperfect Institutionalization: Islam Councils in Europe. This chapter examines the second round of state-mosque relations that produced institutionalized Islam Councils. Interior ministries provided the first impetus to organize Islam as a "national" religion, and the government-led consultations established a variety of national councils between 1992 and 2006, from the *Conseil français du culte musulman*, to the *Comisión Islámica de España*, to the *Exécutif des musulmans de Belgique*, to the *Deutsche Islam Konferenz*, to the Mosques and Imams National Advisory Board in Britain, to the *Consulta per l'Islam italiano*. These national processes are not identical: many place more weight on the role of Embassy Islam and foreign government representatives (e.g., Belgium, Germany, France, Spain), while others rely more heavily on handpicked local civil society organizations (e.g., Italy, United Kingdom).

The cases exhibit strong evidence of institutional parallelism as states seek similar types of alliances. The central commonality of these state-Islam consultations is that they are held with the administrators and delegates of prayer spaces, large mosques, and Islamic religious federations—i.e., not with Muslim *political* leaders. The consultations serve two principal purposes: to routinize and de-politicize Muslims' religious practices, and to force opposing movements within organized Islam (notably, Embassy Islam and Political Islam) to work together under the neutral brokerage of the state.

Chapter 7. The Partial Emancipation: Muslim Responses to State-Islam Consultations. The seventh chapter addresses the achievements of state-mosque relations and the "incorporation" outcomes that can be measured so far. What is the stability and performance of Islam Councils across the countries? How have these policies conditioned integration outcomes and political moderation, and what impact do they have on the long-term prospects of Muslims' everyday integration in Europe? After earlier chapters' emphasis on the State, this chapter empirically traces the effects of European policy approaches and finds that they have had a dramatic effect on Muslim communities: their domestic orientation, their reformed organizational structures, their outspoken distancing from violence and radicalism, and their outward commitment to playing by the rules of the game. Host societies as well as Muslim community leaders—and the scope of their agendas—have been transformed by the experience of institutional integration.

Muslims in Europe today have yet to experience full political integration—their residual foreign citizenship will prevent that until a majority are European citizens over the voting age—but increasing numbers of leaders are being received in the halls of power. The predominant scene of state-Islam interactions is not just of unabated conflict but of government officials sitting down with Muslims to address issues associated with domestic Islamic observance. As a result of meticulous institution-building by Interior Ministries across the continent, these meetings are no longer the ad hoc gatherings of foreign dignitaries they once were. In practice, authorities have effectively opened up communications channels that serve both as a sounding board for the putative Muslim community and as a temporary substitute for the millions of citizens and residents of Muslim origin who are, for the time being, without significant electoral representation. Islam Councils have even begun to achieve some concrete instances of "domestication," such as the oversight of halal slaughter, the nomination of chaplains in the military, the organization of religious education in public schools, the endowment of university departments of Islamic theology, and civic training for imams.

Both the diplomatic religious networks and Political-Islam networks have been profoundly changed by their experience in Europe, in unforeseen ways. The content of "Embassy Islam" has been both multiplied and adapted to the new circumstances of state-mosque relations. And some Islamist groups in Europe have showed signs of a practical-minded evolution. The Islam Councils have begun to demonstrate that over time, a new politics of distinctly European state-mosque relations can emerge.

Chapter 8. Muslim Integration and European Islam in the Next Generation. The concluding chapter discusses the future prospects for Muslims' political and social integration. A number of the social, cultural, and political adjustments that will characterize Europe in coming generations are already under way, although often the results are not visible to the naked eye. This chapter examines the pre-electoral political behavior and earliest known voting preferences and demographic future of the postcolonial—and post-guestworker—Muslim minorities of Europe. The chapter argues that the most serious threats to successful emancipation—violent extremism among Muslims and right-wing nativism among "host societies"—may ultimately be weakened by a confluence of demographic trends and old-fashioned integration processes. The key development will be that as the proportion of Muslims of foreign nationality residing in Europe decreases (because of the increasing share of native-born Muslims), European countries' democratic political institutions increasingly will take effect.

The normalization of Muslims' participation in political life will give a small voice in government to Muslim advocates of all partisan stripes. And the routinization of Islamic religious observance will diminish the significance of religious inequality as a mobilizing issue in Muslim identity politics. National Islam Councils will slowly domesticate the religious leadership, rooting it in a European context, and Muslim politicians will gradually be brought into traditional political institutions.

The advent of a large class of voting Muslim citizens will also contribute to the flowering of a rich civil society. The discussions of Muslims' future in Europe and the compatibility of Islam and democracy—that is, of the question "Can Muslims be good citizens?"—will become less abstract, less hypothetical. The answer to that question will no longer be sought in the publicly stated good intentions of Muslim leaders, on one hand, or in the rabble-rousing of nationalists or Islamists prophesying clashes yet to come, on the other. Conflicts over public prayers, unsanitary animal slaughter, and radical proselytizing in prisons and sermonizing in mosques will be addressed and mostly resolved by the practical accommodations and administrative oversight of governments across the continent. Integration problems will persist, but discussions of how to resolve them will no longer be crudely couched in terms of the clash of civilizations.

Case Selection and a Disclaimer

This book distills the perspective and insights gained from more than a decade of research in four languages and nine countries. Most of the comparative analysis is conducted on empirical data compiled during nearly three years of fieldwork in Western Europe: Belgium, France, Germany, Italy, Ireland, the Netherlands, and the United Kingdom, whose collective Muslim-origin population accounts for roughly 14 million of the approximately 16–17 million Muslims in Europe, as well as during short research visits to Morocco and Turkey. I conducted more than two hundred interviews with civil servants, politicians, diplomats, and ministers; religious federation leaders and local community presidents; and imams and sheikhs—before and during the state-Islam consultation process—and became familiar with the perspectives, complaints, and aspirations of Muslim minorities and their majority societies.[34] The sample of host countries examined is not exhaustive of the European Muslim experience but includes: countries with variations of three different state-church regimes; with relevant colonial histories and without; with Muslim populations that are either predominantly South Asian, Turkish, or North African, i.e., the three main sources of Muslim migration to Europe.

The story of European Islam is about much more than geopolitics and state-building processes discussed in this book. It is wrapped up in complex daily local realities that cannot be fully captured by a work whose aim is to generalize and offer a view of the broad trends. The cross-national parallels I describe, by their nature, impose a "model" on messy empirical data. The book contributes to the existing literature by offering a 30,000-foot view of what is happening across Europe: why European state-mosque relations and "organized Islam" look the way they do in the early twenty-first century. My generalizations will occasionally unfairly lump subtle actors into the two principal categories: "Political Islam" and "Embassy Islam." The usefulness of this shorthand is mostly in the context of understanding the composition of Islam Councils, but they also give a broad sense of a given organization's acceptance of the political status quo and degree of religious observance. My aim is to give a detailed overview of continental patterns, which sometimes means I do not capture the subtle interiors of every rectory or religious affairs office.

The criterion for placing mosques and federations in the Embassy Islam category is whether the leader serves at the pleasure of a foreign government, and whether the mosque is effectively used as a drawing room of the embassy—these are useful heuristics for the broader attempt to measure foreign governments' influence on the religious landscape in a given country. Despite the internal diversity of Embassy Islam, I hope that the next chapter will demonstrate why it is a useful category. The Political Islam category, similarly brimming with diversity, includes any organization with ties to Jama'at-i Islami, Muslim Brotherhood, and Millî Görüş—which, along with a handful of other groups, have been referred to collectively as "the new Muslim Brotherhood" in the West—although individual leaders and members may repudiate entire swaths of those amorphous movements' partisan and ideological platforms in various contexts.[35]

The template of "religious community" that this book applies to a set of nationally and ethnically heterogeneous minority populations with varying degrees of piety or communitarian identity will strike a discordant note for some readers. Ultimately, the integration problems faced by the descendants of immigrants from Muslim-majority countries are not only religious in nature, and in many ways it is unfair to refer to these populations as "Muslims" or to call the leadership of Islamic organizations—mosques and federations, etc.—"community leaders." One could write an entirely different book about "secular" leadership, and those Muslim-origin politicians who refuse the religion template entirely.[36] This book's framework takes advantage of the institutional opportunity structure of state-mosque relations, as they are the only official contact point for millions of Muslims at the cusp of emancipation, without access to traditional political resources (parties, elections, and public bureaucracies).

State-mosque relations in Europe stand at a critical juncture between national and international organizational and political influences. This period shares features of the dynamic process that Seymour Martin Lipset and Stein Rokkan observed at the moment when universal suffrage was granted in the interwar period, during which ideological cleavages were "frozen" in place for much of the remaining century.[37] The jockeying of foreign governments and international NGOs is a contest to set the conditions in which the first fully enfranchised Muslim citizens of Europe come of age, and it will influence the shape of state-mosque relations—and the integration of European Muslims—for generations to come. The two categories of religious actors that are the focus of the policies under examination—Embassy Islam and Political Islam—are not the only relevant movements active in European Islam, but taken together, the federations under these two mantles account for large majorities of "organized" Muslims who have registered religious associations. They are the movements that have tried to confederate the mosques and Islamic houses of worship of Europe and who have sought recognition by European states. They are also the main forces in competition to dominate the institutional life of state-mosque relations, and thereby to speak on behalf of religious—and often, political—questions for millions of Muslims. The policy choices made by European governments during this molten era will be critical to the success of the emancipation process under way.

CHAPTER TWO

European Outsourcing and Embassy Islam

L'ISLAM, C'EST MOI

THE FIRST MONTH OF 2010 brought several reminders of the Muslim world's residual paternalism toward the Islamic diaspora in Europe. The Tunisian presidency organized a conference on "Youth and the Future: Contemporary Challenges," and invited an Italian Muslim leader to participate with a delegation of young Italian Muslims. The Algerian government signaled that it would replace the rector of the Grand Mosque of Paris, the oldest and most prominent Islamic institution in metropolitan France. A columnist in the *Saudi Gazette* reminded the Saudi leadership of the Muslim world's responsibility to protect and promote their minorities abroad. He cited the "Swiss ban on minarets, French aversion to burqa, Danish blasphemy, and the American call for assimilation" to rile his readers out of their inaction. He asked: "What have we done to help those affected minorities?" The answer is: quite a lot, actually. Embassy Islam—in other words, the international advocacy, summitry, and intervention on behalf of the Islamic minority in Europe—has been under way for three decades, and shows no signs of abating, although it is adapting the content of its offerings as the European Muslim population nears the point of being majority native-born.

The religious infrastructure of Muslim communities in Western Europe was, in a sense, decided in advance—not by the communities themselves, but by those who had the power to set the conditions: sending and receiving states. The homeland governments of the majority-Muslim sending states have exercised a strong hand in Islam in Europe since shortly after the first guestworkers first emigrated. European governments were content to "outsource" the day-to-day management of Islamic religious observance, a practice that dovetailed with the interests of the countries of origin. The policies of the host and sending states were entirely convergent for the first decades of Muslim settlement. The Europeans embraced return-oriented integration policies that meshed well with the religious and cultural outreach of three principal labor-exporting states—Algeria, Morocco, and Turkey—as well as the religious-hegemonic aspirations of officials in Pakistan and Saudi Arabia.

European countries gradually found themselves unwitting and often unwilling referees of the modern struggles between religion and politics in the Muslim world. The real-time process of nation-state consolidation in Turkey and Morocco and its shortcomings in Pakistan and Algeria, the effects of the fall of the Ottoman Empire and the rise of the Saudi dynasty, and the Europeans' mid-twentieth-century exit from the region are all tightly intertwined with the still unsettled role of Islam within these Muslim-majority states—and in Europe itself.[1] Distinct variants of official religion emerged as part of each Muslim-majority state's individual self-definition, internal balance of power, and quest for self-preservation. Europeans are no strangers to these discussions, many of them having recent colonial pasts and strong economic and political ties in the Subcontinent, the Levant, and the Maghreb—in addition to their own vivid memories of brokering religious conflicts at home.

But after more than a century of Europeans' military and political presence in the greater Middle East, and the gradual diminution of organized Christianity's influence over society and politics in Europe, the settlement of millions of Muslims in Europe has transformed the vicissitudes of state-religion relations in Muslim-majority countries into an internal political matter. Official and unofficial actors from those countries have gradually intensified their focus on the European Muslim diaspora, supplying a steady stream of funding and personnel in support of competing understandings of religion and politics.

This chapter explores the origins of the privileged status enjoyed by foreign Islamic governments in the first stage (c. 1960–1990) of state-mosque relations in Europe. Several factors help explain why European governments gave them that status. Europeans were interested in a good trade relationship and the even flow of oil, in avoiding the politicization of migrant populations, and above all in orienting the immigrants to eventually go back to their original homelands. A template of *temporary* migration defined the host governments' demand for religious interlocutors during the first stage, during which they experimented with return-oriented policies and the outsourcing of linguistic, cultural, and religious programs. The encouragement of a home-country identity in the domain of religion dovetailed with a mutually perpetuated fiction of a future homecoming (*Rückkehrillusion*) for migrants and even their locally born children.[2] But this did not constitute a fully developed approach: rather, it reflected the absence of a policy toward the new Muslim minority.

In general, European countries in the 1970s and 1980s preferred not to consider themselves countries of immigration. A French interior minister said that despite more than a century of granting citizenship based on *ius soli*, Algerians should be considered "as foreign workers and not as immigrants, and . . . children born in France should not get French citizenship automatically."[3] Conservatives in Germany insisted simply that "Germany is not an immigration country," for example, while political parties like the Bavarian *CSU* or the French *Front National* capitalized on fears of an "immigrant invasion." In response to the judicial rulings liberalizing family reunification, governments offered cash to migrants who would voluntarily return immediately and homeland re-entry preparation for those who stayed.[4] In the end, very few returned voluntarily and many more instead brought family members and fiancés to live with them in Europe.

During the first period of state-mosque relations, European governments came to view their Muslim populations as an object of diplomatic geostrategy. Riven with internal tensions, Europeans' postcolonial policy toward the Muslim majority world—supporting officialdom in the greater Middle East region while granting safe haven to reformers, for example—had unintended consequences that proved difficult to reconcile in their host societies. Not seeing the guestworkers and their offspring as destined for citizenship, and believing Islam, as the religion of foreigners, "an exogenous reality," the host societies tried their best to avoid the hard questions of Islam's status in European societies.[5] Foreign Affairs ministries adapted to cope with the new religious issues raised by the presence of migrant laborers. Bilateral conventions that France signed with Algeria for foreign workers—a kind of mini-shari'a accord—governed questions of inheritance, repatriation of the deceased, polygamy, and divorce, thus reproducing for Muslims in France the situation of North Africans under French colonial rule.[6] In the same spirit, a convention signed by France and Morocco in 1981 even obligated judges to apply Moroccan Islamic law in family law matters (marriage, divorce, and inheritance) for first-generation Moroccans living in France.[7] The French Counselor for Religious Affairs, initially created to re-establish relations with the Holy See following the break in diplomatic relations after the 1905 law separating Church and State, saw his role enhanced in the 1970s with respect to the growing Muslim population.[8] The German Foreign Ministry's office for Dialogue with the Islamic World would later play a similar role vis-à-vis Turkey.[9] Every European government, whether overtly "multicultural" or not, accepted outside funds and allowed outside authorities—from Algeria, Morocco, and Turkey to Saudi Arabia, Libya, and beyond—to influence its local Muslim population.

THE SUBCONTRACTOR'S PERSPECTIVE: FOREIGN GOVERNMENT INTEREST IN DIASPORA MUSLIMS

Throughout the period 1960–2010, the *sending* governments have maintained and amplified these efforts in an attempt to gain control over labor emigration's sometimes beneficial, sometimes threatening, consequences for political legitimacy and economic development.[10]

Two types of Embassy Islam can be distinguished in the first stage: that of the major "sending states" (Algeria, Morocco, and Turkey) that fit the general pattern of emigrant outreach, on the one hand; and that of one major sending state (Pakistan) and a non-sending state (Saudi Arabia) that seek to propagate Islamic institutions more broadly. The Saudi and Pakistani governments, who fashioned their foreign policy in the guise of heirs to the Caliphate, treated European Muslims as the objects of state-led pan-Islamic designs. Their extramural sponsorship of Islamic associations targeted all Muslim minorities worldwide, from India and Nigeria as well as in Italy and Canada. The main sending states aside from Pakistan—namely, Algeria, Morocco, and Turkey— viewed their European diasporas with concern that dissidents abroad might seek to gather forces to effect policy changes, or change of regime, at home. Their governments' attempts to consolidate the work of postcolonial and post-imperial nation-building and thereby control class-based, Islamist and ethnic threats to the unitary nation-state risked being undone by the expansion of dissident religious and political networks in Europe. As one Turkish study analyzed the potential threat from abroad in 1986, "by virtue of living in Europe, the migrants can carry out their commitment to Islam to its most conservative extremes."[11]

In addition to adopting a policy of emigrant outreach for ideological and religious reasons, these states had more prosaic grounds for maintaining links with diasporas: to support economic growth and development in the homeland. Over time, as much as 5 percent of these sending countries' labor force moved to Western Europe, and remittance outflows from European states to these countries increased by billions of dollars annually. Between 1961 and 1967, for example, Turkey signed bilateral agreements with Germany, the European Economic Community, Austria, the Netherlands, Belgium, France, and Sweden, leading to the exportation of 800,000 workers to Europe before the 1974 immigration freeze. Thanks to the labor agreements, Moroccan, Pakistani, Turkish, and Algerian labor migrants sent home billions of dollars annually, the equivalent of anywhere from 2–3 percent of national GDP (Algeria and Turkey) to 8–10 percent (Morocco); indeed, remittances often represent the second or third largest single contribution to GDP.

EUROPEAN OUTSOURCING: A MUTUALLY BENEFICIAL ARRANGEMENT

The Growth of a Religious Infrastructure

Several years after the end of mass migration in 1973–74, national and local governments in Europe realized they would require an interlocutor in order to attend to the basic religious needs of their newly settled foreign populations: e.g., prayer space, imams, facilities for ritual lamb slaughter, and travel visas for pilgrimage to Mecca. This demand determined the type of community interlocutor that governments sought out. Faced with a community of modest means, and given the legal and political difficulties of providing public funding, European governments encouraged embassies and representatives of the official Islams of the Muslim world.[12]

A basic religious infrastructure—mosques and a handful of imams—was installed in the late 1960s and early 1970s in the framework of diplomatic and economic cooperation between Western European and majority-Muslim labor exporting countries on the Mediterranean basin. European governments tolerated the Islamic proselytism of foreign envoys for pragmatic reasons. The large, classical mosques these governments planned and built across Europe—and the prayer rooms they gathered under umbrella organizations guided by their consulates—were a quick fix for the practical needs of local Muslims since they could apply their experience in the practical administration of Islamic religious practice.

European governments thus initiated the habit-forming practice of importing imams and allowing foreign governments to sponsor mosque construction (see figures 2.1, 2.2, and 2.3). With the minor exception of prayer spaces created in some workplaces and public housing units, governments outsourced relations to Muslim representatives to the embassies and consulates of sending states and the regional religious powerhouse, Saudi Arabia. This became known as a *"Gastarbeiter* Islam" or an "Islam *des foyers"* (workers' dormitories).[13] Beginning in the early 1980s, for example, Dutch authorities allowed a branch of the Turkish presidency for religious affairs to appoint around 140 imams for Turkish mosques and granted permission to Moroccans to do the same for an additional one hundred mosques.[14] By the late 1980s, the *Grande Mosquée de Paris* had brought over so much of the official religious apparatus from Algeria that it became known as the "second Algerian embassy."[15] By 1979, there were twenty-six Turkish religious affairs attachés in place in embassies and consulates across Europe.[16] A quarter of a century later, there were nearly eight hundred imams hired under the supervision of the Turkish directorate for religious affairs in Germany alone.

Figure 2.1. Si Hamza Boubakeur, Rector of the *Grande Mosquée de Paris*, 1978. Source: © Tor Eigeland /*Saudi Aramco World*/ PADIA.

Avoiding a Less Desirable Alternative

> Most migrant workers are not politically conscious . . . Their thought is traditional—either Catholic or Muslim; their expectation of change . . . is gathered into hopes of individual and family achievement. It is too soon to know how they might become politicized if they stayed longer . . . Aware of the inconvenience of a politically conscious proletariat, [European governments] plan for a continual "rotation" of foreign labor so that no workers will stay too long.
>
> —John Berger, *A Seventh Man*, 1984, 144

This excerpt from John Berger and Jean Mohr's landmark photo-essay on guestworkers in Europe, composed in 1973–74, evokes the "pre-electoral" mind-set of Europe's migrant minorities and the host governments' interest in keeping things that way. Europeans' reliance on foreign states for the oversight of Muslim populations was initially pursued in part to avoid a less desirable alternative: that trade unionists advancing a class-conscious ideology—or imams representing Islamist opposition in their home countries—would promote political mobilization among Muslims in Europe's receiving societies.[17] Europeans preferred the safer bet, i.e., the official religious infrastructure of Muslim-majority states, which combated extremism in their own national interest, as a "useful bulwark against Islamic radicalism."[18] As former Interior Minister Pierre Joxe describes it, the 1980s had "a generally subversive atmosphere" in

Figure 2.2. A Turkish Mosque in Almelo, the Netherlands, 1978. Source: © Tor Eigeland / *Saudi Aramco
World* / PADIA.

which the French government allowed Islam "to be managed by the
national police," and reinforced by the secret services of the Muslim
states "who aimed to control 'their community' and above all 'their
Islamists.'"[19]

The implantation of "Embassy" Islam in European national land-
scapes thus offered a putative security guarantee. Abdellah Redouane,
a Moroccan diplomat who leads the Islamic Cultural Center of Italy,
recounted in an interview that well into the 1990s, "the countries of
origin were still trying—and this is not a secret—to have a strong influence over their emigrés in Europe for one reason or another, through
amicales, diplomatic representations and consulates."[20] Similarly, a Turk-

Figure 2.3. Inauguration of the Regent's Park Mosque, London, 1978. Source: © Tor Eigeland /*Saudi Aramco World*/PADIA.

ish diplomat argued in another interview that "In the late 1970s and early 1980s it could have been much worse with radicalization tendencies among Turks in Germany if DİTİB had not been here to prevent it. The de-escalation is thanks to DİTİB."[21] As one French interior ministry official confirmed, "Algeria, Morocco, and Turkey were able to offer France a common front that was perhaps not pro-Western but at least anti-terrorist."[22]

Former Italian Prime Minister Giulio Andreotti related an illustrative anecdote from a meeting he held with Libyan leader Moammar Qaddafi in the late 1970s: "He spoke to me of the danger of Islamic fundamentalism, and he said he was the one who saw the danger originally—that the fundamentalists are motivated, religious young people and that they were starting to say terrible things and he repeated one phrase in particular, that they were going to 're-conquer Andalusia,' and then he said these people are worse than your fascists and your Nazis, and that if we're not careful then there will be a real danger."[23] Europeans were happy to outsource this policing and administrative know-how, to governments who were acquainted, first-hand, with violence and terrorism in the Islamic world.

Sand in Water

A further and more surprising point of convergence between sending states and host governments, however, justified the absence of European integration policies to help the Muslim-origin labor force fit into their host societies. The return-oriented administrative practices of Europeans and the aims of Muslim-majority sending states and regional religious hegemons were mirror images of one another. Both the European governments and Muslim states purposely worked against integration for decades by promoting native language retention and the maintenance of distinct cultural and religious identities that did not mingle with the majority society—the very traits that would later be cited as evidence of failure to integrate. In 1980, the Pakistani Minister for Religious Affairs proudly compared Muslims in Europe to "sand in water—they cannot possibly get dissolved and so be assimilated."[24] Unwittingly foreshadowing the arguments of future skeptics of Muslim emancipation in Europe, he wrote:

> There is something in Islam as a religion that somehow an adherent of Islam can never renounce . . . and the hold that his religion has on him is so all-pervading and far-reaching that there is hardly a facet of his life that is not touched by religion. These are some of the reasons why Muslim minorities are hard to assimilate . . . [The] prevalence of secularist philosophy has not made much dent on those who subscribe to the religion of Islam.[25]

When it came to the preservation of these alleged singularities, Muslim-majority governments and European governments found common ground. But whereas the European governments did so in furtherance of a myth of the migrants' eventual return to the homeland, some of their Muslim counterparts had a different understanding: they wanted to calcify and preserve the *Islamic* distinctiveness of labor migrants in Europe. The Secretary General of the OIC wrote at the time that

> The most serious problem that can face a minority is social absorption by the majority. Such an absorption is usually the result of a

long assimilation process that nibbles at the Islamic characteristics of the minority until it disappears altogether, usually after two or three generations.

Therefore, he continued, "learning the language of the [host society] . . . will not be harmful if the Muslims are able to keep on learning Arabic, the language of the Qur'ân."[26] As a speaker in a Saudi-sponsored conference in London said in 1982,

> The English maintain contact with Latin and Greek because they are the languages of their culture. The Muslim world is fortunate to have one common language of faith and culture—the Arabic language in which the Holy Qur'ân was revealed. Every Muslim child learns the Qur'ân and the language of the Qur'ân.[27]

That conference concluded with a declaration that "Arabic, the language of Al Qur'ân, should be developed as the lingua franca of the Muslim *ummah* and every effort should be made to achieve this objective."[28]

As it happened, a European Community directive in 1977 explicitly authorized mother-tongue classes to be sponsored by sending countries. In Germany, this was described in a document for state ministers for religious affairs as "an effort to socially integrate foreign students during the period of their residence [in Germany]" and to facilitate "their reinsertion in the homeland school system."[29] In France and the Netherlands, the door to the homeland was similarly left ajar. French authorities promoted an alternative of "adaptation or return,"[30] while the Dutch pursued a "dual policy" (*tweesporenbeleid*) that would "simultaneously create opportunities for a successful re-integration of immigrants who decided to return, and to equip those who decided to stay with a strong and positive sense of identity."[31]

In conjunction with these efforts on the linguistic front, Europe's foreign ministries created theological scholarships for foreign imams through programs such as ELCO in France (*Enseignement des langues et cultures d'origine*, Teaching the Language and Culture of Origin), a set of eight bilateral accords initiated in 1975—less than a year after the French government suspended the entry of labor migrants and their families—with migration sending states. As a French religious affairs diplomat told the author in an interview, "The ELCO programs allowed many Turks, Algerians, Tunisians and others to come to France to teach the language and cultures of origin to the children of the different communities. Very often these programs have had a very strong religious connotation: the language and culture of origin is taught with the Qur'ân."[32] Between 1984 and 1992, an average of 64,000 Algerian,

Moroccan, Tunisian, and Turkish students were enrolled in these courses annually.[33] The sending states paid for the courses, determined the content, and trained and sent the teachers; the French foreign affairs ministry facilitated their temporary visas. As one former director of the *Fonds d'Action Sociale* said in an interview:

> We began to promote the teaching of the native language in school, but not at all to recognize their literatures. The thinking went that if these kids don't know how to speak their native language any more, then we could never deport them. So we financed radio stations in mother tongues and the teaching of Arabic and Turkish—by teachers who did not speak a word of French—to allow the eventual departure of entire families. This "joke" lasted until the end of the 1980s and cost many hundreds of millions of Francs.[34]

Beginning in the early 1980s, most German *länder* offered Turkish children religious education within the framework of the "native language instruction" (*muttersprachliche Ergänzungsunterricht*), and outsourced responsibility for this to Turkish consular representatives. Teachers were sent for five-year stints.[35] In the German state of North Rhine Westphalia, Turkish officials met with state administrators to set curriculum and a textbook for use in religion class by Turkish schoolchildren. In Bavaria, school administrators introduced a curriculum that closely followed the official Turkish state's curriculum introduced in the wake of the 1980 military coup in Turkey.[36] DİTİB began organizing religion courses in Berlin schools in 1983.[37] In Baden-Württemberg in the late 1980s, 220 teachers sent from Turkey offered religion lessons in Islam in the context of Turkish-language courses. Through the 1990s, hundreds of thousands of Turkish students (nearly half the then roughly 500,000 Turks of school age) were annually enrolled in language and religious instruction offered by Turkish teachers installed by agreement between the state religion ministries and the Turkish foreign ministry in the *länder* home to major migrant populations.[38] In the Netherlands, more than 315,000 school-age students were enrolled in Turkish or Arabic classes in 1989.[39]

In Germany, the issue of foreign interlocutors had first emerged because of the way in which religious education is organized in many of the *Länder*'s public school systems. When the local government in Bavaria created Turkish language religious instruction in public schools in the early 1980s, for example, Turkish consular officials from DİTİB were responsible for curriculum and instruction, avoiding religious instruction in German and insisting on the use of Turkish. And, in the absence of formal religious education for Muslims in public schools in North-Rhine Westphalia, Germany, Saudi Arabia created the King Fahd Akademie. French authorities allotted funds for Arabic language radio and other "cultural programming" through the Social Action Fund (*Fonds d'Action Sociale*) created in 1959.[40] In the Netherlands, support for native languages and cultures could "help in sustaining the possibilities for guestworkers and their family members to successfully re-integrate upon return to the home country."[41] Guestworker programs on public radio stations aimed to construct "a bridge to the homeland" throughout the 1960s and 1970s.[42]

In hindsight, these practices resemble "multicultural" programs intended to highlight the place of migrant cultures in European societies; however, they were in fact designed to facilitate migrants'—and their European-born children's—eventual departure.[43] The sending countries, in turn, took advantage of the opportunity to combat undesirable influences—Islamic radicalism or ethnic separatism—on their emigrants from fundamentalist groups operating in Europe. An early Turkish government study, for example, stated plainly the options facing the diaspora—ignorance or extremism: "Integration is not assimilation. The lack of religious education can lead to: (a) Turkish families losing their cultures, and adopt complete western values. (b) People becoming radicalized as a response."[44]

L'ISLAM, C'EST MOI

> Every Arab government that wanted to survive has traditionally had to defend its legitimacy in three political languages: nationalism, social justice and Islam.
> —Albert Hourani, History of the Arab Peoples, 1992, 451

> I do not accept the thesis that there is no clergy in Islam. There is a clergy in Algeria, in Morocco, in Egypt, in Tunisia. The imams are civil servants, they are paid by the state. In what sense are they not a clergy? They lead prayers, they organize the religion.[45]
> —French interior ministry advisor, author interview, June 2002

What are the defining features of Embassy Islam, and where did the imams, teachers, and school curriculum that it exports to Europe come from? Who were the statesmen exporting it, and what was their ideological and political outlook? Even though some of the countries that have influenced Islam in Europe are technically "lay" states, this does not mean the separation of Islam and state. It means that religion may not be used to influence public policy, but is used in service of national unity and the state more broadly. Governments in the majority-Muslim world have a rich history of bureaucratized religion in the twentieth century. Three phases of religion policy can be identified: A first phase, between roughly 1925 and 1965: Islam's role in modern state formation in the broader Middle East and North Africa began as a self-defensive measure, as governments developed an official Islam for internal consumption. A second phase, beginning in the 1960s: The establishment of an Embassy Islam, for exportation, with a general missionary goal (*Da'wa*) characterized by competition among regional actors for international religious hegemony, which these countries exported to other postcolonial societies, e.g., in Sub-Saharan Africa or Central Asia. And a third phase, beginning in the 1980s: The consular transmission of Embassy Islam to preserve political-religious control—and economic ties— over diaspora groups in Europe. Embassy Islam seeks to retain a guardian status over religious practices abroad. Each sending state contributed to a learning curve: Algerians pioneered the fraternal organizational model and Turks pioneered the Embassy Islam model; Moroccans would eventually synthesize the best practices of both.

Official Islams: Consolidation, Centralization, and Self-Defense

The emergence of an exportable "official religion" in modern Muslim societies—the equivalent of the civil constitution of the clergy in nineteenth-century Europe—resulted from governments' deliberate decision in the early postcolonial period to consolidate political legitimacy and defuse threats within their domestic contexts (see table 2.1). A vibrant fragmentation of nation-state Islams proliferated after pan-Islam's defeat during the First World War. Most of these governments used religion to consolidate rule within their own borders. After the fall of the Ottoman Empire, and then after World War II, Jacob Landau writes, "For the first time, numerous sovereign states could determine their own attitudes towards Islam . . . Nationalism competed increasingly with Islam."[46] With the notable exceptions of Saudi Arabia and Pakistan, Muslim governments abandoned internationalism and focused on national politics. The regimes in Jordan, Algeria, Turkey, Syria, Tunisia, and Morocco first viewed the official co-optation of Islamic activism "as a means to counter secular leftist influences" at the height of the Cold War, and later, after the Iranian revolution, as a way to undermine internal hardliner religious opponents' accusations of "un-Islamic" governance.[47] The project of nation-building in these young states regularly came under attack by influential members of religious circles who "considered secular nationalism especially noxious to Islam itself."[48] In response to Islamist violence or attempted coups, governments responded ruthlessly, executing or imprisoning many opponents while allowing others to go into exile. But they also sought to counter the Islamist threat by venturing into the provision of official religious infrastructure.

Religious consolidation and institutionalization formed a key part of the Muslim world's modernization process. In a first stage, this entailed the attempted elimination of folk Islam and spiritual brotherhoods that undermined centralized control. As Marco Pirrone writes, "Arab nationalism originated on the base of Muslim cultural identity and against the European nation-state model. [. . .] The recourse to Islam and pan-Arabism as a matrix of historical-cultural and religious identity . . . gave additional meaning to the anti-colonial struggle . . . and became the political identity against colonial domination."[49] Later, when governments faced threats from leftist and Islamist movements, co-opting religion came to be viewed not only as a unifying national culture, but "as the best bulwark against communism and religious fanaticism."[50] These measures were taken in order to establish a "nationally oriented" Islam and to limit the spread of "folk Islam" and political opposition that increasingly took the guise of "unapproved" preaching.[51]

In the 1920s and 1930s, Turkey and Saudi Arabia—the original post-Caliphate religious authorities, i.e., Kemalists in Turkey, and Wahhabis in Saudi Arabia—first consolidated their rule through the institutionalized use of religion, followed by Egypt and Pakistan in the 1940s and 1950s. The countries of the Maghreb went through this phase later; during the post-independence period between 1957 and 1962, they consolidated their nascent nation-states against leftist secular and conservative Islamist radicalisms. These governments prophylactically "Islamized" their national laws and legitimized religious practice in the public sphere. They created the functional equivalent of national clergies, chartered seminaries, and religious schools and established religious faculties of higher education. These activities were generally overseen by a Ministry of Religious Affairs or Islamic quasi-NGO (*waqf*) whose appointees enjoyed a monopoly over the designation of imams and religious education. The ministries gradually centralized and took over responsibility for training, appointing a new clerical civil service, and/or the licensing of active imams, and often providing them with pre-approved Friday sermons (*khutba*). Official theology faculties were created in Cairo, Ankara, Tunisia, and Morocco, and governments attempted to nationalize the networks of prayer spaces, sanctioned boards of official religious scholars (*ulama*), and centralized their issuing of religious rulings (*fatwa*). A brief review of the principal steps toward religious consolidation and the establishment of an official Islam in the most important Muslim-majority countries follows here, in order to provide context for the eventual exportation of these institutions to European receiving states.

TABLE 2.1.
Official Islam in Turkey, Egypt, Morocco, Algeria, and Pakistan

Turkey

The founder of modern Turkey, Kemal Mustafa Atatürk, argued that "the modern state would be shored up by *civic religion*."[1] "Hospitable boundaries" now link the state and Islamic actors, says one scholar. Although Atatürk eliminated any "potential Islamic political dissent" in secular Turkey, he did not attack religion directly.[2] The largest expansion of religious infrastructure took place under the rule of the center-right Democratic Party (1950–1960). "We are like a strainer for tea," one senior official said in a newspaper interview in 2004. "We strain the information so that when it reaches the people, it is the best possible interpretation based on the Qur'ân . . . Our mission is to get people to live in peace and harmony."[3]

Egypt

Nasser's Egypt (1956–1970) is often portrayed as the regime that "best illustrates the transfer of Kemalist precepts to the Arab world."[4] The *ulama* were made civil servants in 1961, and the Academy of Islamic Research (and its associated magazine, *Magallat al-Azhar*) was created for missionary purposes (*da'wa*) to help propagate Islam outside Egypt. Since 1961, the grand imam or Sheikh of Al Azhar is named by the president of the republic.[5] Presidents Nasser and Sadat (1970–1981) used Al Azhar for "nationalist Islamic propaganda," creating the Islamic World Center and the Voice of Islam broadcasting service.[6] Religious education, chaplains in prisons, schools, and the armies as well as ritual slaughter all came under state control.

Morocco

In the face of persistent challenges from the periphery against the political center, the 1962 Moroccan constitution enshrined its king as a descendent of the Prophet Muhammad and the Commander of the Faithful ('*Amir al Mu'minin*). At the beginning of the 1960s, King Hassan II "sought out Moroccan Islamic specificity—the religious role of the head of state—in distinction to Nasserism, Arab socialism and communism."[7]

Algeria

President Chadli Benjedid (1979–1992) attempted to "recapture the Islamic initiative away from populist imams and Muslim fundamentalists" by increasing the use of "religious idiom in the official speeches, public statements, and governments pronouncements of the President and his subordinates."[8] Islam was used as an "identity-forming instrument" but not as the basis for legal code or political institutions. Algeria was to be considered a secular state with a strong Islamic cultural component. Religious affairs were institutionalized in the Ministry for Religious Affairs and the Hajj, coming "under the direct and complete control of the centralized authorities."[9]

(continued)

TABLE 2.1. *cont.*
Official Islam in Turkey, Egypt, Morocco, Algeria, and Pakistan

Pakistan
The Pakistani government created an officially sanctioned ulama academy to train religious scholars in 1961, and religion has been included as a critical component of periodic educational reforms since 1955. But despite government efforts, or indeed because of certain officials' pan-Islamic leanings, there has not been much in the way of constitutional state control over madrassas and imam training in Pakistan. The policy of "adopting Islam and supporting Pan-Islam" served several goals: it satisfied popular sentiment since the issue was "popular with rural population and urban lower middle class" and was also useful to buttress its international alliances against the perceived threat posed by its Indian neighbor.

1. Turam, Between Islam *and the State the Politics of Engagement, 2007, 41.*
2. Ibid., 37–41.
3. McMahon and Collins, "State comes first, mosque second in Turkey's system," 2004.
4. Luizard, Laïcités au*toritaires en terres d'Islam, 2008, 9.*
5. Sources: "Islamic Mission in Sub-Saharan Africa. The Perspectives of Some 'Ulama' associated with the Al-Azhar University (196-1970)"; Roy, L'islam mondialisé, 2002, 29, 117; Xavier Ternisien, "Contestations en Egypte après la visite de M. Sarkozy," Le Monde, January 6, 2004.
6. Landau, The *Politics of Pan-Islam, 1990, 256.*
7. el-Ghissassi, "La restructuration du champ religieux marocain, entretien avec Mohamed Tozy," 2007.
8. Entelis, Algeria: The *Revolution Institutionalized, 1986, 88.*
9. Ibid., 81.

The Geopolitics of Laissez-Faire

> If . . . it is acknowledged that certain Muslim communities shall always reside within non-Muslim jurisdictions . . . then the Muslim world must determine precisely what form its interest in Muslim minorities should take. . . . The political caliphate may be a thing of the past, but the well-springs of Islamic thought still flow from this region. Therefore, realistically speaking, no interpretation of religious principle and no statement of Islamic policy can have wide acceptance unless it reflects some consensus of the major constituents of the Muslim world.
>
> — *Syed Abedin, Institute of Muslim Minority Affairs, King Abdul Aziz University (Saudi Arabia), 1980*[52]

The European policies of granting a relatively free hand to foreign governments in the provision of Islamic religious services in Europe served as a diplomatic nod to regional powers in the Muslim world, where a reshuffling of the power balance had taken place in the aftermath of Egypt's military defeat by Israel in 1973, the Iranian Islamic revolution and the religiously inspired coup attempt in Saudi Arabia in 1979.[53] Although some European countries first viewed Iranian revolutionaries benevolently, they later sought to contain the regional aspirations of newly theocratic and Shi'a Iran by supporting its Arab Sunni rivals in Saudi Arabia, Iraq, and in the Maghreb. French President Giscard even sent troops to relieve the House of Saud's difficulties with armed militants in Mecca. Tokens of good faith were offered by European governments eager to be on good terms with the Arab world, the source not only of cheap labor but also of oil. Europeans recognized their growing dependence on the Arab world following the OPEC embargo of the United States and the Netherlands and the threatened oil embargo of the rest of Europe.[54]

Key international institutions in the majority-Muslim world developed their own strategy during this period. One key Saudi-sponsored initiative in close cooperation with Pakistani authorities was called the Islamic Council of Europe (ICE). This organization was established in 1973, when estimates of the Muslim population in Europe had just reached a total of five million, to "monitor the conditions of Muslim minorities and whenever necessary take appropriate measures to deal with any situation of discrimination, injustice and denial of human and civil rights."[55] The Council, in conjunction with Muslim World League and the Organization of the Islamic Conference (OIC, founded in 1972), voiced concerns over the dangers that Muslim labor migrants would assimilate into European host societies. The Secretary General of the OIC viewed the growing Muslim population in Europe as an opportunity to increase missionary activity. The portion of the *ummah* living as minorities in non-Muslim countries, he wrote in 1980, "can help to spread the message of Islam throughout the world and can constitute a source of support in case of serious crisis. Weak, it would be threatened with destruction and would bring in its wake irreparable loss to the Muslim world."[56]

Ali Kettani, an OIC advisor on Muslim minorities, asserted the right to engage with Muslims living in Europe and to address these trends. The "maintenance of ties with the main body of Islam (*dar al-Islam*) is a very potent factor to counteract these developments," he wrote in 1980. "The Hajj plays a major role in the maintenance of these ties [as does the religious and cultural] education of the Muslim children."[57] Deeming the European Muslim minority as "a matter of Islamic duty and a matter of necessity for survival," Kettani wrote that "Muslim countries should make their relationship with the non-Muslims of the world a function of the way these countries treat their Muslim minorities."[58] A missionary leader from Pakistan wrote of the need to "provide facilities for Islamic education, the denial of which would mean the ideological death of the Muslim community," and argued that Muslim minorities in Europe must "remain conscious of their position as an ideological group with values different from those of non-Muslims."[59]

The activities of the Muslim World League and associated organizations in 1970s and 1980s Europe parallel the efforts of nineteenth-century French Catholic or American Protestant missionaries in the countries of the Levant, or the activities of the *Alliance Israëlite Universelle* which sent emissaries throughout North Africa and the Otttoman Empire to develop a transnational religious identity among Jewish minority communities in the Mediterranean.[60] Many observers have characterized this period of Euro-Arab rapprochement in the 1970s and 1980s not as routine cross-border proselytism, however, but rather as the founding moment of "Eurabia."[61] One critic of these diplomatic relations argues that Europeans' accommodation of the diplomatic aims of the Arab world, from "immigrant rights" in Europe to promoting the Palestinian cause in European foreign policy, is nothing short of "the road back to Munich via appeasement, collaboration, *dhimmitude* . . . and subservience."[62] Europeans did indeed engage in an implicit political bargain with the oil-producing Arab states, which were a non-negligible economic partner of the European Community at the time. By the mid-1970s, Artner writes, "Arab purchases from the European Community accounted for 44 percent of all Arab imports and 13.5 percent of the EEC's extra-Community exports"—more than the EEC was exporting to the United States and Japan combined.[63]

The Euro-Arab Dialogue would lead indirectly to the reinforcement of ties between Arab migrants in Europe and homeland religious organizations. It has been observed that European governments and Arab governments "had quite different perceptions and expectations" of the intensification of relations: "The Europeans wished it to be mainly technical and economic while the Arabs stressed the political dimension much more."[64] The two elephants in the room—energy and the Arab-Israeli conflict—were formally excluded from the working agenda, but the latter sometimes made its way into the language of final communiqués.[65] It would be a stretch of the historical record and an anachronism to suggest that the relationship amounted to European subservience to a monolithic Islamic "cause": the Euro-Arab Dialogue was the opening of a tug-of-war over the Muslims of Europe between competing forces in the Islamic world.

Saudi Arabia: Religious Exportation as Geopolitical Strategy

While Saudi Arabia did not send labor migrants to Europe, its government has constantly expanded the kingdom's religious influence in European countries, through the support of international Islamic organizations

Figure 2.4. *Aramco World Magazine*, January/February 1979
[FULL-PAGE]. Source: © Tor Eigeland /*Saudi Aramco
World*/PADIA.

and publications (see figure 2.4).[66] Saudi Arabia became a major commercial and diplomatic player in international Islam and in Middle
East politics thanks to energy politics and its role as custodian of Mecca
and Medina, a role wrested from the Hashemite King Hussein by
Abdel Aziz Ibn Saud upon conquering Mecca in 1924.[67] The Saudis
strategic use of oil resources and revenues dates to the late 1930s, when
the future Arabian-American Oil Company (Aramco) located its first
wells. King Faysal, in power during much of the Cold War, used religion to combat radical Arab nationalism, arguing that Muslim solidarity and Arab unity "faced the same foes—imperialism, Zionism and
Communism."[68]

This goal has been pursued in part through the Muslim World League
(*Rabitat al Alam al Islami*, MWL), a Mecca-based NGO founded in 1962
under Faysal's predecessor, King Saud bin Abdul Aziz. In response to

the rise of Arab nationalism (e.g., Nasserism) and socialism (e.g., Ba'athism) from the mid-1950s through the 1970s, the Saudi government made "systematic use of Islam as an instrument of its foreign and security policy" to safeguard the position and interests of the royal family.[69] Saudi Arabia emerged as a leading oil exporter and creditor and gained an edge in its competition with Egypt for regional hegemony following the latter's defeat by Israel, which marked the collapse of Nasserite ideology and the defeat of its privileged alliance with the Soviet Union.[70] Saudi Arabia emerged to "serve as interlocutor within the Arab state system for the concerns of its western allies."[71] The spread of Wahhabi Islam, therefore, was increasingly "interconnected with the achievement of the [House of Saud's] secular objectives."[72]

King Faysal bin Abdul Aziz (1964–1975) greatly enhanced the activities of the Muslim World League and sought to enable "independent Islamic diplomacy" through commissioners in Saudi embassies who served simultaneously as MWL representatives.[73] A former French ambassador to Saudi Arabia described the MWL's activities as multivaried and "tentacular."[74] Its Paris bureau chief, for example, also acted as an ambassador to UNESCO. The MWL charter called for making "direct contact with Muslim minorities and communities wherever they are [. . .] to close ranks and encourage them to speak with a single voice in defense of Muslims and Islam."[75] The MWL "has perceived its duty," Landau writes, "to be involved in anything and everything of concern to Muslims everywhere."[76] The MWL established 120 offices around the world and several subsidiary institutions, including regional Islamic councils on each continent.

The Islamic Council of Europe, its European headquarters, was located in London. Chaired by an Egyptian Muslim Brotherhood member who had been granted asylum in Saudi Arabia, the ICE aimed to play "an important role" in bringing Muslim organizations in the UK and elsewhere "close to the Muslim League office."[77] In the mid-late 1970s, MWL held numerous international conventions on Muslim minorities on each continent.[78] The World Supreme Council for Mosques (WSCM) was created to oversee mosque construction and maintenance outside of Saudi Arabia (its European headquarters are in Brussels); the King Abdul Aziz University in Jeddah set up an Institute of Muslim Minority Affairs; the OIC created a department of Muslim Communities in Non-Muslim States at the secretariat general in Jeddah; and a private Islamic bank was established in Geneva in 1981.

OPPORTUNITY KNOCKS: OIL SHOCK AND THE EURO-ARAB DIALOGUE

The international expansion of Saudi religious activities took place at a sensitive moment in relations between the Arab world and Western countries, and it occurred just as the immigrant population in Europe was on the verge of permanent settlement. The American military support of Israel during the Yom Kippur War in October 1973 led the Organization of Arab Oil Exporting Countries to raise prices, cut output and, eventually, impose an embargo on the United States and the Netherlands, provoking a widespread economic downturn across the industrialized world. In Europe, the sagging demand for production would spell the end of mass labor migration by the following year. The decision to stop importing labor left the population of several million first-generation migrants of Muslim origin voluntarily "stranded" in the countries they had come to for work. The embargo's deployment of the "oil weapon" revealed the "capacity of the Arab states to change the terms of their relationship with external powers through their control of large supplies of a critical resource—oil."[79] Saudi Arabia, in particular, controlled nearly 22 percent of the world's known oil reserves, and the embargo allowed it to enjoy a new position as the only "marginal supplier" or "swing producer" capable of "fixing or at least containing serious disturbances" in the oil market.[80] As Mustapha Benchenane wrote, "Arabs were finally once again able to change the power dynamics and be agents and full subjects of their own history."[81]

But Europeans, too, sensed a chance to change course. Just over a decade after French withdrawal from Algeria—the symbolic end to the European colonial era in the Arab world—European Community member-states saw an opening for new European-Arab cooperation and a chance to decrease American influence in the Arab world and, as an ancillary benefit, to acknowledge the new presence of millions of Muslims in Western Europe. During the embargo, France refused to participate in a U.S.-led "coordination group" of oil-consuming countries; France, Spain, and the UK were temporarily put on a "preferred list" to spare them the effects of the embargo and a 5 percent decrease in production.[82] Europeans discovered common cause and an opportunity to place a strategic wedge between themselves—and the Arab world—from the United States.

French former foreign minister Michel Jobert said that "European projects, such as the [Euro-Arab] dialogue face a determined opposition . . . The struggle is, how can the [Arab] states escape a system of economic and monetary control by the United States? Saudi Arabia has been American since 1938."[83] Jobert noted the opportunity presented by the Israel-Arab war, saying it "reminded Europe of its singular destiny, which is not simply that of an Atlantic promontory . . . The oil embargo was an alarm bell, not the cause, of the crisis."[84] In a 1974 interview in *Le Monde*, Algerian president Boumediènne suggested that the Europeans' only alternative to U.S. hegemony was "openness to its neighbors" in Africa and the Arab world.[85]

European governments began to seek individual and collective bilateral oil and arms trade agreements with the Saudi Kingdom and other Gulf states.[86] Shireen Hunter argues, "the West viewed Saudi-style Islam as a convenient antidote to both Communism and Arab radicalism."[87] Saudi Arabia, in turn, used the excuse of Cold-War military buildup in the West, "along with its status as custodian of the holy sites to consolidate [a Saudi] presence in the wider Islamic world by supporting the Muslim World League and the Organization of the Islamic Conference."[88] A more ambitious Saudi foreign policy ensued, with expanded influence in Asia, Africa, the Arab world, and even in Saudi Arabia's non-Arab neighbors such as Iran, Turkey, and Pakistan, in "a determined effort to acquire the spiritual and political leadership of the Arab and Islamic worlds."[89] Perhaps an "Islamic Commonwealth" constructed by the Saudi monarchy, wrote one French observer, would be "one of tomorrow's geopolitical realities, and one of the spiritual forces of a world in disarray."[90]

SAUDI EXPANSION IN EUROPE AND BEYOND

The increasing political and economic accords after 1973–74 may be viewed as a de facto peace treaty between the governments of the European Community and Arab League. Diplomatic considerations were paramount given Europeans' growing reliance on the Arab world for oil and trade purposes, as well as aspirations to use European influence in the Middle East to serve as a counterweight to the USSR and the United States.[91] In the aftermath of OPEC's oil embargo of the United States and the Netherlands in 1973–74, the Euro-Arab Dialogue (EAD)—a parliamentary and diplomatic forum between members of the European Community and the Arab League—was institutionalized between twenty-one Arab states and the ten European countries.

The injection of the issue of minority Islam into diplomatic relations between Europe and the Arab world had already begun in the aftermath of the six-day 1967 Arab-Israeli war, six years before the Yom Kippur War and subsequent oil crisis.[92] The Italian Islamic Cultural Center (CICI) was registered by Muslim diplomats in Rome as an Italian association in 1968 and soon "evolved into a way to offer internal help to Muslims in Italy."[93] The Islamic Cultural Center of Brussels, funded in large part by the MWL, was founded in 1969 and chaired by the Saudi Ambassador to Belgium, and would be considered as the official representative body in Belgium for Muslims for decades to follow.[94]

During the regular EAD meetings several times a year, participants moved from their discussion of trade issues to address the theme of "cultural cooperation," which touched on issues affecting Muslim migrants.

One EAD report made specific recommendations for the development of integration policy in Europe:

> The social integration of migrant workers and their families in the host countries would be facilitated by . . . making the general public more aware of the cultural background of migrants, e.g. by promoting cultural activities of the immigrant communities [as well as] assuring that migrants be in a position to receive regular information in their own language about their own culture as well as about the conditions of life in the host country.[95]

In view of the volatility of the situation in the Middle East at the time, following on growing demands of Arab League foreign ministers regarding Palestine-Israel and the sudden delicacy of oil supply, European governments competed with one another outside of the framework of the EAD. French and Italian foreign ministers competed to curry favor with their clients in the oil-rich Gulf region (to the mild consternation of German and American foreign ministers).[96] Giulio Andreotti, who served as Italian Prime Minister and Defense Minister in the period from 1972 to 1974, undertook a series of diplomatic visits throughout the Arab world and attempted to build up a set of "common interests between 'Christian Europe' and Islam, in search of the cohabitation, forced if necessary, between a plethora of states and political proposals."[97]

Grand diplomatic gestures and monuments to the Islamic presence in Europe soon followed, such as permission for construction of an enormous mosque in Rome, which the Saudi King Faysal bin Abdul Aziz formally requested of the Italian government during a visit in 1972.[98] The offer of the land was authorized by the local city council in 1974 in cooperation with Prime Minister Andreotti, who personally asked for the pope's blessing of a minaret in the heart of western Christendom. Andreotti said in an interview that Muslim immigration to Italy, which had just begun in the early 1970s, provided "political, strategic and symbolic" motivations for the Italian government to build the mosque, and Pope Paul VI (1963–1978) said that the mosque "would enrich Rome's civilization."[99] A group of ambassadors from Islamic countries led by Saudi Arabia were "invited to join the effort at first in order to support the idea of constructing a mosque," and they soon became members of the mosques administrative council.[100] The Italian president then recognized the mosque by decree as a legal entity (*ente giuridico*) in 1974, although construction was not completed until the mid-1990s, after the Moroccan government released additional funds.

In 1974, newly elected French President Valérie Giscard d'Estaing proposed the creation of an Institute for the Arab World (*Institut du monde arabe*, IMA), the same year his government halted labor migration. As a French commentator has observed, "It was clear that the immigrant communities would not return to their countries of origin. All the more reason to encourage their integration and to change the image of Arabs [who were] often viewed in the context of explosions of violence or the recurrent problems of oil."[101] The French government authorized the land, a choice parcel on the Seine, six years later, and the IMA's founding documents were signed in February 1980 by France and the seventeen members of the Arab League.[102] In Belgium, the official recognition of Islam as a national religion took place in 1974 (the first in postwar Europe) and the Muslim World League's creation of major Islamic centers in Brussels and Vienna in 1975. The MWL opened an office in Paris in 1976. [103]

The MWL receives dozens of annual funding requests across Europe and has provided hundreds of millions of dollars for mosques across the continent, from Mantes-la-Jolie (1980), Evry (1984), Lyon, and Paris, to Madrid, Rome, Copenhagen, and Kensington (UK). As of 1994, it was calculated that the MWL provided $40 million to French mosques and $40 million in support of Islamic organizations and institutions in the UK.[104] King Fahd (Faysal's successor) contributed more than half of the £2 million total cost of building the East London Mosque, while ambassadors from Saudi Arabia and Egypt were members of the mosque's management committee.[105]

In the subsequent two decades, the Saudis followed up on their investment in the Muslim diaspora in Europe. The Secretary General of the Muslim World League, as well as the Saudi Minister for Religious Affairs, have made regular visits to Europe to inspect premises and meet with community leaders and government officials, and the MWL has also delegated one or two representatives in each European country. The MWL was able to channel support to budding mosque federations in national contexts—not just through its support of their flagship mosques but also through support of leading personnel, at various moments—in the *Fédération nationale des musulmans de France*, the *Zentralrat der Muslime in Deutschland*, and the *Centro Culturale Islamico d'Italia*. The Saudis also provided a safe haven to key Egyptian Muslim Brotherhood figures (including Salem Azzam, the chairman of the Islamic Council of Europe).[106] Representatives of other Embassy Islams have participated in the executive boards of Saudi-funded mosques, but at the beginning of Saudi proselytism in Europe, labor migrant populations were not yet a major political issue for sending states. On occasion, the MWL chose its European representatives to maximize access to government officials. As the first Italian representative of the

MWL, a former Italian diplomat who converted to Islam, noted in an interview that:

> I have the advantage, as a retired ambassador, as a retired civil ser-
> vant, I have open doors everywhere. I go wherever I want to. I have
> access to all the palaces and all the ministries. This is a notable advan-
> tage because the Muslims of Italy do not have this access.[107]

The boom in Saudi proselytism around the world—through the construction of grand mosques, the circulation of millions of free Wahhabi
prayer books, and the dispatching of missionaries and imams—was
funded by petrodollars at an estimated expense of more than $85 bil-
lion between 1975 and 2005, reflecting a determined effort to establish
spiritual and political hegemony over Muslim practice.[108] King Fahd
(1982–2005) "personally financed the building of 210 Islamic centers
and supported more than 1,500 mosques and 202 colleges and almost
2,000 schools for educating Muslim children in non-Islamic countries,
including Europe."[109]

Former Italian Prime Minister Andreotti explained the complicated
relationship between Saudi proselytizing in Europe, and the Western
military and economic presence in the Middle East, that were at the
center of the Euro-Arab Dialogue:

> We try to have good relations with the Arab governments, not be-
> cause we are indifferent, but because it is essential that there be a
> common discussion in the Mediterranean, that we talk to one an-
> other, that we do not prejudicially consider one another enemies . . .
> All the mosques that the Saudis have built around the world became
> elements of propaganda. I'm not naïve. But the important thing is to
> try to have a relationship with them . . . because they too are suspi-
> cious about why we are [in the Middle East].[110]

The dividends of Euro-Arab dialogue for Muslim-majority countries
are difficult to assess. It is dubious whether Europeans were brought
closer to Palestinian views as a result of the EAD. For example, the
central occasion when European and Arab states issued a joint statement in the early 1980s that largely echoed PLO claims for a "compre-
hensive solution, the return of occupied land, and the need to refrain
from changing the status of Jerusalem"; but the declaration was abandoned in 1989.[111] The "oil weapon," three scholars of Saudi-European
relations recently wrote, "brought the oil-exporting countries economic rather than political gains."[112] The expansion of Islam in Europe
that took place during that period left behind a tangible institutional
legacy—grand mosques and privileged relationships with European
governments—that cannot be denied.

MISSION EUROPE: NATIONAL *DA'WA* AND FOREIGN DIRECT INVESTMENT

Turkey, Algeria, Morocco, and Pakistan: Exporting Religion as Emigrant Control

In addition to this Saudi-sponsored pursuit of religious leadership through expansion of its activities in Europe, there is also the national Embassy Islam of labor exporting states, i.e., the traditional, everyday engagement of embassies and consulates that try to maintain influence over emigré populations abroad. The four largest sending countries to Europe—Algeria, Pakistan, Turkey, and Morocco—all developed a robust practice of exporting their official Islam to the diaspora. Each state, concerned for national security and diplomatic influence in the countries of the diaspora, eventually asserted its own right of interference (sometimes euphemistically referred to as a *"droit de regard,"* or oversight) over migrants and their descendants in European host societies, its monopolistic intentions to represent Islam vis-à-vis host government, and its own status as "moderate Islam." Algerian governments worried about Islamist advances within its diaspora and wanted to counter Moroccan influence in Europe; Morocco worried about threats to the ruling regime from Moroccans abroad and hoped to counter Saudi and Algerian influence in Europe; and Turkey was most concerned about its internal legal order, as well as its geopolitical heft as the successor regime to the *Seyh ul Islam* of the Ottoman era.

The "siphoning off" of nearly one million workers during the guest-worker period relieved the unemployment problems in Turkish cities following the exodus from the countryside in the 1960s.[113] But Turkey, like each sending state, hoped to further its own economic growth and development with the help of its residents abroad. In Morocco, for example, remittances make up the largest portion of GDP after tourism and phosphate. Total remittances to the Maghreb are worth $11.5 billion, and in Turkey, which had problems with its balance of payments, remittances played an important role in its recurrent foreign-exchange crises. In this way, Turkish migrants helped cover the country's large trade deficits, a fact that was formally recognized in the Turkish five-year plan published in 1969. In addition to traditional remittances, migrants were often engaged in sizeable direct investment in their countries of origin as well as the transfer of technology and machinery. Despite a degree of "official disenchantment" over the actual impact of remittances on sending-states' economies in the mid-1970s[114]—i.e., its net effect was less than expected—the overall impact of having millions of emigrés abroad remitting, investing, and returning as tourists has proven indispensable to the developing economies. In 1975, remittances to Turkey amounted to 94 percent of exports, and nearly one-half of all

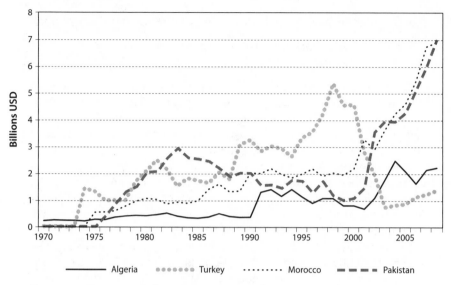

Figure 2.5. Remittances from Europe in US $ (billions) to Algeria, Morocco, Pakistan, and Turkey (1970–2008). Source: World Bank (http://databank. worldbank.org/ddp/home.do).

Moroccan exports; in 1977, they accounted for 88 percent of Pakistani exports.[115] The amount of cash flowing back to the sending countries fluctuated somewhat over the decades, but it remained a critical piece of the economic puzzle for homeland governments (see figures 2.5 and 2.6). A recent study undertaken by the Moroccan government found that most Moroccans living in Europe—2.6 million—expected to return to Morocco during summer vacation; they account for 40% of total tourism revenues annually. Their remittances were worth €4.34 billion in 2006, an increase of 17.2 percent over 2005[116] (the 2005 figure itself marked an increase of 8.2 percent over 2004).[117] This amounts to just under 10 percent of Moroccan GDP. Moreover, French transfers account for more than half of all foreign direct investment in Morocco, accounting for nearly one-quarter of all commerce in the kingdom.[118]

The Era of the Amicales (1960–1980)

Algerian, Moroccan, and Turkish governments supported social and political clubs (amicales) for single male guestworkers. These associations' main task was to "maintain the allegiance" of emigrants and to "prevent its compatriots from succumbing to the 'cancers' of liberalism, socialism, and communism so easily contracted by 'naïve emigrants in the 'decadent' host societies."[119] Beyond the bare minimum of accom-

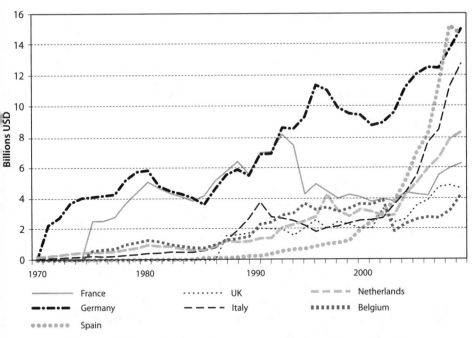

Figure 2.6. Remittance Outflow from Selected EU Countries (1970–2008).
Source: World Bank (http://databank.worldbank.org/ddp/home.do).

modation of ritual observance, scant mention of religion was made in the activities of *amicales* in the 1960s and 1970s. But later, in the 1980s and especially in the 1990s, Morocco, Algeria, and Turkey would add Islamism to the host of ills that migrants risked contracting abroad. Their consulates kept records of the number of citizens in each European city and tabs on associations founded by their nationals abroad, compiled lists of friendly and unfriendly prayer associations, and either offered their support or reported potential trouble makers to authorities of the home country or the host government.[120] Together with the sending of imams and language instructors described earlier in this chapter, the activity of *amicales* did the work of "identity preservation" to keep them "in some way affiliated to the sending country."[121]

The *Amicale des algériens en Europe* (AAE) was the most advanced "homeland fraternal organization . . . the ideal to which other homeland fraternal organizations aspire."[122] There were 100,000 members in France, and several thousand apiece in Switzerland and Germany.[123] In 1967, more than five-thousand AAE meetings took place, bringing together sixty thousand Algerians living in Europe.[124] The AAE maintained a bimonthly magazine and scheduled programming on radio and television.

Similarly, Moroccan *amicales* were "para-governmental" associations that mobilized the male population around homeland political issues and in defense of foreigners' rights, mostly for visas, resident permits, and access to the social welfare state. The *Amicale des Travailleurs et Commerçants Marocains en France* (ATCMF) was not organized as a mass-membership organization, like the AAE, but in 1985, nearly half of the 850 North African associations active in France were constituted as Moroccan *amicales*.[125]

The Exportation of Official Islam (1980–2000)

The exportation of national Islam apparatuses took place in the context of increasing worries of sending countries at home: leftist-inspired violence and instability had helped spur the consolidation of national official Islam, as discussed above. This took place in two phases: first, a partial exportation (late 1970s to late 1980s) in which homeland governments engaged in basic *cooperation* with host states to further native language retention and the sending of imams or chaplains and other basic religious services; during a second exportation (2000–2010), homeland governments intensified their outreach *independently* of the European host states (see chapter 7).

Throughout this entire period, Political-Islam networks also expanded (more on this in chapter 3), spurring the defensive diffusion of Embassy Islam through diplomatic outposts. In the 1980s and 1990s, Political-Islam groups matured into mosque federations which served as umbrella organizations to gather together the hundreds of individual prayer spaces that had been created in the meantime. The fallout from the 1979 Iranian revolution added to the constant background activities of loosely affiliated Islamist networks that were flourishing in Europe and in the sending states. Faced with severe political pressure at home, some of these movements—such as the Moroccan *Al Adl wa al Ihsan*, the Algerian *Front Islamique du Salut*, and groups linked to Turkish and Pakistani Islamist parties—had transplanted some of their operations to Europe and viewed the diaspora populations as natural sources of political and financial support. The survival of the lay order thus depended on keeping Islamist and other minority elements in check at home and abroad.

By the mid-late 1980s and 1990s, immigration and family reunification had built up a substantial enough pool of emigré constituencies to make them an issue of domestic politics for Algeria, Morocco, Pakistan, and Turkey. National sending states and regional hegemons like Saudi Arabia had an interest in keeping a close eye on diaspora populations, both as a source of support and a potential threat. The official exportation of national Islam during the past three decades provides a window into the practices of several of the most important countries "sending" Muslims to Europe. A brief exploration of the origins of each sending state's Embassy Islam follows below.

TURKEY

The Turkish directorate for religious affairs (*Diyanet İşleri Başkanliği*, DİB) developed the quintessential model of exported Embassy Islam. DİB's foreign operations expanded alongside the activities of the Turkish Foreign Ministry and the State Ministry for Religious Affairs and Turks Abroad. The DİB's European branches are generally known by the acronym DİTİB (*Diyanet İşleri Türk İslam Birliği*, Turkish-Islamic Union for Religious Affairs), for most practical matters relating to the practice of Islam: e.g., visas for imams, permits for mosque construction, teachers for religious education in public schools, etc. As the highest religious authority in Turkey, the president of DİB is the honorary chairman of every DİTİB abroad, and he participates in local DİTİB membership and executive meetings (see figure 2.7 for a photograph of the officeholder from 2003 to 2010).

Figure 2.7. Ali Bardakoğlu, President of Diyanet, Ankara, 2004. Source: Website of the Presidency of Religious Affairs, http://www.diyanet.gov.tr/english/default.asp.

Wherever there is a Turkish immigrant minority in Europe, DİTİB offers organizational shelter for existing or newly founded Turkish-Muslim cultural organizations in addition to providing services for pilgrimage to Mecca and burial in Turkey. It is estimated that DİB headquarters in Ankara holds sway over around half of the several thousand Turkish mosques and prayer rooms in Europe. Its prayer spaces in Europe have taken on some traits of Turkish territory. When they join the national DİTİB umbrella organization, the property is usually transferred to DİB and comes under the control of the Turkish government—a Turkish flag is raised and a portrait of Atatürk is hung.[126] Prayer spaces that affiliate with DİTİB are asked to promise to "uphold valid Turkish laws and regulations" on the premises.[127]

Diyanet's Foreign Affairs Department was officially founded in 1984; however, DİB initiated a foreign program as early as 1971 to offer religious services and education for Turks abroad.[128] DİTİB's 1971 mission statement compels it to "instill love of fatherland, flag and religion" abroad, and to "prevent opposition forces from exploiting the religious needs of Turkish migrants and mobilizing them against the interests of the Turkish republic." Like Algerian and Moroccan state Islam, respectively, the DİB lays claim on all Turkish citizens living abroad; it underwrites prayer space and religious education for Turks living abroad through local offices (DİTİB), often staffing them with diplomats from Turkish embassies (Minister Counselors).

DİTİB's European engagement was launched during a tumultuous period in Turkish politics, shortly after the emergence of Islamist political parties in the 1970s, the growing Islamist influence in government, a military dictatorship in 1980 and new constitution in 1982 mandating religious education. Since 1978, the DTİB has sent preachers trained in state-run seminaries (İmam Hatip Lisesi) to Europe, and a 1979 law formally authorized DİB to establish branches outside Turkey.[129] Religious officials started to work as "social help experts" through consulates and embassies. Its first official European branch was established in West Berlin in 1982; within two years, 250 organizations were gathered under the umbrella organization's headquarters in Cologne. At around the same time, DİB also brought a majority of Turkish-run mosques in the Netherlands (around 100, staffed by 75 imams) and Belgium (55) under its indirect control.[130]

Historically, Ankara has aimed to "ensure the attachment of émigré populations to the national ideology of Kemalist rhetoric—a perpetual allegiance linked to a secularized Islam and a unified nation under the control of the central state."[131] The Turkish government offers a prefabricated, export-ready version of the Islamic religion: a Muslim religious practice within the secular Turkish framework, complete with clergy

TABLE 2.2.
Religious Publications Circulated by the
Turkish Government (2006)

Language	Books	Brochures
Turkish	1,307,000	175,000
Azeri	687,000	50,000
Kazakh	502,000	40,000
Uzbek	365,000	40,000
Kirghiz	485,000	40,000
Turkmen	542,000	40,000
Tatar	140,000	40,000
German	72,000	209,000
French	17,000	217,000
Dutch	10,000	3,000
Danish	n/a	5,000
English	n/a	200,000
Total (sum of above)	4,127,000	1,059,000

Source: Statistical Figures on Turkish Islam and
Diyanet Personnel, July 2006 (http://www.diyanet
.gov.tr/english/default.asp).

from the homeland who stick to fifteen-minute sermons centrally approved and posted on *Diyanet's* internal website from Ankara each Friday (see table 2.2 of DİB publications circulated in languages other than Turkish).[132] Since the signing of a bilateral treaty in 1984, the German interior ministry has helped DİTİB with entry visas and three- to four-year German residence permits (and a Turkish-paid salary) for the imams in its employ, and similar arrangements have been struck with all European countries with significant Turkish-origin populations.[133] DİTİB's general secretary in Germany told the author that imams from Ankara are "sent to Germany to spread healthy religious information and encourage peaceful coexistence. This is a benefit to the country, since we cannot wait for Germany to get around to training imams."[134]

For Turkey, the 1970s and 1980s saw the growth of Kurdish and Islamist threats abroad to Kemalist unity at home. While the DİTİB has focused its energies in the past on marginalizing Kurdish nationalists

TABLE 2.3.
Strategy for the Religious Education of Turkish Children in Germany (1993)

- A new chamber should be founded under the Turkish Ministry of Education to deal with this issue of religious education of Turkish children in Europe.

- Turkish cultural houses can be opened in Germany, especially in big cities.

- Teachers and religious officials that are sent to Germany should be trained by the state and university professors to acquire necessary knowledge of the country and the subjects that they will teach.

- Turkish television channel that broadcasts to Europe can increase the amount of religious education showed on TV.

- Teachers and the religious officials in the mosques should cooperate, as many students also attend Koran courses. They should also increase their language skills.

- Religious course material should be adapted to the conditions of Turks in Germany.

Source: Aşıkoğlu 1993, pp. 142–48.

abroad, the largest thorn in its side in recent years has been the German Political-Islam association of *Millî Görüş*. The stakes are highest for the Turkish government in Germany, which is home to three-quarters of all Turkish citizens living abroad (see table 2.3). Sectarian and dissident religious groups had opened their own mosques and created their own unofficial associations. Therefore, by the time DİTİB opened its first European operations, immigrant workers were already under the influence of competing groups.[135] This led DİB to organize its foreign branches with greater attention and vigor. In the wake of the 1980 military coup, the Turkish government claimed that fundamentalist groups had taken root in Europe and formed a danger for the Turkish Republic.[136] "Religious problems come from abroad, especially from Germany," said former Diyanet president Mehmet Nuri Yilmaz.[137] A report in the early 1990s found that the DİTİB's main mosque in Germany was used as a base for Turkish secret services and that DİB imams reported three times a year on their congregants' political views, especially on those of Kurdish Turks.[138]

DİTİB would eventually employ more than 800 imams in Germany, each hired with the status of public servant; roughly one hundred are rotated annually with a salary from the Turkish state for four-year terms.[139] Currently, DİTİB controls more than three hundred associations and around 800–900 prayer spaces in Germany.[140] Its "Missionary and Service" activities are carried out by Religious Services counselors in Turkish embassies to Germany, Austria, Belgium, Denmark, France, Holland, Sweden, Switzerland, and by Religious Services attachés in at least fifteen consulates across Europe (including thirteen in German cities, and one in France and one in the Netherlands).[141]

ALGERIA

The stakes for Algeria are highest in France, which is home to half of Algerians abroad. From its creation in 1921 as a symbol of gratitude to North African soldiers who fought in World War I, the Grande Mosquée de Paris (GMP) was emblematic of the colonialist administration of Islam, a relation involving close cooperation—and occasional disputes— between the French and the Algerian (as well as Moroccan, Tunisian, and Senegalese) governments. After World War I, the French colonial power relied on Algeria and these other countries to establish the Grand Mosque of Paris.[142] The French president personally inaugurated the mosque in 1926 and established an association in charge of holy sites in French Algeria shortly after World War I. Though its first board of directors included Algerians, Moroccans, Tunisians, and Senegalese, the GMP gradually came under Algerian domination in the two decades that followed that country's independence.

In the 1960s and 1970s, the official Algerian amicale sponsored only nine imams "to attend to the spiritual welfare of Algerian migrants" in France.[143] In 1982, the Algerian government took over responsibility for the GMP's finances and began using the mosque as a conduit for spreading its official state Islam, creating prayer spaces, and attempting to co-opt existing ones. In the 1960s and 1970s, the GMP had a decidedly French inflection—it was "the essence of moderate French republican Islam," Boyer writes. "But once it fell into Algerian hands, a series of agreements between the rector Si Hamza Boubakeur and the Algerian government led to the successive nomination of more Algerian rectors—first Abbas Bencheikh el Hocine and then Tedjini Haddam."[144]

The Ministry for Social Affairs (in 1985–86) and then the Ministry for Foreign Affairs encouraged Sheikh Abbas to consolidate French Islam around the GMP.[145] Following the death of Abbas in 1989, the French interior minister requested a reform of the nomination process for the GMP rector. But the Ministry of Foreign Affairs intervened and took over communications with Algeria, after which another Algerian civil servant was sent to head the GMP—Tedjini Haddam—who was then named to the Algerian executive council (i.e., the Algerian presidency).[146] The French government nonetheless attempted to organize French Islam around the GMP in 1995, when the Algerians replaced Haddam, with Dalil Boubakeur (son of the former rector Si Hamza Boubakeur), a "well-integrated" French doctor of Algerian origin. Boubakeur attempted to unify the Muslim community around the Mosquée de Paris—"the same role it had when it was created in the 1920s"—and the French government gave him some tools to do so, namely a monopoly on revenues from the halal certification industry. The GMP drafted a charter of the Muslim faith that outlined a framework for state-mosque relations and which was "acceptable to French authorities of all political persuasions, for the authorities of the Republic."[147] For some Muslims in France, however, Boubakeur is still considered "un fonctionnaire algérien."[148] The GMP is now organized as a federation with five regional Muftis, and it currently controls 250 prayer spaces and associations around France. The GMP's rector has authority over 150 imams (just over 10 percent of all Imams in France), most of whom are imported from Algeria.

MOROCCO

In 1978, the Moroccan government helped establish the Union of Moroccan Muslim Organizations in the Netherlands, with ninety affiliated prayer spaces, facilitating the sending of imams from Morocco especially during Ramadan.[149] By 1990, "official" prayer spaces outnumbered rival Moroccan mosques in the Netherlands by a factor of two to one, and sixty-five paid imams worked in the Dutch community.[150] In France, Morocco was nudged by the Algerian takeover of the *Grande Mosquée de Paris* in 1982 to counter Algerian hegemony and inject its own influence into French Islamic affairs with its support of the *Fédération nationale des musulmans de France* in 1985.[151] As King Hassan II remarked in 1989:

> We are linked by the act of allegiance (*bay'ah*) to Our subjects abroad in the same way as We are to their brothers in Morocco, that We have a paternal, religious, and a moral responsibility to them, Our citizens abroad deserve more concern than their fellow citizens living in Morocco, whose needs are looked into day and night . . . The objective of the mission is to safeguard these ties and the act of allegiance.[152]

That year, the Ministry of Religious Affairs (MRA) embarked on an "Islamic awakening" campaign in universities throughout Morocco and Europe (see table 2.4).[153]

France is home to one-third of all Moroccans living abroad, and Muslims of Moroccan origin form, after Algerians, the second-largest national bloc there. As such, France has been a key arena in which the Kingdom has sought to expand its religious activities abroad. During the first French headscarf affair in 1989, King Hassan II publicly sup-

TABLE 2.4.
Key Strategic Points for Moroccans Living Abroad (2006)

Total mobilization in defense of our vital interests and national causes, foremost territorial integrity

Engaging the Community of MREs as a fundamental human resource in economic development

Consolidating the rights and privileges of the MRE Community

Modernizing emigration policies through the national sensitization of the Moroccan Community and encouraging it to assume its citizen responsibility as well as participation in political, trade union, and associational life

Intensifying cooperation with the host countries

Encourage national tourism of the MRE community by make available competitive offers

Defend our specific national causes and in particular territorial integrity

Create multidisciplinary cultural and polyvalent spaces in the principal foreign capitals

Propagate religious and civilizational values founded on tolerance, dialogue, and cohabitation

Short-term priorities: an MRE website, hotline, national Day of the Emigrant, radio and TV shows for MREs

Medium-term priorities: solving problems related to the emigration of minors, family reunification, and the civil status (*statut personnel*), customs, taxes, road safety, and international recognition of the Moroccan driver's license

---

Source: http://www.marocainsdumonde.gov.ma, July 2006.

ported the high school official who expelled the three girls—against the claims of a Moroccan-led Islamist federation that filed a lawsuit on the girls' behalf. Afterward, Hassan requested that France allow a new Moroccan mosque to be built in order to counter the influence of Algeria and Saudi Arabia, who had recently sponsored the construction of two *grandes mosquées*.[154]

Since the 1960s, this initiative was in continuity with a series of projects originating in Rabat aimed at nurturing the ties between diaspora and homeland:[155] from membership in government-sponsored *amicales*, to the creation of a Ministry for Moroccans Residing Abroad, to the establishment of the Hassan II Foundation—and later, consular support of the FNMF (later RMF) federation in France, and the launching of a new website (in French) for the Moroccan Ministry of Religious Affairs,[156] a thirty-seven-member consultative council for Moroccan residents abroad (CCME) and even an Ulama Council for the Moroccan Community in Europe (see chapter 7). Hassan's governments formally discouraged Moroccan residents abroad from acquiring double citizenship and voting rights in European countries, and in 1986 the King asked his subjects overseas not to participate in municipal elections where local law allowed for it.[157] The networks of embassies, consulates, and *amicales* were allegedly asked to "watch over MREs [*Marocains résidents à l'étranger*] and obstruct [their] political activities—even union involvement or the promotion of Berber culture was not desired," out of concern that such activities could spread to Morocco, and in order to protect the image of Moroccan laborers as "a flexible and reliable workforce."[158] When a Moroccan minister visiting an Amsterdam mosque in 1983 noticed that the imam had pointedly omitted an element of the Moroccan Malekite rite—the part offering a prayer for the Moroccan King as "commander of the faithful—he pressured local leaders to have the imam dismissed.[159]

The Moroccan king created the Hassan II foundation in 1990 to coordinate with the new Ministry for MREs to export Arabic language and Moroccan "culture teachers" to Europe: sixty-six were sent to France, thirty to Italy, ten to Spain, and two to Germany, and sixty-three preachers were sent throughout Europe for Ramadan in 1995. This grew to 206 preachers in 2006, and the Foundation claims to increasingly involve the "community" of MREs in its "conception and execution."[160] When announcing the Foundation in a Paris speech, the king said, "We have decided to entrust, by the grace of god, the presidency of the FHII for MRE to our loyal daughter Lalla Meryem. Thus our ties will not be solely of allegiance but also of family ties, since you [Moroccans abroad] will be like sons and daughters to me."[161] Its mission was "to maintain ties of allegiance with Moroccans living abroad" and to encourage "our community abroad to achieve its potential and enrich the development and modernization of Morocco."[162] It "strives to maintain and develop fundamental ties between Moroccans living abroad with their home country."

Together with the Ministry for *Habous* and Religious Affairs, the Foundation has had an annual budget of $15–$20 million since 1998, much of which was spent on teachers and educational administration in European countries. Moreover, it "supports migrant organizations' projects in Morocco or in the receiving country, sends Arabic teachers and social attachés; leads youth exchange programs, offers social and legal advice and helps with administrative problems."[163] In addition to its administrative structure, it has a research and analysis unit (the Observatory of the MRE Community) and eight operational poles: education, cultural exchange, sport and youth, legal aid, social assistance, economic development, cooperation and partnerships, and communication. Within the first pole, religious leadership (*l'animation religeuse*) is "considered essential for the preservation of the Muslim identity of the Moroccan community." Religious instruction holds a privileged place in the foundation's activities and is implemented in two programs: (1) support for Islamic centers and several grand mosques in Europe through the employment of permanent preachers sent from the Foundation for the MRE; and (2) a special program for the holy month of Ramadan in cooperation with universities, grand mosques, and other branches of the Moroccan administration.

PAKISTAN

For Pakistan, the stakes were highest in the United Kingdom, where more than a million residents would ultimately settle. However, the absence of a strong official state Islam tied to the Pakistani government led to the absence of a strong Embassy Islam in the UK as well as in other destination countries for Pakistani migrants. Despite government efforts, or indeed because of certain government officials' pan-Islamic leanings, there is not much in the way of constitutional state control over madrassas and imam training in Pakistan. This lack of official oversight is evident in the relative lack of state control over Pakistani Islam in the diaspora. Pakistan stands out in strong contrast to Turkey, not only because of the relative weak shielding of religion from political use, but also because the Pakistani military has actively used Islam as a tool of political mobilization. Pakistan more closely resembles Saudi Arabia or Egypt, in that it "sought a leading role in Pan-Islamic politics very soon after attaining statehood. After all, Islam was the main reason for its establishment and existence."[164] Pakistan thus used the rhetoric of religion for political ends, but mostly in a diplomatic context, i.e., to hasten rapprochement with Iran and Turkey, and to facilitate its courting of Arab states.[165]

As a result, the near entirety of Pakistani "export Islam" is not typical Embassy Islam fare. It is a non-nationalist, pan-Islamic variant that reflects the internal bargain that Pakistani authorities struck with local religious leaders—witness the profusion of unofficial madrassas and imam training facilities—and as such is much closer in content to the Saudi export Islam than to Algerian, Moroccan, or Turkish export Islam. Nonetheless, one scholar found that Bradford's mosques "teach Urdu using language textbooks produced for schools in Pakistan by the Punjab Text Book Board. . . . These schoolbooks are full of the heroic exploits of South Asian Sufis."[166] In Blackburn, near Manchester, each of twenty-seven mosques is staffed by an imam and a preacher sent from Pakistan.[167] Moreover, a majority of imams active in the UK are of Pakistani heritage—although the extent of their ties with official Pakistani channels has not been extensively detailed in open sources.

A Hard Habit to Break

Into the mid-1990s, with few exceptions, representatives of Embassy Islam served as the natural, de facto interlocutor for all "Muslim affairs" in European host societies. Embassy-Islam organizations became notorious for their uncooperativeness—each wants to be the exclusive representative of Islam, striving for a representative monopoly with national governments in Europe and hoping to instill cultural continuity between diasporas and the homeland.

The rector of the *Grande Mosquée de Paris* was the lone Muslim leader invited for the traditional new year's greeting at the Elysée palace. Since 1974, the Saudi- and Moroccan-sponsored CICI in Italy has long been the only mosque in Italy to hold the privileged status of "legal entity," which its General Secretary told the author means "the CICI is the only credible interlocutor for Italian authorities on a juridical basis and also on the basis of daily practice."[168] Similarly, the Saudi-sponsored ICC in Belgium gained official recognition for Islam in 1974; a royal decree recognized the center as the *"interlocuteur privilegié"* in 1978, and it remained such until 1996. The German DİTİB was the only Islamic organization to have imam visa and resident permit agreements beginning in 1984. As DİTİB spokesman Bekir Alboğa said in an interview, "In Turkey there is only one office for religious affairs, and all imams are appointed by the executive board of this office. It is the sole representative for religion. And this is why the DİTİB also has this position in Germany: it serves as the representative here [in Germany]—and this is how the DİTİB wants to be perceived."[169] Thus it has, like the Algerian-backed GMP in France, attempted to stymie or dominate any state-led efforts to create representative Islam Councils in European countries. Similarly, Turkey backed out of elections for a High Council of Belgian Muslims in 1991 (though it would later control the EMB).[170] And the Italian CICI has consistently undermined Italian government attempts to involve a broader group of mosques in its consultations with organized Islam.

The sending states want to preserve a say over the nomination of imams and chaplains, and to exert influence over the curriculum of religious education. In the case of Saudi export Islam, single-sex classes were reportedly a condition for a grant offered to Muslim school in

France,[171] and the Saudis have also laid down conditions "as to *Eid* timings and even the content of sermons."[172] Since each government is focused on a strategy of nurturing a close relationship with its *own* emigré population, the profusion of national variants of Embassy Islam—the Moroccan king is the commander of the faithful, the Turkish state is the purveyor of Kemalism, and the Algerian government proffers its own variant of Sunni Malekism—makes cooperation among them in European countries extremely unlikely.

However, Embassy Islam's interests overlapped with, but did not coincide completely with, those of the host countries. In particular, many practices of Embassy Islam representatives did not facilitate or encourage integration. They favored the use of non-European languages (Arabic, Turkish, or Urdu) in religious education, and the imams they exported were also unlikely to have command of the language of the host society. They have encouraged the political participation of Muslims in Europe in elections in the homeland and have continued a pretense of political representation for migrant-origin Muslims who are rapidly becoming a majority of European citizenship holders. Embassy Islam's activities became ever more vigorous in the late 1990s and 2000s, when majority Muslim sending-state governments intensified outreach *independently* of the European host states and sought to extend their grip on state-Islam institutions (more on this in chapter 6).

A growing chorus of denunciations of Embassy Islam arose in the late 1990s, as well as a growing pressure for governments to open talks with Political Islam representatives, as Embassy-Islam organizations proved unable to capture the imagination of second- and third-generation European Muslims. The honeymoon between European and Muslim governments was strategic and short-lived, since the host governments would ultimately judge this bargain to be too costly for domestic cohesion and immigrant integration. Europeans' demand for spokespeople and interlocutors was destined to change once outsourcing and laissez-faire became counterproductive, and when they collectively realized the cost of having intentionally sacrificed immigrant integration on the altar of short-term pragmatism.

CHAPTER THREE

A Politicized Minority

"THE QUR'ÂN IS OUR CONSTITUTION"

AT THE DAWN of the twenty-first century, public authorities in Europe had two options for Islamic interlocutors and mixed emotions about each one. On the one hand, they had in the representatives of Embassy Islam a set of reliable interlocutors whom they knew well and whom they could count on to respect the rule of law. But Embassy-Islam representatives' dedication to immigrant integration was ambivalent. On the other hand, European countries also hosted a growing number of Islamist organizations who were committed to integrating into domestic institutions. But governments were not sure they could trust the democratic instincts of Political-Islam representatives because of Islamist groups' roles in political-religious conflict in their Muslim-majority homelands and their ambiguous relationship with political violence.

Islamist organizational networks in Europe first emerged from the loose association of members-in-exile of the Muslim Brotherhood and the transnational proselytism of the Muslim World League. Since the 1940s, international Political-Islam groups had taken up the mantle of Pan-Islam as the new (or newly independent) nation-states of the majority-Muslim world were preoccupied with state consolidation at home. Many Islamists sought refuge in Europe after encountering repression beginning in the 1960s, leading to what French scholar Olivier Roy called the gradual "delocalization" of Islamist activity. The fact that many of them turned out to be religious hardliners is the result of the specific historical circumstances of the postcolonial Middle East, South Asian Subcontinent, and North Africa. The consideration of Islamism here does not focus on violent extremists or small revolutionary groups and individuals, most of whom were banned or apprehended in Europe.[1] This chapter concentrates on Political-Islam organizations located in the "gray area," those that avoid illicit activities, incitement to violence, or association with terrorists.

Practically none of the first two generations of Islamist leadership in Western Europe arrived as labor migrants or as beneficiaries of family reunification. They emerged instead from a small cohort of religiously minded students in Europe to pursue advanced degrees in engineering, architecture, and medicine, and from political exiles who had fled religious repression in majority-Muslim countries. The Islamic activists who arrived from Egypt, Syria, Saudi Arabia, and other Gulf states in two waves—the 1960s and the 1980s—found in Europe a wide-open berth for nongovernmental participation in the social and religious lives of Europe's Muslims.

Ironically, European governments' ambivalent views of their immigrant populations of Muslim origin led them to permit (or ignore) the arrival of these religious leaders from the Muslim world—who did not come with their home government's stamp of approval. These men left behind semi-authoritarian political situations marked by the strong-arm tactics of many heads of state in the region. European governments provided safe harbor to regime opponents, sometimes granting asylum as retribution for diplomatic slights by their home countries' governments.[2] The political-religious dissidents clearing out of Nasserist Egypt and Baathist Syria, as well as those countries that did send labor migrants—Bhutto's Pakistan, Bourguiba's Tunisia, Hassan II's Morocco, Benjedid's and Boumedienne's Algeria, and Kemalist Turkey—often came to pursue advanced degrees. Many of them created "Muslim student associations" to campaign for religious rights at a time when their economic migrant compatriots were mostly engaged in struggles for labor and civic rights when they were politically organized at all.

These refugees and students—estimated today to number in the low thousands—would eventually "constitute the central core of Western Islamism."[3] Much of today's non-governmental Muslim leadership in Europe can trace their lineage this way, ranging from the Italian *Unione delle comunità ed organizzazioni islamiche* to the French *Union des organisations islamiques*, to the United Kingdom's Muslim Association of Britain, Islamic Mission, and Islamic Society of Britain, to the European branches of *Millî Görüş*. These leaders in turn created or modernized youth sections of their current associations. The prayer rooms gradually affiliated with national branches of Islamist federations, and second and third generations exhibited signs of an increase in religious identity and (selective) religious practice, what some scholars have termed "re-Islamization."[4]

What values and claims do the Political-Islam federations aim to inculcate? In European contexts, their morality campaigns are most aggressive in areas related to co-education and the defense of Islam's presence in the public sphere. Islamists encourage "modesty" among young women, asserting the right of girls to wear headscarves, to be excused from physical education, especially swimming, and frown upon taking class trips without religiously sanctioned chaperones. Indeed, many of the most infamous nonviolent confrontations between "Islam" and "the West" between 1990 and 2010 can be traced to the presence of Political-Islam networks in Europe. Islamist leaders have demonstrated an unmistakable propensity toward censorship. For example, they have objected to the depiction of the Prophet Mohammad in European cultural products old and new: British novels, Italian frescoes, Danish caricatures, and operas staged in Geneva or Berlin. They are litigious, vigorously defending Muslims' (and their own) public image in court. In some ways, their agenda is not so dissimilar from Islamist movements in the homeland countries. Islamist parties there favor the visible expression of religion in the public sphere, and institutional and social equality of religious individuals' ability to lead their own version of a pious life.

Despite Islamists' public assurances, some movement slogans hint at greater aspirations than just equal treatment and integration for Muslims. It has been suggested that the Muslim Brotherhood aphorism, "Allah is our objective; The Prophet is our leader; The Qur'ân is our constitution," reveals affiliated Muslim leaders' true intentions in Europe.[5] The suspicions point to the enduring influence of a small canon of Islamist scholars including Sayyid Qutb (Egypt, 1906–1966), who strived for an "Islamic society" on the basis of Islamic law—which he viewed as "self-sufficient"[6]—without any of the individualist additions of modern constitutional law. The Brotherhood slogan "The Qur'ân is our constitution" was allegedly uttered in an interview by a leader of France's largest Political-Islam federation, the *Union des Organisations Islamiques* (UOIF), although he later denied it. The underlying message of disloyalty to the rule of law is a frequent accusation by German security officials of the Constitutional Protection Office (*Verfassungschutz*), for example, who claim that Islamists pursue an Islamic legal order. The slogan echoes the founding mottos of the Muslim Brotherhood from the interwar period, and those of Brotherhood-inspired political parties in the Maghreb, Turkey, and Middle East in recent years that have suggested that "Islam is the solution" to their countries' political and economic development.

Since 1989, the networks created by Islamist prayer federations have come to pose the strongest challenge to the "secular" rule of law in Europe since native opposition to the liberalization of divorce and abortion in the early 1970s.[7] Given the fact that Muslims will constitute a tiny percentage of voters for many generations to come, the Islamist groups in Europe have avoided electoral politics and focused instead on community organization. When critics of Islam suggest the religion is in need of Reformation, or accuse Muslim leadership of a "double discourse"—preaching conciliation and dialogue in European tongues, while exhorting religious fervor in their native languages—it is Islamist leaders whom they have in mind. To some observers, they appear to be pursuing the creeping Islamization of Europe.

Political Islam's success can be at least partly explained by the first phase of European "outsourcing" of state-mosque relations until 1990. The wholesale exportation of prayer leaders from home governments and the privileged arrangement of Embassy Islam did little to further integration, and competing religious leaders pointed out the contradictions of Europeans' practice of outsourcing with their stated desire for Muslims' integration. In an interview with the author, one community leader described the French rector of Paris's Grande Mosquée as "*un fonctionnaire algérien*" [an Algerian bureaucrat].[8] A Hamburg mosque federation spokesman said plainly that "The prayer leaders sent from Turkey do not know German society. Muslims' religious identity is reinforced in these mosques, but not their integration into German society."[9] A Turkish-German Islamist leader, contrasting his organization's activities with those of the Turkish state-sponsored Directorate for Religious Affairs (*Diyanet*), suggested that German administrators had painted themselves into a corner.

> Some German politicians think that when it comes to question of religious education, for example, that they can work together with the Turkish *Diyanet*. Today the diplomatic ties with Turkey are considered to be more important, but in ten years someone is going to have to decide "what will become of Muslims in Germany?" If Germany still wants the Muslim community to develop outside of German politics, out of the sight of the German state, and the opportunity is granted to control the Muslim community from abroad, from Turkey, then they will know for sure what to do. But German politicians will soon realize that *Diyanet* does not encourage integration. Because it is against a German-speaking religious education. And because *Diyanet* preaches Turkish nationalism in its mosques. In ten years, German politicians will ask what happens to the property that *Diyanet* buys in Germany and transfers to the possession of the Turkish state. A foreign state is creating extra-territorial areas in Germany.

The expansion of Political Islam in Europe is also the underside of the standardization and centralization of "official Islam" in Muslim-majority homelands and its exportation to the diaspora. The reason why Embassy Islam representatives pursued a monopoly of state-Islam relations in Europe so tenaciously—as indicated by their expansion of religious control in Europe during the period 1980–2000—was precisely because they were well aware of the Islamist threat to their religious authority and political influence over diaspora Muslims—including through the maintenance of financial ties. Shadid and Koningsveld wrote in 1991 that because of Moroccan and Turkish bans on "the formation abroad of political parties or branches of those in existence, cultural and religious foundations were founded as a substitute."[10]

Diplomats from Algeria, Egypt, Morocco, and elsewhere consistently warned Western security services against taking in their political and religious dissidents, but these admonitions generally went unheeded. After the experience of the Second World War, Europeans were committed—through constitutions and international treaties—to religious liberty and political asylum and they hesitated to take sides in conflicts taking place in colonial lands that European colonial powers had freshly departed.[11] The host governments' strategy of supporting Embassy Islam made sense when the goal was to encourage return migration, but that framework began to obsolesce with the growth of second and third generations. The arrangement would prove costly for the integration of native-born Muslims who did not identify with their host society or their former homeland. As one German integration official said,

> Since so little was done [by German governments] for the religious needs [of migrants from Turkey], structures developed which have led in part to segregation and ghettoization processes. It was thought that we didn't need to pay attention to this because they were all going home anyway. We therefore missed the opportunity to open German institutions to immigrant groups and did not watch out for what kind of independent structures were developing. This makes today's dialogue and bilateral openness [between Turks and Germans] somewhat problematic.[12]

Some governments were wary of allowing avowed (or convicted) religious fundamentalists past their borders, while others were notoriously lax for a time. France was careful to exclude violent extremists who might appeal to the North African-origin population, and Germany closely observed the anti-democratic tendencies of Turkish-origin Islamists. The most notorious case of laxness in filtering out extremists was "Londonistan," but in the main, no country fared much better or worse at preventing the spread of nonviolent Islamist networks in their mosques and prayer spaces.

Governments awarded a de facto monopoly on Islamic religious representation to foreign states, but they also granted student visas and political asylum to those same states' avowed enemies. Most administrations offered indirect or direct financing of local prayer spaces that were separate from the grand mosques funded by foreign governments. In this way, thousands of small prayer rooms were established throughout Europe that were unaffiliated with the Embassy Islam of immigrants' homelands. Islamist groups drew these prayer rooms into representative federations, and thus grew strong enough to challenge the dominant position of Embassy Islam across Western Europe, recreating the oppositional role these movements have played for decades in their countries of origin. In Europe, however, Islamists achieved what was out of reach in their homelands: a measure of official recognition and institutional power, albeit limited to religious affairs and social integration rather than in a political context.

Islamist federations that began as parties-in-exile have, over time, become European sociopolitical actors. They have left behind homeland politics and instead target their host societies' domestic arenas: Europe's state-Islam relations rather than its foreign policy. This mirrors the transformation that Political-Islam movements have undergone in their native environments since the early 1990s, shifting from opposition and exile to a strategy of participation and moderation. In Europe, their initial homeland orientation has largely yielded to domestication (see chapter 7).

Origins of Political Islam: The Pan-Islamic Dream after the Ottoman Empire

> In countries confronted with Islamism, there is an Islam that is recognized and supported by the state, and then there is a parallel Islam. At the moment of the French Revolution we called these the *clergé réfractaire* and the *clergé constitutionnel*. In Islamic countries it is the same thing.
> —*Advisor on Islam to the French Interior Minister (1988–1993)*[13]

One prominent scholar of global Islam points out the "impossibility of a single theory" to account for the galaxy of Islamist movements, noting that the definition has evolved beyond "a totalizing project seeking to capture state power" to include new demands for "the inclusion of religion in public life and greater recognition of Muslim identity claims within the context of broadly secular societies."[14] However, Political-Islam organizations in Europe share several broad characteristics. The French religion specialist Olivier Roy notes two key commonalities of Islamist groups: an ideological outlook of the "inseparability of religion and politics," and their recruitment patterns, which attract individuals "far removed from traditional ulamas," the scholarly councils that are central to official religious authority in the homeland.[15] Notwithstanding their original goals of undermining the nation-building projects in their countries of origin, these are not simply political movements, Roy argues, but also a sort of religious brotherhood. Another historian of Islamic movements adds that Islamists tend "to interpret all events—domestic as well as external—in the light of their impact on the *ummah* [the global Muslim community], and by extension, on Pan-Islam," i.e., the movement advocating the unity of all Muslims under a single caliphate.[16]

The most influential international organizational networks of Political-Islam activists in Europe are of Arab, South Asian, or Turkish descent, corresponding to the dominant origins of the Muslim diaspora in Europe. There are many antecedents to modern Political Islam, but three movements are central: the Muslim Brotherhood, *Ikhwan al-Muslimin* or MB, of Egyptian inspiration; the Islamic Community, *Jama'at-i Islami* or JI, of Indo-Pakistani origins; and the National Vision, *Millî Görüş* or MG, of Turkish background (see table 3.1). The movements' loosely affiliated branches have aimed to "Islamize" society from below—first in their homelands, then in Europe—by gaining control of religious, academic, cultural, and social institutions. They are loose ideological networks of like-minded leadership figures, yet they also maintain organizational and financial ties with Muslim associations across Europe. While they are far from all-encompassing of Islamic organizations in Europe, these movements' worldviews—forged in the tumultuous post-Ottoman interwar period nearly one century ago—provide a powerful prism for understanding links between religion and identity for migrant-origin populations in Europe.

Unlike the Islamist parties that later emerged in North Africa, parties related to both the Pakistani *Jama'at-i Islami* and Turkish *Millî Görüş* have overcome state repression and rotated in and out of political office. In Turkey, Welfare Party leader Necmettin Erbakan held high political office from 1974 to 1978 and briefly served as prime minister in 1996–97. The JI helped rally theologians behind the Pakistani nation-state; it became "the dominant voice for the interests of the Ulama in the debates leading to the adoption of Pakistan's first constitution, and actively participated in opposition politics from 1950 to 1977."[17] JI found an ally in Muhammad Zia-ul-Haq (president, 1978–88) for whom "Islam was Pakistan's salvation." Zia-ul-Haq found religious parties to be a useful moral bulwark after the corrupt civilian rule under Zulfikar Ali Bhutto (prime minister, 1973–77) and because an Islamic identity served as an important nationalist distinction with neighboring India. *Jama'at-i Islami* became "a pillar of the Zia regime and an ardent supporter of the General's Islamic state"; the party even joined government one year after Zia-ul-Haq's coup, during the trial and execution of Zulfikar Ali Bhutto.[18] Zia-ul-Haq's cooperation with *Jama'at-i Islami* extended to his "efforts to pursue domestic legitimacy through religion," with an "Islamic cargo fleet, Islamic science foundation, and Islamic newsprint industry."[19]

This muddies the distinction between Political Islam and Embassy Islam in the case of Pakistan. The distinction remains clearer in the case of Turkey, where the country's independent religious establishment (*Diyanet*) has been institutionally sealed off from Islamist influence. The Turkish Justice and Development Party (AKP) that gained control of the executive branch in 2007 might eventually change course, but the political sensitivity of this separation is likely to remain. Similarly, although the JI suffered repression at the moment of Pakistani state creation in 1948 and spent years in opposition, it subsequently enjoyed a fruitful period of collaboration. Whereas Turkish pan-Islamic tendencies have tended to be limited to Turkish-speaking populations around the world—though they sometimes claim to speak for other Muslim minorities inhabiting the same territories—Pakistan's official Islam was always hybrid, both nationalist and internationally oriented, similar to that of Saudi Arabia, in that the state itself harbored broader pan-Islamic ambitions.

Kindred Spirits: Modern Islamist Parties

If economic issues led millions of low-skilled men to flee the Middle East and North Africa, it was state repression in Egypt, Syria, Lebanon, and North Africa that would spur the partial exodus of thousands of mostly well-educated Muslim Brotherhood members to Europe. The incomplete process of democratization in Turkey, the Middle East, and North Africa—from the periodic repression in Egypt under Nasser until 1971, and again in the mid-1990s under Egyptian President Mubarak, through party bans and coups in 1980s and 1990s Turkey, to the crackdowns under Hassan II in 1970s–1990s Morocco, and the cancelled elections in Algeria in 1991—led to successive waves of political exile to Europe. The difficulty faced by Islamist opposition movements in creating viable political parties over the decades led MB members to turn to a natural reserve of potential support—informal social networks in Europe—for "sustained mobilization in the face of repression."[20] As Dale Eickelman wrote, "first and second-generation immigrant communities offer[ed] better bases for the exchange of ideas and information than those available in countries of origin."[21]

Well before the mass arrival in the late 1960s and early 1970s of immigrant laborers from the Mediterranean basin, the Muslim Brotherhood and *Jama'at-i Islami* provided glimmers of hope to those who wished to restore the caliphate and dreamed of a modern pan-Islamic

TABLE 3.1.
Three Islamist Movements

Ikhwan al-Muslimin (Muslim Brotherhood)

The quintessential Political Islam movement—the Muslim Brotherhood—was founded in 1928 by Hassan al-Banna (1906–1949) in Egypt, the intellectual and political center of Islamism. The MB grew in response to the aftermath of western colonialism, as "arbitrary and tyrannical" rulers replaced European masters in majority Muslim countries.[1] The early MB leaders stressed Islamic unity across geographical boundaries and sought reestablishment of an Islamic Caliphate following the fall of the Ottoman Empire after World War I. Hassan Al-Banna pursued "his own version of Pan-Islamic nationalism," while "strongly disapproving of local brands of nationalism, particularly if they were Western-inspired and secularly minded."[2] Another leading figure in the Egyptian MB wrote that "Loyalty should be to Islam, not to race. The brotherhood of Muslims is the first connection, even if places and times have distanced."[3] The MB initially took up arms against the ruling Egyptian regime, earning it "the negative image of putschists and seditious rebels," and served as the "intellectual source of revolutionary Jihadist Islamism."[4] Later, it would adopt a non-violent, legalist approach. Central MB texts describe their faith as an "all-inclusive system—religion, country, and nationality [*din wa dunya wa dawla*], religion and state, spirituality and action, book and spade"—and Islamic political thought as "needing no foreign borrowings."[5]

Jama'at-i Islami (Islamic Community)

Mawlana abu al-a'la al-Mawdudi (1903–1979) held similar beliefs in Islam as "an ideology, an activist creed and a legal system."[6] As the founder of the *Jama'at-I Islami* (JI) movement in 1941 Lahore, al-Mawdudi viewed nationalism in the Muslim world as a tool of colonialism, and lamented its debilitating effect on the Pan-Islamic movement. In his early publications, al-Mawdudi "attacked patriotism, based on race, territory, language and culture," and recommended instead "an Islamic union . . . to supersede all other ties."[7] Al-Mawdudi sought to make Pakistan an Islamic state and tried to persuade leaders there to apply *shari'a* law. He created a "well organized and efficient religious and political organization"—the oldest Islamist party in Pakistan—modeled on the Egyptian MB.[8] Like its Arab cousin, the JI aimed its calls for Islamic revival at middle-class professionals and state employees, rather than traditional Mullahs and Ulama.[9] "The country is god's; rule must be by god's law," the JI asserted. "The government should be that of god's pious men."

Millî Görüş (National Vision)

In Turkey, the institutional strength of Kemalist-inflected official Islam—and briefly, single-party rule—delayed the emergence of Political Islam as an organized force until the decade 1969–1979. Starting in 1970, the founding father of Turkish Political Islam, Necmettin Erbakan (1926–2011), established a series of

(continued)

TABLE 3.1. *cont.*
Three Islamist Movements

Millî Görüş (National Vision) *cont.*

Islamist political parties that were successively banned.[10] Erbakan's movement was implicitly more nostalgic for the Caliphate than allowed for by Kemalist secular values strictly defined. In a 1979 speech in London, Erbakan said that increasing "Muslim cooperation" could help assemble "the world's greatest power."[11] The *Millî Görüş* movement originated as a faction within one of Erbakan's parties and claimed to be based on "moral and spiritual values," where Islam was the obvious (although usually unmentioned) foundation. *Millî Görüş* aimed to translate "our basic values" into politics, one government minister said in the 1970s, taking into account the constitutional prohibition on the political use of religion and placing Islam at the core of Turkish values.[12]

[1] Maréchal, *The Strength of the Brothers—Roots and Discourses of the Muslim Brotherhood in Europe, 2008,* 2.
[2] Landau, *The Politics of Pan-Islam,* 1990, 223–24.
[3] Muhammad al-Ghazali, 1917–1996 (1984: 138), cited in Shavit, *The New Imagined Community,* 2009, 125.
[4] Maréchal, *The Strength of the Brothers,* 2 and 30.
[5] Allam and Gritti, *Islam, Italia,* 2001, 54; Ternisien, *Les frères musulmans,* 2005.
[6] Lewis, *Islamic Britain: Religion, Politics and Identity among British Muslims: Bradford in the 1990s,* 1994.
[7] Landau, *The Politics of Pan-Islam,* 1990, 227.
[8] Danièle Joly, *Britannia's Crescent: Making a Place for Muslims in British Society,* 1995.
[9] Haqqānī, *Pakistan: between Mosque and Military,* 2005, 21 and 25.
[10] Millî Nizam (National Order, 1970); Millî Selamet (National Salvation, 1972); Refah (Welfare, 1983). Cf. Turam, *Between Islam and the State: The Politics of Engagement,* 2007, 47.
[11] Landau, *The Politics of Pan-Islam,* 1990, 264.
[12] Atacan, "Explaining Religious Politics at the Crossroad: AKP-SP," 2005, 189.

state. These hopes were dashed in short order, first in Egypt and later in North Africa. Egyptian MB leaders flirted with extremism and violence in the mid-1950s and experienced state repression in the form of prison, torture, and executions. During the 1960s, their most difficult decade, 100 MB members were killed by the police and the army, another 1,450 were sentenced to prison or forced labor, and 61,000 were questioned or arrested. The scholar and MB leader Sayyid Qutb was hanged under President Nasser in 1966.[22]

Many Islamists saw the Iranian Revolution of 1979 as the redemption of a half-century's wait since the first stirrings of al-Mawdudi (*Jama'at-i Islami*) and al-Banna (Muslim Brotherhood). The events in Tehran contributed to "an Islamic awakening" elsewhere, well beyond the Shi'ite world under Iranian sway.[23] The Muslim Brotherhood in Egypt sought to channel momentum, the Belgian scholar Brigitte Maréchal writes, "to implant a real international network . . . consolidating their movement and their leadership . . . in an attempt to set in motion a pan-Islamic movement, capable of bringing about an Islamic state in the Muslim world."[24] In the 1980s and 1990s, Political-Islam parties and movements sprouted across the Maghreb, Turkey, and much of the rest of the Muslim world.

In North Africa, where MB-related political parties emerged, each party shared a similar organizational structure,[25] although the Algerian and Moroccan Islamist offshoots were independent from MB central. Even so, the MB's founding fathers remained influential. The writings of the three Egyptian forerunners, Hassan al-Banna, Muhammad al-Ghazali, and Sayyid Qutb, provided the ideological adhesive that connected religious opposition in Arab countries through shared slogans, manifestos, and references. Maréchal observes that in Morocco the connection often "amounted to no more than a certain recognition, on the part of certain individuals, of a certain ideological affiliation." The Moroccan group *Chabiba Islamiyya* (Islamic Youth) adopted Qutb's *Milestones* as its manifesto in 1969, for example. Three decades later the *Al Adl wa al Ihssan* movement in Morocco took on the Muslim Brotherhood slogan "The Qur'ân is our constitution."[26]

The basic platform of national Islamist parties—to free Muslim lands from the vestiges of colonial rule and to introduce Islamic precepts into constitutions and legal frameworks—was uniformly met with state repression. Western governments helped physically stem the revolutionary tide in the Gulf region with material and political support to Iraq, Kuwait, and Saudi Arabia to help them counter Iranian expansion. Governments in North Africa and the Middle East clamped down on the ideological and political threat posed by Islamist parties in the 1980s and 1990s. The experience of Islamists in Algeria, Morocco, and Tunisia consistently mirrored the trajectory of the Egyptian Muslim Brotherhood: each time they gained in strength, they were shut down. Algerian Islamist leader Mahfoud Nahna (b. 1938–d. 2003) spent fifteen years in prison; Algeria's government cancelled the 1991 elections after an impressive performance by the Islamist party, and later prevented Nahna from participating in the 1999 elections, and kept another Islamist party (Movement for National Reform) from running in the 2007 elections. In Morocco, Islamist leader Abd al-Salam Yassine was imprisoned for years at a time in the 1970s, 1980s, and 1990s. Military coups punctuated a half-century of Turkish politics: coups in 1960 and 1980, two "partial" coups in 1971 and 1997, and an abortive coup in 2007. Recep Tayyip Erdoğan, prime minister since 2006, spent four months in prison in 1999 for religious incitement.

This treatment prompted some Islamist leaders to leave, usually to Europe. Those who stayed adjusted their behavior, if not their goals. Political-Islam groups linked to the Muslim Brotherhood responded to repression by reconsidering their approach. In Egypt, the post-Qutb era (after 1966) initiated a long evolution toward pragmatism during the 1970s. Once the MB realized that "putschist strategies" were dead ends, the group "respected [the] established order" and "played the legalist game."[27] The MB's supreme leader asserted that the movement would henceforth "seek compromise" by viewing Islamic culture "as part of the framework of a modern state." New manifestos published in the 1980s "testified to their increased consideration of the pluralism of Egyptian society."[28] A similar transformation took place in Algeria, Morocco, and Turkey, where most branches of the MB chose to collaborate with existing regimes. Islamists settled upon an "emphasis on pragmatism and policy rather than public virtue," Peter Mandaville argues, "figuring Islam as a discourse of progress and social justice."[29] They abandoned excessive ambiguity with regard to the legitimacy of the state and the rule of law. Parties linked to the Muslim Brotherhood transitioned from being seditious enemies of the state to semi-loyal opposition, but retained an attachment to the religious values that had made them controversial. The result, Hugh Roberts argues, is that Islamists have become rational political actors who accommodate modernist and democratic ideas not as "the result of any necessary affinity between Islam and democratic principles . . . so much as the fruit of an evolution determined by . . . the objective of maintaining and, where possible, extending social and political influence."[30]

In Algeria, the Islamist parties that survived the government's annulment of 1991's legislative election results quickly adopted survival strategies. The parties had spent years underground in the 1970s, spreading their message through civil-society associations concentrating in the fields of education, proselytism, and charity, and campus activism. They rose in importance as legitimate opposition parties through the 1980s, and very nearly took power in 1991. After the *Front Islamique du Salut* was banned in 1992, Islamist parties became the official opposition through the 1990s.[31] After a 1997 law banned the political use of religion, one Islamist party, *Hamas*, re-named itself the Movement of the Society for Peace and changed its MB-esque slogan "Islam is the Solution" to "Peace is the Solution."

In Morocco, Abd al-Salam Yassine had called in the 1990s for Islamization of the Moroccan economy. His network of seven hundred charitable and social associations, *Al Adl wa al Ihsan*, were active in the largest cities, expanding into university life and gradually becoming the "largest political force" among Moroccan students.[32] But Moroccan Islamist parties took care to dispel the impression that they sought the application of shari'a law. In Pakistan, the *Jama'at-i Islami* emphasized constitutionalism and cultivated its image as a mainstream Islamic party and worked closely with Zia ul-Haq's government.[33] In response to repeated party bans in Turkey, the thrice-renamed *Refah* party altered its motto in the late 1990s from the pursuit of an "Islamic order" (*tariqat*) to a "Just Order" (*Adil Düzen*). The *Refah* party emerged victorious in local elections in 1994 and was able to form a national coalition two years later, making Necmettin Erbakan prime minister in 1996. This marked the first time an Islamist leader had acceded to power in modern Turkey. Erbakan pursued an Islam-inflected foreign policy, including a rapprochement with Islamist parties in Algeria, Lebanon, Egypt, and the Palestinian territories.[34] This lasted little more than one year, before his party was banned in early 1998. Some observers view the success of Recep Tayyip Erdoğan's Justice and Development Party (*Adalet ve Kalkınma*, 2001–) several years later as the vindication of Erdoğan's patience in achieving his ultimate goal to govern Turkey, while others view it as the reformed response to its earlier excesses.

Words such as "justice" and "development" in Islamist slogans acted as a nod and a wink to voters who viewed existing regimes as incapable of either. Despite the institutional obstacles in their path, Bernard Lewis notes, Islamist opposition parties enjoyed "several obvious advantages. They express both their critiques and their aspirations in terms that are culturally familiar and easily accepted. . . . In the mosques they have access to a communications network—and therefore tools to disseminate propaganda. . . . They are relatively free from corruption and have a record of helping urban masses."[35] Political-Islam parties' organizational strength—and their occasionally robust electoral performance—in spite of the official hindrances placed in their path—testifies to the resonance of their messages. These movements grew stronger in the countries "afflicted with problems of economic and social development where Western-style states were unable to keep promises made with regard to civic, cultural and economic growth."[36] In other words, the same factors that led to large-scale emigration—the lack of economic development resulting in high unemployment rates—also fed organized Islamism.

The organizational networks that Islamist migrants brought to Europe in the period 1960–2000 can be seen as the religious and civil society counterparts of the Muslim humanitarian NGOs that sprang up at the same time in other parts of the world, including Islamic relief organizations in Bosnia, Chechnya, Turkey, Lebanon, and Central Asia.[37] By happenstance of history, second- and third-generation migrant populations of Muslim background came to maturity in European countries precisely when acute conflict in their countries of origin caused regimes in the broader Muslim world to hemorrhage unwanted Islamist leadership. The Political-Islam federations active in contemporary Europe trace their lineage to dissident movements that, seeking refuge from homeland regimes, staked out operational bases in neutral territory.

The Islamist Settlement in Europe

As might be expected, the first Islamists to arrive in Europe were homeland oriented, like aristocrats who fled the French Revolution and eventually helped restore monarchy in 1815, or members of the Polish diaspora who fueled the Solidarity labor movement from abroad. The Islamist leadership in Europe fit Shain's description of the classic "rear guard . . . composed mainly of overseas students and emigrants and their descendants who, for economic reasons, reside or are naturalized outside their home nation."[38] Those seeking refuge abroad were by definition the ones whose political and religious careers in the homeland were unsalvageable under the existing regime or who otherwise refused to compromise their principles to participate in a diluted loyal opposition. Some remained (or remain) committed to regime change at home. But somewhere along the way, many of the leaders who emerged in this milieu changed their goals, fixing their sights instead on the religious and social life of the growing Muslim populations in Europe.

What began as exile student organizations became fairly traditional immigrant/religious services associations over time. Islamist leaders came to view the European Muslim population as a target of proselytism and re-Islamization, rather than as potential recruits to homeland political causes. The Political-Islam federations gathered prayer spaces into umbrella groups to compete with Embassy Islam, not just for influence over social and spiritual activities, but above all to serve as the legitimate community representatives to local and national administrations in the European host societies.

This section discusses the wave of Islamist arrivals to Europe (1960–2000), the proliferation of Political-Islam organizations in Europe (1980–1990), their links with the Islamist leadership and political parties in the homelands, and how Political-Islam federations have attempted to build a sustainable Islamic subculture within the religious-institutional framework of the European host societies.

Waves of Emigrés: 1960–2000

Unlike its development in the majority-Muslim world, the Muslim Brotherhood in Europe was created by a process of "improvisation,"[39] rather than "group intention or decision."[40] The arrival of Islamist refugees in

Europe varied "in relation to disturbances at the international level."[41] The issuance of arrest warrants and the threat of imprisonment in Egypt and Syria in the 1960s—as well as the expulsion of dissidents and the banning of political parties three decades later, such as *Al-Nahda* in Tunisia, the *Front Islamique du Salut* in Algeria, and the Moroccan repression of *Al Adl wa al Ihsan*—have all fed into a growing pool of exiles in contemporary Europe.[42] Given this pattern of Islamist migration, Europe could have simply become a new base for operations so that political designs could be hatched against autocratic regimes at home. Amel Boubekeur argues, however, that "Islamist parties were not present as such in Europe, preferring to work with cultural associations, either creating new associations, or joining existing organizations."[43]

In addition to the expanding population of exiles, Muslim exchange students pursuing advanced degrees in European universities played an important role in this activist milieu. Campuses in the Middle East and North Africa were often the locus of Muslim Brotherhood–related and other Islamist religious activism against homeland regimes,[44] and many Islamist activists came to study in Belgium, France, Germany, Italy, and Great Britain from the 1960s through the 1980s (see table 3.2). The most effective and dynamic new Islamic associations in Europe—in stark contrast to the staid institutions representing Embassy Islam— were Muslim student organizations which set up educational seminars and preached the movement's tenets. Many of these student groups served as the institutional precursors of the major PI federations active today. They assumed these roles in immigrant communities that otherwise lacked leadership. Given that many labor migrants came from the least educated and least moneyed, it was "natural that MB should play a leadership role among them."[45]

The associations these exiles created eventually took on a life of their own, far removed from concerns over the repressive situations in the countries of origin. The establishment of mosques and affiliations into Europe-based umbrella organizations mirrored, with a delay, developments in the Muslim majority world. They transitioned from holding the perspective of parties-in-exile to that of local community organizers, all the while retaining some attachment to the values that made them controversial to begin with. "At first, they organized inward-facing groups," Brigitte Maréchal writes of the Muslim Brotherhood leadership that sought refuge from repressive regimes. "But since the 1980s, they became a powerful force acting within the community as a whole."[46] They transformed from being homeland-oriented to being Europe-orientated, and from making maximalist claims to taking more pragmatic and moderate stances, which also mirrors broader patterns in Muslim majority countries—opposition/exile, then participation/ moderation—as described in chapter 7. "Association[s] which started off with an Islamist heritage," Amghar and Boubekeur argue, "converted [their] activities to the defense and integration of Muslims in Europe."[47]

POLITICAL ISLAM NETWORKS AND RELIGIOUS INFRASTRUCTURE:
AN ORGANIZATIONAL SUPERNOVA

From the mid-1980s to the mid-1990s, a plethora of new federations founded by Islamists in exile emerged to aggregate the hundreds of local prayer spaces that had been established in European host societies (see table 3.3 and figure 3.1). This organizational burst of activity coincided with a reconsideration of relying on Embassy Islam as the sole legitimate purveyor of new mosques and religious personnel. Political-Islam leaders, estranged from the official Islam in their countries of origin, argued that Embassy-Islam organizations were sclerotic and out of touch with the reality of a growing native European Muslim population which had little experience of their parents' and grandparents' homeland. Events linked to a nascent European Muslim experience bolstered this trend, such as the Rushdie affair in 1988 and the French headscarf affair in 1989: they laid bare the differences between the strategies of state-centered organizations that tended to back European governments and those of federations with civil-society ties who came down on the more populist side.

Many Political-Islam leaders are often better integrated in European societies than Embassy representatives, speaking the local language and being familiar with asserting their rights via European legal and political systems rather than through diplomatic channels. Over the past two decades, they have pursued anti-discrimination lawsuits, established religious instruction, and constructed new mosques. Many have ties to Political-Islam organizations in the Middle East and North Africa.[48] The French UOIF and FNMF organizations, for example, were co-founded by Islamist exiles from Morocco and Tunisia, and Algerian Islamists with links to MSP later joined the UOIF governing structure. In Italy, the UCOII traces its origins to USMI (late 1960s), an organization of Jordanian, Syrian, and Palestinian students in Perugia that merged with six other mosques and thirty-two other leaders to found UCOII. Organizational links with the Muslim Brotherhood are usually indirect, even though these would not be "not illegal per se," as Vidino points out, "since the MB is not considered a terrorist organization nor is it banned in any Western country."[49]

A typical Political-Islam federation in a European country represents several hundreds of prayer spaces and has its headquarters and primary mosque in a former industrial site on the outskirts of a city with a large Muslim population. Each federation maintains a network of preachers, has contacts with a handful of charismatic stars able to draw

TABLE 3.2.
Founding Waves of Political Islam Organizations in Europe

	Name	Founding Location	Founder/Leader and Date	Personal/Organizational Ties
First Wave	Internationale Muslimische Studenten Union e.V. (IMSU)	Aachen, Germany	1960	Established a prayer space that would become the Bilal Mosque, and later, Islamische Zentrum Aachen (IZA, 1978)
	Bilal Moque and Islamic Center	Aachen, Germany	Issam al-Attar, 1964	Syrian Muslim Brotherhood
	Islamisches Zentrum	Munich, Germany	Saïd Ramadan and Ghaleb Himmat, 1960/1973	Egyptian and Syrian Muslim Brotherhood
	Centre Islamique de Genève	Geneva, Switzer-land	Saïd Ramadan, 1961	Egyptian Muslim Brotherhood
	Council of Islamic Communities and Societies in Germany	Mainz, Germany	Saïd Ramadan, 1962	Egyptian Muslim Brotherhood
	Association des Etudiants Islamiques en France (AEIF)	Tunisian Al-Nahda	Paris, France	Muhammad Hamidullah, 1963
	Union Muslimischer Studenten-Oranisationen in Europa e.V.(UMSO)	1963	Bonn, Germany	Mohammad H. Said from the West Bank and Hassan Torabi from Sudan
	l'Union Internationale des Étudiants Musulmans	Belgium	1964	Syrian Muslim Brotherhood
	Islamic Cultural Center of Brussels	Brussels, Belgium	1969	Muslim World League

Second Wave	Tabligh wa Da 'wa (Faith and Observance)	France	Mawlana Muhammad Ilyas, 1927 (India), 1972 (France)	
	Millî Görüs (IGMG)	Germany, France, Netherlands, etc.	Necmettin Erbakan, 1969 (Turkey), 1973 (Germany)	Millî Nizam, Millî Selamet, Refah
	Islamische Gemeinde Köln	Cologne, Germany	Metwaly Mousa, 1976	
	International Institute of Islamic Thought	Lugano, Switzerland	Yusuf al-Qaradawi, Ghaleb Himmat, 1977	
	Groupement Islamique en France	France	1979	Breakaway group from AEIF, wanted to shift ties from Syria Muslim Brotherhood to Egyptian Muslim Brotherhood
	Ad-dawah Mosque (Stalingrad Mosque)	Paris, France	1979	Association Culturelle Islamique
	Islamische Gemeinschaft Deutschland (IGD)	Munich, Germany	1982	Egyptian and Syrian Muslim Brotherhood
	Ligue islamique du nord	Nord-Pas-de-Calais, France	1983	Created the first private Islamic school in France, Lycee Averroes, Involved in the 1994 Hijab case of 20 girls expelled from school
	Union des organisations islamiques en France (UOIF)	Seine St-Denis, France	1984	
	Al-Khalil Mosque	Brussels, Belgium	1985	Abdel-Karim Al-Kebadani,

Sources: Maréchal 2008; Johnson 2010; Lemmen, 2000

TABLE 3.3.
Selected Religious NGOs

Country	Date	Acronym	Full Name
France	1972	Tabligh	Tabligh wa Da'wa (Faith and Practice)
	1983	UOIF	L'union des Organisations Islamiques de France
	1985	FNMF	Federation nationale des musulmans de France
	1989	FFAIACA	Fédération française des associations islamiques d'Afrique, des Comores et des Antilles
	1997	CIMG	Communauté Islamique de *Millî Görüş*
Germany	1973	VIKZ	Verband der Islamischen Kulturzentren
	1985	IGMG	Islamische Gemeinschaft *Millî Görüş*
	1986	IR	Islamrat (Islam Council)
	1994	ZMD	Zentralrat der Muslime in Deutschland
	2007	KRM	Koordinationsrat der Muslime
Belgium	1986	FIB	Fédération Islamique de Belgique (*Millî Görüş*)
	1997	LIIB	Ligue Islamique Interculturelle de Belgique
	2006	LMB	Ligue des Musulmans de Belgique
Netherlands	1975	FION	Federatie Islamitische Organisaties in Nederland
	1981	NIF	Nederlandse Islamitische Federatie (*Millî Görüş*)
	1990	NFMIO	Nederlandse Federatie van Maghrebijnse Islamitische Organisaties
Italy	1982	AMI	Assemblea Musulmana d'Italia
	1990	UCOII	Unione delle Comunità ed Organizzazioni Islamiche in Italia
Spain	1971	AME	La Asociación Musulmana de España
	1979	CME	La Comunidad Musulmana de España
	1981	UCIDE	La Unión de Comunidades Islamicas
	1986	AU	La Asociación Al Umma

(continued)

TABLE 3.3. *cont.*
Selected Religious NGOs

Country	Date	Acronym	Full Name
United Kingdom	1997	MCB	Muslim Council of Britain
	1997	MAB	Muslim Association of Britain
Europe	1989	FIOE	Federation of Islamic Organizations in Europe
	1990	IESH	Institute for the Study of Human Sciences
	1997	ECFR	European Council for Fatwa and Research

a crowd for its annual conferences, and is linked with like-minded federations at the national and European levels. Table 3.4 provides a brief profile of an Islamist federation typical of each major ethnic Islamist group—Arab, Turkish, and South Asian, in three countries where each group is predominant, respectively—in Europe's Muslim diaspora.

GROWING APART FROM THE HOMELAND:
THE BIRTH OF A EUROPEAN *UMMAH*

In the late 1980s, Muslims living in Europe began to feel increasingly distant from the countries of origin and experienced a political awakening leading to more participation and a higher profile in domestic political debates. These trends combined to create a movement toward European Islamic organizations, and away from religious organizations identified with the official religion of the sending states described in chapter 2. Embassy Islam was increasingly "disavowed by the base," leading to the "questioning of the *amicale* system due to the legitimacy crisis of North African regimes" and the "contradictions of [those regimes'] development policies and [their] acute socio-economic problems."[50]

Tariq Ramadan, a Swiss reformist theologian with family ties to the Muslim Brotherhood, characterized the 1985–2000 period as one of political awakening: "the way in which Muslims in Europe have taken root follows a three-fold logic," he wrote in 2000: "active citizenship, social and political participation at all levels, and financial and political independence."[51] The French political scientist Vincent Geisser wrote:

The children of emigration [now] make claims in the public space of the host societies with the intention of being recognized as European citizens, not just as employees. The new generations of young people

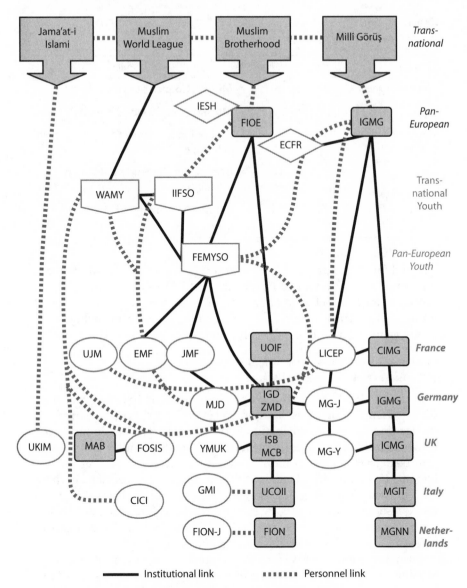

Figure 3.1. Organizational Links Among Religious NGO Networks

TABLE 3.4.
Three Political-Islam Federations of Prayer Spaces

The UOIF in France

The *Union des Organisations Islamiques de France* (UOIF), a charter member of the Federation of Islamic Organizations in Europe (FIOE), is headquartered in a defunct factory in a Parisian suburb. The UOIF was founded in 1983 by Moroccan students who rejected the monopoly on representation by the Grand Mosque of Paris, and as a result of other schisms amongst dissidents of "official" Franco-Algerian Islam. The UOIF federates approximately 250 of cultural, religious, and professional associations. It claims influence over 150 prayer spaces, but directly owns less than a third of these. The UOIF runs a small theological seminary in cooperation with the FIOE at Château-C1hinon in Nièvre. As of 2009, its president and general secretary are both from Morocco, and both came to France to pursue advanced degrees in Bordeaux. Though the organization has no formal links to the Muslim Brotherhood, its president has met regularly with a roving MB ambassador in Europe. UOIF representatives go on regular fundraising trips to the Gulf States and Saudi Arabia, partly with the help of the French offices of the Muslim World League and private donors; the organization's directors speak openly of their wish to decrease their dependence on foreign aid.[2] The federation claims to maintain a "policy of non-intervention" with regard to its donors: the UOIF independently owns and administers the prayer spaces paid for with Saudi or Gulf-state money.[3] The UOIF has sought to dispel any uncertainty about whether its sympathies lie with its adoptive country, however, and in 1990 changed its name to the Union of Islamic Organizations *of* France (rather than "in" France).

The IGMG in Germany

The *Islamische Gemeinschaft Millî Görüş* (Islamic Community of the National Vision, IGMG) headquartered in Kerpen, North Rhine Westphalia, promotes "the application of Islamic principles to the public sphere."[4] Established in Cologne in 1976 as the Islamic Union of Europe (Islamische Union Europa), and refounded in 1985 as *Millî Görüş*, the organization has long been the arch-rival of the directorate for religious affairs (DITIB). IGMG has links to a series of Islamist parties in Turkey associated with Necmettin Erbakan.[5] The party has nurtured an active dissident network in Europe, sending leaders to Germany for service in IGMG. In turn, IGMG has helped finance the political activities of Refah and its successors in Turkey with donations from European members of IGMG. The IGMG maintains fourteen branches across Europe. The Cologne office is responsible for finances, while the Bonn office, established in 1994 and called the Union of the New World Outlook in Europe, oversees religious issues and mosque construction. Local *Millî Görüş* branches (known as *Islamische Föderationen*) have emerged as a major organizational force, principally as the arch-rival of the Embassy Islam of the Turkish state (DİTİB). The IGMG defines itself in contrast to the DİTİB, describing it as a foreign organizations operating

(continued)

TABLE 3.4. *cont.*
Three Political-Islam Federations of Prayer Spaces

The IGMG in Germany cont.

under diplomatic cover, and thus as an obstacle to integration. The federation has approximately 400–600 prayer spaces in Germany and 26,500 dues-paying members there, though it is estimated to have as many as 100,000 sympathizers.[6] The IGMG has founded qur'ânic schools and prayer spaces in competition with the DİTİB, and organizes its own Hajj pilgrimage tour package.[7]

The UKIM in Great Britain

The United Kingdom Islamic Mission (UKIM) and the Islamist party *Jama'at-i Islami* (JI) have historically maintained close ties. The UKIM was founded in East London in 1962 by a group of students and young professionals from Pakistan.[8] By the late 1970s, UKIM controlled 38 mosques and 22 cultural centers. Its network of mosques is centered around Birmingham, with headquarters in London.[9] In 1973, UKIM established the Islamic Foundation (IF) which has evolved into a major center of research and education, first located in Leicester and now Markfield. Other affiliated institutions in its network include Young Muslims UK, the Muslim Education Trust, and a separate institution called *Dawat ul Islam* that is targeted at Bangladeshis.[10] The first directors of the UKIM's Islamic Foundation were followers of JI founder Abu al-ala' al-Mawdudi. An early chairman was Khurshid Ahmed, a Pakistani Senator who joined JI in 1956 and served as a JI vice president. The group spent its early years translating the JI founder's work "to make al-Mawdudi's writing available to South Asian Muslim diaspora in England."[11] The extent of coordination between UKIM and JI is not publicly known: in the words of one UKIM official, "We belong to the international Islamic movement, neither to *Jama'at[-i Islami]* nor to *Ikhwan* [Muslim Brotherhood] nor to the *Refah* Party in Turkey—but all of them are our friends."[12] The organization is also said to have connections with the Islamist *Ahl-i Hadith* party in Pakistan, and it is a member organization of the Council of Mosques in the UK and Ireland, sponsored by the Saudi-based Muslim World League.[13] Beyond its preoccupation with Pakistani politics, the UKIM has been active in organizing Islamic education for migrant-origin Britons in furtherance of "a caring and sharing society . . . based on the ideals, values, and principles of Islam," and has aimed to represent religious community with the British administration. At present, UKIM has forty-six branches, including several with Islamic schools where roughly five thousand British Muslim children are enrolled.[14]

[1] Ternisien, "Un budget encore très dépendant des "généreux donateurs" du Golfe," 2002.
[2] Interview by the author with Fouad Alaoui, General Secretary of the UOIF, 06.2002.
[3] Frégosi 1999.
[4] See "Islamische Gemeinschaft Milli Görüs," www.igmg.de.
[5] First the Refah party, then its successive rump factions, Fazilet and Saadet.

(continued)

TABLE 3.4. *cont.*
Three Political-Islam Federations of Prayer Spaces

[6]Innenministerium Nordrhein-Westfalen, "Islamische Gemeinschaft Milli Gorus," http://www.im.nrw.de/sch/582.htm; IGMG controls 514 prayer associations across Europe and claims 210,000 dues-paying members from across the continent. See: 2005 Verfassungsschutzbericht, p. 223.
[7]Feindt-Riggers and Steinbach, *Islamische Organisationen in Deutschland*, 1997, 40.
[8]Vidino, "Aims and Methods of Europe's Muslim Brotherhood," 2006.
[9]Nielsen, "Transnational Islam and the Integration of Islam in Europe," 2003.
[10]Rex, "Islam in the United Kingdom," 2002, 61.
[11]Mandaville, *Global Political Islam*, 2007, 283.
[12]Vidino, "Aims and Methods of Europe's Muslim Brotherhood," 2006.
[13]Lewis, *Islamic Britain: Religion, Politics, and Identity among British Muslims: Bradford in the 1990s*, 1994.
[14]"U.K. Islamic Mission," http://www.ukim.org/webpages/Branches_Centres.aspx.

of North African origin hold the nationality of the host society, which is not just an administrative process but a clear statement of allegiance to the host nation that they now identify as their own.[52]

Geisser argued that the sending governments' encouragement of certain ties to its diaspora has actually been counterproductive. Emigrés returning to the ancestral homeland encountered "administrative chaos, corruption at customs, and bureaucratic misadventures," leading to "a loss of illusions about the 'accomplishments' of North African regimes since independence." This undermines any nostalgia they might have felt—especially among the younger generation that did not experience colonialism—and leads to "a more critical stance towards the countries of origin."[53]

By the late 1980s, Political-Islam federations were present to accelerate this tendency and to capitalize on it. Their new formulations of political demands are partly the reflection of changing citizenship and nationality regimes.[54] But this is also a reflection of the organizational dynamics of adaptation and pragmatism displayed by Islamist networks across varying European political systems. Representatives of Political Islam in Western Europe do not constitute a political force that aims to win votes and hold elected office; instead, they aspire to be an administrative partner of government. As representatives of a tiny minority, their office-holding aspirations do not extend to the three branches of government: their membership-based civil-society associations seek administrative privileges such as mosque permits, visas for imams, and chaplaincy appointments. They are thus focused primarily on obtaining influence in the realm of religious-service provision.

Their experience of entering public debate in the late 1980s demonstrated, however, that these activities can easily influence the sociopolitical (if not electoral) realm. Their eruption onto their respective national scenes in Europe came as a turning point in 1988–1990. The second generation of Muslims born in Europe came of age during the Rushdie affair, the first headscarf affair, the first Palestinian Intifada, and the 1991 Gulf War. As nervous European governments expressed a need for Muslim interlocutors, Political-Islam federations were the only ones with a legitimate claim of authentic links to the Islam of the streets (*l'Islam de la rue*), the courtyards (*hinterhöfe*), or the cellars (*caves*). They claimed they could decipher what average Muslims were thinking about these international incidents more accurately than any consular representative or ambassador associated with Embassy Islam.

The Second Stage (1990–2010)

Despite the existence of clear linkages of Political-Islam federations with Islamist parties and with pan-Islamic movements such as the Muslim Brotherhood, it would be difficult to describe the federations' activities in Europe as a strategy of global domination, except, perhaps, through a strategy of political integration. These groups behave not as branches of a new "Comintern," but as domestic European organizations with domestic-oriented leadership and exclusively domestic political demands. Political-Islam leaders may retain allegiances to and symbolic membership in international networks, but their daily activities—and their constituencies' interests—are undeniably domestic and routine in nature. These groups are entrenched and involved with their European host societies, whose domestic institutions are at a far more advanced and generally more self-confident stage of democratization.

By portraying themselves as the only segment of European Islamic leadership willing to use local European languages as a working idiom, and the only ones willing to naturalize unconditionally (not an option for diplomats from sending states), they define themselves in contradistinction to the homeland-oriented policies of Embassy Islam organizations. The typical "self-definition" of Political-Islam federations, as one Italian official put it, is that of the "Islam of the base, of the mosques, of the periphery, of the poor."[55]

As with MB-inspired parties elsewhere in the world, national strategies, local chapters, and national branches have often taken divergent positions from the mother organization, as well as from one another.[56] Despite the close relationship with Necmettin Erbakan's Turkish political parties, Yukleyen writes, the *Saadet* party's "failure in the home country has led the European branch of *Millî Görüş* . . . to concentrate more on their local situation and interaction with European authorities."[57] In an interview with the author, a *Millî Görüş* leader argued that "a generational change" occurred in the mid-1990s.

Today, IGMG employees concentrate on the issues of importance to the communities in Germany and Europe—and I object to the German government's characterization of IGMG as fundamentalist or having the Islamist goals of founding an Islamic state. But for today's era, the youth know what they want. Beforehand, *Millî Görüş* was an organization of foreigners who felt like guestworkers. People were interested in Turkish politics, since they intended anyway to return to Turkey, and did not concern themselves for the needs of Muslims in Germany. But today this has changed. We see ourselves as an Islamic religious community in Germany, which addresses the social and culture needs of its membership, which of course also engages in political action since it is also an immigrant organization. Because our proposals are at the end of the day aimed at German politicians. We do not want to be seen as a foreign organization or to be treated as a Turkish political party. We see ourselves as a Germany-founded, Germany-concerned—and also Europe—and evolving community.[58]

Throughout Western Europe, governments are legally precluded from reaching formal religious-recognition agreements with noncitizens. Political-Islam leaders who had become naturalized European citizens sought advantage from this constraint by proposing themselves as more suitable interlocutors for European administrations than the foreign diplomats of Embassy Islam.

LEGITIMATE SUBCULTURE OR ISLAMIST SPACE? ISLAMIST NETWORKS AND THE EUROPEAN *UMMAH*

Political-Islamist organizations have been focused on a second-generation strategy since the mid-1980s. They did so in much the same way as postwar communist parties built up organizational subcultures to "corporative forms of group solidarity by creating a socially encapsulated [. . .] culture" that engaged their followers in related organizations.[59] Islamist networks worked to develop networks that cater to all aspects of their members' social life.[60]

ISLAMIC YOUTH ORGANIZATIONS

The best illustration of how Political-Islam leaders have gone about re-Islamization is to examine their focus on youth groups. The interest of pan-Islamic leaders in developing an Islamic identity to counter "assimilationist" trends was signaled by a Pakistani official in charge of the World Federation of Islamic Missions at a 1980 conference in London. He proposed the establishment of Sunday schools in Europe as well as a "forty-day intensive course of *Islamiyat* for students during long vacations at certain selected schools or other places" in order to "provide basic skills and values but also to help develop a healthy character."[61] Associations linked to the Muslim Brotherhood have emulated the strategies of Evangelical and Jewish communities to establish religious weekend retreats and activism training workshops which take place in a summer camp–like atmosphere. The major PI federations in each European country also host multi-day annual conferences— generally over Christmas or Easter holidays—that focus on how to live as an observant Muslim in the West, and how to navigate European legal systems on behalf of Muslims' religious freedoms.

As with Political-Islam organizations more generally, the creation of Islamic youth organizations (IYOs) in Europe owes much, indirectly, to the transnational proselytism of the Muslim World League and the exile of the various branches of Muslim Brotherhood. Much of today's Muslim leadership in Europe can trace their lineage to the Muslim Student Associations of the 1970s.[62] These leaders and others have in turn created or modernized youth sections of their current associations. IYOs organize lectures, discussions and leisure activities, overnight trips, religious seminars, and annual conferences; many maintain websites for online chatting. They can be a space for political socialization, conferences, and young-leadership training; they offer camaraderie and a common identity to young people coming of age, and thereby offer the consolidation and articulation of a minority voice in a "hostile" environment. IYO members socialize and learn more about Islam. IYO leaders participate in international conferences sponsored by youth sections of UNESCO or the UN, issue statements on behalf of Gazans or the Egyptian Muslim Brotherhood, and offer advice on the most recent public debates surrounding the place of Islam in Western societies.

Each European country with a sizeable Muslim population has at least one IYO (see table 3.5). Some are the successor organizations to Muslim student associations (MSAs) founded in the 1960s and 1970s, while many others were created as youth sections of national Muslim associations; like their "parent" organizations, many of these IYOs are federated at a European level in the Forum of European Muslim Youth and Student Organisations (FEMYSO). Like their PI "parent" organizations, IYOs in each European country are divided along linguistic and ethnic cleavages: Arabic-speaking, Turkish-speaking, or Urdu-speaking. At a pan-European level, however, a linguistic common space has emerged where second- and third-generation young people from Urdu- and Arabic-speaking families converse together in English or French.

TABLE 3.5.
Islamic Youth Organizations in Western Europe

Name	Place	Date
Federation of Student Islamic Societies (FOSIS)	London, England	1962
Islamische Gemeinschaft *Millî Görüş*-Jugendabteilung (IGMG-J)	Kerpen, Germany	1971
World Assembly of Muslim Youth (WAMY)	Riyadh, S. Arabia	1972
Young Muslim Organization (YMO)	London, England	1978
International Islamic Federation of Student Organizations (IIFSO)	Salimiyah, Kuwait	1970s
Muslim Youth Foundation	Manchester, UK	1983
Young Muslims UK (YMUK)	UK, Birmingham	1984
Union des Jeunes Musulmans (UJM)	Lyon, France	1987
Sveriges Unga Muslimer (SUM)	Sweden	1991
United Muslim Student Organisations in Europe	N/A	1991
Conseil de la Jeunesse Pluriculturelle (COJEP) / Ligue cojépienne d'éducation populaire (LICEP)	France	1992
Jeunesse Musulmane de France (JMF)	France	1993
Muslimische Jugend Deutschland (MJD)	Germany	1995
Forum of European Muslim Youth and Student Organisations (FEMYSO)	Brussels, Belgium	1996
Étudiants Musulmans de France (EMF)	Talence, France	1997
Giovani Musulmani d'Italia (GMI)	Milan, Italy	2001
Muslimische Jugend in Österreich (MJÖ)	Austria	2001
Congres des Étudiants Turcs de France (CETF)	France	N/A
Islamische Föderation in Wien–Jugendverein (IFW-J)	Vienna, Austria	N/A

A separate German-speaking space exists among Arab- and Turkish-origin youth in Germany, Austria, and Switzerland. However, these two groups—Arab and Turkish—otherwise remain organizationally segregated throughout Europe.

There is a lack of consensus on the precise number of young Muslims in Europe, but it is estimated that young people under the age of eighteen make up roughly half the European Muslim population of around 16 million.[63] IYO activities involve an organized subpopulation of perhaps tens of thousands or one hundred thousand across Europe: a tiny fraction of young people of Muslim background. The distinction between "youth" and "parent" (or "adult") organizations is not always especially meaningful. Some adult organizations have had prominent young leaders (the *Comunità religiosa islamica in Italia*, e.g., has long had a thirty-something vice president and spokesman; the *Union des organisations islamiques de France* (UOIF) has executives in their thirties and a twenty-three-year-old regional CRCM president). And other adult organizations, such as *Hizb-ut-Tahrir* and *Tablighi Jama'at*, explicitly target youth in their recruitment efforts without maintaining a separate youth section in their organization.

Nonetheless, a field of youth organization has come into existence and thrives as a social and political action network, and as a feeder into the PI political and religious associations that some young Muslims will later join. They are organized as national, regional, and local branches of European networks or as freestanding associations. At the same time, many or most young Muslims involved in IYO activities are citizens of the European states where they were born and/or grew up.[64] This means individuals' potential for traditional political participation through institutional channels is greater than that of the current adult generation, since they enjoy full political rights.

POLITICAL ISLAM IN A MINORITY CONTEXT: THE SOCIAL AND POLITICAL RECEPTION OF ISLAMISTS

Europeans' understanding of Political Islam is colored by their interpretation of the postcolonial history of the Muslim world as well as their own experiments with "official" and "unofficial" religion in their national histories. The respect that European governments accorded to Embassy Islam, seen in chapter 2, reflects a natural solidarity with their governmental counterparts in Muslim states, and a shared perception of dissident Islamic movements as essentially anti-system actors. But European governments' occasional openness to Political Islam hints at an acknowledgment of their own failed efforts to control forms of religious expression in previous centuries, as well.

Muslim sending states made clear that European governments would pay a diplomatic cost for legitimating the European branches—however diluted and estranged—of Islamist opposition groups abroad. Diplomatic pressures were exerted on host states to refrain from engaging dissidents: "by protecting and assisting the political exiles—an insignificant nonrepresentative minority which had conspired against the national interest," the hosts would endanger their relationship.[65] "Home regimes," Yossi Shain writes, "may employ a wide range of symbolic and coercive measures at home and abroad to discredit political exiles as illegitimate and destroy them as a political force." [66] Thus, the Egyptians persuaded the French to ban Tariq Ramadan from entering French territory for a year in the mid-1990s, and the Turks pressured the Germans to deny official recognition to leaders of *Millî Görüş*.

Some European observers see the Islamists' strategy of adaptation, such as *Millî Görüş*'s shift from seeking *"eine islamische Ordnung"* (an Islamic order) to *"eine gerechte Ordnung"* (a just order) as a coded language that proves they are wolves in sheep's clothing. Critics argue that European Islamists are merely deferring their dream, and waiting to become "50% plus one" when they will show their true colors and limited commitment to democracy: what Martin Kramer has referred to as "one man, one vote, one time."[67] These attitudes do not follow partisan lines: European political figures on both right and left are uncomfortable with PI federations because of their promotion of such issues as the headscarf and their defensiveness regarding Islam's image in the public sphere.

The most frequent accusation is that MB-related organizations and individuals engage in double-speak and harbor the same worrisome agenda pursued by Islamist parties in the Muslim-majority world: Islamization, or the creation of an Islamic sub-culture.[68] One scholar, Lorenzo Vidino, has argued that European Islamists "often show a moderate façade" when speaking with journalists or government officials,

> Yet, in their mosques, revivalist organizations espouse a diametrically different rhetoric, still embracing the ideology of the organization to which they trace their origins. . . . Their aim . . . is the radicalization of European Muslim communities and the creation of . . . "non-territorial Islamic states"—separate Islamic states within the state, in which Muslims would have separate social spaces (from schools to swimming pools) and separate jurisdiction.[69]

All Muslim Brotherhood organizations, Vidino asserts, "aim at swaying the Muslim population to [their] strict interpretation through the activities of [their] capillary network of mosques. . . . Given the lack of other structures . . . many Muslim immigrants seeking the comfort of familiar faces, languages and smells congregate in mosques, which are often seen more as community centers rather than simply places of worship."[70]

Islamists' turn away from homeland politics and toward the European arena does not reassure everyone. Indeed, it has raised the antennae of security officials across Europe who view this in terms of a long-term Islamist strategy of global domination. An observer of German Islamists asked, "Does anyone doubt this is part of a plan?"

> The key is that this isn't a natural outgrowth of European Islam. This isn't civil society taking root and sending out shoots. Instead, it's like a plant that has been given a super dose of fertilizer or growth steroids. And like such a plant, its fruit is unsafe for human consumption. . . . Nowadays, our bar is so low that if groups aren't al Qaeda, we're happy. If they're not overtly supporting terrorism, we think they're okay. We don't stop to think where the terrorism comes from, where the fish swim.[71]

A former interior ministry official in France told the author in an interview, similarly, that

> One can speak with [the] secretary general of the UOIF, but he is attached to a general Islamist strategy for Europe, for the world over. Which is the strategy of the Muslim Brotherhood—of which there are many different expressions. Whenever I say something like this, everyone says "this guy is completely crazy, he's agitated, he sees Islamists everywhere just as one used to see Bolsheviks everywhere—he thinks there's a new International." But the Federation of Islamic Organizations in Europe (FIOE), which administers the problem of French Islam from a European perspective, treats the national federations as subsidiaries."[72]

Nonetheless, Islamists come under harsh scrutiny from state security services, who suspect a basic terrorist connection—or at least a slippery slope from Islamism to violent radicalism: the intellectual foundation of jihadism, after all, was laid by the framers of the Muslim Brotherhood movement. Hassan Al-Banna's *Risalat al-Jihad* is still "required reading for jihadist indoctrination."[73] Despite the primordial connection between Political Islam and violent Jihadism, there have been irreparable rifts. Political-Islam activists prioritize political action over religious proselytism, Roberts argues, and they "seek power by political rather than violent means."[74]

In fact, their pragmatism has been the cause of much strife. They come in for criticism from another realm—violent Islamist extremists—and this is one raft of criticism that may actually help their case in Europe. Many *jihadis* criticize Political-Islam activists for their pragmatic tendencies, for "dividing the *ummah* (community) and tending to *fitna* (dissension/civil strife)" and for using Islam as "party-political stock in trade."[75] The fact that Muslim Brotherhood leaders "admit the importance of juridical methods of reasoning and the results obtained therewith by ulamas who came after the first three generations of Islam," Maréchal writes, has led to tense relations with purist Wahabi-Salafist elements.[76]

The Case of Germany and Millî Görüş

German political leaders' fears of Islamism are reflected in the *Länder*'s relationship with *Millî Görüş* (IGMG). State offices for the protection of the constitution (*Verfassungsschutzbehörden*) monitor the publications, public statements, and meetings of potentially violent radicals and potential terrorists, as well as those of explicitly non-violent Islamists. IGMG has been the subject of *Verfassungsschutz* investigations of anti-constitutional activities at the federal level and in nearly every German *Land* where it is active. Its followers are frequently demonized in the German press as rampant fundamentalists.[77] "The number of Islamists is not the same thing as the number of potential terrorists," Interior Minister Schäuble said in May 2006, but "Islamists have a vision of state order that we do not share. . . . We do not want terrorists, but we also do not want Islamists. Instead, we want [Muslims to have a] passion for this country . . . We must insist that Muslims in Germany identify with the constitution." German constitutional protection reports enumerate Islamists' offenses to the democratic spirit, regardless of whether organizations espouse violence, eschew it, or denounce it. While nonviolent Islamists' law-abiding nature is not directly questioned, their organizations are often accused of practicing social or political self-segregation, of promoting intolerant attitudes, and of using legal means to "create Islamist milieux, where there is a danger of continuing radicalization." A typical report on the IGMG by the government of Hamburg excludes the possibility of administrative contact with the organization so long as *Millî Görüş* does not renounce what the government calls the fundaments of Political Islam, that "Islamists want God, not the people, as the highest authority, with shari'a as the basis for this state."

IGMG's focus on developing Islamic identity among young German Muslims has aroused concern that they wish to segregate German-born second- and third-generation Muslims. Critics believe that the organization brainwashes young participants in its activities so they have an Islamist, anti-Western viewpoint. A Berlin teacher in a heavily immigrant school said, "I have students who take a bus and go away for the weekend to a *Millî Görüş* sponsored workshop in North Rhine West-phalia and they come back 'knowing' exactly how the world works."[78] The IGMG came under state surveillance for a combination of cultural and security-related reasons. The *Verfassungsschutz* reports note with alarm the organization's "conflation of religion and politics, which has a negative consequence for democracy and the Turkish popula-tions"[79]; its ties to foreign political parties such as offshoots of *Refah* in Turkey; its alleged support of Bosnian and Algerian extremists in their civil wars during the 1990s; the repeated expressions of anti-Semitism in *Millî Gazete* (although disavowed by IGMG), thought to be one of the organization's press organs; use of the Turkish language in educational materials; its conception of gender relations and segregation of the sexes; and the report's assumption that IGMG aims to found a political party one day.[80] *Millî Görüş's* attempts to disassociate itself from the *Refah* party, or to disown its association *Millî Gazete*, are deemed im-plausible by security officials and political leaders alike. In the words of one security official, "The problem is that they want to create a separate space."

> The IGMG is problematic when it comes to the role of women, and the fact that it is tied to political parties in Turkey. . . . They are not independent—they get orders from abroad and even send money back. They claim that the ties with Erbakan no longer exist . . . and they set off flares to distract attention and claim that the *Millî Gazete* isn't theirs—yet ask anyone![81]

Unlike other policy questions related to immigration and integration, which often divide political leaders along party lines, the evaluation of *Millî Görüş* is a matter of elite consensus. A research director at a foun-dation tied to the German Socialist Party concurred: "*Millî Görüş* lead-ers still don't fulfill certain basic conditions to remove all doubts that they're fully compatible with democracy and they still have no distance from Erbakan's ideology."[82]

This intense state surveillance has disqualified Islamists from any formal status as a community representative for state-Islam affairs in Germany. A federal interior ministry official in Berlin stated in 2003:

> The general question of the status of MG is difficult because it is a heterogeneous organization, and there are reformist movements within it, as could be seen in the most recent elections in Turkey. . . . There is a very lively discussion in academic circles about the best way to engage MG. It is important to have these discussions and to work through these conflicts. But we cannot engage the organization so long as it is considered extremist by the government. That would

be a contradiction of our security policy. In other words, discussions with MG must be held, but we in the [state-religion relations office] must have a passive role. As a security office we naturally have other responsibilities.

As the influence of Embassy Islam over prayer spaces in Germany and Europe diminishes and that of Political Islam grows, the desire to engage *Millî Görüş* and similar organizations has continued to spread among administrators who need reasonably representative spokespeople with whom to negotiate the details of state-religion affairs.

Can Political Islam Be Engaged in Europe?

In political matters, Political-Islam forums tend to be critical of Western foreign policy toward the Arab and majority-Muslim world, to express solidarity with the Palestinian cause and against Zionism, and to be broadly worried about the rise of Islamophobia in the West. Since 9/11, however, they have openly and often renounced political violence. Thus, while they acknowledge the misdeeds of fellow Muslims, such as instances of terrorism or anti-Semitism, Political-Islam leaders tend to be more worried about the vulnerability of the Muslim world to external attack and the precariousness of the Muslim minority in Europe. This fits in with broader narratives of "victimization" and Islamophobia popular among Islamists around the world. Many critics of Islamist groups in the West focus on their dissident foreign policy views and their general lack of introspection regarding unsavory associations in their movement's past. But Political-Islam leaders have not emerged from a siege mentality that still characterizes their movement's experience in Muslim-majority societies, and, increasingly, in countries where Muslims are a minority as well. In this latter context, Political-Islam organizations learned from the example of non-Muslim advocacy groups that the best offense is defense. Political-Islam groups are mostly involved in the vaguely defined "defense" of the religion in the public sphere, for example by denouncing incidences of blasphemy or the restriction of Islamic practices.

However, they are not the source of one particular set of local tensions stemming from improvised religious observance in European villages, towns, and cities. Islamists would greatly prefer that Muslims pray in proper mosques rather than the streets, for example, or that the faithful donate to charity rather than slaughter lambs in their bathtubs during Eid-al-Adha. They want Islam to be fully recognized in Europe and for their religion to be practiced in a dignified manner, claiming the same types of autonomous spaces enjoyed by other religions: seminaries, places of worship, and a place in public institutions.

In domestic European contexts, Political-Islam organizations are a more effective version of Embassy Islam's *amicales*, the homeland fraternal organizations geared toward first-generation migrants, precisely because they are not oriented toward a return "home." By definition, they are adapted to the European institutional context: local authorities are their addressees. The two competing forces in organized European Islam—Embassy Islam and Political Islam— has each in its own way posed a challenge to immigrant integration and European states' control over their populations. But each also wants something from European states: control over community institutions, and an upper hand in the broader contest of official versus unofficial religion. Over time, the question for European governments became less whether to engage them but rather, what institutional configuration would best suit the triangle of interest groups that had taken shape? European states became increasingly convinced of the need to enact policies to actively encourage a degree of religious-community-based integration into their societies, rather than continuing to hope it would occur spontaneously.

CHAPTER FOUR

Citizens, Groups, and the State

THE RELIGIOUS PRACTICES of a population of "guestworkers" pose different policy challenges than do those of a permanent religious minority. Since the arrival in Western Europe of Muslim labor migrants in the 1960s and 1970s, their status changed from guests to residents, and from immigrants to natives. The governments' administrative interaction with Muslim communities underwent a corresponding paradigm shift.[1] The dominant policy paradigm in the 1960s, 1970s, and 1980s held that a monopoly of immigrants' sending states over organized Islam in Europe was a sensible solution for temporarily guaranteeing religious freedoms without violating prohibitions on the public financing of religion. European governments avoided the direct regulation of Islam while diplomatic representatives provided imams, prayer space, and practical advice on religious accommodation. This was possible during the first decades of Europe's demographic transformation because labor migrants were not considered an element of domestic politics: the new presence raised issues of diplomacy, not internal democracy.

In the 1990s, however, a number of developments converged to convince policymakers that Muslims in Europe needed to be emancipated from the overbearing influence of foreign governments and brought into the domestic institutional life. In particular, migrants' right to family reunification—upheld in a series of court decisions—transformed the formerly single male group into a population with women and children. In 1991, 51 percent of Pakistanis in the UK had been born in the UK.[2] France, the Netherlands, and Germany reached a similar milestone by the end of the decade.[3] Nearly half a million Moroccans were born in Europe in the 1990s. As the second generation came of age, more individuals of Muslim background used public services—from education to health care and the welfare state—and issues related to religious and cultural observance became more visible in the public sphere.

The objective material inadequacy of Muslims' religious infrastructure was of key importance to this growth in visibility. Despite the activity of Political-Islam and Embassy-Islam groups, Muslims in Europe still experience restricted religious freedoms. This was due in part to their relatively recent arrival, but it could be explained largely by European governments' lack of involvement in guaranteeing Muslims the same rights to religious practice afforded to other religious communities.

The state's absence was most obvious in the shortage of mosques and imams, but several other images of Islamic religiosity—and thus, their alienation from European practices—have been seared into the public imagination: the slaughtering of lambs in bathtubs for the *Eid al-Adha* holiday; the sidewalk congestion caused by men praying on rugs in public streets outside overflowing prayer spaces; children attending informal Qur'ân schools; the transportation of the deceased to be buried in the country "of origin"; the extremist preaching of rogue imams and of fundamentalist chaplains in prisons.

Each one can be traced to a deficit in ordinary state-religion oversight and accommodation. Administrative agreements with the other major religious communities—Jewish, Protestant, and Catholic—mean that those who so desire have access to ritual animal slaughter facilities, separate cemetery sections, sufficient places of worship, recognized parochial schools and/or religious education in public schools, routine procedures for the appointment of chaplains in public institutions, and so forth.

Governments that initially subjugated Islam policy to their foreign policy priorities were forced to reckon with the reality of Muslims as a new domestic social group. The children of labor migrants living in housing projects suffered disproportionate rates of unemployment, and there were few European-born economic elites or parliamentarians of Muslim origin—even as the number of Muslim consumers and voters increased. Many politicians and policymakers agreed that Muslims, in being left on their own or abandoned by the state, were thus vulnerable to extremist tendencies. There were insufficient Muslim prayer spaces and not enough imams; those that were in place were largely foreign-sponsored and not conversant in a European language. The rise of Political Islam federations and the emergence of the geopolitical dimension of the *ummah* raised the question of national security. Well-organized networks of Islamist activists who hold more conservative, politicized, and assertive views of religion flourished on the margins of immigrant communities.

Their activism and the natural growth of Muslim populations thrust the issue of Islam onto governments' domestic agendas, leading to an administrative awakening that would ultimately lead to the incorporation of Islam into national state-religion relations. The debates ranged from the propriety of religious garb in public institutions and the inadequate financing of mosques and imams, to the causes of young Muslims' integration difficulties and unemployment, to the appropriate response to Islamists' demands for censorship and to religiously justified terror plots. The lack of local interlocutors on Muslim issues highlighted the unintended side effects of outsourcing; it made little sense to speak with foreign diplomats about the challenges of integration, and yet the governments' contacts in local Muslim communities were few and far between.

As European frustration with foreign governments' influence over immigrants reached a boiling point between 1990 and 2005, the period in which integration failures became impossible to ignore, European governments refined their assessment of the cost of Islam's remaining outside of national state-church institutions. This would end the era of "outsourcing" and inaugurate a phase of "domestication" for Islamic prayer spaces and religious leadership in Europe. Many politicians and policymakers agreed that Muslims were being left on their own or abandoned by the state. During this fifteen-year period, European governments pursued an array of policies to facilitate integration and "domesticate" Islam—encouraging civic participation and citizenship acquisition—and to assert their national sovereignty over Muslim populations.[4]

The "domestication" of state-mosque relations emerged as the primary arena of integration policy. As the president of the German Bundestag said three months after 9/11:

> I wish for a Euro-Islam to emerge, an Islam that really allows for the separation of church and state, and willingly recognizes human rights, pluralism and religious tolerance. . . . There is still no Islamic theology in European universities and no European mosques. When these emerge then it would be more apparent that Islam is more multiform than it has appeared until now.[5]

"The state can not afford to ignore the [. . .] dynamics and potentially explosive nature of religious questions," said the German interior minister Otto Schily in September 2002. "Integration will only succeed when we take into account the new religious needs of Muslims." And Giuseppe Pisanu, the Italian interior minister, said several months later, "We do not want the implantation of Islam to be hostile, foreign or indifferent to the Italian State—Italian Islam must harmonize with Italian identity and Italian rules." Officials in every European country with a new Muslim minority expressed similar sentiments of wishing to oversee the liberalization and reform of Islam.

There were many legal and philosophical obstacles to the domestication of Islam in Europe. The array of Islamist groups and diplomatic representatives was one daunting obstacle. The vaunted unity of faith and politics in Islam, which seemed to rule out an easy cohabitation, was another, and many commentators and scholars argued that Islam and liberal democracy are inherently incompatible. A fourth was the constitutional limits of what European authorities could claim when injecting themselves into the internal workings of a religious community.

Several administrative angles justified official intervention in the organization of Islam. Interior ministries in continental Europe are charged with guaranteeing freedom of religious exercise as well as with the policing of faith communities to ensure their compliance with the rule of law. The thousands of informal Islamic prayer spaces on national territory are thus subject to ministerial oversight by existing religion offices. The near exclusive foreign origin of imams and prayer leaders, additionally, meant that the granting of visas and residence permits—or their revocation—could be used as an administrative tool to shape the nature of religious leadership through consular screening in the countries of origin, and by way of domestic intelligence on European soil.

The concurrent extension of *individual* political rights and *group* status in public law raises a fundamental question about the role of communities in contemporary political life: is the unit of incorporation here the individual with a Muslim background or rather Muslims as a group? This chapter situates this unresolved tension within the literature on modern state-building and European state-society relations, from Reinhard Bendix's (1977) identification of evolving forms of representation, to explorations by Alessandro Pizzorno (1981) and Charles Maier (1988) of what came after the nineteenth century's "liberal parenthesis." The analysis of religious leaders' responses to this process brings the material into a discussion of Theodore Lowi's (1964) observation that "new policies create a new politics." Seymour Lipset's (1983) focus on rights-granting regimes in response to radical working-class movements—and how they influenced workers' political integration—is also relevant here.

This chapter places contemporary European governments' responses to the "Islamic challenge" in historical and theoretical context. The first two-thirds of the chapter will draw lessons from highlights of the modern state's experience with organized religions, and the last third will examine the institutional legacy of the emergence of working-class associations and their institutionalization through neo-corporatism.

Doctrinal Incompatibility?

The political incorporation of religion has required the modern state to alter, over time, its conception of nation-building. Recognizing religious practices through toleration can require liberal states to forsake some of their liberalism, at least in its nineteenth-century variants. The desire to regulate and help to centralize Islamic organizations operating within Europeans' national borders is reminiscent of the steps taken by activist states in response to the challenges posed by religious and ideological communities and civil-society organizations with international linkages outside national borders.

Since the nineteenth century, centralized and local bodies representing Jewish, Protestant, and Catholic hierarchies already have served as interlocutors for administrators to address challenges of religious observance in a formal and relatively transparent process that takes conflicts over religious practices out of the "public sphere": for example, to license kosher slaughterhouses and butchers; grant permits for synagogues or churches; organize religious class in public schools or in parochial schools recognized by state authorities; create confessional graveyards (or sections in public cemeteries).[6] The contemporary outreach to Muslim communities aims to give them the same interlocutors: to prepare the ground for practical local- and national-level solutions to a series of controversial issues related to religious practices that had long interfered with the social acceptance and integration of Muslims in their adopted European societies. This chapter will explore the similarities and differences between Islam and these earlier political challenges to the nation-state.

The incorporation of Muslims in contemporary Europe is a challenge of historical proportions. Christopher Caldwell correctly notes that "there is no precedent for the mass immigration that Europe has seen over the last five decades."[7] But there is clearly precedent for the nature of this challenge: the phases of nation-building that have taken place at fifty- or hundred-year intervals over the past two centuries. European Muslims' religious "needs" stand out not simply because the societies they inhabit have long undergone a general "secularization,"[8] but because other religious communities—notably Jewish and Christian denominations—settled their equivalent practical requirements in consultative structures in the nineteenth and early twentieth centuries. The trope of Islam's incompatibility with "Western" religious practices is well worn in public and media discourses surrounding Muslim integration in Europe.[9] The kindest commentary that Caldwell, a well-regarded critic of Muslim integration, had to offer was that Islam's compatibility with liberal institutions "is hard to gauge."[10]

Religious belonging challenges the nation-state's reference points of territory and citizenship by setting constitutions in competition with a "higher law." Pressed with the need to resolve urgent practical issues of religious observance, European states have not treated Islam as doctrinally impossible to integrate and institutionalize. The widespread concern with Muslims' ultimate loyalty is what the political theorist Nancy Rosenblum calls the "painful conflict between the obligations of citizenship and the demands of faith."[11] Its line of questioning is also remarkably similar to John Locke's skepticism about the suitability of Christians as republican citizens. But it additionally recalls the Enlightenment-era logic of Mirabeau or Von Dohm, who argued that only by emancipating and domestically orienting the Jews would they become more useful members of society, as full citizens.[12] As one scholar aptly paraphrased Rousseau, "your citizenship can be in Heaven or in France, but not in both."[13] States' management of religious diversity reflects the "liberal democratic aspiration to create conditions that encourage mutual toleration among religious groups."[14]

More generally, these questions call to mind previous efforts of the centralizing modern state to integrate groups—from peasants to workers to Catholics, Protestants, and Jews—whose particular interests, especially their transnational connections, and their apparently different set of moral and political values, it perceived to pose a threat to national political unity. This point comes through especially clearly in accounts of Jewish emancipation in nineteenth-century Europe.

In the mind of the skeptics, Islam is different and more threatening to the rule of law than other monotheisms.[15] On the one hand, critics in the host societies often judge Muslims in Europe by the practices of their traditional societies: since, for example, Saudi women are not allowed to drive, or Iranian women are obliged to wear a headscarf, or Sub-Saharan African women live in polygamous households, or "honor killings" are tolerated in Pakistan, or because non-Muslims may not pray openly in Saudi Arabia, Muslim migrants are said to be inevitably misogynous and unable to accept the Western understanding of the equality of the sexes and religious pluralism. Any residue of these homeland traits in their thoughts or actions is taken as proof that the same spirit of intolerance or inequality pervades the diaspora population.[16] As one widely cited study of opinion in the Netherlands put it, "Western Europeans take exception to Muslim treatment of women and children" and "many Dutch take strong exception to Muslim practices." For all the evocation of "Muslim culture," however, the authors never specify exactly what they mean beyond "commonalities in the way of life in countries where the majority are Muslims."[17] To resort to this level of generalization about Muslims reinforces the very confusion that contributes to prejudice in the first place. The authors write that Muslim children are likely to be "kept under strict surveillance and control," and are often subject to "threat, verbal violence, and corporal punishment." An entire religious and cultural group, in all its diversity, is dealt with as a uniform bloc, without recourse to any polling or statistics of the Muslim population to gauge the extent of the offending behavior. The diversity of views and practices among Muslims and non-Muslims is left unspoken, as are the distinctions between Moroccan, Tunisian, or Saudi Islam, e.g., from its Indonesian or Turkish variants. This shortcut in reasoning characterizes the view of Muslim populations in Europe as a static, wholesale import from the homeland. As a result, it is sometimes unclear in studies of Islam in Europe whether the subject is "Muslims" or "immigrants."

Many observers have fused their cultural complaints about Muslims with two structural obstacles to integrating Islam in the West—its decentralized nature and its reluctance to accept basic liberal precepts that distinguish spiritual rule from temporal authority,[18] to argue that Islam as an organized religion is doctrinally unsuited for state-church separation in contemporary Western democracies to the point of utter incompatibility.[19] In the words of Jean-Louis Debré, a French interior minister who suspended state-Islam consultations in the mid-1990s:

> Catholicism contains the seeds of *laïcité* (the French separation of church and state). *Laïcité* is the practical application of the gospel: render unto Caesar. [. . .] This cannot be taken for granted with Islam—which only exists in the context of 'shari'a-craties' where there is no separation of state and religion.[20]

Similarly, René Rémond, the late dean of French religious studies, referred to the "fundamental obstacle" to integrating Islam: "contrary to Christianity, which, even if it sometimes rejects the consequences, admits a natural distinction between religious community and civil and political society, Islam is presented as a unified whole."[21] The political scientist Stathis Kalyvas argues, furthermore, that the "languages of Muslim countries have no words for 'secularism' or 'layman.'"[22]

The problem of integrating Muslims is compounded by the belief among these skeptics that they are systemically incapable of producing centralized representatives for the government to address—i.e., a single organization that can "communicate and negotiate" on behalf of Muslims.[23] The organizational disarray of newly settled immigrant groups is interpreted as proof of a systemic problem. Indeed, local and national officials used this as a convenient excuse in the 1990s for avoiding official contacts with Muslim communities. In the words of one Berlin official responsible for state-church relations: "Cooperation could exist [with Islam] but the Turks are rather unorganized. Islam itself is a structure-poor religion, very diffuse and informal."[24] Similarly, a former French minister of urban affairs observed that consultations risked failure because "the Muslim community has been a victim of its divisions [. . .] It is enough to have two Muslims in a room to have three different political viewpoints."[25]

This perspective has influenced explanations of the patterns of state-mosque relations. "In contrast to Catholicism," Carolyn Warner and Manfred Wenner write, "the Islamic religion is not conducive to large-scale collective action [. . .] It is a decentralized, non-hierarchical religion with multiple, competing schools [. . .] and has no central authority to enforce cooperation or structure activity."[26] They further note that in Sunni Muslim countries, where the vast majority of these immigrants originate, *ulamas* do not have legal standing in the Islamic system of any other Muslim state, setting the stage for a competitive relationship among different national variants of Islam. Warner argues elsewhere that an additional problem stems from Islam's claim of being "universally applicable" and that the religion thus constitutes a "principal rival to national governments for authority over people, power and resources."[27]

If the Islamic religion tends to fuse religion and politics, then according to this logic, any official recognition of Islam or establishment of policies that benefit Muslims' religious claims-making will inevitably weaken the foundations of liberal democracy.[28] When awarding recognition rights to Islam, therefore, some theorists have stressed the need to differentiate between society's need for "pluralism" and the capitulation of "multiculturalism." For sociologist Alain Touraine and political scientist Giovanni Sartori, who have been among the foremost critics of Islam's eventual integration into European societies, contemporary Muslim demands—whether for the right to wear headscarves or the adoption of aspects of shari'a law—are direct challenges to liberal society. Sartori writes of a "theocratic Islam" (an echo of Debré's "shari'a-cracy") and declares fundamentalist Muslims to be "open and aggressive cultural enemies," "that Islam means 'submission,' and that the Arabic word for 'freedom' only refers to a situation of non-slavery, and that unlike our separation of church and state, there is the Islamic notion of religion-and-state."[29]

Why Accommodate Religion?

The arguments for Islam's doctrinal incompatibility with liberal government rest on the curious assumption that Western democracies have never before faced such a rigorous religious challenge to the state's authority. But they have. For example, José Casanova sees "some similarities between transnational *jihādism* today and Catholic ultramontanism in the nineteenth century. Both were parallel responses of transnational religious groups to the threats of the modern system of nation-states and the political opportunities of globalization."[30] Moreover, he argues, there are parallels between

> today's discourse on Islam as a fundamentalist anti-modern religion incompatible with democracy and yesterday's discourse on Catholicism . . . [and] the widely held perception on both sides of the French republican-laicist and monarchist-Catholic divide that Catholicism was incompatible with modern democracy and with individual freedoms (96). . . . Even after its official accommodation with secular modernity and after relinquishing its identity as a monopolistic state church, the Catholic Church refuses to become just a private religion, just an individual private belief. It wants to be both modern and public. (99)

As Carolyn Warner has written about the organized religious background to the development of Christian Democratic parties, "The Church is an atypical interest group in that it claims its principles are universally applicable. It is not one political actor among many, but the principal rival to national governments for authority over people, power, resources."[31] In the gradual process of secularization, Françoise Champion argues, the state has tried to limit the influence of the Churches in social life, and the Churches try to acquire maximal rights and possibilities of influence: "It is a difficult path by which religion becomes 'one institution among others.'"[32] The liberal democratic promise of universal citizenship has been strained by doubts about religious, particularly minority religious, group compatibility with national membership norms.

On the other hand, Didier Motchane, an advisor to the French interior ministry who oversaw consultation with Islamic organizations, argued in a party memorandum that organized elements of most religions could be interpreted as being opposed to secularism:

> Laïcité is not the spontaneous philosophical product of any religion. The integration of Catholics in the Republic is the touchstone of Republican integration, and it will be the same for the near future of Muslim integration. [. . .] Even though it be true that no religion or church can find Laïcité in its cradle, Islam has no reason to fear more than others to find its grave therein.[33]

Notwithstanding the Interior Minister Jean-Louis Debré's argument that Christianity contains the "seed of secularism," European history abounds with evidence that the Church did not always acknowledge that openly.[34] In the *Social Contract*, Rousseau considers whether religious duties interfere with loyalty to the state—that is, whether religious Christians could be good citizens.[35] The central problem, in his view, can be illustrated by the failed aftermath of military defeats in Jewish history. Once Jews refused to obey the obligatory "law of the vanquished" to convert upon defeat, their presence as citizens became forever suspect. Christian citizens pose a particular problem: their refusal to recognize the god of the victor eventually poses an existential problem for the legitimacy of the state and raises the question of whether Christians can be good citizens.

Rousseau doubted that believers could be trusted to choose between priest and prince. Christians are persecuted, he argues, because of the well-founded suspicion that at every turn they await an opportunity to usurp state sovereignty. "The sacred cult of Christianity aimed to become independent of the sovereign, and had no natural or necessary bond with the body of the state."[36] He warns that religious belonging independent of politics can be incompatible with citizenship. True Christian religion—"not that of today, but that of the Gospel"—is actually "contrary to the social spirit," for it "has no particular relation to the body politic. . . . Far from attaching citizens' hearts to the State, it detaches them from it as from all worldly things."[37] Even if a Christian "does his [civic] duty," he does it without apparent relish or concern for its outcome.

Rousseau is even less optimistic about the nature of religious minorities and their respect for the state. They do not just seek tolerance for their religious faith: if they are left alone, he thinks they will plot actively against the state. The pagan mistrust of Christians is, he argues, wholly founded. In this sense, he blames the victim: the Christians themselves are the "cause of the persecutions"—they are true rebels, who are only "hypocritically" submissive, and await the right moment to "usurp adroitly." The phrase "Christian republic" is a "mutually exclusive" term.[38] Since true Christianity does not have any relation to the state, how could its devout followers be good citizens? Each Christian citizen is in a sense a sleeping conspirator, waiting to awaken to the call of the "dominating spirit of Christianity."[39]

In the aftermath of the liberal democratic revolutions of the eighteenth and nineteenth centuries, the Enlightenment's legacy brought on the beginnings of "emancipation from religion," reflected in the radically secular goals of the French Revolution.[40] The de-legitimization of intermediary structures during the birth of the modern nation-state, Wendehorst argues, was part of a general "hostility towards collective manifestations" of religious groups—and "not necessarily directed against a particular community as such."[41] Nonetheless, the nascent French and Italian nation-states aimed to weaken the influence of the transnational Catholic network by eliminating its monopolistic or dominant position in state-church discussions. Soon after taking power in

France and Italy, respectively, Napoleon Bonaparte and Camillo Cavour recognized religious minorities and subjected the Catholic clergy to the civil code (in addition to taxing and seizing their property and wealth). They wanted to create a docile church, one unable to interfere in political affairs and submissive to the state. Post–Revolution era priests in France, for example, were forced to pledge loyalty to the state: "I recognize that the universality of the French citizenry is the sovereign, and I hereby promise to submit and obey the laws of the Republic."[42] This provoked violent reactions from the Church. As the nineteenth-century historian Antonin Debidour put it, "the high clergy denounced the Civil Constitution as heretical and schismatic and preached holy war (*guerre sainte*) against it, and promised to annihilate it in France with fire and blood."[43]

Less than a century later, Pope Pius IX released the well-known encyclical *Non expedit*, which argued that it did not behoove good Catholics to participate in Italian political life. Nonetheless, the Concordat that Napoleon negotiated with the Church was a relatively accommodating "blueprint [for finding a] modus vivendi with the new secular states," which spread to other Catholic-majority countries. "Free operation within national state borders" was granted "in exchange for agreement not to interfere with the state's sovereign power."[44]

CHURCHES, GROUPS, AND THE ROAD FROM OPPRESSION TO SEDITION

The two centuries between the Glorious Revolution in England and the late nineteenth century witnessed the birth of a modern state that sought to liberate national society from Church monopolies and temporal political influence. This period corresponded with the rise of parliamentary sovereignty and a recrudescence of negative attitudes toward secondary associations between the citizen and the state. Each of these broad movements against religion and other intermediary groups engendered a backlash in the context of the reality of group belonging and the persistent power of organized religion. During the half-century between 1880 and 1930, state-church renegotiation ceded symbolic powers to religious organizations, all while increasing administrative ties, regulation, and the ultimate "domestication" of religion.

The recognition of religious groups and the historical conciliation with the churches is part of a larger trend that modified the idealized conception of citizenship as the French Revolution had defined it. Governments moved past the ideal of only direct, unmediated links between citizen and state, and went from prohibiting secondary associations to recognizing the social reality of different kinds of interest groups. Churches were not the only "civil society" organizations targeted by the highly influential French post-revolutionary political model. But they were the problematic interest association par excellence. The tension between organized religion and modernizing Western European states originated in the states' rejection of feudalism as an organizational model for social relations. The "modern fixation on the sovereign state and its individual citizens" so sacred to proponents of secular states and anti-clericalism is the radically democratic and modern "antithesis of the medieval theory of community life."[45]

The concern about national unity dominated the debate over secondary affiliations. Ernest Barker, a British theorist of the state who espoused this antithesis, warned in 1915 that the "public law sanctioning" of associations reduces the state to a "community of communities which embraces not only economic, but also ecclesiastical and national attempts to belittle the state." Group demands, he argued, imperil the sovereignty of republics or otherwise "discredit the state."[46] The question of state sovereignty is the fundamental issue of how citizens "experience authority." "Political world pictures and attitudes towards the accommodation of interests" are revealed by the "character of authority relations within the 'associative bonds.'"[47]

This is a zero-sum vision in which political authority emanates either from communities and intermediary associations or from within the state. Along these lines, Hobbes likened corporations to "many lesser Common-wealths in the bowels of a greater [commonwealth], like worms in the entrayles of a naturall man," and Hume "detested and hated" the founders of sects and factions as much as he "honored and respected" legislators.[48] The "privileges" of group personality request exemption from general laws and special consideration of their improbable claim to represent a sector of the population.[49]

The French Le Chapelier law dissolving guilds, issued in 1791, just two years after the National Assembly voided feudal arrangements, reflected the ideological extremism of the nascent republic. The law's passage and repeal nearly a century later could be seen as two competing approaches to "groupness." The motivation behind the law was to establish that "citizens are such, and all relations in society are undertaken à titre individuel. . . . [If] masters are not to have associations then neither are workers."[50] For example, Article 2 prohibited "citizens of the same estate or profession" from naming "a president, secretaries, representatives," and from "collecting records or making decisions, deliberations or regulations regarding their presumed common interests." It thus refuses to recognize the "real personality" of associations and withholds legal status from interest groups, either out of discomfort with the group or in deference to the state and to the availability of general political institutions for equal members (citizens) of the polity.[51]

The Stubborn Reality of Interest Groups

In the post-revolutionary era of emancipation and industrialization, however, the state eventually had no choice but to acknowledge the existence of groups, including religious associations. The birth of "the collectivist era" saw the rise of new "producer groups": business associations and worker groups who demanded political representation.[52] Individual citizenship did not fully capture the reality of economic interest, and parliaments failed to reflect socioeconomic aggregations.[53] Emile Durkheim, the founding father of French sociology and a forerunner of corporatist theory, argued that the state is essentially a "society composed of naturally occurring societies": "Secondary groups form the primary condition for any higher organization . . . the state exists only where they exist. No secondary groups, no political authority."[54] The "new group politics" offer the advantages of checking state supremacy: "a counterbalance to the extension and centralization of government control."[55] And contra Adam Smith, Keynes weighed in on this debate in the United Kingdom with the conclusion that "individuals are not less clear-sighted when they make up a social unit than when they act separately."[56]

Other historical reasons for this trend of legal recognition stem from the weakness or "un-representativeness" of nineteenth-century parliaments and from the fact that the socioeconomic interest blocs, shattered by the legislated end of feudalism in August 1789, were to be reconfigured in the Industrial age; and some types of groups proved insoluble in their "group-ness," namely religion. In the nineteenth century, parties and parliaments did not fulfill the general roles that theorists hoped would obviate the need for interest groups. In the 1820s, political associations in England represented a new kind of political power; there emerged "extra-parliamentary political parties," often single-issue coalitions, "not unlike the limited liability companies that were springing up"—the nineteenth century was the "era of joint-stock politics."[57]

The expansion of the franchise in the nineteenth and early twentieth centuries was a watershed moment for democratic politics, but suffrage had transformed representation into a party-based system, and the working classes had serious difficulty gaining entry into party leadership, or for their own new parties to make electoral headway.[58] Its impact was undermined by the fact that legislators were unsalaried, and by the "gentleman's club" atmosphere that persisted in national parliaments well through the First World War. Continuing restrictions on voter registration kept working men disenfranchised long after the Reform Acts in the United Kingdom.[59] Overall, the effects of working-class voters on the composition of the nation's political elite, as one scholar of the Edwardian era put it, was "slow to be felt."[60] There were no working-class members in parliament by 1869, and no son of working-class parents had risen to become a member of cabinet from 1801 to 1905; Epstein writes that "not a single exception [. . .] was available to symbolize the possibility of rising from humble origins to high office."[61]

The need for alternative modes of political participation and interest representation soon led to institutional innovation. "As parliamentary mediation encountered difficulties," Maier writes of the twentieth century's interwar period, "differing mixtures of bureaucratically sponsored interest-group mediation seemed to offer possible alternatives."[62] In other words, if government needed a labor perspective on policy questions, it could turn only to representatives of industrial workers' civil society: the trade union movement and labor leagues. This bears striking similarities to the role of Islam Councils with respect to the state of Muslims' representation in elected institutions at the dawn of the twenty-first century.

Parliament proved inadequate for certain tasks because it was unable to provide certain kinds of information about society and because it excluded some social and economic interests. The legitimacy necessary to execute certain policies, then, may perforce have to come from outside that most sovereign body. Therefore, the "liberal parenthesis" that characterized the first hundred years of the modern nation-state was quickly followed by what has been called the "corporate bracketing" of the individual.[63] The "period of individualistic liberalism was quite short and incomplete," writes Philippe Schmitter. "By the latter quarter of the nineteenth century, the 'art of association' could no longer be formally denied."[64]

Arguments for the legal recognition of professional groups found parliamentary vindication in a series of laws permitting associations and interest groups in France (1884/1901), labor unions in Britain (1824–25), and private associations in German states (1860s).[65] In France, the repeal of Le Chapelier with the Waldeck-Rousseau law of 1884 opened the way for public law to recognize unions in acknowledgment of their special claims to represent a given constituency (this was expanded to general interest associations in the better-known 1901 law). After Waldeck-Rousseau, "interest group brokerage gradually changed from a suspicious innovation to a convenient channel of representation . . . the web of interest groups offered to dampen the distributive conflicts of industrial society. The web of interest groups offered to allow religious communities to preserve their cultural identity in secular society."[66]

CHURCHES AND THE CENTRIPETAL FORCE OF THE MODERN STATE

The institutionalization of state-church relations can be viewed as the intersection of two vectors: the centripetal force of the modern state and an increasing acknowledgment of the need for extra-parliamentary consultation to legitimate and facilitate the increasingly complex work of government. In the late nineteenth century, administrations began to execute more ambitious government policies, and state rationalization was powered by an agenda of classification and control. The state designed a "centralized administrative system in order to 'penetrate' society to effect policies and to acquire legitimacy."[67] In Eugen Weber's account of late-nineteenth-century modernization, when Paris overran the French countryside, metropolitan France could "itself be seen as a colonial empire shaped over the centuries." The French state "conquered, annexed and integrated in a political and administrative whole" disparate territorial groups—from Bretons to Basques—some of whom had "specifically un- or anti-French" traditions.[68] In James Scott's language, the state got "a handle" on its subjects and the "in-between spaces" of their environment, rendering its population "legible," through administrative surveillance and control in the interest of better social and economic government.[69]

The use of churches for the purposes of government has a long legacy. Michel Foucault recounts the sixteenth-century shift wherein the national population became "an object in the hands of government, the object about which the government will have to take into account in its observations, knowledge . . . to govern rationally and thoughtfully."[70] In Louis XIV's military reviews and Bentham's prisons, Foucault perceives "the unavoidable visibility of the subjects," slowly "entering the age of infinite examination."[71] The panopticon's "enclosed, segmented space, observed at every point, in which the individuals are inserted in a fixed place" symbolizes the new "permanent visibility that assures the automatic functioning of power."[72] From the design of prisons to the widening of boulevards, one can see reflections of new ways of organizing the state. The halls of bureaucracy can be seen as Haussmann-like alleys through the population, offering the state's agents easy access and surveillance possibilities. The population is the principal target of the "triangle of sovereignty-discipline-administration,"[73] and churches and religious associations had long facilitated this task of legibility. Religious populations are ready-made community units; their simplification of the social landscape naturally lends itself to "miniaturization" and a "more easily controlled micro-order."[74] Jews across Europe had used the legally incorporated community structure for centuries as a survival mechanism and tool of government.[75] And, as Foucault observes, private religious groups in England "carried out, for a long time, the functions of social discipline."[76]

Governments encouraged this role, for example through the regulation of charity associations in parishes: "The territory to be covered was divided into quarters and cantons and the members of the associations divided themselves up along the same lines." This permitted a high degree of surveillance of a local population through visits to the poor to check on their housing and their professional and spiritual situations. Religious groups and charity organizations had long played the role of "disciplining" the population.[77] Such closed apparatuses, Foucault argues, add to their internal and specific function a role of external surveillance that can be quite useful to the state—a prototype of corporatist church-state relations.

CITIZENSHIP OR COMMUNITY?

The practical effect of using religious groups to serve the ends of government is to legally reconstitute the very group borders—economic, religious, or other—that the equalizing force of liberal citizenship itself was designed to dissolve. But public recognition for these and other interest groups can be seen as a prudent response to the representative insufficiency of parliament in the modern state. Like emancipation or suffrage themselves, recognition in public law of secondary associations grants groups entry to the decision-making process, and this entry was "a counterpart to the extension of citizenship."[78]

Through the peaks and troughs of religious toleration and state secularism, and better or worse relationships with the church structures of organized religion, however, states could never simply "wish away" religious groups. Some theorists suggest that at least some of the nineteenth-century zeal against majority or minority churches was an ideologically driven, and untenable, misstatement of social reality. Max Weber describes how the French Revolutionary "trend" against juridical personality was "reversed" not only by the "economic needs of capitalism," the market economy (syndicalism), and party politics, but also "the growing substantive differentiation of the cultural demands in connection with the personal differentiation of cultural interests among individuals."[79]

There are also significant incentives to recognize the existence even of "troublesome" religious groups. As John Neville Figgis, a contemporary of Max Weber, writes, "The fact is, to deny smaller societies a real life and meaning [. . .] is not anti-clerical, or illiberal, or unwise, or oppressive—it is untrue."[80] Religious oppression through the state's denial of official recognition is futile: for example, though "starved of material resources," the Scottish church "continued to exist in the activities of its members."[81] Locke's *Letter on Toleration* makes the case, furthermore, that the state represses religious groups at its own peril, and that it is counterproductive to public order: "Only one thing gathers People into Seditious Commotions: Oppression."[82]

As Nicolas Sarkozy argued when defending his pursuit of a representative interlocutor for Islam in France, it was "catastrophic [to deny] the cultural and religious identity of Muslims. An identity denied is an identity that radicalizes. We saw this with what would later be called 'urban violence.'"[83] But with recognition comes legitimacy, and with legitimacy comes the danger of legal religious activity that could undermine the authority of the state.

Making Good Citizens: The Jewish Roots of Muslim Moderation

EMANCIPATION DEBATES

> There are only two possible solutions: either to reform the Jews, or to expel them, as there is no compromise between these two solutions for a wise government. [. . .] To expel the Jews would be a show of weakness; to reform them would be a sign of strength.
> —*Rapporteur to Napoleon Bonaparte, 1806*[84]

The arguments against Jewish emancipation and enfranchisement foreshadow objections to the integration of Muslim migrants and their kin two hundred years later: accusations of dual loyalties, particularistic values, and a general inability to separate religion and politics. In addition to the relevance of State-Church history for dominant groups, the path to Muslim leaders' contemporary attestations of good citizenship can also be traced back to critical junctures in the consolidation of citizenship for marginal groups in nineteenth- and twentieth-century Europe.[85]

In the 1780s, Christian von Dohm and Moses Mendelssohn exchanged polemics with Johann David Michaelis about the wisdom of Jewish emancipation in Prussia, while Count Stanislas Clermont-Tonnerre's and Abbé Henri Grégoire's spirited defense of citizenship for Jews clashed with the objections of Abbé Maury and Bishop de la Fare in the French National Assembly debate after the Revolution.[86] Nineteenth-century stereotypes about Jews bore the same pattern; Wendy Brown points out the state's perception that Jews "obeyed a different legal code." A report to Napoleon declared that "the code of the Jews includes at the same time the religion, the political and the civil laws, the habits, the manners and all of the customs of life. These diverse things, which everywhere else are separated, are here mixed in the same code."[87] Consider this summary of arguments against Jewish emancipation:

(1) Their fealty to another (higher) god and another (higher) legal order preempts their fealty to the Christian or secular state.

(2) They live a partial [religious] life, and do not . . . participate in the universality the modern state is held to embody.

(3) Their religion cannot be easily rendered a purely private affair— holiday requirements, as well as public worship and prayer, contour their daily civic life and thus prevent them from the eligibility for tolerance, available to Protestant sects, in which religion can be rendered a purely individual and private order of belief . . . Community, law and/or ethnic affiliation leak into the domain where the abstract and universal equality, liberty and community of man are held to reign.[88]

Along these same lines, additional concerns about Jews' suitability for citizenship in the early nineteenth century regarded their alleged parochialism and rootlessness. The movement for Jewish emancipation can be seen as part of governments' "goal of constructing and defending the sovereignty of the nation-state."[89] It would take place, Christian von Dohm wrote, "as a great education project with the help of and under the watchful eye of the state."[90] For von Dohm, "the field of administration" was more compelling than the realm of theory and morality; "He saw emancipation in terms of an overall transformation of German society."[91]

Just as the path to Muslim leaders' contemporary attestations of good citizenship can be traced back to the earlier Jewish experience, so the concessions sought by governments in consultations with Muslim leaders today share interesting commonalities with the responses furnished two centuries ago by Jewish notables to the pointed questions (*questions gênantes*) posed by Napoleon Bonaparte in France and Kaiser Wilhelm I in Prussia as a condition for the public recognition of Judaism.[92] The Jewish notables were polled on their positions on polygamy, divorce, and intermarriage, on their attitudes toward fellow citizens and respect for the law, on rabbinical appointments, community policy, and economic integration. These questions "obliged Jews to choose regarding the crucial problems between Jewish law and citizenship: it forced them to reform both religiously and civilly."[93]

The nineteenth century witnessed the creation of state-led Jewish *consistoires* and *Körperschaften* that guaranteed community leaders a thriving religious infrastructure, though under state oversight, as well as the promise of political integration and access to elected office for individual Jewish citizens. The subsequent accords signed between community and state representatives were what Markell calls "a double bind": they "secured recognition for the Jews, yet [they] also secured recognition for [the state] by placing Jews into a new relationship with the state."[94] This is a common thread in corporatist and neo-corporatist style negotiations: interest groups act as partners of the state, and "not only represent the interests of their members vis-à-vis the state but also the state's interests vis-à-vis their members."[95]

What exactly did governments hope to achieve by extending citizenship and communal recognition to their Jewish populations? The public policy purposes were relevant to citizens' relationship to the state. If a recurring objection to Jewish or Muslim minorities' ability to integrate has relied on the assumption that the institutions of western government are foreign to them, overcoming the group's estrangement from the state could logically lead the group closer to the majority's social mores. In other words, the winning arguments for Jewish emancipation are *rational* state-building conceits, not *universalistic* principles of enlightenment. In von Dohm's view, the improvement of the Jews would be both *sittlich und politisch* (moral and political), since "humanity and politics are one and the same."[96] Emancipation sought to "cultivate identification with the state" among Jews. Granting Jews equal rights would "enable them to recognize these remote and alien institutions as *theirs*."[97] This process entails the assertion of state power over communal bonds, but comes with the compensation of self-recognition in the state.

Assuaging Fears of Dual Loyalty: State Pressure for Community Re-Organization

The process of emancipation led to a new relationship between Jews and their religious community *and* between the Jewish community and the state during the nineteenth and early twentieth centuries. In the ensuing process of state-led community re-organization, "the modern state did not abolish intermediary structures separating the Jew from the center of authority but rather reshaped, rationalized, and regulated those intermediary bodies as best suited [the state's] interests."[98] Ironically, recognizing the existence of the community may "redraw the very configurations and effects of power that they seek to vanquish."[99] One observer calls this a "partial rolling back of emancipatory process,"[100] while another refers to it as a Hegelian contradiction: "the recognition of the sovereignty of the state [requires that] the institutions of the state maintain a vigilant surveillance of the Jews to be sure that they are conforming to the terms of their emancipation."[101] Emancipation and universal citizenship called for an end to the corporatist bodies of the *ancien régime*.[102] Crucial to the evolution of community recognition in the modern era, Jewish communities in Europe were no longer ascriptive; rather, they were a "reorganized voluntary community."[103]

The recognition of difference in the 1812 Prussian Emancipation legislation can be understood as "an instrument of, rather than a threat to, [state] sovereignty."[104] This tradeoff occurs at the highest theoretical level of state-building, Markell argues: "[Emancipation] was not conceived merely as the fulfillment of liberal principles of fairness or equality, nor was it simply the gift of an indifferent king who expected nothing in return. It secured recognition for the Jews, yet it also secured recognition for Prussia by placing Jews into a new relationship with the state."[105]

Community recognition represented the first step toward the incorporation and dissolution of the religious minority into the national polity. According to one of Friedrich Wilhelm II's ministers in 1808, emancipating the Jews would "undermine and abolish their nationality, and gradually . . . produce a situation in which they will no longer seek to form a state within a state."[106] Emancipation was a contract—a tradeoff that served the designs on sovereignty of both group and state.

In France, the most significant accomplishment following formal emancipation was the creation of the Jewish *Consistoire* in 1806–1807. Napoleon invited eighty-two delegates (a mixture of merchants, rabbis, and community leaders) from all regions to constitute an assembly of notables asked to answer twelve questions regarding the compatibility of Jewish law (*halacha*) and the French civil code. This assembly was eventually converted into a Grand Sanhedrin (a rabbinical high court) of seventy members, two-thirds of whom were rabbis, which in turn led to the creation of national and local *consistoires* formed around synagogues, later a system of community representation as interlocutors for the French state.

Napoleon's 1806 letter of instructions to the commissioners of the Assembly of Jewish Notables included a list of questions to be submitted to delegates "reconciling the belief of the Jews with the duties of Frenchmen, and to turn them into useful citizens."[107] The Assembly of Notables was thus intended to demonstrate the state's universality over the particularisms of religious community; its first meeting was even held on the Sabbath, "perhaps to show that the French state did business on the Sabbath, and that all citizens were to take cognizance of this fact."[108] The list presented to the Jewish notables included:

1. Is it lawful for Jews to have more than one wife?
2. Is divorce allowed by the Jewish religion? Is divorce valid, although pronounced not by courts of justice but by virtue of laws in contradiction to the French code?

3. May a Jewess marry a Christian, or a Jew a Christian woman? or does Jewish law order that the Jews should only intermarry among themselves?
4. In the eyes of Jews are Frenchmen not of the Jewish religion considered as brethren or as strangers?
5. What conduct does Jewish law prescribe toward Frenchmen not of the Jewish religion?
6. Do the Jews born in France, and treated by the law as French citizens, acknowledge France as their country? Are they bound to defend it? Are they bound to obey the laws and follow the directions of the civil code?
7. Who elects the rabbis?
8. What kind of police jurisdiction do the rabbis exercise over the Jews? What judicial power do they exercise over them?[109]

Trigano writes that "these eight difficult questions to the Grand Sanhedrin obligated the Jews to choose regarding the crucial problems between Jewish law and French citizenship: It forced them to reform both religiously and civilly."[110] The Jewish élites needed to satisfy the government that Jewish law did not contradict French law. The integrating effects of emancipation included complete freedom of movement (and thus extensive urban settlement), intermarriage, and army service. A French scholar of Jewish emancipation concludes that the

> systematic regulation of Jewish life . . . [was] a turning-point in the long history of Judaism . . . [and offered] compelling reasons for French Jewry to consider possible modes of existence in the modern free world. . . . A new definition of Judaism was inescapable . . . [to provide] an answer to the new problems which confronted the Jewish population as a consequence of its emancipation.[111]

In Prussia, Prime Minister Karl August von Hardenberg took a proactive stance towards Jewish emancipation. In 1812, thirty-nine articles gave Jews near civil equality with Prussian Protestants but also forced them to assimilate culturally. There would be no more residency or professional restrictions, nor bans on intermarriage, though Jews were still banned from government posts, except as teachers.

At the same time, the articles abolished the rabbinical courts in favor of civil courts and required Jews to complete military service (even on the Sabbath and in potential violation of Kashruth) and attend compulsory secular education. The articles ordered Jews to "keep their ledgers in German rather than in Hebrew characters"; adopt "fixed official family names"; and banned foreign rabbis from Prussia.[112] Hardenberg even oversaw the establishment of special seminaries for the education of rabbis so they could learn to "speak one of the current languages of

Europe" and would learn only to perform marriages and divorces after civil ceremonies had taken place.[113] In Italy, where the Jewish community was formally recognized by decree in 1930, the Interior Minister had approval rights over the nomination of rabbis.[114] The role of religious communities was limited to worship, religious education, and the supervision of charitable institutions.[115]

It is no accident of chance that the Jewish community's reorganization coincided, in France, with the temporary restoration of the guilds. One scholar suggests that in the Napoleonic era, governments proposed corporatist answers to the central "social and political and economic question: How does one bring order to a society in flux?"[116] Another historian of Judaism writes that "much of Jewish communal evolution can be explained only by *the state's self-interest* in the effective fiscal and ecclesiastical organization of Jewish subjects."[117]

To understand the form that community organizations took on, he points to the "general evolution of corporate bodies in a particular society and the forces of imitation of institutional and legal patterns developed by the non-Jewish nations."[118] The establishment of the first German central organization of citizens of Jewish descent (*Centralverein deutscher Staatsbürger jüdischen Glaubens*) in 1893, similarly, reflected the fact that "extra-parliamentary political influence through economic or other special interest representation was a legitimate, generally accepted method in the political practice of the time."[119]

The Corporatist Roots of State-Islam Consultations

> The workers have no country [. . .] In the case of war among the great powers, the workers will respond with the declaration of a revolutionary strike.
> —*Declaration of CGT, 10th Congress, Marseille (1908)*[120]

The author of an influential book on Muslims in Europe asks his readership to imagine, by way of comparison with the millions of Muslims in Europe today, "that the West, at the height of the Cold War, had received a mass inflow of immigrants from Communist countries who were ambivalent about which side they supported."[121] But it is sufficient to look back to the history of large Communist parties and active trade unions in the decades of the teens, twenties, and seventies of the twentieth century to get an idea of what kind of challenges such an ambivalent group could represent—with the added menace that the group in question were not foreigners but fully enfranchised citizens who sympathized with revolutionary movements.

Muslims in Europe have something in common with the "mass of disorganized workers" from the dawn of the industrial era to the harder edges of far-left movements of the 1960s and 1970s. Working-class voters found that in the decades following the expansion of universal suffrage, practical obstacles delayed their democratic representation, and political parties showed limited interest in them as a new constituency—an experience Muslim citizens can identify with today. Moreover, just as the Communist Party and trade unions aimed to represent all working classes, and the Catholic Church claimed to speak for Italian and Polish and Portuguese immigrations in the mid-twentieth century, international actors and multiple, competing associations claim to speak for them as a whole.[122] Some scholars have drawn explicit comparisons between nineteenth-century working classes, known as the *"classes laborieuses, classes dangereuses,"* and Muslims, who "are similarly considered with a mix of fear and distrust" to that once reserved for working classes.[123] "The behavior of these [Arab or Muslim] young men," writes another, "is not unlike that of working class youth living in the same neighborhoods fifty years ago."[124]

Small, potentially violent minority wings of underrepresented groups have threatened social peace and political stability in earlier, critical moments of democratic consolidation in Western Europe and the United States.[125] Contemporary political Islamist movements share commonalities with other political movements that served as philosophical ground for violent offshoots such as anarchist and syndicalist groups in the 1920s, and the Red Brigades and the Red Army Faction in the 1970s.[126] Militant organizations that committed political violence posed a similar terrorist threat to that posed by the violent fringes of contemporary Political Islam.[127] The challenge is, once again, how to incorporate transnational movements with potentially extremist elements into a democratic institutional framework.

Neo-corporatist institutions aim to depoliticize conflicts and lead to the moderation of demands through the establishment of a set of moderate elites/leaders.[128] Neo-corporatism played a key role in reducing labor's capacity to strike, a goal of behavioral reformation that recalls the nineteenth-century era of emancipation and organization of representative consultative bodies for Jewish Communities. Instead of reducing strike days or inducing wage restraint, however, governments seeking behavioral transformation of religious leaders may look for other indications of success, such as political moderation of religious demands, including even the number of headscarves being worn in schools. Religious behavioral reformation could also mean simple "adaptation" of religious law to the national context, as the Grand Sanhedrin was asked to do by Napoleon. In the case of Islam, one could imagine the adaptation of *fiqh* (jurisprudence) and *shari'a* (Qur'ânic law) to satisfy the integration requirements of Muslims in the West—such as the right to borrow with interest (mortgages); alter the times of prayers to coincide with working times in Western societies; or the adaptation of standards for marriage, divorce, and inheritance rights.

The state offers incentives for participation by granting the parties a role within intermediary bodies that are established under the state's patronage.[129] The control mechanisms allow an exchange to take place: the state accords a representative monopoly and the chance to have input on public policy decisions concerning the group. In return, groups submit to state influence over "leadership selection as well as limits on the articulation of their demands."[130] The representative centralization is artificial, but it receives an effective monopoly and it is eventually responsible for executing the policies. But one must also recognize the State's relative powerlessness: it cannot impose a solution on conflicting interests, whether of a socioeconomic nature or religious-cultural. It can, though, create institutions that structure peaceful negotiations among interest parties.[131]

Some detected a "whiff of fascism" in the neo-corporatist revival of the 1970s, but in reality its contours had already been softened.[132] As one scholar convincingly argued, this is "not your grandfather's corporatism."[133] Unlike its fascist or authoritarian predecessors, where interest groups were "managed" in a police state, neo-corporatism stands for "a kinder, gentler corporatism . . . [that] allows liberal societies to accommodate class and interest-group conflict without authoritarianism."[134] Neo-corporatism requires "the opposite of a bully state," Keeler writes. It needs, rather, "a wheeling and dealing type of public authority seeking out allies, probing and maneuvering for their active consensus."[135]

In the past, governments pursued a broad institutional engagement of "moderates" to help defuse class, racial, or religious tensions. They used "summit diplomacy" among peak civil society associations to create a dynamic of administrative behavioral incentives and disincentives.[136] Many governing coalitions sought trade unions' help to pursue economic modernization policies and contribute to social peace in potentially pre-revolutionary situations.[137] These civil society organizations, acting as extra-parliamentary institutions, were given an exclusive role in administering specific practical tasks.

In addition to this technical role, a political behavioral agenda undergirded the institutional process: to encourage moderate demands and traditional political participation.[138] A central claim of the neo-corporatist literature is that interest groups "exercise restraint in pursuing their goals in return for their official recognition and privileges."[139] The advantages and privileges of institutional access for organized interest groups are balanced by a set of restrictions and obligations: interest organizations will "behave responsibly, predictably and will refrain from nonnegotiable demands or unacceptable tactics."[140]

Although national governments have taken different national paths and exhibit a good degree of institutional variety, state-mosque consultations with these very goals now exist in nearly every European state with a sizeable Muslim minority. The Muslim charters that formed the foundation of state-mosque relations in early twentieth-century Europe, discussed in chapter 5, have an analog from the era of class warfare: the *Charte d'Amiens*, signed in 1906 by the Confédération Générale du Travail (CGT), the Communist trade union, a year after the failed Russian revolution. In it, the CGT assuaged fears of its own revolutionary intentions by recognizing the legitimacy of political parties and "the imperative of engaging in dialogue with the state." The labor leaders who signed at Amiens asserted their right to call general strikes, but they also issued a call to end "reciprocal exclusion" in favor of "mutual recognition."[141] Within fourteen years, the CGT affirmed "the superiority of the administrator over the militant"; in effect, the former syndicalists had adopted a *socialisme d'institutions*, in the words of one contemporary observer.[142] The labor leadership was rewarded with minimal representation (three spots) on a ministerial committee in 1918; this would eventually become the *Conseil national économique*, where forty-seven representatives were appointed by labor and employer organizations.[143] By 1920, CGT leaders agreed that their struggle was no longer about "reversing the social order but rather to improve it and transform it gradually . . . the pursuit of practical and limited goals . . . 'Red blood' syndicalism had morphed into a state socialism with syndicalist bases."[144]

CONCLUSION

> If you find Islam to be incompatible with the Republic, then what do you do with the five million people of Muslim origin living in France? Do you kick them out, or make them convert, or ask them not to practice their religion? [. . .] With the French Council for the Muslim Religion, we are organizing an Islam that is compatible with the values of the Republic.
> —*French Interior Minister Nicolas Sarkozy, 2003*[145]

What community leaders aimed to achieve by asserting their movement's compatibility with the legal order and political system is not so much to fulfill the conditions for individual emancipation—after all, many of their constituents were already citizens with full political and associational rights at the time. Instead, it is an attempt to meet the criteria for the state's institutional engagement with civil society organizations. In other words, their concern is not simply private legal status, but equal recognition and access to representation of their interests within an administrative regime of state-society relations. They re-structure and reorient themselves in response to a perceived political opportunity structure that would allow them to gain representation in institutions and access to organizational resources.

What do governments try to achieve with an institutionalized dialogue? Most importantly, authorities engage with the assumption that a client role for the concerned interest groups includes an obligation to "behave responsibly."[146] This form of state-society relationship also makes possible a certain relationship to the "base," i.e., the faithful masses. Wilson's position was that "interest groups *constrain and discipline* their own members [. . .] as well as or even instead of *representing* them."[147] The state's desire for community interlocutors is about fitting religious organizations into round pegs of the interior ministries' religion bureaus. Institutionalization, or the assignment of political status to interest groups, Claus Offe writes:

> is always two-sided in its effects . . . Groups gain advantages and privileges although . . . they have to accept certain constraints and restrictive obligations . . .They gain access to government decision-making positions . . . but are subject to more or less formalized obligations. . . .[148]

Former Prime Minister Michel Rocard, who oversaw the creation of the first state-Islam consultation in France, compared the situation of Muslims to nineteenth-century Jews in an interview with the author:

> Napoleon recognized the necessity of having religious authorities in France accept the Convention [*Concordat*] of 1801/2. The Jews were very dispersed, there was no Jewish authority capable of making common statements, and so he succeeded with a "coup formidable" and held a meeting of the Sanhedrin [in 1806/7], which had not taken place since the destruction of the second temple. I don't know how the Jewish community deals with the question of that Sanhedrin's legitimacy, but it was a move of efficient democracy—and the Civil Code was accepted! It is difficult for the French to think anew about the problem that is posed by the Muslims and their institutionalization. But the relationship between the Jewish community and France shows that it can work—we don't have any more problems with the Jews. It must be possible to create a recognized and accepted meeting place whose function is not disputed. The legal relationship between the Jewish community and the State is now stable, and no matter what happens within the community, whether the majority's attempt

to achieve complete integration or, on the contrary, a reactivation of identity, including religious practice, does not bother anyone. There is an absolute separation of the church and the state, which facilitates everything.[149]

Nineteenth-century European states pursued state-religion policies with the aim of rendering communal organizations and churches (whether majority or minority) compatible with—and loyal to—the larger, national political community. In exchange for measures of accommodation, governments demanded a redefinition of religious citizens' relationship to their faith and, in particular, the explicit prioritization of constitutional law over religious liturgy—what Owen terms "the political (if not complete) subordination of religion to liberal constitutionalism."[150] Diner (2007) objects to the Jewish comparison, citing the inclusion of *"dina demalchuta dina"* (the law of the land is the law) in the preamble to Napoleon's agreement with the Jewish community. Yet that is precisely what state-Islam consultations and the use of neo-corporatist arrangements have also done.

Jews experienced millennia living in diasporas as a minority religion and had become accustomed to the contractual respect for the laws of the land, and had developed a system of self-government that would disappear only with emancipation in the late eighteenth and early nineteenth centuries. State-Mosque relations reenact the struggle that existed between the boundary of public and private in the nineteenth century, when European governments encouraged the emergence of domesticated religious practices—especially among Catholics and Jews—while avoiding the establishment of official religions. Unlike Judaism and Christianity, the institutions and liturgy of Islam have had limited experience outside of *dar al-Islam*.

States have behaved in the modern era as though they can "do something" about the place of religion in the public sphere, and European states sought to domesticate Catholic and Jewish communities—and the political loyalties of the working-class organizations—in the past. Today, the governments of Western Europe are engaging in state-Islam consultations with the aim of promoting the integration of Muslim citizens. By taking the initiative to incorporate and nationalize Islam in their respective institutional orders, European states have attempted to influence what kind of Islam young people discover—whether they search out religion as a reaction against European societies, or whether they are just satisfying curiosity about their heritage, or carrying on family traditions. The institutionalized relations between state and religion are predicated on the prioritization of national laws over religious texts and aspire to steep religious leaders in the secular precepts of a society in which church and state are separate.

The religion bureaus of contemporary European interior ministries structure and mediate the relationship of citizens and their chosen or native religion: to "ensure that the centrifugal push of religious loyalties that transnational religious regimes foster does not grow strong enough to overcome the centripetal pull toward national unity that the state must nurture."[151] These bureaus are the administrative tools to "deal with the demands that their relationship with the rest of the world has placed on [a state's own] policy towards religious believers among their own citizens."[152]

We can see contemporary centralization and institutionalization of Islam as damage control in defense of national unity. The mechanisms of re-territorialization and "de-transnationalization" are not new to Europe: these states initiated similar institutionalization to resolve the dilemmas of loyalty and identity in the nineteenth and twentieth centuries. Just as the state acted to *collectively* integrate their Jewish and working-class communities, so have recent governments attempted to "transform" the major representatives of Islam in Europe. The parallel efforts of European states to confront the transnational nature of the Islamic communities have led to a head-on confrontation and redefinition of religious communities' internal structures and their relationship to state and society.

Despite the crucial differences between Muslims in Europe today, and Jews and working-class groups in previous centuries, there are interesting similarities in their passage from a stage of pre-citizenship to citizenship as well as in the theoretical challenges posed by their full participation in politics and society. Governments feared sedition and disloyalty—and, in the case of the working classes, threats to social peace. Granting universal citizenship and the right to association does not solve the threat that secondary associations can pose to state sovereignty; it can make the problem more acute. It was with the justification of domestication and institution-building that the work of state-building got under way. The following chapter examines the national paths to state-Islam consultations in the context of this historic process.

CHAPTER FIVE

The Domestication of State-Mosque Relations

THE ESTABLISHMENT OF Islam Councils by national interior ministries is the most striking policy response of recent years to the growth of Islam in Europe, and the only campaign to date to have mobilized a majority of Muslim leaders to rise above their divisions in common purpose. In the first institutional acknowledgment of Muslim minorities' permanence, European governments between 1990 and 2010 have overseen a proliferation of state-led consultations, councils, conferences, and commissions established to represent the Muslim faith in state-mosque relations. Their institutional activism in Islamic affairs has been largely overlooked or hastily dismissed as ineffective because it conflicts with the portrayal of European governments as weak, unprepared for, and overrun by the diverse Muslim organizations that have sprung up on their territories. National governments follow the same two phases of state-mosque relations—outsourcing followed by incorporation—and this chapter demonstrates that these policy developments are due neither to "post-nationalism" nor to "shared values." They take place instead through parallel processes in which each state seeks similar alliances within its Islamic community in order to assert its *national* sovereignty.

By the mid- to late 1980s, the children and grandchildren of labor migrants had grown up, and the largely civic-based integration strategy had not achieved the desired results in the second and third generations. The half-hearted strategies of inclusion that had stressed anti-racism or citizenship and electoral participation had, to a large extent, fallen flat: schools in the large urban centers that are home to populations of immigrant origin suffered from budgetary crises; military service was no longer obligatory; and voting rights had not led to much parliamentary representation. By the late 1980s, the convenient bargain of outsourcing was ultimately judged to be counterproductive in terms of the integration of Muslims. Islamic NGOs associated with the Political-Islam movements of transnational Muslim civil society in the diaspora were increasingly assertive and behaved similarly to the peak associations of Embassy Islam. They agglomerated sympathetic prayer rooms and cultural associations under common-law umbrella organizations that were ineligible for the status of state-church associations, and therefore beyond the oversight and control of the government. The shortcomings of the promise of integration and socioeconomic mobility were clear for all to see, which contributed to the crystallizing sentiment that, as Hugh Heclo describes the moment preceding important policy shifts, "spread a general conviction that something must be done."[1]

With the state-led creation of Islam Councils, governments have acted as a broker between a persistently strong Embassy Islam and a growing Political Islam—the two competing organizational networks exported from Muslim-majority countries. Governments seek a mediated settlement that would grant full religious freedoms while subjecting Islamic infrastructure (mosques, chaplains, imams, etc.) to oversight of their financial and personnel links with foreign governments and NGO networks abroad.

Without the existence of a state-mosque track in governments' relationship with organized Muslim communities, the focus on the "Islamization" and security threats could have dominated interactions in the period from the first to second Gulf War. This population was increasingly beckoned by religious appeals to lend moral, political, or financial support to victims of conflicts and Islamist organizations, both in their countries of residence and abroad.

Authorities' attitudes toward Embassy Islam changed significantly during the period of "incorporation" since 1989. This was not because European governments suddenly discovered the Islam of "sending" states to be anti-democratic or even fundamentalist; indeed, the Embassy Islam of Algeria, Morocco, and Turkey aimed by definition for a peaceful relationship between religion and state. But their religious emissaries perpetuated a competing foreign tie among populations of immigrant origin. A growing perception of transnational threats linked to global Islam coincided with the maturation of migrant-origin Muslim communities with strong organizational ties to homeland governments and Political-Islam organizations.[2]

It would be a mistake to view the intervention of European states in Islamic affairs as a concession or capitulation to Muslim religious groups, even though this governmental activism stands out in contrast with its relatively unchanging official support for other national religious communities with a historic presence. But even so, the contemporary institutionalization of Islam grants only a semi-sovereign, stripped-down version of official recognition compared to the rights and financing available to Catholicism, Protestant and Jewish communities under agreements first crafted between the early nineteenth and early twentieth centuries.

European governments began using religious recognition as an instrument of oversight and state-mosque relations emerged as the primary category of integration policy.[3] This shift from outsourcing to incorporation changed the kind of desired interlocutors that they sought out in the practical and politically symbolic realm. It led to sustained efforts to institutionalize relations between religion offices and Muslim organizations along the lines of existing arrangements for other religions. Since September 11, officials have accelerated efforts to "detransnationalize" the cross-border solidarity of Muslims in Europe. From the 1999 German citizenship law forcing Turks to decide between German and Turkish nationality to the 2004 French law banning religious symbols in primary and secondary schools, governments have aimed to forcibly shelter Muslim minorities from transnational political and religious pressures.

State policies toward Islam between 1990 and 2010 have consisted of governments soliciting assurances directly from a broad range of Muslim groups in order to bring them into a regime of religious recognition for Islam, and doing so without significantly altering European state-church institutions. Western European governments who have gotten in on the game of bending Islamist organizations toward a national institutional framework are expressing the same survival instinct demonstrated by governments in some Muslim-majority countries, albeit in a small-scale, liberal democratic framework. But in this case, the overture to Islamist groups is for the highly circumscribed purpose of state-religion relations, not parliamentary politics and national law.

This chapter argues that the state-building spirit and institutional logic behind Islam councils in contemporary Europe is comparable to policies pursued in the earlier era of neo-corporatism, and it is therefore worth pausing briefly to explore the state-building logic at work here. At the very least, Islam Councils share similarities with workers' councils in that they serve a function of "elite recruitment" into institutional life, but they also do much more. The Islam Councils are state-convened organizations that bring together the leadership of opposing camps (à la capital and labor) to marginalize extremists and achieve "moderate" outcomes. The state-mosque forums are not as monopolistic or hierarchical as workers' councils. But they do share the aims of neo-corporatist councils to marginalize a fringe, vocal, and occasionally violent minority by incorporating the moderate silent majority—and by asserting the national state as the broker and enforcer in this equation. Moreover, Islam councils are similarly extra-parliamentary, consultative bodies to whom certain practical tasks are delegated, as in the case of *cogestion*—co-administration of member services—in neo-corporatist arrangements. Workers' councils were not meant to supplant elective democracy, but to enhance institutional representation and ideological "domestication" by other means. This is a remarkably similar process to what we observe in state-mosque relations.

Many religious needs of Muslims are easily accommodated in theory (confessional burial grounds or ritual animal slaughter, for example), but the practical arrangements of *who* is representative enough to organize these tasks on behalf of the Muslim community in Europe have always stirred controversy. The consultations and councils thus tried to answer these questions of who could serve as the state's interlocutor for the appointment of chaplains in the prisons or receive construction permits for a new mosque. Once it became clear in the late 1980s that the traditional diplomatic spokesmen from the home state governments would no longer be accepted, the focus of European governments shifted to an attempt to transform Muslim civil society through the institutional balancing act of neo-corporatist arrangements. This approach meant putting the weight of the state behind an oft-stated goal of creating an Islam *of*—not merely *in*—Europe.

While not exactly analogous to the historical state-religion consultations for Jews, Catholics, or Protestants of previous centuries, these councils share the same broad goal of encouraging religious practice that is compatible with national citizenship. Prayer associations and federations have indeed changed greatly as a result of their participation in Islam Councils, and the councils themselves have produced measurable policy outcomes. As the Turkish-German author Zafer şenocak argues, "A Muslim march through the institutions would have an emancipatory character by breaking through the metaphorical ghetto walls and leading to a critical relationship to Muslims' own traditions."[4]

State-mosque relations in Europe have developed as a way to elicit Islamic leaders' acceptance of the authority of modern, secular states. This has usually taken place in the ministry of the interior, which maintains similar contacts with representatives of other major recognized world religions. European governments have engaged in separate but strikingly similar confrontations with the transnational nature of Muslim organizations operating under their national legal system.[5] The consultations with Islam united diverse-minded participants around a set of common ground rules by drafting of charters for consultation participants and the establishment of working groups with the power to propose and implement policy solutions for Muslims' religious requirements. Authorities became more involved with internal community dynamics and forced rivals to interact with one another.

By the mid-1990s, all European governments had stopped purely "outsourcing" state-mosque relations. Interior ministers wrested Islamic affairs from the foreign policy desk and advertised a vacancy in their existing religion bureaucracies for "moderate" Muslim voices. The ministries in charge of overseeing religious freedom and public order provided the first impetus to organize Islam as a "national" religion subject to previously established state-religion relations. They spearheaded the government-led consultations that led to the establishment of national Islam Councils. The consultations went through two phases. The first, without the full investment of government intervention, involved tentative national attempts to identify interlocutors in the early to mid-1990s. A second phase of intensive negotiations between public authorities and community leaders produced more durable arrangements (the subject of chapter 6).

As a result, in 1989, France began its fifteen-year journey to the *Conseil français du culte musulman*, established in 2004. Between 1989 and 1992, Spain developed a *Comisión Islámica de España*. From 1994 to 1998, Belgium created an *Exécutif des musulmans*. Between 2004 and 2005, the Netherlands established the *Contactorgaan Moslims en Overheid* and the *Contact Groep Islam*. Between 2001 and 2006, state-mosque relations in Germany were formalized in the *Deutsche Islam Konferenz*. Between 2003 and 2006, the Italian interior ministry created the *Consulta per l'Islam*. And, between 1997 and 2008, the UK government laid the groundwork for the National Imam and Mosques Advisory Board.

The predominant scene in recent years is therefore no longer one of unrelieved conflict between Islam and the West, but rather of Muslim leaders sitting down with European leaders in historic halls of power: the French Interior Minister at Chateau Nainville-les-roches, the German Interior Minister in the Charlottenburg Castle, the Pope at Castelgandolfo, and the Italian President in the Quirinale palace. As a result of meticulous institution-building by Interior Ministries, these encounters between European officials and Muslim leaders are not random, ad hoc gatherings.

The meetings of state and mosque might be compared to the *Grand Sanhedrins*, the official emancipatory congresses that governments held with Jewish citizens in the nineteenth century, or with the *Concordat* and the *Lateran Accords* which negotiated a truce between the Catholic Church and the Italian Kingdom. Europe's Muslim religion councils have their parallels to a corporatist inspiration typical of the nineteenth-century law-and-order state. But if the authoritarian specters of Napoleon and Mussolini are present in the attempts to centralize and domesticate the Islamic faith in contemporary Europe, so are the spirits of the noblemen and legislators who supported the emancipation of European Jewry by arguing that "better citizens" are fashioned through the recognition of a minority's religious faith, and through the minority's acceptance of the primacy of national legal and administrative frameworks.

These national councils have forced together, under their respective governmental auspices, representatives of hundreds of Muslim prayer

TABLE 5.1.
Typical Agenda Items for Islam Councils

Religious Education, Islam in schools, religious teacher training
Cemetery sections for Muslims so graves may face Mecca, burial without coffins
Chaplains in prisons, military and public hospitals
Imam training, civic and theological education
Halal slaughter, Eid el Adha slaughterhouses
Hajj issues: consumer fraud protection, Saudi visas
Broadcasting time on state-supported mass media
Prayer spaces and mosques: permits, funding
Interreligious and intercultural dialogue

spaces in each country and worked closely with them to begin resolving the practical challenges of religious observance facing Muslim populations (see table 5.1). Such cooperation institutionalizes equal access to religious freedom and helps resolve controversial issues surrounding Muslims' religious observance; they thus smooth out the jagged edges of religious observance that would otherwise catch on the majority society's sensibilities. At the same time, they aid in the reform of the ties of Europe's Muslim communities with foreign governments and international Islamic NGOs, which is a key element in the establishment of nascent Islam Councils that have legitimacy in the eyes of both the Muslim communities and the state. The councils are the principal point of contact between governments and Muslim religious associations at a time when Muslims' political integration in elected and appointed capacities is practically non-existent. They have begun to resolve many practical issues that are at the core of tensions with host societies.

By acknowledging the place of Islam in their state-religion institutions and by placing a national imprimatur on organized Muslim communities in their societies, authorities open a formal communication channel to reduce the points of cultural tension between majority society and Muslim minorities that could hinder social and political integration. State-Islam consultations could undermine native resistance to believers in a "foreign" religion by helping adapt the practice of Islam to local institutional norms. And politicians' engagement with the "moderate majority" of Muslim religious leaders could weaken extremists' exhortations for the necessity of a "parallel society" or for parallel institutions for education or other purposes. The salutary image of Muslim religious leaders sitting down with ministers signals the community's arrival as part of the national fabric. While this does not suggest the arrival of full political integration, it is a powerful sign of respect. As a historian invoked by French interior minister Jean-Pierre Chevènement wrote, if there is space for three religions—Catholics, Protestants, and Jews—then why not for four? "Rest assured that there is room for Islam at the table of the Republic," Chevènement said, shortly before launching the process that would lead to the French Council for the Muslim Faith.[6]

But who among the Muslim contenders would take their rightful seat at the table? Since 1990, European states have sought to exert national sovereignty over the informal influence of international religious NGOs and foreign embassies, or Embassy Islam. Thus, the first task of the "domestication" of Muslim incorporation was to undo the outsourcing arrangement of the 1970s and 1980s that had allowed Saudi Arabia and Muslim labor-sending states to dominate the practice of Islam in Europe. The second task was to rein in the unregulated associations of transnational Political Islam active on Europeans' national territories. But after decades of informal arrangements, administrators needed some way of prioritizing and ranking and formalizing their relationships with Muslim federations. It would take two rounds of negotiations to arrive at a durable framework: an exploratory set of consultations between 1990 and 2000, and a second phase between 2000 and 2010 that produced the Islam Councils currently in operation (which is the subject of chapter 6).

The next section of this chapter addresses the failures of the "outsourcing" phase described briefly in chapter 2, and other events and issues that prompted European interior ministries to wrest control of state-mosque relations from their foreign-ministry counterparts and undertake efforts to bring Islam to the table. First, there is a discussion of socioeconomic indicators of integration, followed by the growing problem of foreign government control over Muslims' religious life, an increasingly felt inadequacy of prayer space and imams, and finally, the rise of Political-Islam activism and Islamist terrorism. Then, the chapter delves into the first of two phases of these efforts that culminated in the establishment of Islamic councils in the ten European states with sizable Muslim populations.

Socioeconomic Indicators

By the mid- to late 1980s, the children and grandchildren of labor migrants had grown up, and the integration strategy based on citizenship and nationality policies had not achieved impressive results for the second and third generations. Scholars evoked the possibility of "second-generation decline" and the "danger of underclass formation"[7] and noted the ever-rising costs of not engaging this new minority in its full organizational reality. Young people of Muslim background had higher unemployment rates than average, were overrepresented in the incarcerated population, and were underrepresented in higher education.[8] Such political and economic indicators helped discredit the notion that second- and third-generation immigrant youth would follow an easy path toward integration.

With few exceptions, Muslims were not yet successfully entering electoral politics or other high-status professions, but they were beginning to display more curiosity about their cultural heritage. In the words of one association leader, "I go to the mosque because down there, I exist."[9] As Olivier Roy writes: "The state is not engaging in a grand strategy but rather making the observation that the spontaneous organization of Islam in the West is still the mosque, not political parties, unions or national movements."[10]

The second- and third-generation migrants who had been expected to assimilate or to "return home" instead discovered religious identity—and not only in the mold of the "embassy" Islam promoted by the sending governments. Surveys showed that many of these young people identified more with their inherited religion than with their nationality, place of residence, or even gender. This re-Islamization, or the "*ummah* phenomenon,"[11] has been called "Muslim cosmopolitanism—a doctrine asserting the unity of all Muslims as members of a transnational, transethnic community—the *ummah*—which recognized a universalistic Islamic law, shari'a."[12]

Religious representation was the sole legitimate area where a government ministry could pursue contacts with Muslims *as such*. Even if the socioeconomic difficulties could not be easily explained by purely religious heritage, administrators discovered that the pursuit of religion policy was a sure and easy approach to at least convey government's interest in Muslims' symbolic integration into European polities. As the French interior minister from 1998 to 2000, Jean-Pierre Chevènement, said in an interview,

> It was only upon discovering that Islam was a form of identity affirmation for people who do not have much else that I got to know Islam little by little. . . . I thought it important to engage in dialogue with those who are having an identity crisis [*angoisse identitaire*]. . . . One must not let these young people stew in an isolated environment. One must not leave Islam outside. One must get used to working with them, listening to them, recognizing them. And Muslims are obliged to adapt to French society.[13]

Two studies carried out for the French Ministry of the Interior in the early 2000s suggested that religious identification was rising among Muslim youth and associational leaders. The first found that religious beliefs were "very important" for 85 percent of Muslim students, whereas the same was true for only 35 percent of non-Muslim students.[14] A third of Muslim students said they identified most with their religious group, much more so than by their skin color (10 percent) or where they live (11 percent). Only 4 percent of non-Muslim students felt defined by their religion, and many more by their gender (24 percent) and place of residence (27 percent). The authors concluded that although Islam was practically absent from the concerns of students of North African descent up until the 1980s, it has now become a major factor: Islam gives meaning to these students' daily lives and defines their identity in the public sphere. The second study, which examined twelve "socio-culturally Muslim" associations, found that Islam was the "principal reference that justifies associational participation" for all leaders under observation, who appealed more or less openly to religion in their activities. This was true whether the associations were offering study tutors, holding civic education courses, or organizing sports events.[15] A more recent study commissioned by the German government found a relationship between religiosity and lack of sociopolitical integration among young men of Muslim background, in particular claiming to show results that propensity toward violence was correlated with higher levels of religiosity.[16] These studies contributed to governments' impetus to become more involved in overseeing the supply of religious infrastructure on their national territories.

The Challenge of Foreign Government Control

The initial convergence of interests between receiving and sending governments was epitomized by the way in which policies favoring mother tongue instruction and religious outsourcing dovetailed with the goal of return migration. Once the temporary labor force turned into a permanent resident minority, however, these practices became objectively counterproductive to immigrant integration. Authorities in Europe began to object to the fact that religious leaders, and the financial backers of prayer spaces, were almost exclusively the representatives of foreign governments. In 1991, the Christian Democratic leader of the Dutch parliament called for an end to importing imams, who would be phased out through the establishment of an Islamic theology chair at a public university.[17] The wholesale importation of religious emissaries from sending states meant that populations of immigrant origin were practicing Islam "in" Europe rather than "of" Europe, in many politicians' shorthand.

In Germany and the Netherlands, representatives of the Turkish government in the DİTİB organizations insisted on providing religious instruction for all students of Turkish background, taught by teachers from the homeland in Turkish language, not German or Dutch. In Germany, frustration grew as every new DİTİB general secretary was sent directly from Ankara and served simultaneously as a diplomatic counselor (Botschaftsrat) to the Turkish ambassador in Berlin. One advisor to the Chancellor said in an interview, "The DİTİB says that all Turks are Muslim, but I do not say so!"[18] In France, the Algerian government insisted on sending prominent politicians—even government ministers— to serve as rectors of the Grand Mosque of Paris. At one particularly sensitive moment in Algerian politics, after the cancellation of the 1991 elections, the rector appointed by Algiers was recalled to the Algerian capital to serve simultaneously on the government's executive board. Despite French displeasure at this dual role, the rector was reluctant to give up his post, and even kept the keys to his apartment in the mosque compound, while his eventual replacement—a French citizen of Algerian origin—was forced to live elsewhere.[19] In Italy, the sole mosque in possession of the appropriate legal status (ente morale) to enter into state-religion relations with the Italian government is led by a board of diplomats in the Rome mosque; these diplomats did their best to block Italians' outreach efforts to invite additional organizations to the table.[20]

Material Inadequacy

Politicians, bureaucrats, and Muslim leaders alike have all deplored the lack of appropriate material conditions in which to practice Islam in European countries. The role played by imams and mosques is not precisely analogous to the clergy and prayer spaces in Judeo-Christian traditions: imams need no formal training and can be elected by the community they serve, and observant Muslims are not required to regularly attend mosque. But these are key pillars of Muslim communities: the gathering places and the moral leadership. As the general secretary of the French UOIF federation said in an interview, "The role of mosques is not just as a place for prayer. A mosque has a social role, it is a welcoming space where discussions and meetings are held."[21] The material condition of Islamic places of worship and the ratio of prayer spaces to Muslims, however, left much to be desired (see figure 5.1).

Less than 10 percent of mosques in France, Germany, the Netherlands, Spain, and the United Kingdom were "purpose-built," i.e., constructed as proper mosques.[22] The vast majority of Islamic prayer spaces

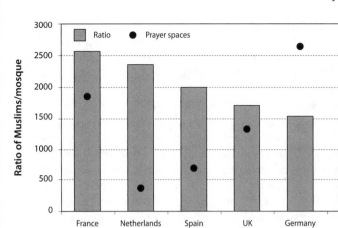

Figure 5.1. Availability of Islamic Prayer Space. Source: Allievi, 2009.

are converted common rooms—"micromosques"—in housing projects, garages, or even basements, whose capacity often does not exceed fifty people. In the most popular prayer spaces, there is regularly a spillover of prayer rugs onto adjoining courtyards or even sidewalks. The typical places of worship at present are thus improvised and are not identifiable as mosques from the outside. A pious businessman, for example, may simply rent a neighborhood storefront and lay down some rugs.

A former director of the Social Action Fund in France described the state of Muslim prayer spaces in the following vivid way: "you'll find garages, basements in housing projects, two or three bedrooms in workers hostels, with torn pieces of carpet on the floor, unheated—it is undignified. For those who wish to practice the religion, it is very humiliating."[23] Half of Marseille's seventy-three prayer spaces, for example, were thought to be without hot water or proper plumbing.[24] "It is indecent that Muslims are constrained to pray in prayer spaces incompatible with their devotion," said Jean-Pierre Chevènement. "I am aware of the legal difficulties that undermine state intervention in this area. But I also know the ravages provoked by feelings of humiliation; it would be unjust to let them fester." [25] As future President Nicolas Sarkozy would later state, it is not minarets that the public should fear, but rather garages and basements. The proliferation of small, improvised prayer spaces built a reputation of back alley (*Hinterhöfe*) Islam in Germany, for example, and elsewhere contributed to the impression of a rampant and obscure underground religion—both literally and figuratively.

There also have been quantitative and qualitative problems with imams. One of the major difficulties of creating a "European" Islam stems from the fact that most imams were born, raised, and trained outside of Europe—if they were trained at all.[26] Turkey sends a total of eight hundred imams, the near totality of imams in Germany, while Morocco, Algeria, Pakistan, and Tunisia rotate hundreds of imams in and out of Europe each year.

In France, only one of every five imams is a French citizen and even those were recently naturalized.[27] In Britain, only about one in ten have British nationality.[28] In Germany, there was not a single imam of German nationality in a Turkish mosque until 2007. Just under half of imams in France are regular salaried employees, paid either by the association that runs the prayer spaces or by foreign countries.[29] In France, only one-quarter are proficient in French language; the respective percentages are even smaller in Germany and Italy. Those who have received formal training usually attended universities in North Africa, Turkey, or Saudi Arabia, given the lack of equivalent seminary options in Europe.[30] Beyond the basic shortage of imams in France today, many of them are linguistically and culturally disconnected from the context in which they operate—half of them are over the age of fifty, only one-third are proficient in the French language, and two-thirds of them are on welfare.[31] "Imams are mainly confined to performing their 'internal' functions," Shadid and Koningsveld wrote in 1991, "and they are incapable of establishing intercultural and interreligious contacts. . . . The lack of qualified leadership forms a structural barrier to the flexibility in tehological thining."[32]

For several Interior Ministers in a row, the creation of French-trained imams is one of the main impulses behind the state's support for the organization of French Islam. As Nicolas Sarkozy stated in 2002, "imams are not adapted to the reality of French society and the needs of Muslims. . . . The current situation leads to clandestine behavior, which leaves room for extremism."[33] Jacques Berque, the late specialist of North Africa, argued in the 1980s that there could be a "Gallic Islam, just as there is an Islam of the Maghreb," and that would require creation of a Muslim theological faculty and seminary to train imams.[34]

POLITICAL-ISLAM ACTIVISM AND ISLAMIST TERRORISM

At the end of the "outsourcing" stage, in the 1980s and 1990s, a growing perception of transnational threats—from cultural clashes to terrorist incidents—linked to global Islam made interior ministries wary not only of migrants' organizational ties to homeland governments, but their connections with almost entirely unregulated Political-Islam organizations— i.e., the Islam "of the street" or "of the mosques."[35] Organizations affiliated with Political Islam, which had grown in size and number of prayer spaces to rival the homeland's Embassy Islam organizations, had remained largely unregulated and excluded, yet were now poised to challenge the monopoly of Embassy Islam over state-mosque relations in Europe. Their dynamism would ultimately contribute to the decision to revise the list of organizations governments consulted as interlocutors for their Muslim communities.

National federations inspired by Political-Islam movements were both fiercely independent from their "native" consulates and embassies and more assertive in the realm of religious rights, demanding cultural recognition and calling for an end to the foreign governmental control over Islam.[36] The UOIF in France, for example, waged a media campaign during the *affaire du foulard* in 1989 and hired lawyers to represent the schoolgirls who had been expelled from secondary school for wearing a headscarf. Political-Islam federations gathered sympathetic prayer rooms and cultural associations under common-law umbrella organizations that were ineligible for the status of state-church associations, and therefore beyond the oversight and control of the government.

The events of 1989–90 led to a new phase of state-mosque relations during which governments sought to bring in the Political-Islam networks under the existing institutional state-mosque relations. The Iranian fatwa of February 14, 1989, against Salman Rushdie (for his novel *The Satanic Verses*) definitively "moved the frontlines of Islamist contestation, situated in Southeast Asia during the 1980s, beyond the traditional historic boundaries of the Community of Believers, towards Western Europe where Salman Rushdie lives."[37] Pro-Fatwa demonstrations in Hyde Park and press releases from French and German Muslims denounced Rushdie. Later that year, three headscarf-wearing girls were expelled from a junior high school outside Paris, sparking a widespread controversy across Europe that would last fifteen years and eventually lead to legislation in France and Germany restricting the wearing of religious garb (not just Islamic garb) in public schools.[38] Also that year, after the Soviet troops withdrew from Afghanistan, the post-Communist void there and in central Asia revealed to Europe the extent of Saudi (and later, Turkish) institutional and financial deployment and proselytizing outside of the Arab world. This encouraged many governments to take a second look at the practices of these Islamic networks within the European context.

The subsequent Gulf War (1990–91) provoked further ripples across Muslim populations' public opinion. French officials worried that French Muslims "might follow the siren calls of Saddam Hussein's appeal for holy war."[39] There were some expressions of sympathy for President Saddam Hussein and signs of a discontent among some communities against the alliance sealed between the very exporters of Embassy Islam with the U.S.-led coalition.[40] The Gulf War marked a crisis in faith between the Muslim populations of Europe and the representatives of Embassy Islam: a number of Arab governments supported the allied war, and Saudi Arabia requested military assistance. The Mecca-based Muslim World League, a major funder of mosques across Europe, was in the awkward situation of justifying to European Muslims the presence of foreign troops on Saudi soil. As one participant in state-Islam consultations in France at the time recalled:

> Muslim associations in France wanted to distinguish themselves from the Iraqi position while still being against the US position. Saudi Arabia's support for the US had a chaotic effect on the position of Muslims here. Muslims in France couldn't quite support the Saudis, and everyone supported France, which had joined the coalition.[41]

Together, these events pointed governments to the reality of transnational memberships among the minority populations. The accumulation of bad news added up to a grim outlook for integration and common values among Muslim citizens in the eyes of many policymakers. Government officials were forced to wonder if "their" Muslim population could be next to rise up in protest. This internal debate was all the more intense because the protest arose "at the initiative of Muslim minorities deprived of access to political representation and participation, who mobilized in the name of a 'global Muslim community.'"[42] Later incidents such as the mobilization against Danish publication of caricatures of the Prophet Muhammad in Denmark would further highlight the absence of local reliable interlocutors in Muslim communities.[43]

What finally hardened governments' resolve to encourage the development of European Islam, however, was the Europeanization of Islamist terrorism and the advent of European-born terrorists of Muslim background. The first serious signs of problems with the social integration of the younger generations coincided with the emergence of a terrorist threat connected with Iranian and Algerian Islamist movements active in Europe in the 1980s and 1990s. First associated with Iran's theological revolution in the 1980s, it swept across North Africa and Israel-Palestine in the early 1990s, and finally reached Western capitals—first Paris (1995), then Washington (2001), then Madrid (2004) and London (2005) (see figure 5.2). The experience highlighted the failure of social integration, which would require a more precise domestic response than had been forthcoming in the first stage of state-mosque relations.

The devastating incidents of "homegrown" terrorism between 2000 and 2005—when young men born and raised in European Muslim

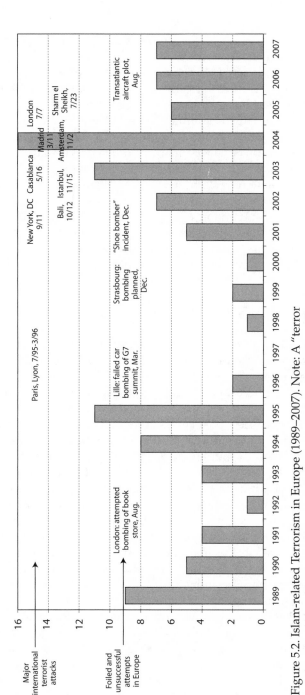

Figure 5.2. Islam-related Terrorism in Europe (1989–2007). Note: A "terror incident" is defined herein as an attempted or successfully executed attack by Muslim extremists in Europe. Source: Country Reports on Terrorism, 2008, April 2009, U.S. Department of State. MIPT Lawson Library, http://www .terrorisminfo.mipt.org/Patterns-of-Global-Terrorism.asp.

communities targeted their fellow citizens—did the most to push governments in the direction of stronger state intervention in Islamic affairs. The Frenchman Zacarias Moussaoui claimed to be part of the 9/11 plot, British suicide bombers were discovered in Israel in 2003, the Dutchman Muhammad Bouyeri murdered Theo Van Gogh in Amsterdam in 2004, and Mohamed Siddique Khan led the London four in suicide bombings of public transportation in 2005. The mosques frequented by these men were at the margins of state oversight, which until then European governments had deliberately avoided engaging in the manner that state-religion framework would allow them to do. Their vulnerability to rogue preachers who openly preached violence against the Western world and its allies in the Middle East (Israel, Morocco, Egypt, etc.) highlighted the unregulated state of Islamic "clergy" across Europe. Laissez-faire outsourcing, which had permitted the freedom to glorify violence, had gone too far; something needed to be done.

Bringing Islam to the Table of the Republic: Background

Government attention to the practical aspects of the "who, what and how" of State-Mosque relations did not increase quickly or uniformly across European countries. But between 1990 and 2010, religiously justified terrorist acts with European links, and the recalcitrant indicators of social and political integration for second- and third-generation Muslim Europeans, caused policymakers to shift their emphasis toward this population. Religion had previously been but one characteristic of this population of immigrant origin. Religious belonging became *the* relevant characteristic for policymakers, and as such, the door through which social integration of this minority population would come to pass. "It did not just have to do with terrorism," a German interior ministry advisor told the author in an interview. "Rather, it was the growing awareness that Islam is a societal reality, that more than half a million Muslim citizens live in Germany. Just based on the fact that the number is growing is reason alone that one can no longer say it is a foreign phenomenon. It is now a reality of internal politics which needs to be addressed in a range of regulatory areas."[44]

The logic was that, if Islam could be incorporated into the institutions of the republic, then Muslims could identify with the state, too, rather than just with their community—and by extension, the global *ummah*. A French official said in an interview that incorporating Islam was a way to send a welcoming message: "With the effort to integrate the Muslim religion by way of the consultation, and by treating its representatives with consideration, the public authorities symbolically demonstrated their desire to integrate *the entirety of the population of Muslim origin or culture.*"[45] Similarly, the British minister for communities argued that "Strong mosques positioned at the centre of the community and effectively governed will be better able to withstand attempts to hijack them by certain groups supporting violent extremist interpretations of Islam."[46] Thus, the goal of state outreach to Muslim communities was twofold: vaccination against radicalism, on the one hand, and the routinization of religious observance for Muslims, on the other. If everyday religious practice could be rendered mundane and freed of avoidable conflicts and tension by state oversight—such as the unavailability of prayer spaces or halal meat—then everyday social and political integration could be unencumbered by the additional weight of a foreign-run religion in its European habitat.

Despite the difficulty of counting Muslims and their diverse national origins, and categorizing or assessing their religious affiliation and levels of piety—national policymakers sought to treat their mosque-going Muslim populations as a national collectivity. This was made more difficult by the organizational topography of Islam in European countries, and the fact that religious observance in Islam is highly individualized. Even though many signs of outward piety are high—such as fasting on Ramadan or attending mosque—formal membership in Islamic organizations is very low. Precise numbers are elusive, but in most European countries, the best available evidence is that only 10–20 percent of Muslims are active participants or dues-paying members of Islamic religious and cultural associations;[47] perhaps twice that number attend prayer and fast on Ramadan. However, governments needed an interlocutor, and therefore the federations representing prayer spaces became the main target of policymaking toward Islam.

Beginning in the 1990s, governments sought to treat organized Islam as they had with previous transnational religious challenges: to mold Islam into an organizational shape that can serve as an administrative counterpart, they sought to weaken ties abroad and strengthen institutional connections at home, in the hope of enhancing the authority of the nation-state over potentially competing demands on citizens' sociopolitical loyalties. "Immigration in our country is heterogeneous," the Italian interior minister said in 2005, "but the *Consulta per l'Islam* aims to develop dialogue with [Muslims, who are] the most distinct and culturally furthest from us."[48] The German interior minister justified his creation of the German Islam Conference with the unsentimentality of a political realist: many of Germany's Muslims "have forgotten about going back home," they are "no longer a foreign population group," and they "have become a component of our society. . . . Their children and grandchildren have long felt themselves to be Germans of Turkish or Arab origin." However, he also expressed the widely held desire to demand something in exchange: if a country grants recognition and acceptance, then it "also has the right to ask [Muslims] to renounce certain aspects of [their] culture."[49] The German Islamic Conference thus aims "To improve the religious and socio-political integration of the Muslim population, to prevent violent Islamism and extremism, to counter the trend towards isolation of Muslims in Germany . . . [and] to preserve and respect the liberal democratic order."[50] Improving integration was thus integral to the removal of threats to identification with and loyalty to the nation.

National interior ministries pursued these goals with a set of mundane administrative instruments: bringing Muslim representatives into the state apparatus so as to regulate areas where religious observance meets the public domain. Authorities sought to nationalize the organized practice of Islam by domesticating the extra-territorial ties—of Muslim religious organizations, prayer spaces, and their personnel. Governments used the formal recognition of Islam as an opportunity to recruit a "moderate" Muslim leadership—those willing to affirm the supremacy of the national constitution—from a broad range of backgrounds. This and the state's encouragement of locally based centers of religious authority, such as training for religion teachers and theological seminaries for imams, was aimed at creating a context for the sociopolitical integration of all Muslims in Europe.

Notwithstanding these countries' distinct State-Church institutions and state-society traditions, they have enacted broadly analogous policies of outreach to organized Muslim religious communities. There is a common search among states for "moderate" elements in locally based Muslim communities and a common emphasis on pragmatic details of religious freedoms and practice. This observation goes against the grain of cumulative academic wisdom on the theme of contemporary state-religion relations.

AN OVERVIEW OF ALTERNATIVE VIEWS IN STATE-CHURCH STUDIES

One tendency in scholarship on Islam in Europe has been to characterize European nation-states' policy responses to the emergence of Islam as falling into their respective national state-church models in an entirely predictable fashion. This school of thought holds that policies can be explained according to resource mobilization and opportunity structures. The Belgian scholar Felice Dassetto argues, for example, "the position of states with regard to Islam does not only differ along ideological lines in the area of historical state-religion relations, in their past experience with intra-Christian religious pluralism . . . state attitudes towards religion vary in function of the relationship between state and civil society."[51] A French sociologist of religion, Jocelyne Cesari, similarly writes that "different institutional arrangements tend to shape the agendas of Islamic mobilization and claims in different countries."[52] In this view, it is the available options for a religious community's public legal status that influence—and constrain—the path of institutionalization. As the German political scientist Michael Minkenburg writes, "church-state relations represent an institutional arrangement which provides an 'opportunity structure' for religious interests in the political process."[53]

Many scholars have relied on this kind of strictly national institutional perspective to explain the development of specific institutional forms of consultation with Islam. They argue that cross-national differences in state-church regimes—which are the product of state secularization, toleration for Protestants and Catholics, Jewish emancipation, etc.—"reveal how host states and their foreigners encounter each other."[54] An often-cited book by American scholars Joel Fetzer and Christopher Soper concludes that the outcomes of religious incorporation and secularization reflect accepted "ideas about the role of religion in [national] public life." "Political disputes over religion," they write, "will inevitably be played out through church-state patterns inherited from the past."[55] In this view, state-church regimes are considered simply a subset of group-state organization within state apparatus, analogous to European states' "incorporation regimes."[56] Church-state relations reflect "different collective modes of understanding and organizing membership in host polities," and provide an opportunity structure for religious groups that aspire to public recognition or support for their activities.[57] The question from an institutional perspective then becomes, what does "emancipation" mean in a given national context: do religious minorities encounter the state as corporatist groups or as individuals?[58]

The fundamental right to freedom of conscience and religious practice exists throughout contemporary Europe, but states' approaches toward organized religion are generally either "negotiated or unilateral": negotiations with Catholics take the form of a Concordat (or international treaty) with the Catholic Church; or, when dealing with other religions, of a domestic contract, voted in parliament or by executive decree. Three ideal-typical categories roughly map the European division amongst "secular, Protestant and Roman Catholic countries": (1) separation/universal (France, Netherlands); (2) concordatarian/recognition (Italy, Germany, Spain); and (3) national church (UK, Denmark, Norway).[59]

According to this school of thought, national institutions make up the political opportunity structure for state-Islam interaction. France, Germany, and Italy have state-church regimes that, as Messner describes them, range from "cooperation-and-coordination" between the state and religions (Germany and Italy), to the more modest "taken-into-consideration" status in France.[60] Yet all three "cultivate a tradition of neutrality and separation" (as opposed to the Greek and Scandinavian "fusion approach" for state-religion relations). Messner defines neutrality as a system of non-establishment of churches, yet one which also "create[s] a place for the expression of religious convictions within society."[61] But neutrality can also mean "active and interventionist: the concrete construction of religious freedom," or, as is the case in Germany, the "protection of religious communities from the state" rather than vice versa.

In "National Church" models (United Kingdom, Denmark, Norway, Sweden, Greece), the state recognizes and finances only one religion, and tends to restrict *de jure* or *de facto* the institutionalization of minority religions—though these may obtain simple associational status and a lower tier of rights available in common law. National church systems have a state church, which receives preferential treatment but is subject to state influence in its leadership, for example the British Queen's appointment of the archbishop of Canterbury and the Prime Minister's naming of twenty-seven bishops to the House of Lords.

In "Concordatarian/Recognition" regimes (Italy, Germany, Spain), churches may be eligible for legal advantages, privileged juridical status, and even significant financial support.[62] "Relations with religious groups" in these regimes, Ferrari writes, "are regulated through bilateral provisions, negotiated between the state and each religious group."[63] In the "recognition" model, religious communities can apply for recognition or sign protocols in the framework of sometimes hierarchical but pluralist church law—sometimes known as a regime of *ententes*.

In the "Separation/Universal" model (France, Netherlands, Ireland), finally, the lay state guarantees religious equality but is not in the business of recognizing or financing religions.[64] Religious activity in universal regimes is regulated, and the government accords certain status and rights to religious organizations and their leaders—this is sometimes referred to as a "separatist" regime. Organizational pillars may allow for the autonomous activities of religious communities, but there are somewhat coordinated relations between religious representatives and the state.

In keeping with the perspective of state-church institutions, the most avid proponents of the strict institutionalist perspective suggest that the incorporation of Muslims simply reflects different "inherited pasts."[65]

In a similar vein, Litt Woon Long and Ari Zolberg conclude that any status improvements for Islam in Europe follow a routine trajectory of pluralist minority incorporation in different national settings.[66] Franck Frégosi argues that regimes of "recognition" constitute a "more favorable environment for the institutionalization of Islam"—it is "not chance" that Islam's status is most advanced in European states with a recognition regime: Austria, Belgium, Spain, and Italy.[67]

But this view of accommodation sketches a stylized image that does not resemble the developments in state-Islam relations in the past several decades. Using this same reasoning, for example, Fetzer and Soper predict "hostility" to Islam in France but "accommodation and compromise in Germany"—which is close to the opposite of what has transpired.[68] In each national case, local and national governments have taken the initiative to centralize religious representation of Islam alongside other established religious communities. These legally personified institutions would serve as interlocutors for local and national governments where religion meets the public sphere, in the same way that Catholic dioceses, Protestant federations, and Jewish consistories have done for over a century. These organizations oversee life cycle events (birth, marriage, divorce, death) and the material needs of minions (prayer space and leadership, ritual animal slaughter, cemeteries); they maintain a presence in state institutions (military, hospital, and prison chaplains); and they serve as symbolic leaders for ceremonial events (such as state dinners or new year's receptions) or in times of international or domestic crisis.

Recent scholarship has questioned the relevance of the state-church typologies to actual policy outcomes. Minkenburg argues against the strict reliance on the institutionalist perspective: "Taken alone, patterns of church-state relations as conceptualized in the 'inherited' typology show a limited relevance for policy outputs."[69] Valérie Amiraux also laments the "weak analytic worth of the schematic classifications" of state-church relations. "They allow us to distinguish between the national experiences of Catholic and Protestant cultures, or their participation in the larger movement towards secularization."[70] A law may allow for mosque-building, for example, but the reality of local politics could prohibit its realization.

Several authors have come to the conclusion that the notions of neutrality and state-church opportunity structures mean different things in reality than in theory. Silvio Ferrari, for example, writes that "the traditional distinction made between systems of separation, Concordat systems and national churches is decreasingly operational . . . general attitude of state neutrality, and allows for treatment of favor reserved in the framework of a 'public sector' where they occupy a recognized place: so that state can intervene in religious question in order to make itself respected and prescribe the rules of the game."[71] Ferrari, along-side others, therefore argues for a reconsideration of state-church categories and, especially, of the definition of "neutrality."[72] Hollerbach points to the existence of "adaptive—not indifferent—neutrality."[73] The liberal state, Ferrari says, was "neutral by default and by ignorance—it professed agnosticism and declared itself incompetent for religious affairs." But, he concludes, it is unclear if such a fair and equal state ever really existed; he finds, instead, that this concept was replaced by a "neutrality of intervention" to assure religious needs of citizens.[74]

At the other end of the spectrum are those scholars who espouse another theoretical view: a "post-national" world of state-church relations. They foretell the end of the Westphalian nation-state system, which they claim has become "outmoded and incapable of keeping pace with changes" in a globalizing world.[75] These scholars predict that accommodation of Islam will indeed occur—but only over the dead body of the nation-state. In this view, the decline of state sovereignty is magnified by the particular challenges posed by contemporary migration flows and international Muslim populations that straddle national borders and cultures.[76] Yasemin Soysal, a proponent of "post-national" rights acquisition, argues that national institutions are further eroded by the development of "constitutionally interconnected states with a multiplicity of memberships."[77] Saskia Sassen similarly claims to observe the state's reduced autonomy in immigration policy as a result of globalization pressures and "international human rights norms and discourses."[78] As Steven Krasner does in his account of the progression of minority rights in post–World War I Europe through contemporary international treaties, Soysal suggests that contemporary third country nationals in 1980s and early 1990s Europe benefited from their host states' membership in supranational organizations.

According to the post-national view, the integration of Islam will take place when national governments lose power and institutions associated with post-national processes and transnational movements gain authority. But there is reason to be skeptical about the two underlying premises of this development: first, the limited nature of European competence in cultural and religious policies or the "third pillar" affairs of Justice and Home Affairs that affect immigrant populations. This area is still mostly subject to unanimous decision-making within the EU. And, second, the reality is that non-governmental organizations focused on immigrant rights have an extremely modest impact on policymaking in Brussels. There is some academic consensus that the judiciary and the bureaucracy (not elected offices) are the institutions best positioned to aid the cause of third country nationals. Virginie Guiraudon has written how decisions made behind "gilded doors" are freed from public relations considerations.[79] Andrew Geddes, too, contends that "technocratic and legalistic processes offer scope for protection of electorally unpopular interests of migrants, as judges and technocrats are insulated from the harsh electoral gaze."[80] Moreover, Europeanization has not integrated cultural competences, although the implication of post-national theorists is that the development of European citizenship could eventually offer Muslims a higher set of rights than that which is guaranteed them as residents or citizens of individual member-states.

Ruud Koopmans and Paul Statham authored a definitive refutation of "post-national challenges to the nation-state"—by bringing to bear empirical evidence that shows the endurance of national immigrant integration models on claims-making activity in the first half of the 1990s: "Neither the post-national nor the multicultural model is able to explain why British minorities identify as racial or religious groups and their German counterparts identify on the basis of their homeland national or ethnic origin."[81] They note "the virtual absence of European-level migrant organizations"—and find that just 1.2 percent and 2.2 percent of claims-making in Germany and the UK, respectively, had a "supra or transnational" scope; just 1.1 percent and 0.7 percent had a "European" scope; and that the vast majority of claims-making was directed at either "Homeland governments" (26 percent Germany, 6 percent UK) or "national authorities" (73 percent Germany, 95 percent UK). When Koopmans and Statham turn their attention to cultural and religious rights in an elaborate five-country study, similarly, they still find that "the factors that have led to the extension of rights to immigrants have been domestic rather than post-national in any meaningful sense."[82]

My findings therefore contradict the view represented by the "inherited institutions" perspective, in which the pre-existing opportunity structure alone determines the shape of Muslim accommodation. Instead, I find that governments have recognized that many integration challenges with regard to the population of Muslim origin require the reining in of certain transnational characteristics of religious communities.

Across a striking range of countries, Islam Councils would later become the instrument through which Islamic organizations and the state cooperate on a broad and substantive range of issues, including appointing chaplains in prisons and the armies, the civic education of imams, mosque construction, faculty chairs, religion teacher training, as well as symbolic roles like sitting on public broadcasting or overseeing *halal* slaughter rituals (see chapter 6). Contrary to the strict institutionalists' expectations, we find similar debates over the place of religion in

Table 5.2.
European Democracies with State Support Policies for Religion

Form of State Policies of Support (or monitoring) of Religion	Percentage
Government funding of religious schools or education	100
Religious education standard (optional in schools)	76
Government collects taxes for religious organizations	52
Official government department for religious affairs	44
Government positions or funding for clergy	40
Government funding of religious charitable organizations	36
Established religion	36
Some clerical positions made by government appointment	24

Source: Stepan, 2010, p. 7.

the public sphere across national cases (e.g., religious education, head-scarves); and institutional opportunities for some form of organized Muslim representation, in effect, exist in each of the national cases at hand (see table 5.2). As Alfred Stepan suggests in his research on state-religion models in Europe, religious interlocutors are required in each type he examines: from the separatist to the established church, from positive accommodation to the equal treatment of all religion.

At a bare minimum, organizational partners must be present to administer religious education, whether organized as an option in public school or under special arrangement as a taxpayer-subsidized parochial school.[83] Many other areas of state-church areas exist as opportunities for institutionalized relations. This illuminates a further reason why strict adherence to an institutional perspective is unsatisfactory for understanding dynamics of state-Islam interactions: it fails to consider "underlying policy goals," or the ways in which ideas of the role of religion in public life can change over time, as Erik Bleich helpfully observed.[84]

The emergence of organized Islam as a permanent fixture in the European religious landscape was under way long before the Hamburg cell began planning the attacks of September 11, before a surge in anti-Semitic acts in France, and before the departure of young European Muslims on suicide bombing missions abroad and at home. Contrary to the prediction of the state's imminent death in the face of globalization and transnationalism, government activity—and assertion of the state's interest—in religious accommodation processes was alive and well between 1990 and 2010. European nation-states have established routine contacts with Muslim leaders, leading to a new level of mutual acquaintance and a slow but steady process of nationalization of religious authority.

Muslim populations did not "go home" after the era of labor importation, and the networks of embassies and NGOs whose religious activities and proselytism European governments had uncritically tolerated for years turned out to be more tenacious than expected. But states roundly judged as a failure the first period's strategy of keeping religion a private affair, of keeping Islam out of the public sphere, and of using international diplomacy to manage the religion of immigrants. The national governments assumed an active posture in state-religion affairs because Islam has emerged as a major factor of individual and group identity among the descendants of labor migrants. Church-state relations are of vital importance because institutional links with religious communities can provide a basic element of political integration for a minority group. If unattended to, however, as was the case during the first period of "outsourcing," transnational religious networks have the potential to threaten the authority of the state and its maintenance of social order. Church-state relations are instrumental to achieving the state's core duties of stability and security. Governments took into consideration the unintended consequences of their previous laissez-faire strategies in state-Islam relations and took stock of unanticipated developments among the immigrant populations.

Since the usual lens of analysis employed in state-church studies has insisted on the different paths states have taken to secular rule, scholars tend to predict divergent policy approaches to Islam based on institutional pre-history. My approach focuses an analytic lens on this lower common denominator: the act of institutional outreach and how it changes the civil society organizations that are engaged by it.

THE FIRST ATTEMPT AT REDEFINING STATE-MOSQUE RELATIONS (1990–1999)

A first attempt to end the outsourcing phase and begin the incorporation of Islam within national institutions took place in the 1990s. This early period was spurred by governments' desire to identify local Muslim interlocutors during controversial episodes in international politics—the Persian Gulf and the Bosnian wars. However, the lack of structure and commitment meant that these early Islam Councils would play a mostly symbolic role. For example, French interior minister Pierre Joxe was moved to found the Council for Reflection on Islam in

France because he wanted someone to represent Islam at official functions, "A Muslim in the *Elysée* palace for next New Year's reception, together with [the Cardinal, the Grand Rabbi and the president of the Protestant Federation], that would be a nice symbol."[85]

Ministerial disagreements over which organizations should be invited to consultations had progressed since the end of the outsourcing arrangements of the 1970s and 1980s. However, disputes persisted over the government's competence to play the role of power broker among the competing successors to Embassy Islam. Many competing mosque federations sought the state's recognition, choosing all-encompassing names to try to appear to be the inevitable choice for administrators who cast about for authentic voices, e.g., the "Central Council of Muslims in Germany," the "Muslim Association of Britain," the "Union of Islamic Communities and Organizations of France," or the "Religious Islamic Community." In reality, however, these names overstated their case: none was ever truly centralized, representative, or unified.

Officials were wary of getting too involved in distinguishing between these claims of representativeness. Authorities argued that they were handicapped by the strictures of state-church norms in their respective countries and thus could not attempt to help Muslims resolve internal differences. For example, a German interior ministry official said in an interview:

> The Basic Law states that religious communities must organize and administer their own affairs . . . It would be basically unconstitutional to say that we are now going to create a central organization. . . . They must organize themselves without the help of the [German] State, and without the help of the Homeland . . . It would be desirable if the Muslim organizations could undertake these duties, then one could see that they are capable of it, and then one could ask what status do they need, it would be more difficult to grant status first.[86]

In Italy, only one organization requesting recognition by the state had the proper legal status to proceed—and it was the Embassy-Islam federation. "But if they get an Intesa," an Italian interior ministry official said in an interview, referring to the official religious recognition available under the constitution, "then the rest of Islam—the real Islam, which is made up of ordinary people, people who get up every morning and go to work, they are not represented. So you risk creating serious conflicts within the confession . . . so we need to find a unity of intentions among the contenders."[87] He continued, with reference to the three principal organizations requesting recognition, "We say 'find an agreement amongst yourselves' because otherwise we can't give you a favorable opinion, what are we supposed to do, have four different consultations with the same confession? The problem is always the same: with whom are we supposed to sign? If I sign an agreement with one group, what will the other organizations say? And how do I justify it? Then the second group says to me that the third group doesn't represent anyone. Then the third group tells me that they represent half a million people and that the second group only represents ambassadors. What am I supposed to do? Call up the *carabinieri* and have them do a head count?"[88]

As befits administrative consultations, not all councils have strived for "democratic" solutions but rather for efficacy and legitimacy. The French interior minister Pierre Joxe, for example, did not set out to create an institution that would be "continuous, precise, profound, or methodical," he said, but rather wanted simply to "gather a few people together, tell them what the problems were, ask them what they think and what we should do."[89] It would be more about symbols: "since you cannot gather 'representatives,' try to 'symbolize' Islam in France by bringing together men who will reflect together."[90] The Council for Reflection on Islam in France convened fifteen handpicked "wise men" (*sages*) in the spring of 1990 to advise the religion office and interior ministry staff in an ad hoc and non-binding capacity.[91] The ministry wanted to have a set of interlocutors after worries had emerged about Muslims' loyalty to France during the first Gulf War in 1990. But some Muslim federations were excluded from the council, and the loose institutional form made consensus elusive. Members helped settle some minor issues such as the provision of halal food in the French armed forces (there were only several hundred Muslims in service at the time) and the starting time for Ramadan, but not much else. When the interior minister who initiated the Council left to take on the government's defense portfolio, the forum limped on briefly, but the official government interlocutor eventually reverted to the same Embassy-Islam representative (*Grande Mosquée de Paris*) that had dominated French Islam until the late 1980s.

Upon the German Constitution's fiftieth anniversary in May 1999, the newly inaugurated President Johannes Rau said in his inaugural address that he would represent all Germans, "especially those still without a German passport." He made a small historical step by being the first head of state to routinely invite the head of the *Zentralrat der Muslime in Deutschland* to official state receptions. In a speech on the first anniversary of the attacks of September 11, 2001, Interior Minister Otto Schily announced an inter-ministerial working group on Islam to meet periodically and resolve familiar and new issues regarding the exercise of the Muslim faith. The Working Group involved three of the four major federations alongside representatives from all ministries having anything to do with Islam—from agricultural (animal slaughter) to construction (prayer space) to interior and even the chancellor's office. This case-by-case, piecemeal solution aimed to "deepen coordination amongst the individual *Bundesländer* and eventually lead to a common Islam policy of the federal government."[92] But they sidestepped the most crucial issues of state-mosque relations, such as the provision of religious education, and they excluded from participation one of the largest Political-Islam federations. Ultimately, the negotiations served only to enthrone the Embassy-Islam representative (from the Turkish-state-inspired DİTİB) rather than truly institutionalize a broader swath of interlocutors.

In Italy in 1998, a newly appointed prime minister made it known to the main Muslim federations representing Embassy Islam and Political Islam, respectively, that his Center-Left government wanted to sign an *Intesa* (bilateral state-church agreement) with Islam.[93] The Embassy-Islam group established the Italian Islamic Council (Consiglio Islamico d'Italia or CII) between 1998 and 2000 as an agreement of friendship between the major federations.[94] Its ten founding members were all Italian citizens.[95] This cooperation among Italian Muslim federations was ephemeral. Almost immediately, there was dissent between the Political and Embassy Islam groups over practical matters of the *intesa*'s content as well as the nature of interaction between Muslim representatives and with state institutions.[96] The federations did not meet long enough to settle anything practical. When it fell apart, the person in charge of religion commissions at the prime minister's office said, "this is their problem, not ours."[97]

In the late 1980s, the Netherlands began to experiment with consultative mechanisms in order to provide "more uniform contact with the state."[98] The Council of Local Islamic Organizations came first,[99] followed by the National Islamic Committee and later, in the mid-1990s, the Islam and Citizenship committee. While each of these instances facilitated dialogue between Muslim groups and government authorities for a time,[100] none was permanent, nor definitively settled the status of their interlocutors, and so they fell into disuse.

In the mid-1990s in the United Kingdom, an attempt to create a single interlocutor for government produced the Muslim Council of Britain (MCB): "a mélange of the top-down and bottom-up initiative."[101] The MCB was officially founded in 1997 after several years of broad consultation by representatives from over 250 Muslim British organizations, and it was intended to be an improvement on the UK Action Committee on Islamic Affairs (made up of British Muslim professionals and some diplomats) that had formed in the wake of the "Rushdie affair" in 1989.[102] The MCB claimed that the home secretary had repeatedly requested a single interlocutor for government from the Muslim community. The MCB's first General Assembly meeting was held in 1998.

Figure 5.3. Prime Minister Tony Blair attends a Muslim Council of Britain meeting, 2004. Source: © Thomson Reuters.

It is possible to identify direct official sponsorship of MCB. Press reports have spoken of "heavy government involvement" in its creation, and some evidence of this relationship emerged in a series of leaked memos (see figure 5.3). "The idea for an umbrella organization for British Islam was first floated [with the] Home Secretary in the last Conservative Government. But the idea was taken up with particular alacrity by [his Labour Party successor], and Government ministers met early and often with MCB in 1999, a moment when government needed an interlocutor on Kosovo war and high profile hate crimes against Muslims."[103] Official approbation was granted to MCB in the critical year of 1999, when the UK had joined the Kosovo conflict. An inherent tension was built into the government's relationship with MCB. Since rival organizations were excluded, moreover, MCB participants were stigmatized by what one observer called the "kiss-of-death" dilemma:

> The more [the government] tries to accommodate leading Muslims, the more its partners risk being seen as patsies. The [MCB] has spoken out boldly in favor of co-operation with police against terrorism. But some Muslim grandees learned a hard lesson in 2001 when Tony Blair persuaded a number of them to endorse the Anglo-American attack on Afghanistan. They have not regained the credibility they lost on the street. That's partly why the MCB is careful to wag its finger at the government over issues ranging from female attire to foreign policy, everywhere from the Middle East to Kashmir to Chechnya.[104]

The British government also became aware of this conundrum: "Some young Muslims are disillusioned with mainstream Muslim organizations that are perceived as pedestrian, ineffective and in many cases, as 'sell-outs' to Her Majesty's Government," the *Economist* wrote in 2006.[105] In other words, any actual rapprochement with the government had to be balanced by the MCB's efforts to retain credibility, at the very moments when the government needed to show it was being tough and demanding on Muslim community leaders. Moreover, the MCB's existence did little prevent urban unrest from occurring in 2001—just several years after a similar set of riots helped build momentum to create the MCB. Within the MCB umbrella group was a highly controversial subgroup that played a central role in the anti-war coalition protests during 2002–3. In January 2005, MCB embarrassed its official patrons by refusing an invitation to attend ceremonies commemorating the sixtieth anniversary of the liberation of Auschwitz.[106]

Conclusion

All of the informal consultations during the first phase of state-mosque relations in Europe met the same fate: they could not arrive at a final status agreement granting official recognition to Islam, and they could not convince participants to agree among themselves. The early councils could not reliably guarantee religious freedoms, and the bringing together of Embassy Islam and Political Islam proved untenable. The Embassy Islam group would torpedo the forums when they strayed too far out of their control. Political-Islam representatives had no real incentive to compromise. Because the state was still tentative in its intervention, the institutionalization—and therefore the benefits of a strong administrative framework to regulate the interaction of competing federations—was also tentative. None of the participants felt stakes were high enough to stick with it. In each case, governments threw up their hands in frustration with their interlocutors. Participants were not asked to explicitly recognize the authority of national law over religious law. Unsurprisingly, they could not deliver either on "moderation" or in terms of practical authority. The next chapter will explore how terrorism spurred governments' collective adaptation and decision to make a more committed effort at institutionalization. Across Europe, the years 2001–2006 would see a ramping up in the investment of political capital to establish national state-mosque relations.

CHAPTER SIX

Imperfect Institutionalization

ISLAM COUNCILS IN EUROPE

EUROPEAN GOVERNMENTS LEARNED valuable lessons in institutional design from the early, ineffective efforts at organizing Muslim communities in the 1990s. The idling of the initial consultations with Muslim groups and their lack of legitimacy and an enforceable consensus had frustrated ministry officials across the continent. The "Europeanization" of Islamist terrorism in the mid-1990s and early 2000s, however, led to a second and more enduring attempt at organizing Islam Councils between 2000 and 2010.

A succession of harrowing experiences contributed to the impetus to accelerate state-mosque relations: the Hamburg cell that committed the attacks of September 11, 2001, the murder of Dutch filmmaker and Islam-critic Theo Van Gogh in 2002, the involvement of residents of Spain and France in the Casablanca bombings in May 2003, the Madrid bombings of March 11, 2004, and the London Underground suicide attacks of July 7, 2005, in addition to reports of European Muslims traveling to fight U.S. and European troops in Iraq and Afghanistan. Beyond the repressive measures that governments could (and did) take to combat the radicalization of young Muslims—such as deportations of extremists and radical imams, and the usual activities of counter-terrorism policies, including political and financial surveillance—authorities also pursued a constructive response to the challenge of Islamist terrorism. Indeed, the international events renewed governments' determination to press forward with state-Islam consultations, and added to the arguments for regulation of the still unsettled status of Islam in Europe.

National governments have followed the same two phases of state-mosque relations—outsourcing followed by incorporation—and this is due neither to "post-nationalism" nor to "shared values." It has taken place instead through parallel processes in which each country asserted its *national* sovereignty in the face of potential social conflict influenced by transnational political actors. With this second phase of reshaping state-mosque relations, European governments engaged in a partial revival of an institutional arrangement that earlier had been used in the realm of postwar economic policymaking. The Islam councils share some of the characteristics of neo-corporatist mediation between "capital" and "labor," as codified by political scientists in the 1970s and 1980s on institutionalized class relations in Western Europe.[1] Rather than favoring one or more "partial" interests, states designed neo-corporatist arrangements to affirm their role as guarantor of public order and as a broker between opposing sides. States granted "peak associations" a representational monopoly and privileged access to government decision-making—including "a high degree of collaboration among the groups themselves in the shaping of policy"— in exchange for "observing controls on selection of leaders and articulation of demands and supports."[2] Governments have again placed themselves in the role of a self-interested broker, now representing the state's interest between the powerful force of Political Islam—by analogy, in the role of the "outsider" trade unions—and the Embassy Islams—whose dominant position could be compared to employers' groups.[3]

State consultations with Islamic religious representatives are properly understood as "Councils for the Muslim Religion," not as "Muslim Councils." In other words, these should not be mistaken for instances of political representation—no more than the French bishops' conference can claim to represent Catholics on non-religious matters or Jewish central councils or grand rabbis can speak for all Jews. The councils provide a regular administrative forum in which to discuss the technical and practical challenges at the intersection of religious practice and public policy—but their institutional mandate stops short of "politics."

To the extent that an Islamic infrastructure in sync with constitutional and state-church norms in European countries emerges, it will be from this crucible: a state-brokered framework with indirect representatives of the two main "blocs" of mosques and prayer spaces—Embassy Islam and Political Islam (see figure 6.1). The working agenda of these bodies is statutorily limited to state-religion affairs, that is, for the practical needs of an organized religion, and is not intended to convey the political interests of Muslim minorities. Nevertheless, European governments are attempting to foster the social and political integration of Muslim populations by creating the institutional conditions for the development of a British or German Islam, for example, rather than just tolerating Islam "in" the United Kingdom or Germany.

The European governments' parallel strategies with regard to Islam come up head-to-head against the pursuit by Islamic religious representatives of their own organizations' competing and distinct ideological interests. These interests, while not easily divisible nor strictly material as in the case of capital and labor, nonetheless include a contest with concrete stakes: namely, the privilege of being recognized as the legitimate representatives of organized Islam. This prize determines which groups will be involved in the training and appointment of religion teachers in publicly financed schools or chaplains in public institutions, for example. It may also lead to financial gains that, while modest, can be crucial to the organizations' self-perpetuation by influencing who is chosen to certify (and tax) halal slaughter, who organizes pilgrimage tours to Mecca, and who receives tax-exempt status or is permitted to indirectly collect "church taxes," etc. Moreover, representatives are engaged in a less worldly competition for spiritual hegemony over European Muslims through scriptural interpretations and public pronouncements—through rival boards for fatwas and *ulama* in Europe—of how to be a good Muslim in a non-Muslim land.

Governments in the second phase undertook three significant steps to try to avoid the kind of instability that had plagued attempts in the 1990s to forge consensus among Muslim groups (see table 6.1). Taking a series of steps that were reminiscent of neo-corporatist relations, authorities became more involved with Muslims' internal community dynamics. In particular, states made use (explicitly or implicitly) of several mechanisms in creating Islam Councils: first, the nomination of a council of rival organizations, to co-opt some leaders and provide a training ground for a new generation of state-oriented elites; second, the promulgation of a charter affirming signatories' respect for the constitution and its fundamental principles and for the legal authority of the government; and third, the granting of an effective monopoly of representation in specific issue areas through the establishment of technical working groups to reach consensus and collaboration over issues relating to prayer outside the home.

In the effort to resolve the state-Islam relationship, governments have helped establish and empower Islam Councils that gather competing Muslim federations under the umbrella of one predominant interlocutor. As with economic neo-corporatism, the government-led consultations aim to have a moderating influence on this competition by setting ground rules and offering institutional incentives, e.g., by rewarding successful compromise with monopolistic control over specific delegated tasks of religious administrative control—this could be seen as a modern-day, religious version of "co-administration" familiar from the economic policymaking realm. That is, the representatives of the state and interest groups "collaborate to define the goals and content of policy and to implement the policies agreed upon to realize those goals."[4] This also furthers the state's agenda of selecting amenable leadership from among elites who will engage in more or less predictable behavior and moderate claims-making activities.[5] As one scholar of neo-corporatist arrangements has observed, "Interest groups not only represent the interest of their members vis-à-vis the state but also the state's interest vis-à-vis their members."[6] Neo-corporatism in the 1970s and 1980s sought to reduce tensions between representatives of labor and capital

TABLE 6.1.
Two Phases of State-Mosque Relations

	Phase One Consultations, 1990–1999	*Phase Two Consultations, 1999–2006*
Belgium	Conseil des Sages (1990)	Exécutif des musulmans de Belgique (1994)
France	Conseil de refléxion sur l'Islam en France (1990)	Al-Istîchara (1999), Conseil Français du Culte Musulman (CFCM) (2003)
Germany	Interministerielle Arbeits- gruppe Islam (2002)	Deutsche Islam Konferenz (DIK) (2006)
Italy	Consiglio islamico d'Italia (1998)	Consulta per l'Islam in Italia (2004), Comitato per L'Islam Italiano (2010)
Netherlands	Islamitische Raad Nederland (1990)	Contactorgaan Moslims en Overheid (2004), Contact Groep Islam (2005)
Spain	Comisión islámica de España (1992)	(negotiations for reform of CIE began in 2010)
UK	Muslim Council of Britain (1997)	Preventing Extremism Together (PET) (2005), Mosques and Imams National Advisory Board (MINAB) (2006)

and to avoid strikes in pursuit of macroeconomic benchmarks. Similarly, its revival to address state-Islam issues in the first decade after 2000 has aimed to minimize religious conflicts and tensions.

A key feature of late twentieth-century neo-corporatist arrangements is the hierarchical ordering of a limited number of interest groups.[7] They are bound—voluntarily—into a single organization. These bodies might be advisory or consultative, enshrined by decree or in legislation; they are indirectly elected from a college of delegates, directly appointed, or a mixture of the two. The standard metaphor for neo-corporatism in postwar Europe was of a "round table" where government, employers, and employees would sit and negotiate policy and administrative practice. Participants might be selected by national government officials or indirectly elected by membership organizations (e.g., by trade unions or employer organizations), and convened in a three-way conference representing the state, labor, and capital.

What distinguishes the Islamic councils from corporatist predecessors in the nineteenth century is that participation in them is strictly voluntary, and they do not enjoy an unqualified monopoly: the government may consult other interlocutors, and no mosques are obliged to participate. But centralized official interlocutors are officially recognized as privileged partners of government. Participants in consultative councils are the physical representatives of their community's acceptance in national institutions, by way of personal invitation and interaction with politicians and civil servants.

Variation in the Design of Islam Councils

While this chapter insists on the importance of common national processes of state-Islam consultations, it is important to retain the obvious fact that no two Islam Councils are identical. While all European countries with a Muslim minority engage in some form of state-mosque relations, not all consultations have been formalized to the same degree, and there is variation in terms of the extent of community reorganization that a government is willing to attempt, especially in terms of whom it invites to participate and what it chooses to put on the working agenda. All governments continue to reserve an outsized role for Embassy-Islam representatives, but they have also opened the door to participation by Political-Islam activists and handpicked local civil society organizations.

The focus of the *working agendas* also varies. In the UK, for example, a security focus has dominated state-mosque relations, reflecting the impetus to outreach of the July 7, 2005, bombings in London. In Germany, on the other hand, consultations have been infused with an emphasis on shared "social values." The religion bureaus of European interior ministries aimed to neutralize the threat posed by religion in general to national community by structuring and mediating the activities of religious organizations. But these efforts also target the specific challenge of transnational Islamic solidarity. Europeans' attempts to organize domestic Islam have never been simply about fitting the religion of a new minority into their existing state-church relations. Rather, in managing a set of religious organizations with transnational linkages, their state-mosque relations are bound up in geopolitics and issues of sovereignty. The reassertion of state authority through the incorporation of organized Islam into a state-brokered arrangement situates competing transnational Muslim networks within a national institutional context. In other words, European nation-states have exercised their sovereign prerogative to manage the external threats associated with their citizens' religious membership by using the institutions of national state-church relations.

An exploration follows of the significant challenges that these efforts encountered: first, the selection of participants; then, an explicit acceptance of the precedence of national laws and constitutions; and finally, the granting of a quasi-monopoly of representation on state-mosque affairs. The chapter concludes with a discussion of the ways in which Islam Councils have varied in both design and output; some have been successful at gearing religious practices toward local compatibility, while others have failed to accomplish many concrete acts.

Who: Selecting Participants for Islam Councils

In a crucial change from previous models of consultation with Muslim leaders, the key innovation of the new councils is to have definitively broken the monopoly of Embassy Islam. The precise formula has varied but in general, participants in formal state-Islam consultations come from federations of prayer spaces affiliated with Embassy Islam, Political-Islam federations, and individual Muslim intellectuals or "native" converts recruited by the government (see figure 6.1).

Muslim groups had already won some rights from individual ministries and local municipalities in the first phase of incorporation. However, the basic dilemma remained unresolved: who should be put in charge of these new rights if not Embassy Islam representatives? Umbrella organizations of Islamic prayer spaces vied for recognition and a permanent role in the religious infrastructure—mosques, imams, chaplains, religion teachers, etc.—which was formerly dominated by the foreign embassies of predominantly Muslim sending states. For example, if Muslims had an equal right to religious education, or to halal meals, or to chaplains in public institutions, then administrators had to choose whether to grant the new right to the non-governmental Islamic federations, who were usually affiliated with Political Islam, or to continue to tap the consular networks of Embassy Islam who were already in place. Or, they could turn to local converts who had citizenship but not much legitimacy among the immigrant-heavy Muslim communities. The increasingly popular option would be to seek a synthesis of the three. But without the right institutional mechanism in place, that could be a recipe for community conflict. Governments thus set about convening consultative councils, and altered their institutional formulas—bringing them into parallel with one another by trial and error—as they went along.

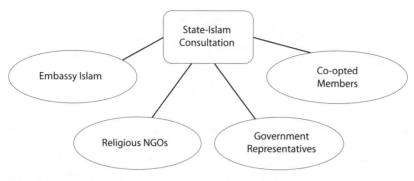

Figure 6.1. The formula of an Islam Council

Whom did governments aim to represent in these councils? As an interior ministry official in Germany stated in an interview,

> Given that part of the Muslims in Germany still have very strong ties to the home countries, and organizations in the home country, it is difficult to view these meetings as taking place in a "politics-free zone." So in the future we need to look at these ties and acknowledge that there are not going to be representatives (*Repräsentanten*) of Muslims, no central organization for Muslims, but rather a multiplicity of organizations which will serve as stand-ins (*Vertreter*) for segments of the Muslim community. No one can represent everybody, but each will stand in for a different large segment. We can never just speak with one organization, and this way we can take them all into account.[8]

French officials said that their council is "only concerned with the 'Muslim faithful' (*fidèles*)" who regularly attend mosque—which they judge to be anywhere from 7 percent to 20 percent.[9] In Italy, the interior minister used a nontraditional formula to make individual appointments to the consultative council. Because the council has no representative ambitions, the Italian interior minister argued that it does not need to correspond to the balance of power among Muslim federations and prayer spaces in Italy. "The *Consulta per l'Islam* does not want to be and cannot ever be a place for effective representation of the Muslims of Italy," he said. "My project is only an organism of consultative character, composed of people of my trust whom I will choose among Muslims who speak Italian, are of certain democratic faith and proven institutional loyalty."[10] This was in contrast with the French government's *Conseil français du culte musulman*, which explicitly aims to represent the mosque-going public. The Italian Council targets those whom the Italian interior minister called the "95% of moderate Muslims who attend neither mosques, nor madrassas nor Islamic cultural centers and who only came to our countries to improve their living conditions and with the sincere intention to respect our law and order."[11]

In the United Kingdom, the Home Office asked the four leading Muslim organizations to help constitute the founding membership of "Preventing Extremism Together" in the weeks after the London bombings of July 7, 2005. The group's first meeting was held on the fourth anniversary of the attacks of September 11, 2001. After some jockeying by participants and internal confusion regarding the board's hierarchy, the Home Office established a steering committee for the Mosques and Imams National Advisory Board.[12]

In Spain, after the Justice Ministry approved recognition of Islam in principle in 1992, the government asked the Islamic communities to form a single federation to negotiate and sign a Cooperation Agreement.[13] The resulting *Comisión Islámica de España* was created to resolve a dispute between two rival federations.[14] Unable to achieve a similar feat, the Dutch created two consultations in 2004 and 2005 that are divided along sectarian lines.[15]

Consulates and embassies of the sending countries jockeyed for position in the electoral rules and regulations to dissuade interior ministries from demoting them, as national Political-Islam federations sought to assure their own place in the hierarchy.[16] Although the French scheme, like other systems for choosing interlocutors, allowed for a continued role by Embassy-Islam representatives, it also definitively opened the door to Political Islam. When the Italian interior minister announced that the government would engage only with "moderate Muslims," the leader of the Italian Political-Islam federation demanded to know: "Who is a moderate? Someone who prays only four times a day?" (Pious Muslims pray five times daily.) The debates within French, German, and Italian ministries responsible for establishing State-Islam consultations have followed similar patterns. As a former advisor to the interior minister in France said:

> The problem with consultation is with whom are we willing to deal? It's a bit of a caricature: we want to deal with the "moderates." But what is a moderate? We could say that we're not going to have Islam with people who plant bombs. Very well, we'll do it with the moderates, so find me the moderates [. . .] We need to draw a red line: there is an Islam that we can organize and administer, to which we can give respectability and visibility, and which has its symbols. And then there is another Islam, which we cannot accept, which we must contain and marginalize.[17]

Another French interior ministry advisor rejected use of the term "moderate Muslim" in any official memorandums:

> I slowly realized that all "moderate Muslims" meant was "those who don't bother the police." The only three categories used were: moderates, Islamists and Terrorists. I decided to classify them according to their desire to integrate: those who want to integrate completely, those who want to integrate halfway, and those who refuse all integration and are ready to conduct Jihad in France.[18]

But even such a gradated scale does not capture the overlapping swaths of potential *sympathizers* with violence or intolerance, what the religious affairs advisor to the German chancellor called a *grey zone*: "It is not enough to be 'a nice guy'—one must also be loyal to the constitution. We need to draw a border—a no-go area—and then decide how we go about interacting with political Islamists in the grey zone."

Political authorities were faced with the choice between marginalizing hardliners or including them in state institutions. As Giovanni Capoccia has written about another instance of European political development, "inclusive strategies aimed at extremist elites" have attempted to "bring at least their more moderate sectors into the democratic process."[19] One London security official pursued a policy of "negotiation leading to partnership with Muslim groups conventionally deemed to be subversive to democracy."[20] When deciding to bring in the controversial participants, the Italian interior minister used the following reasoning: "I took into account what the UCOII is today—not its past—and the efforts it has made for a positive evolution of the Muslim Brotherhood in the whole world."[21] A French official reported a similar thought process: "Should we include them or exclude them? Well, they represent one part of the Muslim [community]—and they are obliged to take account of other peoples' opinion. If we exclude them, then we cannot communicate any messages from one part of the community to another. We have no reason to exclude them—other than the fact that the [Algeria-backed] *Grande Mosquée de Paris* (GMP) representatives don't appreciate their presence. The GMP is leading the charge against them, against the demographic reality." He then spoke a key phrase that interior ministries across Europe were counting on Embassy Islam federations to understand: "But if the GMP doesn't participate they will marginalize themselves."[22]

Ultimately, officials needed to find a credible way to balance the competing segments of the organized community. With governments' insistence on a single interlocutor, and given the fractured state of the Muslim community, European states had practically no choice but to increase their involvement in the composition of Muslim councils. One way would be to take account of which groups controlled the most prayer spaces. In France, Germany, and Italy, governments invited several umbrella groups to state-mosque relations. France invited six federations and six *grandes mosquées* to form part of its council, and Italy invited three federations to join its consultation; in Germany, the five main federations invited to the Islam conference are together estimated to represent as many as 15–20 percent of the general Muslim population.[23] The most creative solution for assigning weight across the country's mosques has taken place in France, where officials left a small space in the process for the participation of the "masses" by allowing participating mosques to appoint electoral delegates based on the mosque's square footage.[24] A complex—and controversial—districting formula was drawn up that assigned delegates and electors based on the number of mosques in a given region and the square footage of prayer space available in each mosque, a policy that favored larger mosques controlled by foreign embassies (which did not necessarily have more prayer-goers).[25] The size of the sanctuary, plus a portion of the space dedicated to other purposes, determines a mosque's weight in elections.[26] As one ministry official explained, "The square footage corresponds to the needs of a given local community—if a prayer room is too small, then an association will rent or buy another one."[27] And, another added, "Some people even wanted to do it according to the *value* of square footage, which wasn't as dumb as it sounds—because the mosques in the north and east of France are enormous where real estate is cheap."[28]

But how could organizational weight in councils be determined solely by the number of prayer spaces, when Islam is a religion without obligatory mosque attendance? As a German official said, "Our big problem is what do we do with the un-organized Muslims? The well-organized federations are empty shells (*Köpfe ohne Bauch*)."[29] An Italian Muslim leader who sat on the *Consulta* noted in parliamentary testimony, similarly, that "Not everyone who goes to pray in a mosque can be considered a member of that mosque. One cannot compare a mosque to a union or a party where there are membership cards. There is a great confusion at the moment regarding who has granted whom the right to represent them."[30]

A third group would be added to consultations: individual Muslims who had no formal constituency but whose views correspond with the "silent majority" of everyday Muslims who do not regularly attend mosque but for whom religion is an element of their cultural identity.

The presence of the "appointed individuals" may reinforce a state's goals of creating a framework for law-abiding, integrated Islam. In the words of a German interior minister, the ten appointees are "representatives of a modern and secular Islam from business, society, science and culture." And they are also there to represent minority views, as a French interior minister put it: "The goal of elections is to elicit a sense of the majority groups; so it makes sense to represent the minority groups with another method, which can only be by ministerial appointment (*cooptation*, in French)."[31] A letter of invitation was sent to six Islam experts to take a seat at the table of the republic.[32] In Germany, the appointees comprise Muslim authors, academics, artists, and entrepreneurs—three of whom have written books about oppressive patriarchal tendencies in traditional Turkish families.[33] In France, the invited experts included an academic Sufi convert, an anthropologist, and a liberal theologian. In Italy, the invited individuals were three journalists, two health workers, a literature professor, a student leader, an author, and a charity worker. The issue in Germany is not the inclusion of "independent personalities" but that they so outweigh the mosque federations, by ten to five; in Italy, similarly, the proportion was eleven co-opted individuals to five federation/mosque leaders. In France, it is the opposite ratio, in favor of twelve mosque and federation representatives versus six "*personnalités qualifiées*" who sat in the executive office of the first *Conseil français du culte musulman*.

Government's efforts to stack the deck with such individuals—known as "qualified personalities," "appointed individuals," or just "experts"—is a way to dilute Islamists, to recognize the "democratic deficit" posed by the large federations, and to enhance the voice of European citizens on the councils, given that not all federation leaders are naturalized citizens. This was a potentially problematic development because the remit of consultations was intended to be limited to practical questions of administering religious practices in a given country, and would seem to be most appropriately addressed by those actually involved in the business of organizing prayer and observance. This logic has a negative effect on the presence of two categories of Muslims who may in fact represent a numerical majority of the Muslim population: women's groups and youth groups—that is, until they open prayer spaces of their own or reach leadership positions in existing mosques. The authorities' efforts to include women and younger leaders by direct appointment addresses that gap, and makes further sense in cases where questions of society and education are on the agenda of consultations—and thus affect more than just the mosque-going public, e.g., the offering of religious class in German or Italian public schools, or the availability of visas to go on pilgrimage or halal meat for domestic consumption.

Muslim Organizations' Acceptance of Constitutional Law

In state-Islam consultations, the recognition of the national government's legal authority has often taken the form of a charter in which consultation participants solemnly affirm their religious organization's attachment to the fundamental principles of the republic. European states' decision to include Political-Islam activists in contemporary state-Islam arrangements has sometimes been judged as a recipe for self-defeat.[34] After all, Islamist parties in the Middle East and North Africa have pursued the implementation of Islamic law and jurisprudence, and are thought to have "limited tolerance for democratic pluralism," as seeking to rule from divine authority, and as demonstrating a broad "intolerance of secular forms of education, entertainment and political representation."[35] An important task for European governments, therefore, has been to solicit the broad agreement or confirmation of respect for the rule of law (as superior to shari'a law) from council participants and their renunciation of an "Islamic Order."

These charters are a small but important part of the nexus between public recognition, interest representation, and political moderation in state-mosque relations in Western Europe. They force participants to take positions on the themes that have made the presence of Islam in Europe so controversial—and that recall the "questions gênantes" asked of Jewish communities two centuries earlier: Is their primary loyalty to the nation or to their religious community? What is the place of religion in public life? Are social integration and political participation necessary? The answers to these questions may seem obvious— one critic calls it meaningless, saying that requiring respect for the law is "to demand exactly nothing"[36]—but given the suspicions about Political Islam and the influence of foreign potentates and princes, securing the explicit acquiescence of participants seemed reasonable.[37] Charters are the price of admission, but they can also be used as an excuse to exclude unwilling participants: the failure to sign or abide by its principles gives governments a way to throw participants out and avoid stalemate due to the presence of people who refuse to cooperate. The document permits the interior ministry to be inclusive while providing some cover against accusations that it allows extremists to participate.[38]

As an official who helped establish the French Council for the Muslim Faith put it, "The charter represents what was given to Muslims to accept in order to enter into the common framework of laïcité. It's a sort of entry ticket—you buy it, you get in. If you don't pay for whatever reason, we're not angry, but you won't get in. But you won't be part of the play that's being produced."[39] The consultation's eighteen members were asked to sign a document of "Principles and foundations regulating the relations between public authorities and the Muslim religion in France." After some debate over language, the representatives of three groups of assembled Muslim dignitaries—the federations, the *grandes mosquées*, and the *personnalités qualifiées*—signed their names in "solemn confirmation of their attachment to the fundamental principles of the French republic." Signature to the "principles," in the ministry's view, affirmed the "desire to join and be integrated into the legal framework that organizes and guarantees the free exercise of religion *and* the lay character of institutions in France."[40] "The label of 'fundamentalist' doesn't concern me," said Vianney Sevaistre, a director of the French *bureau central des cultes*. "What matters to me is if you disturb public order. Those who violated the [charter] were excluded from the consultation."[41]

The German interior minister explained the Islam conference's guiding principles, which participants have endorsed in the course of the consultations proceedings: "Our state order is not unfamiliar with religion [but] we have the separation of state and religion. We will make constitutional standards clear in the German Islam Conference."[42] In the conference's mid-term report, participants presented a document that stated unambiguously: "The constitution is the substantive foundation for the relationship between the State and citizens," and continues, "it is a Muslim desire to develop an understanding of Islamic sources in harmony with the reality of the constitutional order, the self-organization rights of religious communities and religious pluralism, that takes into consideration the present-day living conditions and the creation of a Muslim identity in Europe."[43]

In the Netherlands, the prime minister presided over the signing of a "Behavioral code against extremism/Contract with society" (*Gedragscode tegen extremisme/Contract met de Samenleving*, 2005) with a group of mosques in Amsterdam. In the UK, the draft constitution of the Mosques and Imams National Advisory Board (MINAB) requires that signatories have transparent organizational structures and finances, and equal opportunity policies. The board has produced a "Mosques Good Practice Guide" which lays out core standards—counter-extremism programs, community relations schemes, support and proper conditions for imams, and greater condemnation of "un-Islamic" activity—and called for British prayer spaces to "reform and modernize." In return, mosques that sign on to a specified good-practice framework are promised "practical advice, guidance and support." Board members have sought "spot-check powers" in order to make unannounced visits to review mosque standards, and they are furthermore expected to come up with guidelines for imam accreditation and ensure the "profession is attractive to young British Muslims."[44] Areas of action regarding mosques and imams have come under discussion, in particular, establishing a set of standards for British mosques that address: (1) democratic and accountable practices; (2) transparent finances; (3) openness to women and youth; (4) counter-extremism programs; (5) interfaith schemes; (6) combatting forced marriage.[45]

The Italian "values charter" (*Carta dei Valori*) that *Consulta* participants were asked to sign stands out because the interior ministry there appears to have pursued a charter with the aim of eliminating one of the more controversial organizations. The founding minister of the consultation had said in 2003 that he would choose "advisors he trusted, people who recognize the values of the Republic."[46] But the next interior minister, four years after the initial announcement of the *Consulta*, and just a year and a half after his nomination of its sixteen members, introduced a charter that included some elements unrelated to the organization of religious infrastructure: for example, it referred to the rights of immigrants, and it discussed polygamy and burkas. The new minister stated, moreover, that "Whoever does not sign the charter cannot participate in organizations convened by my ministry."[47] The Islamist federation took offense at the proposed charter: "We have been Italians for 35 generations in my family," said the leader of UCOII, a Muslim convert. "So the charter of values for foreigners doesn't interest us; it is simply a rough draft (*brutta copia*) of the Italian constitution." The *Consulta* was renamed the *Comitato* in 2010, and the UCOII was not invited back.

In France, similarly, parts of a proposed charter were initially opposed by associations of young Muslims who were born and raised in France and found the document's tone to be insulting. This was resolved by changing the verb regarding participants' commitment to respect the law, from "affirm" to "confirm."[48] The UCOII signaled its willingness to sign the document one year later, but ministry officials claimed in an interview that when the UCOII's representative signed the document, he first crossed out the sections to which the organization took exception.[49] Where charters have failed to achieve unanimity, they have threatened the precarious balance of the new councils, but they have nonetheless achieved their primary goal: to offer the opportunity for participation to those who explicitly agree to accept the priority of the national laws and constitution.[50]

Monopoly of Representation

In addition to a state role in selecting participants and setting ground rules for the legal framework, another defining feature of neo-corporatist arrangements is the creation of a de facto monopoly for the consultative council. Islam Councils do not have the only word in state-mosque relations, but they do have some monopolistic traits. Without the government's seal of approval that is granted to consultation participants, it is more difficult for individual prayer spaces to gain access to mosque construction permits or other "goods" that the councils seek to negotiate on behalf of the Muslim communities. As a French official stated, "There is no obligation to adhere to decisions made, but the nature of dialogue with the state does matter. A mosque that does not participate in the CFCM," he said, "will not have its imam chosen as a chaplain" in a public institution.[51]

Even the most successful Islam Councils and consultations, however, are registered as private law associations and do not enjoy the same public law status of religious interlocutor as set out in national state-church regimes.[52] Such status brings privileges in different contexts, such as the collection of "church taxes" or the ability to receive tax-deductible gifts. Being chartered as a corporation of public law in Germany—or as a 1905-law association in France or religious entity in Italy—status grants groups "special rights which allow individual contact with bureaucratic offices."[53] And, even more importantly, in Germany "corporations have legal independence" and may engage in self-administration and are allowed to negotiate as legal entities.[54] But they often require a unified front (*Einheitsgemeinde*) from the religious community—which Muslim groups have been unable to provide—and a long-term administrative commitment from public authorities, which have been hesitant to grant the permanent recognition to any single Muslim organization.

There are also legal obstacles posed by the foreign nationality of many Muslim representatives. For example, the only association that has the appropriate legal status to sign an *intesa* in Italy is governed by a board of Arab and Muslim diplomats, but foreign nationals cannot sign an *intesa*. Any pretense of monopoly for consultation participants in the UK has been quickly dashed. The MINAB's role in religious governance has been supplemented by other government initiatives. For example, the government established a UK fatwa council (Board of Theologians) and has sought advice from international and local partners on how to foster "moderation" within British Islam. A German official said that granting corporation status to a German Muslim group "would be a leap into modernity" but that the government does not deem any Muslim organization to be ready for it.[55]

The negotiations under way with Muslim groups, however, reflect a desire to actively help religious leaders organize themselves in preparation for an eventual application. The German government gave the *Islam Konferenz* an initial timeframe of two and a half years, after which Muslim leaders may agree to "make a kind of round table, elect a leader and rotate, along the model of the charity organizations that have several umbrella organizations."[56] But the subsequent DIK round begun in 2011, resembled the first round with some minor institutional adjustments—notably, a move from fixed working groups to "flexible project groups"—and personnel changes.[57] There is a danger is that any spinoff groups frustrated with the slow pace of second-phase consultations will seek their own alternative arrangements with the government—such as the *Koordinierungsrat der Muslime* in Germany (KRM, 2007), the *Federazione per l'Islam moderato e pluralista* (2008) in Italy, or the *Consejo Islámico Español* (CIE, 2011)—thus reproducing the obstacles in the first phase of government outreach during the 1990s. These groups exclude competitors and thus represent only a small fraction of existing prayer spaces, jeopardizing their own legitimacy and that of the Councils. The Islam Councils are thus a medium-term solution to the longer-term question of final legal status—which is the only adequate dissuasion to would-be splinter groups.

Nonetheless, European governments have accepted the authority of Islam Councils to speak on behalf of most Muslim groups in negotiation with state administrations and have accorded them official approval in one form or another. The CFCM was announced in the *journal officiel*; and the decree creating the Italian Consultation was similarly registered in the *gazzetta ufficiale*. Government representatives preside over the consultations in Italy and Germany, chairing meetings in the interior ministries and overseeing the activities of working groups and the publication of their findings. The number of German government participants in the *Deutsche Islam Konferenz* is roughly equivalent to the Muslim representatives: fifteen officials from the federal, *Länder*, and municipal levels.[58] In France, officials from the justice and interior ministries act as observers and technical legal advisors.

The role of government in the initial composition of the councils was also quite pronounced. The French interior minister, for example, personally negotiated the composition of the CFCM's executive office between representatives of the Moroccan and Algerian embassies, the World Muslim League, and the major federations, all of whom he invited for separate (and, occasionally, joint) meetings between October and November 2002. He holed up with participants in a state-owned château at Nainville-les-Roches in December 2002, where arithmetic calculations of majorities and coalitions were worked out and disputed, and the meeting ended only once agreement was reached over the composition of the governing board, and dates were set for the next elections. Even though the ministry delegated any organizational activity that could be devolved to an association independently run by Muslim leaders, such as the organization of council elections, the government vowed to "accompany" Muslims on their path to representation. In the UK, the communities secretary said that the reforms initiated by the Mosque and Imams National Advisory Board "are important because they are coming from within the community itself."[59] But the open involvement of the Home Office in the launching of MINAB fed fears that the board would be too close to government.[60] As the communities secretary said, "We want to reassure them that it is a Muslim initiative."[61]

Despite official support for the councils, it is worth noting just how small these operations are. Even France's CFCM, arguably the most robust of these institutions, has no permanent offices or dedicated staff, and its annual budget is just 150,000 euros. It is entirely financed by the fees of delegates, which range from 30 to 500 euros per prayer space—although the interior ministry does grant it the unusual favor of having interior ministry officials collect dues, a service it does not do for other civil society organizations.[62] Even though as many as 80 percent of French prayer spaces participated in the consultations, elected CFCM delegates in the council's general assembly can only afford to gather twice a year. A French official said in an interview, "We support it politically but we don't give any money."[63] The German Islam Conference also has only two plenary sessions a year, but its working groups meet every two months. The Italian *Consulta* is supposed to meet three times a year, but after a skeptical political party (Lega Nord) took over the Interior Ministry in 2008, the *Consulta* was not convened for more than two years, and then in reduced form. The permanence and power of Islam Councils is precarious, but some have begun to exert a moderate amount of influence in the organization of religious practice in European countries.

Co-administration and Delegation

The final step in state-Islam consultations is to coordinate the formation of working groups or committees on the concrete tasks to be accomplished (see table 6.2). As Philippe Schmitter wrote about neo-corporatism a generation ago, the representatives of the state and participating interest groups "collaborate to define the goals and content of policy and to implement the policies agreed upon to realize those goals." Interlocutors are granted control over valuable services. They are "not mere interest intermediaries, but co-responsible 'partners' in governance."[64] Successful membership in Islam Councils has been rewarded with control over specific delegated tasks of state-mosque relations.

Whether or not they are in fact inspired by grand designs of religious reform, the everyday agenda of the consultations and their practical orientation allows for regular discussions between Muslims and the

Table 6.2.
What Is on the Agenda? Working Groups of Nine State-Islam Consultations

Conseil français du culte musulman (France, 2008)

1. Audiovisual communications
2. Chaplains in public institutions
3. Cemeteries and Muslim sections
4. Interreligious dialogue
5. Teaching and religious instruction
6. Imams and training
7. Legal questions and observatory of Islamophobia
8. History of the Muslims of France
9. Oversight of the pilgrimage to Mecca
10. Halal meat and ritual slaughter

Executif Musulman Belge (Belgium, 1998)

1. Islamic education practices
2. Proper burial of Muslims in Belgium
3. Muslim chaplains in prisons and in hospitals [...]

Deutsche Islam Konferenz (Germany, 2006)

Working Group 1: The German social order and values consensus
Working Group 2: Religious questions in the German constitutional context
Working Group 3: The building of bridges in the economy and the media
Dialogue Group 4: Security and Islamism

Consulta per l'Islam Italiano (Italy, 2004)

1. Integration issues at home, school, and the workplace
2. Safeguarding the specificities of religion and Muslim traditions including men's and women's rights, use of the veil, observance of Muslim holidays and precepts, ritual animal slaughter, and Muslim cemeteries
3. Italian-language sermons in mosques and the training of imams
4. Registration of prayer spaces to normalize "critical situations" [in small cities]
5. Social conditions and rights of immigrants including asylum, humanitarian protection, residence permits, family reunification, and citizenship
6. Access of Muslim chaplains to prisons and hospital

Contactorgaan Moslems en de Overheid (Netherlands, 2004)

1. Broadcasting time on public television and radio
2. Chaplains in prisons and the army
3. Imam training
4. Islamic religious instruction in public schools
5. Bridging the gap between Muslims and Dutch society

Islamische Glaubensgemeinschaft in Österreich (Austria, 1979)

1. The establishment and administration of Islamic cemeteries
2. Accordance with Islamic ritual
3. Issuance of certificates (for naming, military service, death, etc.)

(continued)

TABLE 6.2. *cont.*
What Is on the Agenda? Working Groups of Nine State-Islam Consultations

4. Organization of symposia of the Imam conference
5. Interreligious dialogue
6. Chaplains and social services to hospitals and prisons
7. Teaching Islam in schools
8. Training teachers of Islam

Comisión Islámica de España (Spain, 1992)

1. Staffing contracts
2. Conscientious objection (defending the Spanish homeland)
3. Marriage contract and the regulation of succession. Civil validity of marriage ceremonies held pursuant to Muslim rites.
4. Overseeing financial arrangements, or collaboration of the state financial support, given to Islamic communities
5. Social security for community leaders and imams
6. Chaplains in prisons
7. The expansion of Islamic religious instruction in the peninsula and in particular the creation of the Foundation Pluralism and Coexistence
8. The status of Islamic Religious Leaders and Imams
9. Spanish Muslims' personal status in areas of such importance as Social Security and military duties
10. Legal protection for mosques
11. Religious services in public centers or establishments
12. Muslim religious education in schools
13. Tax benefits applicable to certain property pertaining to the Federations that constitute the Islamic Commission of Spain
14. Commemoration of Muslim religious holidays
15. Cooperation between the State and such Commission for the conservation and furthering of Islamic Historic and Artistic Heritage

Sveriges Muslimska Råd (Sweden, 2006)

1. Spiritual care / chaplains—prisons and hospitals
2. Help with employment
3. Crisis management
4. Aid for Muslim families with disabled children
5. Religious dialogue group inclusive of all Sweden's religions

Mosques and Imams National Advisory Board (UK, 2006)

1. Self-regulation and standards
2. Capacity-building and governance of mosques and training institutions
3. Engagement of women
4. Engagement of youth
5. Community cohesion, citizenship, and stakeholder engagement
6. Media and public affairs
7. Membership
8. Fundraising
9. Interfaith
10. Standing order / constitution

highest administrative levels of practical policy issues relating to religious observance, from mosque construction and religious education to halal slaughter and chaplains in public institutions. In France and in the United Kingdom, representatives of the participating federations sit on ten committees in CFCM and MINAB, respectively. In Germany, the DIK is divided into four thirty-person working groups, which issue reports once or twice annually and make relevant administrative proposals.[65] The Italian *Consulta* can be asked to formulate opinions and proposals pertaining to the social integration of Muslims in Italy, specifically chaplains in hospitals and prisons, cemeteries, workers' rights. An undersecretary at the interior ministry said that the *Consulta* would "act as a group of advisors who can point out problems" that need to be resolved with the aid of the public administration.[66]

Operation of the Islam Councils

While much of the state-mosque relations agenda contains routine items, it is telling what some countries left out, and what others inserted. Germany and the Netherlands, for example, have an interest and legal competency to resolve the issue of religious education. Germany and some other countries raise the topic of social values. Some avoid addressing imam training because of strong existing arrangements with third parties (Germany), while others go so far as to tackle unemployment (Sweden). Consultation members in Britain organized a series of workshops with twenty-five Muslim leaders, including representatives from four main federations, which were accompanied by meetings between ministers and communities around the country.[67] Participants in seven working groups were asked the question "what makes British Muslims tick?" in seven thematic areas: education; engaging with women; imams and the role of mosques; regional and local initiatives; security and policing; tackling extremism; and radicalization.[68] Some initial results of the councils have begun to emerge.

Germany. The German Islam Conference has produced basic agreements on the future of mosque construction and Islamic burials in Germany, the necessity of offering Islamic religious education in the German language, and the creation of a "clearinghouse" to facilitate a national network of interlocutors in security offices and Muslim organizations (see figures 6.2 and 6.3).[69] Theology departments in Munster and Frankfurt have also endowed chairs in Islamic studies (*Lehrstühle*), and more than half of DİTİB imams sent to Germany from Turkey now take part in pre-departure training in Ankara. At the end of its first full term in 2010, the DIK's achievements included several rhetorical agreements, such as definitions of "integration" and a commitment to up-

Figure 6.2. Working Session of the *Deutsche Islam Konferenz*, 2009.
Source: © Fotografie Katy Otto / Deutsche Islam Konferenz.

holding German laws and values, as well as smaller concrete measures (a handbook for parents and teachers, an internet portal) and the pledge to pursue further cooperation in the DIK's subsequent session, from Islamic burials to the counter-extremism programs. The DIK has served as the framework for civic education training programs for imams in six German cities initiated by the government in 2010.

Despite continued refinement of the organizations and individuals included in the DIK, the conference and its local offshoots have established

Figure 6.3. Group portrait of the *Deutsche Islam Konferenz*, 2009.
Source: © Fotografie Katy Otto / Deutsche Islam Konferenz.

Islam as a permanent feature on the agenda of German state-religion relations. A new interior minister in 2010 adjusted the list of partici-pants.[70] In the first round of the DIK, six "secular" experts were in-cluded alongside the heads of the major mosque federations, but sur-prisingly, the new minister took a different route. The most controver-sial and aggressively "anti-clerical" among the participants were not invited back to the *Deutsche Islam Konferenz* when it reconvened. Addi-tionally, the *Millî Görüş* federation attended DIK proceedings at least three times before the government formally disinvited IGMG's parent organization, Islamrat, in 2010.[71]

A German commentator wrote favorably of the government's efforts: "The Interior Minister paid respect to Muslims not by forcing them into a negotiation with the state, but because he treated them as citizens with multiple rights and duties." He noted the inherently give-and-take nature of the exchange: "The minister became their advocate for Islamic religious instruction, theological faculties and school holidays on religious festivals. On the other hand, he also requested that girls under fourteen years of age not wear headscarves and that they partici-pate on school trips, as well as that Muslim organizations open their finances for inspection, that they accept the reigning laws and values, and that they tolerate other religious convictions."[72] A 2010 study eval-uating the "reach" of the DIK gave reason for optimism: 56 percent of Muslims polled in Germany had heard of the organization or were well acquainted with it (the figure was closer to two-thirds of those with more than elementary school education).[73]

France. In France, the national and local councils announced consen-sus agreements to nominate national and regional chaplains for the armed forces and the prison system in 2006, as well as a decision in 2007 to create a central foundation for mosque financing (*Fondation pour les oeuvres de l'Islam de France*),[74] and a temporary agreement on a civic training course for imams in Paris (see figures 6.4 and 6.5). The French Interior Ministry estimated in 2008 that public authorities are now con-tributing as much as 30 percent of financing for the boom of new prayer spaces.[75] In May 2009, the city of Bourg-en-Bresse inaugurated its first Muslim section of a cemetery, with the cooperation of the local CRCM (*Conseil régional du culte musulman*). Agricultural authorities have pur-sued the possibility of designing a system to trace products and inform consumers, to certify halal products, which would come under "the re-sponsibility of the French Council for the Muslim Faith (CFCM) or the CRCM."[76] CFCM representatives participated in the working group meeting on "Animals and Society" at the Agricultural Ministry in May 2008 to convey the Muslim proscription against stunning animals be-fore slaughter. For the 2009 pilgrimage to Mecca, the CFCM and three

Figure 6.4. Bureau exécutif of the *Conseil français du culte musulman*, 2003.
Source: © Bernard Godard.

CRCMs in the Paris region informed Muslims of the administrative
steps necessary to undertake before pilgrimage, and also set up information desks in French airports.[77] In France, when the chamber of commerce in Limoges was looking for expertise and advice on employment
policies affecting holidays and prayer times, they went to the CRCM in
the Île de France department.[78]

Figure 6.5. Portrait of the *Conseil français du culte musulman*, 2003.
Source: © Bernard Godard.

There are currently more than 2,300 Islamic prayer spaces in France—and two hundred additional places of worship are in final planning stages.[79] Moreover, many of these are made possible by city councils that are less reticent to subsidize mosque construction with public land-use grants (*baux emphytéotiques*). The CRCM in Alsace offered a series of seminars for administrators of local Muslim associations and developed a brochure on "The Construction of Muslim Prayer Spaces" to facilitate contacts with local administrators. In the Rhone Alpes region, ten mosque projects have been approved by four-party agreements among the local prefect, mayor, CRCM and the local association applying to run the mosque. Two hundred additional places of worship are in final planning stages,[80] many of whose existence will have the administrative intervention of the *Conseils régionaux du culte musulman* to thank. A French researcher recently returning from a study on mosque-building reported that: "Whatever the criticism of the CFCM . . . I discovered that the process of consultation that led to the creation of the CFCM unblocked a situation so that now mayors feel authorized to seek practical solutions whereas beforehand they acted with great hesitation."[81]

Some of these accomplishments are the result of community decisions, in others the hand of the state is clearly visible, such as the CFCM declaration that people should avoid pilgrimage to Mecca during the outbreak of H1A1 flu in August 2009. After untiringly (and unsuccessfully) attempting to arrange for the views of the CFCM to be represented in a European Parliament hearing on ritual animal slaughter this spring, the director of the *Bureau central des cultes* said, with a degree of exasperation: "The head of the CFCM is the director of the *Bureau central des cultes!*"[82] Officials in the Interior Ministry also help instruct future Muslim religious personnel in a course on basic religious history, civic and administration knowledge. The first thirty graduates of the training course—held at the Institut Catholique de Paris—recently received their diplomas, and the second class of forty students began coursework in January 2009. Subjects include an introduction to French law and the French political system, as well as the study of other religions in France and the financial-administrative basics of how to run a mosque. The idea is to help imams "become credible interlocutors for public authorities" and show them "how to run a religious community with the framework of republican legality."[83]

Netherlands. The Dutch government introduced an obligatory six-month training program in language, social and political institutions, and the "Dutch ways of life" for imams coming to serve in Dutch Muslim communities. The Free University of Amsterdam now offers bachelors and masters degrees in Islamic theology, as well as training for chaplains who will serve in public institutions. The *Contactorgaan Moslims en Overheid* (CMO) organized a meeting with five Muslim organizations and the Integration and Education ministries to create a university program to train imams in 2005.[84] Domestic politics in the Netherlands, however, subsequently created an inopportune climate for the accommodation of Islam. Interior ministers became less willing to engage in the negotiations and cajoling required to keep the *Contactorgaan* together; it was defunded in 2009 and had fallen into disuse by 2011.

Spain. In Spain, the Islamic Commission proposed curricula for Islamic education in public school and state subsidized schools that were approved in 1996. That same year, the Justice and Education Ministries signed an agreement allowing for the appointment of religion teachers to be paid with public funds.[85] The Islamic Commission has also come to agreement with the Spanish government for the civil recognition for religious marriage, chaplains in public institutions, the public recognition of Muslim holidays, the establishment of cemeteries, and the creation of tax-deductible status for recognized Muslim groups, and to register halal slaughtering procedures as a trademark under the Commission's oversight.[86] The Spanish *Comisión Islámica* had a 2010 budget of 623,000 euros, and has met regularly to approve internal administrative measures and to voice support for topics ranging from interreligious dialogue, to the use of Arabic in Islamic religion class, as well as the right of female students to wear a headscarf in class.[87] Nonetheless, legitimacy across the entire community has eluded the Commission. As Arigita writes, "From the beginning, the contacts between the State and the Muslim community were the result of political desire more than a real process of interaction." She argues that for the government, the agreement leading to the *Comisión's* establishment in 1992 "was not a beginning but an end to its interaction with the Muslim minority."[88]

The issue of inclusiveness has dogged the Commission, in particular with regard to the domination of the UCIDE federation over its rivals. In 2010, the director for religious affairs urged the consultative body to undertake internal reforms in order to achieve "greater representativeness." The justice ministry official reckoned that "the reality of Islam has nothing to do with what it was twenty years ago" when the Commission was founded.[89] The UCIDE responded by creating a new spinoff organization the following year—the *Consejo Islámico Español*— which it intended to use as a new institutional base for state-Islam relations; the government's response will determine the survival of the twenty-year-old *Comisión*.[90]

Italy. In Italy, the *Consulta* created a set of interlocutors for public authorities (see figures 6.6 and 6.7). In January 2007, they were invited to testify at the hearings on the Law on Religious Freedom. As one representative said, "It is the first time that the various actors of the Italian Muslim Community have addressed the Italian Parliament. The Interior Minister did something positive and you are part of it—otherwise it would have been difficult to identify our interlocutors."[91] The *Consulta* members were also invited by Pope Benedict to inter-religious dialogues in 2007 and 2008.

Nonetheless, in the Italian tradition of dissolving and reshuffling a dysfunctional representative body and declaring it something new, in 2010 Interior Minister Roberto Maroni inaugurated a new *Comitato per l'Islam italiano*.[92] Italy, which notoriously experienced fifty governing coalitions in as many years following World War II, actually only had twelve parliamentary elections between 1948 and 1998. This was thanks to the recycling of ministers and a precise re-division of the spoils of governing that took place behind the doors of the presidential palace. This tradition of "trasformismo" can be traced to parliamentary habits formed in the Italian Kingdom one hundred and fifty years ago. Similarly, the Interior Ministry's new Committee for Italian Islam has dropped some community leaders from the former Consulta (2004–2008) and added others, all without endeavoring to establish any form of direct (or indirect) democratic consultation of Italy's mosque-going public. The working agenda is the same as the Consulta's, but the Committee's mandate and status have been demoted: "It is neither a consultation nor a representative organ, it is created to provide a series of brain storming sessions."[93] The generous interpretation of the downgraded institutional design, however, is that it is in fact cutting-edge; one participant described it as a "think tank" that "puts experts from different backgrounds together with Muslims who want to promote an Italian Islam in a laboratory of ideas that will propose innovative solutions: e.g., on the question of the veil, imam training, the protection of minors (forced marriages, etc.), and burial regulations, etc."[94]

What else is different about the Committee? Most noticeable are the omissions. The most prominent community leaders left out of the current group of nineteen include: the head of the Political-Islam federation (UCOII) and the founder of the UCOII's one-time youth group, Young Muslims of Italy (GMI). Both have testified to parliament and served as advisors to Interior Ministers Pisanu and Amato. The UCOII, while far from enjoying a representative majority, represents a plurality (130 or so) of Italy's 750 mosques; the GMI is the country's largest and most visible Muslim youth organization. The UCOII's ties to international Muslim Brotherhood networks have rendered it politically suspect, but former Christian Democrat Giuseppe Pisanu pointedly invited them into the constitutional order when he designed the *Consulta*

Figure 6.6. Meeting of the *Comitato per l'Islam italiano*, 2010. Source: © Ministero dell'Interno.

(much as Nicolas Sarkozy did with the UOIF in France). The decision to exclude the UCOII unilaterally is the fruit of the efforts of officials at the Interior Ministry to expel the UCOII from the *Consulta* since its inception. Once Interior Minister Giuliano Amato succeeded Giuseppe Pisanu in 2006, the ministry required all *Consulta* members to sign a "values charter" that it could be certain the UCOII would not approve. The influence of a former *Consulta* member who later became a member of parliament also contributed to the UCOII's eventual exclusion. Interior Minister Roberto Maroni has expressed general reservations about the usefulness of an Islamic consultation, and said upon taking office in 2008 that it made no sense to convene the *Consulta* without UCOII. His lack of interest in the topic made it easier for lower-level officials with an opinion to have their way. Italy seems to be attempting both to entrench "Muslim secularists" in state-mosque relations and to silence the more challenging voices from the milieu of political Islam. The *Comitato* issued two reports in 2010–2011: one on "good practices" in Italian mosques and another on the impact of the North African "Arab spring" on Italian Islam. Experience in neighboring countries suggests that this

Figure 6.7. Imam Yahya Pallavicini, Interior Minister Giuliano Amato and ministerial advisor Carlo Cardia, 2008. Source: © Yahya Pallavicini.

Committee, too, will undergo more transformations before arriving at its final institutional form.

United Kingdom. Officials have concentrated on two central, inter-related policy goals: religious governance (i.e., state-church relations) and counter-radicalization. After eight years (1997–2005) in which the Muslim Council of Britain held a near-monopoly as the privileged interlocutor of government on religious affairs, authorities have expanded official contacts to include competing federations, prominent Muslim Britons, youth groups, local mosques, and religious authority figures abroad. The government has crafted a loose set of national consultative boards to coordinate UK-wide standards and broad theological guidance. But the UK government has also deliberately moved beyond a narrow focus on large umbrella organizations and now provides extensive funding and administrative support for myriad local actors. This diversification of outreach had already begun after September 2001, but it metastasized following the London underground and bus bombings by four young British men on 7/7/05 (see table 6.3). Since then, the government has attempted to influence the conditions "on the ground" by bringing substantial financial means to bear on the formation of British Islam's religious personnel and infrastructure. This has had two central components: the active development of reliable national-level interlocutors, and an investment in local-level institutional configurations to which the actual business of counter-radicalization can be partially delegated.

In seeking credible alternatives to religiously motivated hate speech, the British government has engaged the fringes of radical Islam and singled out religious leaders it can comfortably support. Recent projects in religious governance include the Preventing Extremism Together program, which led to the creation of a brand new set of institutions for state-Islam relations in the UK: the Mosque and Imams National Advisory Board; a Board of Theologians; and a Muslim Women's National Advisory Group alongside other consultations and international outreach by the Prime Minister's office and the Foreign Office. Likewise, a profusion of working groups has sprouted up in the field of counter-radicalization and anti-terrorism policy: e.g., the Muslim Safety Forum, the Radical Middle Way, the Prevent strategy, and the Muslim Contact Unit. The groups are also useful as a mechanism to manage community relations in the context of increased surveillance, "stops and searches," high-profile terrorism arrests, and prosecutions. In each local forum, a set of favored interlocutors has emerged. But at the national level, no single forum is predominant—indeed, the government has demonstrated a keen desire to encourage the proliferation of programs and groups.

TABLE 6.3.
British Government Outreach, Consultations, and Organizational Support

Program / Name	Type of Outreach/Partnership	Date
Muslim Council of Britain	National Federation of prayer spaces/ associations	1997–2005
Muslim Contact Unit	Local partners, London Metropolitan Police	2001–
Muslim Safety Forum	Local partners, Metropolitan PoliceService/ACPO	2001–
Preventing Violent Extremism	Counter-Radicalization/ Pathfinder Fund	2005–8
Preventing Extrem- ism Together	25 members total; including MCB, BMF, AKF, MAB	2005
Roadshows/ Radical Middle way	30 scholars; Q News, FOSIS, YMO	2005–
Mosques & Imams National	5 WGs; Steering Committee: MCB, BMF, AKF, MAB	2005–6; launch 2007–8
	Advisory Board (MINAB)	
British Sufi Council	National Federation of prayer spaces/ intellectuals	2006–
Board of Theologians	20 scholars, Oxford/ Cambridge	2008–
Scottish Islamic Foundation	Regional Federation	2008–

Institutionalized dialogue has been a hallmark of the UK's counter-radicalization strategy in the aftermath of terrorist attacks in London (see figure 6.8). The government has offered public and private encouragement to law-abiding hardliners and "former radicals," such as the Quilliam Foundation, who have rejected their extremist pasts and are thus considered to be well positioned to vaccinate young Muslims in Britain against the seductive but logically inconsistent arguments of would-be radicalizers and recruiters. Officials have kept close in mind the fact that members of the 7/7 cell (and the Hofstad cell in Slotervaart, Holland), were native-born, often ostensibly well-integrated, local

Figure 6.8. British Muslim community leaders and politicians leave 10 Downing Street after meeting with the Prime Minister, 2005. Source: © Thomson Reuters.

Muslim boys—this was qualitatively different than the 2001 Hamburg cell and to a lesser extent, the 2004 Madrid cell. These young men's lack of exposure to a recognized, mainstream European Islam left them susceptible to extremists who proffer a dangerous mixture of foreign policy criticism and political violence. British authorities gradually came to believe that the best hope for a local, moderate Islam is not a defanged official variant. A newspaper editorial summarized the official view neatly:

> Show young British Muslims that their faith is compatible with the shared values that go with being a British citizen . . . A religious context is a plus rather than a minus. Secularist solutions will not hold much sway with the Muslim community. Indeed, many disenchanted

young British Asians need more Islam, not less: unless they have a proper understanding of what Islam is really about, they can all too easily become easy prey for the distortions of jihadists later in life.[95]

Former radicals deploy a set of arguments to counter the worldview of religious extremists, e.g., that the Qur'ân does not explicitly call for a unified Muslim state or caliphate and that Muslims have the inalienable right to textual interpretation to their given contexts.[96] The religious turn of government policies toward Muslim-origin populations does not signal a decision to treat citizens as Muslims rather than vice versa, so much as it aims to overcome a certain religious subculture that threatens to be an obstacle to social and political integration.

In 2007, the Home Office secured cabinet approval for a "£90m-a-year" plan to prevent the spread of violent extremism in Britain, and a sizable portion of this budget (£45 million) was reserved for use by local authorities, to be disbursed by the new communities and local government secretary.[97] Without a detailed examination of the actual approved budgetary appropriations, it is not possible to gauge the exact amount of resources the government has dedicated to its consultation with domestic Muslim groups and its fight against radicalization. But the amount appears to be in the neighborhood of hundreds of millions of British pounds (over $500 million).

This policy diffusion was not a foreordained outcome. Despite a high degree of policy centralization and the general weakness of local government, British officials have effectively pursued a set of decentralized policy approaches. What was once the domain of the Home Office and Foreign Office is now handled on a day-to-day basis by a new department: the Secretary of State for Communities and Local Government (CLG), whose office distributed the considerable bounty that the government budgeted to combat violent extremist views within the British Muslim population. This cabinet position replaced the Office of the Deputy Prime Minister; Ruth Kelly was the first to hold it (2006–7), followed by Hazel Blears in June 2007 and John Denham in 2009, who served one year before a new coalition government was elected.[98]

Each cabinet secretary brought a different approach to state-mosque relations. A series of interviews by the author with members of the Communities and Local Government administration produced a useful shorthand description of each phase.[99] Kelly emphasized the engagement of organizations with "shared values" and helped establish state-led bodies to represent the "silent majority" of moderates. Blears, by contrast, brought the CLG out into less comfortable terrain and endeavored to interact with individuals and groups who may be in disagreement with government policy: this would avoid "leaving a vacuum" in those community spaces where the government voice often remained unheard. Denham, the final CLG Secretary to serve in the Labour government, aimed for what his staff called a "critical mass approach." He brought discussions with Muslim communities even further beyond the "new comfort zone" pioneered by Blears, and asked the simple question: "are we in government talking to a critical mass or majority of Muslim communities? If not, why not?" The thinking behind this outreach was to view dialogue as "a form of 'primary care' that prevents vulnerability to violent extremism and radicalization." In 2010, a CLG official stated in an interview with the author that

> The Mosques and Imams National Advisory Board is only two years old. In the absence of any Islamic hierarchy, it is the dream of the community that they will have one national body that oversees mosques and imams' training standards. We are very much hopeful that by nurturing and giving them autonomy and a kick-start, that will be the institution compared to Lambeth Palace [the office of the Archbishop of Canterbury] for Muslims.

The MINAB held 26 "internal consultations" in 2008 alone, a relatively high frequency compared to its continental Islam Council counterparts.[100] Yet the official remained mindful of the taint that government involvement could imply—what the *Economist* called the "kiss of death." The official continued, "Today, we must have a relationship of semi-autonomy and arms-length distance, including criticizing where due, to keep the credibility within the Muslim communities themselves—many of whom are not happy with internal policies or the foreign policies of the UK government. That space is crucial to the credibility of the new council or board."

With the arrival of the Conservative/Liberal Democrat coalition in 2010, the British government abruptly changed tack. Despite the statements of Labour politicians suggesting the contrary, their time in government is being portrayed as one in which multiculturalism thrived unchecked and separate identities were permitted to run amok. The new government led by David Cameron placed its mark on the future shape of the British state: the austerity measures cut on average 19 percent in government departments across the board; the Department for Community and Local Government's (CLG) budget for Community outreach was even more dramatically slashed, by 51 percent.[101] The incoming coalition clearly did not appreciate the general situation of state-Islam relations that it inherited from the previous government. Generous CLG spending had been the crown jewel of both New and "Old" Labour's approach to counter-radicalization and counter-terrorism. The new security minister said there would be "less emphasis on 'multiculturalist' approaches than the previous government, and more on better social and cultural integration."[102]

Local Level Success in State-Mosque Relations

While some of the achievements cited above were negotiated within the Councils and their Working Groups, others were accomplished outside the framework of the official consultation. The creation of Councils and Working Groups has clarified some of the confusion over whom mayors and ministers are supposed to speak to when negotiating religious needs with Muslim representatives. In particular, local pragmatism has sometimes been more effective than national Muslim consultations.[103] At the national level, expectations are sometimes too high: governments want to resolve all their worries about security and political stability, while on the Muslim side, there is rivalry between ethnic groups and a compulsion to flex muscles. For local deals to work, there has to be some national consensus about the limits of cultural freedom, an issue indirectly addressed in every working day of national-level consultations.

National interior ministries began serious outreach to mosques and domestic Islamic associations as a result of national political pressure based on concerns over national security, and as a result, every detail of national-level consultations is magnified. Officials insist on ritual declarations of "political moderation" among Muslim leaders. Federations must be seen to defend their constituencies. These attitudes lend themselves to defensiveness and stalemate. By contrast, local consultations set up to address practical issues of religious observance need not be as security-focused (although better working relationships between administrations and communities will enhance trust and cooperation in general). It is often hard to achieve consensus on the national level among Muslim leadership because the embassies retain a certain possessiveness over their emigrants (and their form of Islam), and the limelight of national politics is ill-suited to pragmatic compromises of local administration.

At a national level, expectations for state-mosque relations have been raised so high—each interaction needs to demonstrate the very compatibility between Islam and democracy—that critics will not be satisfied without a modern-day Grand Sanhedrin or Lateran Accord for Islam. The variety of solutions at the local level is better suited to the reality of localized practices within Islamic countries, from Maghreb to Indonesia; even though "there is only one Islam," the variation in practices testifies to real diversity of Muslim populations and of diasporas. So this process furthers integration in the grand tradition of adapting religious loyalty to democratic polities, i.e., by allowing diasporas to find their own solutions rather than worrying about apostasy.

A virtuous circle has thus emerged in some local municipalities. The resolution of practical local problems associated with sudden presence of Muslims in urban neighborhoods helps reduce the tensions created by Islam's inadequate religious infrastructure: e.g., prayer-goers lying prone on sidewalks or blocking traffic; slaughtering lambs in the bathtub; proselytism in prisons—combined with international terrorism, this contributes to Europeans' negative impression of Islam, and made the religion seem more foreign. Muslim religious leaders have demonstrated they are willing to engage in negotiations with local governments, in order to improve conditions for religious freedom. They have no particular desire to violate local health or building codes. Indeed, building cemeteries is a powerful sign of commitment to integration; it indicates that one's "real" home is not elsewhere.

Nonetheless, the councils cannot be described as unadulterated successes. As the above section illustrates, emancipation will remain incomplete as long as state-mosque relations are subject to national coalition politics and the absence of incentives to cooperate. The Spanish Islamic Commission has been riven by internal disputes, the Italian *Consulta* was demoted to a "committee" and shed some participants, the Dutch *Contactorgaan* is in danger of obsolescence, the British MINAB may fail to gain the government's attention, and the CFCM has been described as being in a state of "permanent crisis"—even by some of its main participants.[104] But these organizations' persistence—not their productivity in a given calendar year—will form their legacy for the ages. As the president of a regional council for the Muslim Faith in France said, "the CFCM's survival is an achievement in itself. . . . The CFCM has been able to stay alive even though it is constantly breaking down. It is part of what French Muslims have earned in France."[105] Rather than viewing a given Islam Council's paralysis as a disadvantage, some officials have come to see this as a kind of institutional equilibrium: so long as representatives are haggling and cutting deals at the table, they are not attacking each other in the press. Every time one of the principal federation leaders in the CFCM threatened to resign or withdraw participation of his federation, he quickly realized that there were few other options for interacting with public authorities.[106]

Islam Councils have not yet managed to settle all outstanding state-mosque issues, but they do reflect a main benefit of neo-corporatist statecraft. States have been able to recruit and maintain a core of elites from the underrepresented group to engage in exchanges with administrators. As one Muslim participant in the German Islam Conference said recently:

I was long of the opinion that we were working without achieving any results. That was frustrating. Today I must correct that assessment. We have achieved results at all levels. Islamic organizations and representatives who were not able to speak to one another have now found dialogue and discussion. We have also managed to dismantle some prejudices in Germany. The black box of Islam has become more transparent.[107]

This was facilitated by the naming of interlocutors and by the recognition that consultation affords. In practice, authorities have effectively opened up communications channels to bring the observance of Islam out from *subterranea* and into the national landscape; the Councils simultaneously serve as a sounding board for the Muslim community as a whole, and as a temporary representative for the millions of citizens and residents of Muslim origin who are, for the time being, without significant electoral representation.

CHAPTER SEVEN

The Partial Emancipation

MUSLIM RESPONSES TO THE STATE-ISLAM CONSULTATIONS

How HAVE THE TWO organizational protagonists of European Muslim communities —Political Islam and Embassy Islam—responded to Europeans' state-building efforts? The main mosque federations have undergone a process of "domestication" in two significant ways: by participating in the state-mosque relations, and by taking steps to become less "foreign" in terms of personnel and religious content. The state's recognition, however imperfect, has reduced the stridency of organized Muslims' religious demands and taken federation leaders out of a defensive posture. This chapter makes the argument that Islam Councils have helped achieve an important degree of organizational incorporation, as defined in terms of certain "moderated" and "adapted" behaviors by the representatives of Embassy Islam and Political Islam. Where states adopt a more "neo-corporatist" path—as defined by the formalization of state-mosque relations in a hierarchical and monopolistic Islam Council—we observe a more successful path to the institutionalization, predictability, and moderation of Islamic organizations and the religious accommodation they expect from majority societies. Each Muslim sending state refined its Embassy Islam in response to specific incentives in national host states, and Political Islam groups—originating in Turkey, South Asia, and North Africa—also adapted their own goals to each European country in which they operate. This occurred in the second stage of "incorporation" and not during the earlier "outsourcing phase," suggesting that Islam Councils have provided a set of effective institutional incentives.

Although the measurable "outputs" of the first five to ten years of consultations can appear modest, political and institutional processes are now in place to establish a domestic context for state-mosque relations. The Islam Councils that government ministers trumpet in press conferences, however, are merely the most visible manifestation of a working relationship that has been established between public authorities and Muslim groups, and that extends down through the administration. A set of mosque federations has entered a new routine as interlocutors in state-mosque relations of nearly every European state, a privilege that they do their utmost to guard and preserve. This will contribute over time to Islam's rootedness in national institutions, and indirectly to the sociopolitical integration of all Muslims, pious or not.

During the 1980s and early 1990s, before the inclusion of Political-Islam groups in state-Islam consultations in Europe, many Islamist leaders still exhibited an "old country" mentality reminiscent of the tensions between government-sponsored religion and Islamist political parties in North Africa and Turkey. Embassy-Islam federations ignored their competitors or berated them for their fundamentalism, and Political-Islam groups were in turn confrontational with public authorities and made maximalist demands for religious accommodation in the public sphere.

In the first decade of the twenty-first century, by contrast, Political-Islam federations have demonstrated a willingness to work within the system and have toned down their most controversial stances. For Political-Islam groups, the influence of being *included* in state-led consultations—or, often, the mere possibility of being chosen for government consultation—has had a moderating effect. Between the late 1990s and early 2000s, they adopted repertoires of collective action that are typical of their new national contexts. They also asserted their independence from Islamist positions in the "homeland" and, at times, even from the positions taken by European "headquarters" (e.g., the UK-based Federation of Islamic Organizations in Europe).

Participants have repeatedly declined to engage in inflammatory rhetoric when presented with the opportunity to defend Islam in public debate, such as during the 2003–2004 legislation against headscarves in France and Germany; the 2006 Danish "prophet cartoon" controversy; the Pope's Regensburg speech; the 2008 Dutch "Fitna" movie broadcast on the internet; or the 2008–2009 legislation against burkas in France, Italy, and the UK. Italian Muslim leaders no longer speak of a Muslim's right to polygamy, French Muslim leaders no longer insist upon ritual burial without coffins, German Muslim leaders have dropped their insistence on religious education in Turkish language, British Muslim leaders avoid any ambiguity regarding death sentences for blasphemous authors. Islamist leaders have eschewed street demonstrations in favor of lobbying and lawsuits, and demonstrated an interest in keeping hold over administrative gains in the technical realm of state-mosque relations. Political-Islam federations' response to the political violence committed in the name of Islam—notably, the series of the terrorist attacks and hostage-takings between 2001 and 2006—proved to be decisive in eliciting clear denunciations of violence. The institutional opportunity of state-Islam consultations created a channel of communication and a political opportunity structure.

For Embassy Islam, on the other hand, the possibility of being *excluded* from government consultations—or at least seeing their role greatly diminished—has led to a similarly dramatic overhaul. Embassy-Islam federations that once did business only in their mother tongue, staffed their operations with diplomats, and refused to acknowledge the existence of unofficial religious groups, have changed their ways. The offering of official Islam from the erstwhile "sending countries" has been multiplied and adapted to the new circumstances of greater national oversight in European host states. And Turkish, Moroccan, and Algerian ministries of religious affairs have begun to accept greater scrutiny by European governments over the religious infrastructure they organize for Muslim diasporas. Thus, even while more personnel and infrastructure are exported toward Europe, a degree of autonomy has also been granted to national European branches of Embassy-Islam networks, and the sending states are more likely to work in concert with European governments. They have oriented and adapted their religious programs to the national contexts of European receiving societies. Imams who arrive from national capitals in Algeria, Morocco, Pakistan, and Turkey, for example, now attend destination-specific civic, political, and linguistic training courses. Groups with close home-country links have appointed greater numbers of European-born Muslims to executive positions, and regularly meet with rival federations in official contexts.

These changes have been gradual: neither of these political-religious forces—Embassy or Political Islam—is unrecognizable in their current state. Political Islam continues to push against secular sensibilities and can give the impression of lying in wait, while Embassy Islam resists relinquishing its dominant position within state-Islam affairs. But each has become accustomed to the power-sharing arrangements of the national state-Islam consultations in which they participate. The effect that institutional inclusion has had on the attitudes and behavior of the key Islamic organizations active in Europe, therefore, could arguably be characterized as a *partial* emancipation. Citizens and residents of Muslim background may potentially affiliate with a variety of religious groups (or choose not to do so), including some mosques and associations that operate independently of Embassy-Islam and Political-Islam networks. But these two networks remain the most visible and the most frequently consulted by governments seeking to institutionalize aspects of state-mosque relations.

An understanding of Islamic politics in Europe today must take account of the nuances among Political- and Embassy-Islam organizations' stances toward Islam's "domestication" and institutionalization in these new national contexts, not only with respect to one another as competitors, but also in comparison to their own previous incarnations before the advent of state-Islam consultations.

Councils are in their relative infancy compared with state-religion organs for Christians and Jews. Some Islam Councils have already experienced crises of legitimacy, instances of corruption, and, occasionally, resignations. Even the most "successful" consultations—e.g., in France and Germany—are not a panacea for eliminating extremism and all undesired foreign influences over religious practice, but they do provide a crucial institutional link between the state and community leaders. This relationship has already served the mundane purposes of technical accommodation of religious needs and acted as a sounding board during extraordinary times of crisis. Populations of Muslim origin in Europe today are not yet politically integrated, but institutionalized government consultations on religious matters involve evergreater numbers of Muslim association leaders. As a result of meticulous institution-building by interior ministries across the continent, authorities have opened up new conduits for addressing the material needs and religious sensibilities of a minority population that is, for the time being, without significant electoral representation.

The impact of cross-national variation in the design of Islam Councils is observable in the councils' institutional stability and concrete outcomes, and the main factor appears to be the organizational strength and mobilizational capacity of the principal sending states' religious institutions, i.e., Embassy Islam. Where it is more institutionalized and dominant in the homeland, its indirect mediation offers European governments a stronger interlocutor. Where it is weaker, the religious landscape tends to be dominated by religious NGOs with more political views, and institutional progress stalls. The most successful councils are sturdy enough to contain these religious NGOs. Embassy Islam plays a moderating role and foil for extremists. The irony of this situation is that it perpetuates foreign governments' influence on "European" Islam, and this explains why it is still premature to speak of an "Italian Islam" or "French Islam" or "Euro-Islam."

This chapter examines the political behavior of Islamic associations before and after incorporation and shows how they have responded to the neo-corporatist political opportunity structure. "Radicals" have moderated their demands, trading in their earlier ideological and obstructionist positions for newly pragmatic and cooperative stances: they went from street protests and intimations of violence, to lobbying and pledges of constitutional loyalty. Sending states are adapting the content of their religious programming to the new demands of European host societies. In many cases their adaptations are attempts to seek a competitive edge vis-à-vis their public interlocutors: a French official compared this dynamic to "each pupil wanting to showcase his merits to the teacher."[1] If we examine the positions of leaders of federations in the periods before and after consultations, the contrast in attitudes and behavior is striking.

THE ADAPTATION OF POLITICAL ISLAM TO STATE-MOSQUE RELATIONS

Institutional outreach in the second stage of state-Islam consultations has led to a change in Islamist federations' political behavior—in the sense of moderation and domestication—in response to state initiatives. Yet several years into their operation, many observers disparage the Islam Councils with contradictory arguments: that they have legitimized radicals and let the proverbial fox into the chicken coop, or that they are hopelessly paralyzed and accomplish almost nothing. Scholarly consensus judges the decision to include Political-Islam leaders in contemporary state-Islam arrangements as self-defeating—an act of capitulation that endangers democratic institutions. One political scientist wrote that the CFCM in France, for example, was destined "to empower the very same radicals it seeks to constrain."[2] Or, as a French politician recently argued, "When one recognizes 'moderate Islamist' organizations as official interlocutors . . . are we aware that these are allies of Islamist totalitarianism who betray democracy as well as liberal Muslims . . . If they proclaim their 'pacifism' in France, they support jihad elsewhere, and their ambition is to place veils on all women and prevent the integration of [the second and third generations] into a set of 'unholy' values."[3]

To separate reformists from extremists and guard against such subversive acts, European governments have been compelled to come up with some measure of what moderation looks like. A central claim of the neo-corporatist literature is that interest groups "exercise restraint in pursuing their goals in return for their official recognition and privileges."[4] The advantages and privileges of institutional access for organized interest groups, as one scholar describes it, are balanced by a set of restrictions and obligations: interest organizations will "behave responsibly, predictably and will refrain from nonnegotiable demands or unacceptable tactics."[5] This argument holds that the organization of interests will have an influence on political moderation. The notion is that granting basic religious freedoms (and diversifying the pool of interlocutors) in favor of a localized Islam—from mosque construction to the recruitment of chaplains, imams, and religion teachers—has helped give way to a predictable, institutionalized give and take. Where it has been implemented, this routinization has had a moderating effect on hardliners.

Governments' approaches to state-mosque relations have shaped the nature of Muslim leaders' political participation and the extent of Islam's integration in their respective national settings. Countries that successfully pursued incorporation have elicited a more moderate political participation from Political-Islam groups. The institutional form of state-Islam consultations on the pragmatic issues described here influenced the attitudes of mosque federation leaders toward national governments' Islam-related policies. This process therefore shares many characteristics with earlier state-society governance arrangements, in particular those gleaned from the literature on neo-corporatism for labor-capital disputes. Just as the prospect of economic development could be improved by union leaders' agreeing to wage restraint and limited strikes, then, by analogy, the accommodation of Islam would be accompanied by Muslim leaders who can deliver moderate religious demands.[6] A political behavioral agenda undergirded the institutional process: to encourage moderate demands and institutionalized political participation. The transformation of Islamist leaders' positioning—from an ideological and obstructionist posture to a pragmatic and co-operative one—can be measured using outward manifestations of extremism or moderation:

1. Recognizing the legal authority of the national government;
2. A change in tactics of political participation and the use of institutional forms of protest;
3. The softening of participants' negotiating stance;
4. Establishing nonviolent credentials; and
5. Demonstrating a commitment to intra-religious tolerance and inter-religious dialogue.

The exact measures for the efficacy of socioeconomic interest representation cannot be used to judge the success of state-religion relations. A decrease in the number of workdays lost to labor action does not easily compare with, say, a decline in the number of headscarves worn by Muslim girls in public schools. The goal of "moderation" in state-religion relations is not to eliminate religious expression, in any case, but rather implies a broader behavioral agenda that places a cap on the aspirations and scope of claims-making by community leadership in exchange for an institutional voice. Convincing militant leaders in the "gray zone" to work within "accepted channels" is a slow process of gaining their allegiance and bringing them into participatory processes.[7]

In other words, "moderation" summarizes the basic conditions for integration into institutional politics. It is not merely about a set of positions, but also the attitude accompanying those positions. The cumulative effect of these arrangements has had a broader impact on the political behavior of mosque federations, including in times of crisis.

Without passing judgment on the desirability of one policy position over another, the institutionalization of Islam has had important effects on the decisions made by mosque federations when they voice their objections to state policies regarding Islam—and, ultimately, on their integration into western European political systems. Political-Islam leaders have been conditioned by years of administrative politics and softened into reliable dialogue partners willing to work within state institutions. Professionalization is also a key component of political moderation: the structuring of the group's organizational apparatus to gain control of institutions—"achieving the strategic implantation of their groups into the government machine"[8]—i.e., creating associations and representation at the regional level, to accompany national-level representation—as well as a willingness and ability to interact with other rival organizations and public authorities.[9]

Between 2002 and 2006, four major Political-Islam organizations were invited—directly or indirectly—to participate in official state-Islam consultations: in France, the UOIF (2002); in Italy, the UCOII (2004); in Germany, the IGMG (2006); in the UK, the MCB (2006).[10] One measure of the impact of state-Islam consultations can be seen in these groups' claims-making activities before and during participation in the recently established Islam Councils. Whereas Political-Islam leaders started off standoffish in administrative negotiations and were reluctant to denounce fellow Muslims' use of political violence, their participation in neo-corporatist councils has coincided with their evolution into interlocutors who are more likely to distance themselves from extremism and who have become amenable to discussion and debate. It is useful to compare the reactions and behavior of Political-Islam federations during crises of religious sensibility in the first period (1990–1999) with roughly equivalent moments in the second period (1999—2009).

Early Consultations: "It's in the Qur'ân"

Because of Embassy Islam's dominant position, Political-Islam leaders had little invested in early consultations, and acted as though they had little to lose. In negotiations with administrators, they took an all or nothing approach, they defended literalist interpretations of Qur'ânic injunctions, and they would obstinately repeat themselves when administrations asked for clarification of their intentions.

Upon making their first overtures of consultation at the outset of the second stage, administrators encountered in Political-Islam organizations an inflexible negotiating partner. It is important to recall that Political-Islam organizations' interaction with interior ministries was confrontational from the beginning. Interviews with administrators in Berlin and Paris produce evidence that contacts with Political-Islam organizations were often fraught with conflict: from the Islamische Föderation in Berlin (linked to *Millî Görüş*) which in the late 1990s declined the standard ministerial oversight for its religion curriculum; to the UCOII in Italy, which demanded the rearrangement of work schedules around Muslim holidays and free land on which to build mosques.[11] The Islamische Gemeinschaft-Hamburg published a fatwa restricting schoolgirls' participation in school trips if their male chaperones were more than one day's camel ride away.[12] One advisor on Islam to three French Interior Ministers in the late 1980s and early 1990s said in an interview that these federations made for difficult negotiation partners:

> All interior ministers encountered the problem of Political Islamism, which methodically pursues privileged treatment in a demanding manner [. . .] One cannot negotiate with the Islamists—it's "my way or the highway" with them, because what's in the Qur'ân is law and superior to any administrative or historic arguments you can make [as an administrator].[13]

It was not rare for Political-Islam leadership to call for street protests and at times they issued thinly veiled threats of unrest, fueling criticism that their leadership and ideology were fundamentally at odds with Western democratic values and the prevailing settlement separating religion and state. Political-Islam leadership did not display much interest in establishing nonviolent credentials; some were accused of downplaying Islamist violence—especially in Israel and the occupied territories—or even silently granting their approbation of terrorist methods. Islamist leaders in Europe did not have many incentives to demonstrate tolerance toward other religious groups or to engage in interreligious dialogue, and similarly, they had no real institutional opportunity structure to compel them to engage in professionalization.

During the transition from "outsourcing" to "incorporation," Political-Islam leaders lived up to administrators' low expectations. Advisors to the French, German, and Italian interior ministries said in interviews that Political-Islam leaders discussed issues such as Muslim sections in cemeteries (in France) or religious curriculum (in Germany) in a confrontational fashion. These early proto-consultations, which were mostly informal and never officially institutionalized, encountered Political-Islam leaders who were contemptuous of bureaucratic inquiries. As a result, these initial attempts at state-mosque relations suffered from blockage and even collapse at the hands of uncooperative Political-Islam leadership.

A French advisor to the first interior minister who took on the Islam dossier described the first meeting of Political-Islam leaders with French administrators in 1990, held in the halls of the Ministry in the Place Beauveau in Paris:

> The first demand of the members of the UOIF was that in Islam one cannot be buried in a coffin, only in a sheet in the ground. This was the first time that Muslim leaders had come into the *grands salons* of the Interior Ministry and they were sitting across from the Minister, his chief of staff, the general director of all French prefects, the general director of public liberties and juridical affairs, and the general director of local collectivities as well as the head of the central office for religion. They have in front of them the entirety of the French administration and they state simply "we do not want to use coffins." Just to give you an idea of the tone. The general director of prefects replies, "we acknowledge your request but that is not possible. We can discuss other things—such as allowing a separate section for Muslims—but for health reasons we cannot allow burials without coffins." Their response was that "Islam requires it, it's in the Qur'ân, the Prophet said it, no coffins!"[14]

In Berlin, a judge granted the IGMG-affiliated *Islamische Föderation* the right to organize religious instruction for students in a number of public schools in the year 2000. The education ministry's local administrator in charge of approving the religion syllabus found that, unlike other religious communities, the group was reluctant to enter into a discussion of their curriculum plans. The administrator related the interaction in an interview:

> Their first proposed syllabus was just like it would be in a Qur'ânic school. But religion hour in public schools is not just supposed to be a lesson from the Qur'ân! Simply citing the Qur'ân is not religious education. And they refused to give any bibliographical information: Who wrote the syllabus? Whose Qur'ân translation is this? They chose the worst one. A school administrator needs to know this, and they did not want to share this information. *They submitted four different versions of the syllabus to us without changing the fundamental outline*: just verses from the Qur'ân followed by "intention" and "didactic": what kind of pedagogy is that?[15]

That same year in Rome, the interior ministry attempted to bring together Political-Islam leadership of the UCOII into a short-lived Islamic

Council of Italy (1998–2001), which included just five leaders from religious federations, and which fell apart because of differences in attitude toward state administrators and politicians. As one observer recalled, the Political-Islam federation's spontaneity and confrontational instinct led to the Council's downfall:

> There were practical disagreements with regard to how to manage relations with state institutions. When the minister in charge of domestic intelligence told a reporter the Italian converts represented a dangerous element because there were some from the extreme left and extreme right who had joined mosques, two members of the UCOII published an open letter to the minister in which they violently attacked him in heavy tones, leading to the resignation of several other members of the council.[16]

They occasionally made valid objections. When an Embassy-Islam representative suggested that French Muslims need not observe the obligation to consume only meat that has been slaughtered according to halal requirements, a Political-Islam leader said "Maybe Sheikh Abbas is fine with buying his meat in [any] supermarket, but we don't want this kind of low-grade Islam."[17]

1989: The Rushdie and Headscarf Affairs

Three defining moments for Political Islam's public position in European societies took place between 1988–1990—the Rushdie affair, the first headscarf affairs, and the first Gulf War—and each incident elicited decidedly confrontational behavior and maximalist rhetoric from Political-Islam leaders at the time. Whereas Embassy-Islam envoys reacted limply, with diplomatic aplomb, the recently created Political-Islam federations found their niche as public defenders of Islam. Their confrontational stances and sharp rhetoric were a mark of their outsider status, as they were excluded from state-mosque relations such as they existed in the late 1980s. This helped raise concerns within interior ministries and contributed to a reassessment of their exclusion and the eventual end of Embassy Islam's monopoly.

The publication of the *Satanic Verses* elicited much scorn from Political-Islam groups. Millî Görüş (IGMG) affiliates in Germany asserted that *Satanic Verses* had been published by the CIA, and that the UK government was participating in a "slander campaign" against Muslims. The head of the IGMG in Denmark said that Judaism was the source of decay and social unrest, and that the ideologies of capitalism and communism could be traced back to Jewish origins.[18] In France, UOIF spokesmen warned that they could not hold their constituents back from taking to the streets. Some associations even expressed support for the fatwa against the author Salman Rushdie. The UOIF and FNMF held demonstrations in February and March of 1989 in Paris to demand the book's withdrawal, and other Political-Islam associations held a protest in March in Lyon. UOIF and FNMF leaders used ominous rhetoric while asserting their demands. A FNMF spokesman said, "There are going to be confrontations. We risk being overcome by uncontrollable elements";[19] and a UOIF leader warned, "If the book is displayed in store windows there could be spontaneous reactions."[20] The Socialist Party spokesman equated the subsequent demonstration of one thousand opponents to the publication of Rushdie's novel to a "call for murder."[21] The culture minister and his Socialist Party supported demonstrations in favor of the book's publication in France, and the Mayor of Paris, Jacques Chirac, expressed his "outrage" at the image of Muslim demonstrators in Paris: "If they're French, they must be prosecuted and if they're foreign they must be deported . . . we cannot tolerate calls for murder in the capital of human rights."[22] A UOIF leader said he "would have expected more neutrality from the government."

Similarly, when three schoolgirls were expelled from a Creil middle school for wearing headscarves in 1989, the UOIF took up their case, vowing resistance and calling for street demonstrations to protest the decision. Across Europe, Political-Islam leadership, which was just beginning to form peak associations to compete with Embassy-Islam organizations on European soil, took a hard line. One German Muslim activist, who nearly two decades later would become head of the ZMD, defended headscarves with the comment: "Girls lose their sense of modesty as early as elementary school." A French FNMF co-founder said on the topic of the obligation to wear the headscarf, "if the Conseil d'Etat does not decide in our favor, we will withdraw our girls from French schools."[23] While the leader of the Embassy Islam-affiliated *Grande Mosquée de Paris* (GMP) spoke of finding "amicable solutions," and tried to tamp down the confrontation, competing Political-Islam federations held demonstrations in Paris on October 22 and November 5, 1989 (the GMP leader called those street protests "regrettable").[24]

After: Auditioning for the Role of "Privileged Interlocutor"

Many of the most prominent Political-Islam federations across Europe have moderated their stances and repertoires of political participation: the Muslim Association of Britain (a constituent organization of the Muslim Council of Britain), *the Union des Organisations Islamiques de France* (UOIF is part of the CFCM), *Unione delle Comunità e Organizzazzioni Islamiche in Italia* (UCOII was a member of the *Consulta per l'Islam*), *Islamische Gemeinschaft Millî Görüş* and *Zentralrat der Muslime* in Deutschland (member organizations of the *Islamrat* and the *Koordinierungsrat der Muslime*, respectively, both of which participated in the *Deutsche Islam Konferenz*). The effect seems to have been atmospheric and not merely tied to the circumstance of being officially "co-opted" as an official interlocutor. Even for those Political-Islam federations not currently consulted by the interior ministry in a given European country, their public statements and policy positions appear to reflect a fundamentally system-oriented stance.

In various political contexts, Islamist leaders have gradually bound their organizations to institutional confines, political norms, and expectations of state-mosque relations. They no longer made "maximalist" demands for immediate religious accommodation; they countenanced restrictive policies on religious freedom like headscarf wearing; they increased their denunciations of terrorism committed in the name of Islam; in response to perceived attacks on Islam in the public sphere, they opted for lobbying and lawsuits over street protests; without abandoning their solidarity with Palestinians (nor, often, their disdain for Israeli leaders), they distanced themselves from expressions of anti-Semitism (see figures 7.1 and 7.2).[25] The CFCM in France has met regularly with the Jewish umbrella organization CRIF; the Italian Political-Islam federation, UCOII, organized a visit for its leaders to the extermination camp at Auschwitz-Birkenau in the spring of 2009.

More generally, Political-Islam federations have sought to influence policymaking and administrative practice through institutional channels (see figure 7.3). This was signaled by the extent to which public posturing to demonstrate loyalty and obedience to the legal framework—an unabashed quest for *Salonfähigkeit*—has become a recurring spectacle among European-based Political-Islam activists in the past two decades. Unlike the charters handed down from above during the actual process of state-Islam consultations described in chapter 5, these are independent initiatives by Muslim federations in response to the political opportunity presented by state-church relations.

The "Charter of Muslims in Europe" signed in Brussels in 2008, for example, can be evaluated in light of the political opportunity structure created by state-Islam consultations. The six pages of bullet points— pledging allegiance to their host societies—were issued by the Federation of Islamic Organizations of Europe (FIOE), the thriving network of mosques and prayer spaces in twenty-seven countries that is considered the European branch of the Muslim Brotherhood movement. The charter outlines "how we should act as positive citizens and not be a threat," a spokesman said. The document, ratified by FIOE representatives in all European Union member-states, includes a call for all Muslims in

Figure 7.1. A delegation from the *Conseil français du culte musulman* visits the *Conseil représentatif des institutions juives de France*, 2008. Source: Jean Corcos, http://rencontrejfm.blogspot.com/.

Europe to "enhance the values of mutual understanding, work for peace and the welfare of society, moderation and inter-cultural dialogue, removed from all inclinations of extremism and exclusion." By enjoining its membership to strike "a harmonious balance between preservation of Muslim identity and the duties of citizenship," the FIOE charter of January 2008 continues down a path strewn with earlier such unilateral declarations of good intentions: a 1990 *Bozza d'Intesa* in Italy, the 1995 *Charte du culte musulman en France*, and the 2002 *islamische Charta* in Germany, among others. In response to the Italian interior ministry's announcement of plans for the Council, a number of prominent Muslims published a "Loyalty Pact to the Italian Republic" in May 2003.

Though all Political-Islam federations strongly denounced the 9/11 attacks, they also issued statements condemning the American-led in-

Figure 7.2. Interreligious Dialogue Workshop including members of the *Deutsche Islam Konferenz*, 2008. Source: IGMG, e.V.; www.igmg.de.

vasion of Afghanistan and later, Iraq. But they also routinely condemned the deaths of Western journalists and aid workers—and even soldiers—in the two battle zones (e.g., Italian Carabinieri who died in Nassiriya in 2004 and French soldiers killed in Afghanistan in 2008).[26] In the last six years, Political-Islam federations across Europe have loudly condemned terrorist incidents from Madrid to London, Glasgow, and Mumbai, as well as hostage situations involving European citizens and aid workers in Iraq, Afghanistan, and Yemen. This too represents a change in behavior and message from an earlier era. Oğuz Üçüncü, general secretary of *Millî Görüş* in Germany, said that his federation was committed to using sermons and programming in mosques as a counter-terrorism measure:

> We condemned the terrorist attacks of March 11 [in Madrid] as we did on September 11, and we condemned any other act of terror. So as a Muslim organization we did our duty and we condemned the terror on the very first day of any such attack. . . . . But what we did as an Islamic organization is more than just demonstrating. We have been using our infrastructure in order to condemn the terrorist attacks and violence in general, but also to inform our people to not give any kind of support or sympathy to terrorists.[27]

At regular intervals since 2003, Political-Islam federations involved with State-Islam consultations in Germany, France, and Italy have proposed sending delegations to help free hostages. A CFCM delegation including the UOIF addressed kidnappers of two French journalists at a Baghdad press conference in 2004: "Show us you are good Muslims like us and hand over the hostages." Political-Islam leaders in France refused to call for a repeal of the headscarf law at the time as the kidnappers demanded, saying that amounted to "odious blackmail."[28] Nadeem Elyas of the German Zentralrat der Muslime even offered to take the place of German hostages in Iraq, and the Muslim Association of Britain called for the unconditional release of British hostages on the Al Jazeera news network.

ITALY: THE UCOII — MODERATION DESPITE EXCLUSION?

The trajectory of the *Unione delle Comunità e Organizzazioni Islamiche* is significant because it had originally been excluded from the preparatory meetings in the lead-up to the Italian consultation, and it has been repeatedly sidelined from Italian state-mosque relations with changes in government: each occupant of the Italian interior ministry tends to view the organization differently. Its behavioral adjustment is interesting because it indicates a spillover effect of the opportunity structure of state-mosque relations, which provide a model—and incentives—to

Figure 7.3. Members of the *Conseil français du culte musulman* leave the presidential Elysée Palace in Paris, 2009

aspire to participate in them. The UCOII general secretary questioned the definition of "moderate" Muslims. "Islam is Islam," he said. "One must pray five times a day, so what is meant by a 'moderate'—someone who only prays three times a day?"[29] Thinking he might eventually be tapped for the Consulta, however, Dachan proceeded to say and do all the "right" things. He publicly laid out the duty of Muslims in Italy to participate as full citizens:

> Italian and European Muslims must be first and foremost citizens of their respective state, with full responsibilities and rights, financially independent from any sticky charity groups, structurally integrated in the societies they live in, social and political subjects and politically active, capable of establishing their own representative frameworks and new ways of spreading Islam.[30]

Further re-branding its public image as "moderate"—with the hope of improving its candidacy for the Consulta—the UCOII released a "manifesto against terrorism and for life" in September 2004, and held peace marches in several Italian cities on September 11, 2004, to demand the release of Italian hostages in Iraq.[31] The UCOII leader even traveled personally (in the image of his French counterparts of the CFCM) to press for the release of the two Italian aid workers in Afghanistan. The UCOII adopted two slogans on posters and banners for this campaign: "We Muslims of Italy are united against all violence" and "Absolute loyalty towards the country, its values, and its ordinances."[32] Moreover, it was supportive of the government's effort to secure the release of Italian hostages in Yemen in December 2005. There are also indications that the UCOII is looking to consolidate its control over Muslim associations to achieve a degree of organizational unity.[33]

In 2008 and 2009, the conservative government suspended the Consulta and created a new "committee for Italian Islam" which re-introduced the primacy of Embassy Islam as the preferred interlocutor and relegated the UCOII to supplicant status. Nonetheless, the UCOII leadership still made a point of demonstrating their commitment to the Italian Republic: the general secretary attended the state funerals of paratroopers who died in Afghanistan, as well as earthquake and flood victims, and issued statements of condolences. "I want to make clear that we are for the respect of the Italian constitution," the general secretary said in an interview in 2009.[34] A UCOII spokesman welcomed a court ruling protecting women from domestic abuse by calling it "a step forward in the public's getting to know what Islam is really about." Another UCOII leader visited the extermination camps at Auschwitz-Birkenau and stated that "During these times, prejudice among Muslims denying the Holocaust is widespread. In this context, as a Muslim and a leader of the Muslim community, I went to Auschwitz to show that we, Muslims do not deny the Holocaust and we are not anti-Semites, even if we criticize Israel's policies."[35] The general secretary participated in an official ceremony at the Prefecture of Ancona where survivors were awarded a medal of honor, and he presented a medal to a veteran. When two politicians proposed that Muslim children be given the option of Islamic religious education during the weekly period allotted for religious instruction in Italian public schools, they set off a lively debate. Surprisingly, one of the voices that rejected the proposal was the UCOII spokesman, who said: "we have to be realistic—they're cutting teachers and school funding right now, and religious instruction requires training people, creating a curriculum, securing resources. And above all, we need a cultural maturation of the overall society. All these conditions are not yet met in Italy."[36] Following Pope Benedict XVI's Regensburg speech in 2006, the UCOII sent him a letter inviting him to a dialogue, citing a Qur'ânic imperative to "engage in dialogue with the people of the book"[37] and attended a meeting with the pope at his retreat in Castelgandolfo. In 2009, a UCOII leader stated unambiguously, "The incident is closed, and we have maximum respect for the pope."[38]

FRANCE: MODERATION THROUGH INSTITUTIONALIZATION

During crises, members of the French CFCM pursued legal remedies and expressed their outrage through institutional channels, explicitly shunning public demonstrations. The CFCM called for "Calm and serenity" in the aftermath of Chirac's December 2003 speech that announced the legislative project including a headscarf ban. The CFCM again issued an appeal for "calme, dignité et serenité" before the U.S.-led invasion of Iraq, on March 21, 2003, even while noting French Muslims' "consternation over this aggression, which is contrary to international law."[39] During the 2005 French riots, the UOIF issued a fatwa declaring participation in riots and the destruction of property to be "un-Islamic."

When the French parliament passed a law banning headscarves in primary and secondary schools in 2004, the CFCM had been in place for just over one year. Six months before the law was passed, the interior minister at the time called upon the Regional Councils for the Muslim Faith (CRCMs) to join in discussions of the headscarf issue with local authorities and offered them a choice: "confrontation or accompaniment."[40] The CFCM issued a statement in October 2003, containing mild language which indicated that headscarves were "a religious prescription" (i.e., not an "obligation") and requested that the Conseil d'État ruling of 1989 be applied. Doing so would allow for the discretion of school principals in setting guidelines. The UOIF leadership avoided confrontational behavior and called off participation in street demonstrations, and even went so far as to remove a student leader who had agitated against the law.

The CFCM president sent a memorandum to CRCM representatives to avoid participating in demonstrations against the headscarf law and, instead, to lobby parliamentary deputies: "if our discussions with parliamentarians are conducted methodically and with determination, we can ensure that the law is applied as close as possible to the jurisprudence of the Conseil d'État," which was seen to be more tolerant of headscarf wearing. "Because the UOIF was co-opted by officialdom," the *Economist* editorialized in March 2004, "it was unable to support protests against a ban on Muslim headscarves in public schools and other state institutions." But the federations saw a no-win situation and sought to mitigate the law in its application. Through their newfound institutional contacts, the UOIF helped shape the implementation memorandum (*circulaire d'application*) by influencing the language used, eliminating mention of a ban on "all head coverings" (thus leaving open the possibility of wearing bandanas) and assuring the right of "interested third parties," i.e., CRCMs, to contact local educational officials in cases of conflict.[41] Brèze said in an interview that UOIF stopped granting financial support to lawyers of girls wearing headscarves who make judicial appeals in 1998.[42]

The headscarf proved to be just the first phase of policymaking around Muslims' religious garb. After U.S. President Barack Obama spoke out in his Cairo address against legislating what Muslims could wear, French President Sarkozy initially supported him. But he used a later speech to dispatch any attempt to outflank him in French politics and called the burka "unwelcome in France." The French—and later, Italian—governments moved to ban the niqab and burka in the fall of 2009. But none of the major Islamic federations defended wearing a full-body veil, although some were troubled by the prospect of another round of negative publicity and restrictive legislation centered on Islam. The general secretary of the Italian UCOII stated simply that "The niqab is against the law, which requires everyone's faces to be recognizable," but later questioned the necessity of a school ban on niqabs since no students had been reported as attending school in a full veil. The French CFCM stated that it "would not ask French society to accept the burka," and that "Muslims should pay attention to the society in which they live, and its cultural code, and adopt a religious practice that is appropriate."[43] The UOIF later railed against the law—as it had against the March 15 headscarf law—but in both cases spoke in favor of legislative reform rather than civil disobedience. A prominent UOIF imam added: "the only Muslims who will survive spiritually are those who know how to moderate, adapt and negotiate their practices with the reality of French society."[44]

Despite violent reactions to publication of Danish cartoons mocking the prophet Muhammad, the absence of unrest on the European continent was noteworthy.[45] When the caricatures deemed offensive to the image of the Prophet Mohammed were republished in two French periodicals, furthermore, the UOIF did not take to the streets but instead joined a lawsuit (together with the *Grande Mosquée de Paris*, a rival Embassy-Islam federation).[46] The UOIF "judged that [the cartoons] went beyond freedom of expression and constitute an aggression," but asked French Muslims to "take a responsible attitude . . . and allow the law to sort it out."[47] This response is a far cry from the "broken bookshop windows" evoked by UOIF leaders seventeen years earlier (see table 7.1).

ISLAMIC YOUTH ORGANIZATIONS (IYOS): MODERATION
THROUGH EUROPEANIZATION

A further measure of the domestication of Political-Islam federations is provided by the positions and behavior of the youth branches they have spawned (discussed in chapter 2). Those who participate in formal Islamic youth organizations or pass through their leadership positions experience a political socialization that influences their views on

TABLE 7.1.
Islamic Religious "Outrage" in Europe

Caricatures Affair (2005–2010). In the Italian Consultative Council's first meeting, members condemned violent protests against caricatures of the prophet Muhammad, as well as the caricatures themselves: like their French counterparts, the UCOII called for the application of an existing law against inciting racial hatred (*Legge Mancini*) against newspapers that reprinted the cartoons. Italian Interior minister Pisanu commented after the meeting that "anyone participating in this meeting would have understood that there is a moderate Islam in Italy." Following the Mohammad caricature controversy, the UCOII held talks with Danish diplomats in Italy and released a common press declaration with the Danish embassy. Klausen observes that the Muslim Association of Britain framed its protest of the cartoons in terms of "Muslims' right to equal treatment in European law and civic life," complaining about "discriminatory treatment rather than matters of faith."[1]

Idomeneo at the Deutsche Oper (2006). The staging of Mozart's *Idomeneo* at the Deutsche Oper—which included a decapitated Islamic prophet—was in walking distance to the Charlottenburg castle where the Deutsche Islam Konferenz held its opening meeting. A proposal was made that all thirty DIK members go to see the opera together. The Islamrat representative demurred, saying that "even though it would have pleased the Minister, artistic freedom doesn't mean you have to go see everything."[2] Later, however, Kizilkaya joined the group of DIK participants at the Opera house for a coffee during intermission.

Another Cartoon Incident (2007). The European Council for Fatwa and Research and the Federation of Islamic Organizations in Europe issued condemnations of a death threat that had been issued against a Swedish cartoonist who had drawn Mohammed with a dog's body.

"Fitna" Webcast (2008). The Dutch National Moroccans Council called for a "calm and sensible response" to Dutch politician Geert Wilders's polemical "anti-Qurân" video montage. Its president said, "Our call to Muslims abroad is follow our strategy and don't frustrate it with any violent incidents,"[4] Muhammad al-Rabi'i, chairman of the Moroccan and Islamic Societies Coordination, said: "We call on all Muslims in the Netherlands and all citizens who might be offended by the film's contents to exercise self-restraint and not be carried away by the perversion." The Coordination contacted the Muslim countries' embassies in the Netherlands and the Organization of Islamic Conference "to urge them not to boycott Netherlands' products."[5] The Council secured the approval of Egyptian grand mufti and even of Yusuf al-Qaradawi for the Dutch government's handling of the issue; the council eventually filed a lawsuit asking for an injunction against the webcast, which was refused.

---

[1] Klausen, *The Cartoons that Shook the World*, 2009, 124.

[2] "Kizilkaya will Idomeneo nicht sehen," www.stern.de, 29 September 2006.

[3] Canadian Broadcasting Company, "Dutch officials report calm following release of anti-Islamic film," 2009.

[4] Soares, "Netherlands Braced for Muslim Anger as Politician Releases 'Anti-Islam' Film," *The Independent*, 2008.

[5] el Madkoury, "How a film which spreads hate had a healing effect on relations between Muslims and non-Muslims in the Netherlands," Conference on "Violent extremism in Europe," 2008.

national and international debates. Their ties to homeland govern-ments are less pronounced than those of the current generation of adult leadership. These youth organizations' advocacy, published materials, positions taken in political debates, and organized activities offer in-sights into the political affinities, ideologies, and political worldview. The current generation was born and raised in Europe, and is less likely to have lived at great length in Muslim-majority countries. They are less connected to the homeland politics that influence many parent or-ganizations and they are much less likely to have personal ties to over-seas donors in the Gulf and elsewhere.

Islamic youth organizations may have inherited some of what could be considered sexist attitudes and "hate literature"—mostly regarding Jews, Israelis, and Shi'as—from their distant sponsors of the Muslim World League and Muslim Brotherhood-affiliated parent organiza-tions. It is nonetheless hard to detect a dominant Muslim Brother-hood or Muslim World League influence on most IYO's behavior and political positions. Almost without exception, IYOs at the national and pan-European levels are heavily involved with "interreligious" and "intercultural" dialogue with Christian and Jewish groups. At the pan-European level, furthermore, the degree of gender diversity is un-precedented for Muslim associational activity in Europe. In the adult organizations, women are generally segregated into separate female branches. In IYOs, however, young women participate as near-equals (though they are still under-represented) and some have even taken on leadership roles (e.g., in the Forum of European Muslim Youth and Stu-dent Organizations, or FEMYSO). This openness to other religions and to feminism can no doubt be justified exegetically, but here they prob-ably result from the influence of the Council on Europe and the Euro-pean Commission. Even if European-level institutions have no real competence to act in national religious affairs, and their means are lim-ited to modest subsidies for individual associations, the Council and Commission's support of IYOs has helped nurture a reasonably neutral and tolerant space of European Islamic associations.

Overall, IYOs demonstrate their autonomy by engaging in political dialogue and compromise more actively than their parent associations. There is considerably greater interfaith activity with Jewish communi-ties and Catholic and Protestant groups at the IYO level than at the adult Muslim associational level. When, for example, a Rome imam canceled a high-profile visit to the Italian capital's main synagogue in January 2008, the Young Italian Muslims (GMI) kept their meeting with the Union of Young Italian Jews and planned a synagogue visit of their own. Thus, IYOs are less likely to fall into the kind of erratic and politically tone-deaf behavior that reflects internal divisions in adult associations, e.g., the GMI's then-parent organization's (UCOII) full-page newspaper advertisement in 2006 comparing Israeli occupation to Nazi massacres. IYOs have sometimes been reined in by adult organizations. For example, during the lead-up to the 2004 French headscarf law, when the *Jeunes Musulmans de France* tried to organize a street protest that the UOIF did not endorse, the rally was called off. On the other hand, adult associations may sometimes use IYOs to make gestures that they cannot themselves easily make for internal reasons.

THE ADAPTATION OF EMBASSY ISLAM TO STATE-MOSQUE RELATIONS

With the creation of the Islam Councils, European governments intended to end Embassy Islam's monopoly over religious representation and domination over mosques and imams. The transformation of Embassy-Islam federations and their sending-state sponsors has been less dramatic than that of Political-Islam leadership, but it is no less significant in the emancipation of Europe's Muslims. Embassy-Islam leaders were initially reluctant to accept any change in the formula of state-Islam consultations. European governments' inclusion of Political-Islam federations and other religious figures and institutions in state-Islam dialogues in the 1990s and 2000s ended the monopoly over religious representation that Embassy Islam had enjoyed for more than two decades. Embassy-Islam federations in every national context have tried to defend their advantageous position, and they have employed a variety of obstructive and then adaptive techniques.

The indirect representatives of Turkey, Algeria, and Morocco have responded to Europeans' efforts to create Islamic Councils in the last fifteen to twenty years by undergoing a process of qualified "domestication": (1) They have accepted to participate in state-mosque relations and have sought to retain a dominant position. (2) When their relative importance has been diminished by the inclusion of other representatives, they have tried to block or obstruct the progress of state-mosque relations. (3) Finally, they have taken steps to become less "foreign" in terms of personnel (e.g., imams, spokesmen), the use of European languages, cooperation with European governments on the training of religion teachers and imams and adapting religious content (e.g., school curriculum, Friday sermons) to the European context. They have also begun to accept the legitimacy of rival organizations in European Muslim communities. Nonetheless, these same countries' authorities have increased their targeting of the diasporas with the exportation of personnel and religious institutions. There has been a flurry of state cooperation with Embassy Islam at all levels of government, most of which has taken place *since* the creation of the Islam Councils.

In the 1980s, Embassy Islam in France, Germany, and Italy worked to win over new mosques and to consolidate control over rising federations. They did this first by blocking or boycotting state-Islam consultations that included rival organizations, then by insisting on presiding over the consultations, and occasionally working outside the margins of official consultations in side agreements with individual ministries (or threatening to sabotage Islam Councils) when they feel marginalized. Embassy-Islam officials—some of whom hold diplomatic status in the European host country—are not a natural match for national state-Islam consultations, which are supposed to oversee the "citizenization" (*citoyennisation* or *Einbürgerung*) of Islam. Foreign governments have displayed a cautious interest in immigrant participation in host societies: Turkish Prime Minister Erdoğan famously referred to assimilation as "a crime against humanity," and the Moroccan minister for Moroccan community abroad stated simply that "Integration is an objective, but it must not constitute a rupture with the mother country."[48]

European governments have reserved a leadership role for Embassy Islam within Islam Councils for the same reasons that made their leadership such palatable interlocutors in the first place—these official representatives projected a reassuring appearance of an Islam at peace with the rule of law. They come with the sending governments' implicit "guarantee" of law-abiding behavior, and they have the expertise to provide trained imams, and they have experience building and administering mosques and religious communities. Despite the pessimistic predictions regarding the inclusion of Political-Islam leaders in consultations, the reality is that they have been co-opted. They participate and grant their implicit and explicit approval of the state's religion policy without being granted full control of anything. If European governments could not countenance the direct participation of foreign government representatives in the late 1980s and early 1990s, they encouraged the transition to the use of European nationals as local Embassy-Islam personnel. Both the GMP and DİTİB adapted to French consultations (in 1992 and 2004, respectively) by replacing their diplomatic leadership with French citizens.[49] In Germany, DİTİB created the post of "dialogue commissioner" so that German officials would have someone to interface with beyond the general secretary (who is a diplomat and ex-officio counselor to the Turkish embassy in Berlin).

Embassy-Islam representatives in state-Islam consultations did not stand by quietly during the consultation process. They vigorously asserted themselves and increased their activities. They were motivated

by several fears: of losing influence within Muslim communities—
exacerbating their vulnerability to radicalization that host societies
have not adequately addressed— as well as of losing remittances, and
of losing a chance to have a voice in European institutions. Some of this
resistance was rooted in national rivalries between competing homeland governments, e.g., Moroccans or Algerians in France, or between
dominant sects and minority sects, e.g., Sunnis and Alevites in Turkey.
When the rector of the Grand Mosque of Paris rails against "fundamentalists," for example, he is sometimes just expressing his competitive
spirit vis-à-vis the rising power of Moroccans, who are numerically superior to—and more likely to attend mosques than—Algerians in France.

Embassy Islam Strikes Back

The content of "Embassy Islam" has been both multiplied and adapted
to the new circumstances of state-mosque relations. Thus, even while
homeland governments export more personnel and infrastructure, a
degree of autonomy has also been granted to national European
branches of Embassy-Islam networks, and the sending states are more
likely to work in concert with European governments. They have appointed greater numbers of European-born Muslims to executive positions, begun to address gender disparities on governing boards and
among prayer leaders, and regularly meet with rival federations in official contexts. Imams who arrive from Algeria, Morocco, Pakistan, and
Turkey now increasingly attend destination-specific civic, political, and
linguistic training courses.

Although sending states have redoubled their involvement in providing religious infrastructure in Europe—increasing the number of
imams they send and mosques they build—they no longer operate as
independent subcontractors. They have been constrained to work together with Political-Islam leaders in the Islam Councils, or they work
in cooperation with European governments on the design and content
of training for religious personnel. Thus, even while Political-Islam federations have been allowed into consultations, the prominent leadership positions in Islam Councils remain in the hands of Embassy Islam.
In 2010 as in 1990, Embassy-Islam leaders are the face and voice of
Muslim communities in European countries. If one looks at three of the
most advanced cases of state-mosque relations where a formal council
has been created—France, Germany, and Italy—the Turkish DİTİB's
"dialogue commissioner" is the only German Muslim invited to speak
at joint *Deutsche Islam Konferenz* press conferences with the interior minister; the Moroccan-endorsed RMF leader Mohamed Moussaoui succeeded the two-term Algerian-sponsored GMP leader Dalil Boubakeur

as head of the CFCM; and the Moroccan diplomat who leads Italy's Islamic Cultural Center is often the only Muslim leader invited to official government events in Rome. This reflects the general reluctance by European governments to sever ties with homeland states, despite a growing pressure to "domesticate" religious personnel and mosque financing.

The full-blown media controversies over the construction of large new mosques in Cologne and Turin in 2008–2009 raised a familiar dilemma: European governments are not able to sponsor mosques directly (although municipalities are increasingly making land available at cut rates) and communities are not yet economically independent enough to come up with the millions of euros required to construct from the ground up. As the dialogue commissioner for the Turkish DİTİB in Germany, put it, "There can be no 'German Islam' if there is no money available from the German state . . . if the Turkish state didn't pay for imam salaries, or the costs of mosque maintenance and rent, then who would?"[50] Diplomatic representatives continue to make the additional argument that Embassy Islam remains the best point of reference for immigrant communities in the diaspora:

> Until now, has the Muslim presence—this is the key question—produced an elite that is capable of administrating and taking over the financing of the [Rome Mosque]? As you can see, such a building—just at the level of the basic costs, maintenance, electricity, water, preparing the place—requires enormous funds which are beyond the means of the community. This is what explains the continuity of these ambassadors in the Administrative council . . . To be totally frank, how is Islam lived in Europe today? What I see, personally, is that many immigrants ask themselves the question "who am I" after they arrive here. Once an immigrant encounters another society which is new to him, another way of life, another way of seeing things, he starts to ask questions of identity and he finds that the first response that comes to him is religion and nation. . . . And sometimes, nationalism, sometimes belonging to a nation, belonging to a religion can give comfort.[51]

Embassy Islam stances can vary from country to country, but they share the understandable reluctance to be demoted. Algerian representatives twice delayed the elections of the French Council for the Muslim Faith and threatened to walk away or resign from the CFCM on several occasions when its influence appeared to be declining. The Turkish-sponsored DİTİB in Germany, for example, initially protested any attempt by German officials or by rival Muslim organizations to modify the DİTİB's de facto monopoly over contacts with government offices.

It declined to participate in several community organization efforts by other Muslim associations in Hamburg and Hessen in the early 2000s, and did not reply to an invitation by Bavarian authorities to join a "round table" with the state government to discuss Islamic religious instruction in public schools because two rival federations were also invited.[52] This attitude has persisted in the realm of educational privileges: Baden-Württemberg wants to introduce Islamic religion courses in twelve schools, and DİTİB is helping train the teachers, which the DİTİB spokesman said "would be impossible if other organizations were involved."[53] Even while participating in the German Islam Conference, DİTİB still seeks a monopoly over religious representation: "We suggest that the German state try recognizing DİTİB as a Corporation of Public Law and take it from there. Try the experience of making DİTİB the monopoly, the official interlocutor of the government. If every federation is going to be treated equally, what is the motivation to refuse radicalism?"[54]

The case of Saudi Arabia's de-railing of the Italian government's attempt to create a consultative body with Italian Muslims in the fall of 2001 is also instructive in this regard (although it ultimately relented and participated briefly in the *Consulta per l'Islam italiano* three years later). Gianni Letta, Prime Minister Berlusconi's undersecretary for policy, held a meeting with Mario Scialoja of MWL-Italy and the Saudi ambassador, Prince Mohammed Bin Nawaf Al Saud, to discuss the scenario. The government told the CICI to establish a representative assembly, activate their legal status as an *ente morale* (which they have had for more than three decades), and elect an administrative council, president, and vice president. But the Saudi ambassador refused. In an interview, one person involved with these discussions said:

> What the Saudis feared was a governing body within the CICI that could exert pressure to undertake certain activities and to spend money . . . Nothing is going to happen on this front unless the MWL headquarters tells the CICI "Okay, let's create an assembly of members, admit forty Italian citizens as members, and go ahead with the plan."[55]

The protectiveness of Embassy Islam undermined the Italian government's hopes of gaining a domestic institutional counterpart for Islam, and in Italy's case may have fumbled a once-in-a-generation opportunity. "We were offered an intesa on a silver platter and we blew it," said one person close to the CICI in an interview.[56] Even seven years later, following the CICI's brief participation in the *Consulta per l'Islam*, the mosque's general secretary said that "I am convinced—not out of presumption but by personal conviction, that the Grand Mosque of Rome must always be an essential reference point and an indispensible protagonist of Italian Islam."[57] When the CICI finally convened a constituent assembly eight years after 9/11, the organizers stated with pride: "It is the first time in Europe that an Islamic representative body has been created without any compromise with the fundamentalist organizations, which we purposely left out."[58]

A central objection voiced by Embassy-Islam organizations had been that consultations offered legitimacy to their sworn enemies in the context of homeland politics: the representatives of Political Islam. They insisted on the danger of granting recognition to "fundamentalists," and world events tended to reinforce their narrative, from terrorism-related incidents and arrests in Europe, but also in Iraq, Afghanistan, Indonesia, Egypt, and Morocco. The rise of regional terrorist groups in the sending countries—such as the GICM (*groupe islamique combatant marocain*), GSPC (*groupe salafiste de combat et predication*), Al Qaeda in the Maghreb (AQIM)—all reinforced the case that homeland governments made to extend their predominance over European Muslim diasporas. The increase in terrorist threats led to a resurgence of bilateral cooperation and consultation between Europeans' interior and foreign ministries, with the religion and foreign ministries of predominantly Muslim countries. European governments still prefer interlocutors and religious personnel who "see like a state." An advisor to the French interior ministry said in an interview that:

> The Algerian-supported *Grande Mosquée de Paris* argued that the consultation played into the hands of extremists, fundamentalists and therefore terrorists. His point was that "the only country that can efficiently combat terrorists was Algeria, therefore you should trust only the Mosquée de Paris." But obviously the Moroccan King says that he too is doing something in this area, and Turkey says that it too is doing something and that moreover it is an ally of the West.[59]

Another French official said, "A line of communication is open with Algiers, Tunis, Rabat, and Tripoli on the question of Muslims—we cannot do anything except rely on these states which have a certain vision of Islam in their own countries, because they are engaged in a real fight. And we are asking them to join the grand battle against terrorism."[60] A Moroccan ambassador formerly stationed in Paris and Rome told the author in an interview: "Western governments did not believe us that this would eventually be their security concern as well; now, they do."

In a demonstration of the connection between France's CFCM and its international counterterrorism policies, the Algerian and French Interior Minister exchanged visits in 2007 and 2008 in advance of CFCM elections, to discuss the GMP's participation in the elections and to discuss security cooperation.[61] The Spanish government initiated in spring 2004—within the context of reestablishing bilateral relations with Morocco—"a policy of more active cooperation with the Moroccan authorities in their search for more effective formulas to control religious activities that may lead to radicalism." When the Spanish justice minister met the Moroccan religious affairs minister in 2005, he declared his government's agenda to be the "deepening and increasing of our understanding of the Islamic community in Spain."[62] Between 2007 and 2009, the Moroccan government successfully used its good connections with the network of Moroccan communities residing abroad to position their allies in key federations in Spain (FEERI), France (RMF), and Italy (CICI) to enjoy strong support for its positions within state-mosque relations in each of these countries at the end of the decade.[63]

This reversion to an almost pre-consultation, outsourcing state of affairs more typical of the 1970s and 1980s has led some officials involved in the construction of state-mosque relations, as well as some leaders of Political Islam federations, to despair that there is no hope for a European Islam. "To say that we're going to build a French Islam," an advisor to the French interior ministry said, "all that is over now."[64] As former interior minister Jean-Pierre Chevènement put it in an interview, "the problem is that we haven't been successful in weakening the ties between the various French Muslim communities and the countries of origin which are trying to keep the influence they have in France."[65] This is in part because these states' cooperation remains necessary to combat terrorism, and in part because it is unclear what alternative sources of financing exist to pay for mosques and imams. An advisor in the Italian interior ministry said in an interview that "it is difficult in any Western country to construct a national Islam," because:

> no matter what, there will always be the influence of the country of origin. Even if you succeed in organizing the religion according to your own national rules, including from a financial perspective, with oversight of the financial flow. But there will always be this foreign influence—I can keep an eye on the 500,000 Italian Muslims who may one day pay a church tax to Islam, but who can ever tell me that money isn't also coming in from Kosovo, from Montenegro, from Saudi Arabia, from Iran? I have no way of controlling this.[66]

BACK TO SQUARE ONE?

In reality, both European and homeland governments have been complicit in extending the dominance of Embassy Islam in state-led consultations (see figure 7.4). The French and Italian officials quoted

Figure 7.4. French Interior minister Brice Hortefeux attends a ceremony to mark the breaking of the fast in Paris, 2009. Source: Thomson Reuters.

above highlight an important limitation of state organization of religious communities and the compelling reasons for continued strong relations with Embassy Islam: the requirement of international cooperation on terrorism, and the inability to cut off financing from abroad. "The fate of French Islam is not being played out in the consultation," said a leader of one of France's five grand mosques. "It is being decided in the chancelleries" of Paris.[67]

European states never intended that consultations meet the standards of direct democratic procedures: the state-Islam dialogue was always meant to be a compromise among competing interests, using indirect elections and ministerial appointments to determine the composition. But Political-Islam leaders have nonetheless expressed disappointment at the prominent role accorded to Embassy-Islam federations and homeland governments in the CFCM and the DIK. As the UOIF general secretary said in an interview in the months leading up to the creation of the CFCM:

> It's realpolitik: they prefer to deal with foreign governments rather than with organizations here. We had always known that we would have to reckon with a role for foreign states, but we never thought it would come to the point where there would be a total shift by the

French state towards foreign domination of Islam in France. There needs to be balance, that's understandable—give a little to the Moroccans, to the Algerians, but on the whole we thought there would be a decision in favor of democracy and Muslims' own choices. But that's just on paper.[68]

In Germany, the deputy general secretary of Millî Görüş argued similarly that German authorities continue to rely on Embassy Islam at the cost of legitimacy and efficiency for state-mosque relations:

How are you supposed to build national structures for Islam in Germany if you do not engage with organizations that have their headquarters here, that are organized here, that see their future in Germany? What does the German state do instead? They go to Ankara to negotiate the problems of Muslims in Germany. Just recently the NRW education minister traveled twice to Ankara to negotiate the model of religious education in NRW . . . Diyanet says "either us alone or we're not participating."[69]

A regional UOIF leader in France wrote an opinion piece arguing that the consultation project was undermined by foreign governments who place "national" and "ethnic" templates over religion during CFCM elections:

One of our Moroccan consuls in France . . . taking the lead from the French Interior minister, called in several mosque leaders for a quick lesson in geography . . . Certain consuls were even kind enough to prepare sample ballots in their offices. Talk about service to one's citizens! And on the day of the vote, other Moroccan consuls prepared a generous meal in honor of the grand electors, [. . .] but only the electors on *their* lists were invited . . . Long live moderate Islam, French Islam! . . . This Islam which is nothing but that of the consular mosques . . . So go ahead and grant more visas for the Moroccan, Algerian and Turkish imams, above all those who can't even find France on a Michelin map, who will consolidate "the moderates."[70]

The UOIF leader goes on to claim that this will endanger French-language preaching, women delegates and CRCM presidents, and inter-religious dialogue. In an interview with Dhao Meskine, the director of a French imams association in 2007, he said:

"Islam of France" is a joke. It is the Islam of Morocco, Algeria and Saudi Arabia . . . Why is it necessary to join a foreign association to be represented? I have been preaching in French since 1986, to speak to young people in their language and bring them closer to their citizenship. The Grande Mosquee de Paris still doesn't translate its Friday sermon![71]

Further evidence of the enduring role played by homeland governments in European Islam comes in the form of their continued funding to build mosques in Europe and their increased exportation of imams for rotation and Ramadan service (see table 7.2). Embassy Islam's reluctance to relinquish political control over Islam among the diaspora—and their collective realization that European governments were determined to "domesticate" Islam—led Embassy-Islam federations to frame their activities within the spirit of the state-led Europeanization movement. "One of the only advantages of a state-led consultation," a French official stated, is that it gave the homeland governments "a wake-up call: they realized that their influence and their implantation had been somewhat diminished."[72] An important transition has taken place: the gradual domestication of Embassy Islam's religious exports. There has been an intensification of bilateral cooperation between homeland governments and European states in the areas of imam training, imam importation, and security affairs. But nearly all of these initiatives are undertaken in collaboration with national authorities, who must issue travel visas and residence permits, and grant the authority to teach Islam in public schools.

European governments have created training programs to help acclimatize the newly arrived religious personnel from abroad each year, to lessen their "foreignness" and orient them to their new surroundings. The Dutch government established a complementary training program for imams arriving from abroad. Munich and Berlin have set up pilot programs between imams and local administrative officials to familiarize Islamic prayer leaders with the German school system and bureaucracy.[73] DİTİB sends imams to participate in the civic training program begun in 2007 by the French interior ministry at the Institut Catholique in Paris, and collaborates with a pre-departure training program at the German Goethe Institute in Ankara. In April 2008, the British home secretary announced a plan to bring "moderate imams" from Pakistan and Bangladesh to "counter the threat of violent extremism," claiming that this would "complement work already underway to ensure imams are firmly rooted in the communities they serve." Germany has a similar agreement with Turkey, and the Netherlands, Belgium, and France also arranged such an exchange with Morocco. The CFCM president called the program at the Institut Catholique "an important but limited experiment," given that there have been just thirty to forty

TABLE 7.2.
Recent Examples of Support for Islam in Europe by Algeria

2005: Algeria sends 29 imams and two "mourchidates" (female religious instructors) to be deployed in Algerian prayer spaces across France.[1]

2009: €490,000 for the construction of a mosque of the city of Tours; €270,000 for a mosque in Toulouse; €250,000 per annum for the administration of the Grande Mosquée de Paris; €1,000,000 for the Mosquée de Marseilles[2]

2009: Algerian Religious Affairs minister personally gives instructions to Algerian Imams in a meeting held at the Grande Mosquée de Paris; he asked the group to dedicate their Friday khutba before the April 4–9 vote to "raise the awareness of Algerian voters" about the upcoming election. This marks the first time Algerian mosques in France have been "officially solicited to play a political role." The government spends €6 Million on get-out-the-vote effort in France, sponsoring buses leaving from community associations and more than doubling the number of polling places in France to 134.[3]

2009: Algerian foreign affairs ministry instructs consulates in Europe to "offer aid and assistance" to help the "Algerian diaspora assert itself in host countries"; an Algerian consul general in France convenes Algerian associations "to tell them what Algeria expects of them."[4]

2010: Algerian religious affairs minister announces that 52 imams and an unspecified number of "mourchidates" (female religious instructors) would be sent to France on missions of "orientation, education and culture" for the Muslim community.[5]

---

[1] *Liberté* Rédaction, "29 imams algériens à pied d'oeuvre," *Liberté*, 2005.

[2] Qattab, "L'Islam en France: Le Maroc et l'Algérie à couteaux tirés," *Le Soir Échos*, 2009.

[3] The 776,000 Algerian voters residing in France (out of an Algerian electorate of 20 million) have been a target of information campaigns from the country's embassies and consulates in the past, and 2010 was no exception. There were new efforts aimed at reducing the inconvenience of travelling to vote (only one-third of the million or so Algerian voters abroad bothered to vote in legislative elections in 2007, down from 43% in 2004). The effort is also conceived, one assumes, to reduce Islamist penetration of the diaspora vote (familiar to Moroccan and Turkish governments as well). In 1997, the first time Algerians abroad could vote in consular stations, the MSP/Hamas-Algeria candidate Mahfoud Nahnah was the winner —at least in Strasbourg, Nice and Grenoble—coming in well ahead of the national victor Liamine Zeroual. The novelty in spring 2009 were the It's unclear whether the efforts paid — even though Bouteflika improved his national score to 90 percent from 85 percent in 2004.

[4] website,OrganisationdelaDiasporaalgérienne.http://www.mnr-nord.com/actualites-monde/organisation-de-la-diaspora-algerienne.html.

[5] "52 imams algériens seront envoyés en France en mission spéciale," Atlasinfo.fr, 26 May 2010, http://www.atlasinfo.fr/52-imams-algeriens-seront-envoyes-en-France-en-mission-speciale_a3625.html?preaction=nl&id=13864685&idnl=68949&

students per semester (out of circa 1,800 imams). "The new generation has a hard time engaging in dialogue with foreign imams," said CFCM President Mohamed Moussaoui in an interview. "Therefore we need to train them on site, in France." Nonetheless, he said that exchanges would continue and include reciters of the Qur'ân, for example, who carry on an "artistic tradition" and "fill a void" in French Islam.[74] The fact that governments continue to import imams reflects the difficulty of hiring locally trained imams who are considered legitimate by local European Muslim communities, and who are willing and able to work for the relatively low wages that these congregations can afford to pay.[75]

MOROCCO

The Moroccan government has tried to influence religious developments abroad—the 3.2 million abroad constitute 10 percent of the total Moroccan population—by sponsoring mosques and Arab language instructors, and nurturing relationships with key Moroccan nationals residing abroad. King Muhammad VI (1999–) has pursued an activist policy of exporting the kingdom's religious practices, including the annual delegations of imams and Qur'ân reciters sent throughout Europe as well as a new Ulama Council for Europe in Brussels—a group of learned religious scholars who aim to influence religious observance by Moroccans in Europe. Armed with a budget of circa 12 million euros, a handful of institutions in the Moroccan capital, Rabat, offer support and guidance for the religious practices of MREs: the Hassan II Foundation, the Ministry for *Habous* and Religious Affairs, the Ministry for Moroccans Living Abroad (located within the foreign ministry), and the Council for the Morocan Community Abroad (CCME, see figure 7.5).

A "restructuration" of the religious affairs ministry in 2005 led to an increase in the exportation of religious personnel (see table 7.3). In 2005, King Mohammed VI announced the creation of a Council of the Moroccan Community Abroad (*Conseil de la communauté marocaine de l'étranger*, or CCME) which would hold conferences and publish books on best practices of Islam in Europe, from mosques and imam training to the religion's legal status in host societies. The Hassan II Foundation announced a program "in continuous expansion" to locate imams and preachers from Moroccan universities, grand mosques, and civil service.[76] In 2004, Morocco sent only twelve year-round imams to Europe— mostly from Moroccan universities—of whom four resided in France.[77] In 1998, 60 preachers were sent, but by 2009, this number increased to 206 imams (both seasonal and temporary) in addition to hundreds of language instructors.[78]

Figure 7.5. Islam in Europe Conference sponsored by the *Conseil de la communauté marocaine à l'étranger* in Casablanca, 2008. Source: CCME.

TURKEY

The *Diyanet İşleri Başkanliği* (DİB) has also pursued the international-ization of Turkish religious activities in an effort to expand Turkish in-fluence over the country's European diaspora (see figure 7.6). DİB has funded chairs of theology departments in a handful of European univer-sities, trained teachers in religious education, and developed religious curriculum for use in European schools.[79] At a 2004 conference, DİB leaders adopted a policy of "preference for Turkish religion teachers over European teachers, and for religion lessons conducted in Turkish over lessons conducted in any other language" and resolved to "in-crease the quota of Turkish imams and muftis overseas."[80] At a DİB conference in Ankara in September 2004, Turkish Prime Minister Recep Tayyip Erdoğan proclaimed his ambition that the European branches of DİTİB would one day "be accepted as the EU's only partner on related issues" in recognition of the "leading role played by Turkey

TABLE 7.3.
Recent Examples of Support for Islam in Europe by Morocco

2004: Moroccan King MVI helps fund €4 million Mosque in Clichy[1]

2004: 179 teachers selected to work with Hassan II Foundation, to be sent to work with Turkish communities in Belgium (71), France (66), Italy (30), Spain (10), and Germany (2)[2]

2004: Three representatives from FEERI federation in Spain are invited to Moroccan Religious Affairs Ministry, leading to the "Mixed Commission of Cooperation and Advice on Religious Affairs"[3]

2006: Morocco sent 100 imams to Europe accompanied by unknown number of "reciters" of the Holy Qur'ân— France, Italy, Spain, Germany, Belgium, Netherlands, and Scandinavian countries[4]

2008: Morocco invites 40 imams from the Netherlands— approximately one-quarter of all imams in the country— on a government-paid trip to Morocco to support the spread of moderate, Moroccan Islam[5]

2008: Morocco announces the creation of Moroccan cultural centers in Germany and other European countries to improve Arabic language instruction for the children of Moroccans: "this will consolidate the presence in host societies of authentic Moroccan culture founded on the values of moderation, dialogue, and openness[6]

2008: Morocco sends artisans to help build a mosque in the city of Créteil (France)[7]

2008: Morocco sends 176 imams to Europe for Ramadan: 100 to France, 31 to Belgium, 7 to the Netherlands, the rest to Denmark, Sweden, Norway, Switzerland, and the UK: to "answer the religious needs of the Moroccan community abroad, to protect it from any speeches of extremism or irregular nature, and to shelter it from extremism and fanaticism," according to the religious affairs ministry in Rabat;[8]

2008: Council of the Moroccan Community Residing Abroad (CCME) holds its first meeting with the Moroccan Prime Minister presiding in February; the CCME's plenary assembly meets in June 2008 in Rabat, with 37 members including 31 from Europe (1 from Germany, 3 from Belgium, 5 from Spain, 14 from France, 2 from Italy, 4 from Netherlands, 1 from UK, 1 from DK).[9]

2008: Moroccan government reportedly allocates €50,000 to campaign for favored candidates in CFCM and CRCM elections in each of twenty-five electoral districts in France[10]

2009: First meeting of the official Moroccan Ulama Council for Europe to offer religious interpretations and train imams and female religious leaders in each host country; to offer a religious structure for the holy month of Ramadan, and contribute to the selection of imams and female religious leaders sent by Morocco to Europe[11]

(continued)

TABLE 7.3. *cont.*

Recent Examples of Support for Islam in Europe by Morocco

2009: Moroccan government transfers funds to Italian Muslim Association to finance a new mosque in Turin (in the Piedmont region of northeast Italy) at a cost of nearly €2 million.

2009–2010: Council of the Moroccan Community Residing Abroad (CCME) organizes a March conference in Fes on "the legal statute of Islam in Europe, convening Moroccan foreign ministry officials, French interior ministry officials, and CFCM president.[12] The CCME organizes two conferences: "Languages in Immigration: Changes and New Challenges" in Rabat, and the "First Forum of Young Moroccans of the World" in Ifrane (in cooperation with the Ministry of the Moroccan Community Living Abroad)[13]

---

[1] *Le Parisien*, "Enfin une mosquée à Clichy," *Le Parisien, Marocain du Monde*, 2004.

[2] L'Economiste, "MRE: Enseignement de la langue arabe et de la culture marocaine," *l'Economiste* and MAP (Maghreb Arab Press), 2004.

[3] Arigita, "Represnting Islam in Spain," 2006, 563–84, 573.

[4] Gadi, "100 prédicateurs," *Le Matin*, 2006.

[5] Hes, "Morocco invites at least 40 imams for visit," *Expatica.com*, 2008.

[6] el Ghissassi, "Le gouvernement marocain pour la création de centres culturels en Europe," Sezamemag.net, 2008.

[7] *Le Parisien*, "Islam de France: La mosquée de Créteil prête pour accueillir les fidèles dès le mois du Ramadan, " 2008 (just three years after creating an Ulama Council for Morocco).

[8] Belga press agency, "176 marokkaanse Predikanten naar Europa," 2008.

[9] el Ghissassi, "Première Assemblée plénière du Conseil de la comunauté Marocaine à l'étranger," 2008.

[10] Yahmid, "Countries Fight Over French Muslims," 2008.

[11] el Ghissassi, "Principaux axes du programme 2009 du Conseil marocain des ouléma pour l'Europe," www.sezamemag.net, January 30, 2009.

[12] Chartier, "Du rififi au Conseil français du culte musulman," l'Express, 2009.

[13] http://www.atlasinfo.fr/Le-CCME-organise-une-conference-internationale-sur-le-theme-Langues-en-immigration-mutations-et-nouveaux-enjeux_a5017.html?preaction=nl&id=13864685&idnl=70607&; http://www.atlasinfo.fr/Maroc-1er-Forum-des-Jeunes-Marocains-du-Monde-les-27-et-28-juillet_a6749.html?preaction=nl&id=13864685&idnl=72241&

in the Islamic world." The conference adopted a policy of "preference for Turkish religion teachers over European teachers, and for religion lessons to be conducted in Turkish over lessons conducted in any other language"; they also resolved to "increase the quota of Turkish imams and muftis overseas" and that the organization should ensure there is "at least one Islamic cleric in the catchment area of each consulate."[81]

There is a great potential for tensions between European governments, who are actively "domesticating" their state-mosque relations,

Figure 7.6. The Turkish Minister for Turks living abroad, the chairman of the office for religious affairs in Turkey, and Cologne's mayor take part in the ceremony for laying the foundation stone for a DİTİB mosque in Cologne, Germany, 2009. Source: AP Photo/Hermann J. Knippertz.

and sending states who seek to retain influence over immigrant-origin populations in Europe. A 2006 German Embassy memorandum indicates that the DİB in Ankara voiced dissatisfaction with a German state government's decision to train instructors for religious education:

> Although the *Diyanet* is open to bilateral cooperation in education with German government offices, it has not been satisfied with the [German creation of education programs] for religion teachers . . . The appointment of [the director] in Münster was difficult for *Diyanet* to accept [. . .] The job "should have gone to" a Hanafi Turk,

since these constitute the majority of Muslims in Germany [. . .] the cooperation with the Osnabrück Hochschule for the training of Islamic culture teachers was also unsatisfactory for *Diyanet* . . . the previously intensive cooperation with Turkey was reduced to a measly two-week excursion in Turkey [. . .] *Diyanet* accused Germany of ignoring the needs of the majority of Muslims under the mantel of a German desire for "pluralism."[82]

The author of the German Embassy memorandum interprets Ankara's creation of an international theology faculty aimed at Turks abroad as a "a reaction to what *Diyanet* views as insufficient religious educational cooperation in target countries of Turkish migration."[83]

DİTİB is a key partner of the federal government in the *Deutsche Islam Konferenz*, and *Diyanet* sponsors two theology professors at Goethe–University of Frankfurt. Since 2006, the German government has arranged for hundreds of these Turkish imams to receive preparation before departing for Germany. The *Goethe Institut* provides German-language instruction, and the *Konrad Adenauer Stiftung* (affiliated with the majority Christian Democratic Union) conducts acculturation courses. In cooperation with the German Islam Conference, the government has recently added local Imam civic training programs in Munich, Berlin, Frankfurt, and Stuttgart that have attracted hundreds of participants.[84] This and related developments will likely further weaken the position in Germany of the Turkish directorate of religious affairs (*Diyanet*) and its local branch (DİTİB). The German government has announced an imam seminary program in cooperation with four universities—Tübingen, Münster, und Osnabrück and one other to be announced—but excluding DİTİB. Up to five hundred new students could be enrolled in academic courses aimed at training imams and Islamic religious teachers by September 2011 (see table 7.4).[85]

Despite the experience of working together, sending states' resistance to Europeans' taking matters into their own hands is still palpable. When imam training in four German universities was announced in 2010, the *Diyanet* vice president regretted that his organization was not consulted. When asked why he thought Turkey was being excluded from the project, he ventured that "Germany has been in a phase of cultural decline, and it is not good for the country to give in to its fears."[86] The journalist then inquired whether Germany might simply be copying the Turkish model of imposing state control over imam training; the official said: "There is no state control of Islam in Turkey. Knowledge is the basis of our content, not politics." The German government, like others, is looking to inject *national German culture* into the basis of religious content, as well. Adding insult to injury for the DİTİB,

TABLE 7.4.
Recent Examples of Support for Islam in Europe by Turkey

2002: The Goethe Institute in collaboration with the German embassy and *Diyanet* offer a 400- or 600-hour German language course to imams preparing to depart for Germany.[1] 50 took part in pilot project in 2006, all 100 who are being sent to Germany after training will take part in the intensive course in German language and culture in 2007.[2]

2003: The Turkish Directorate for Religious Affairs (DİB) allocated funds to finance two chairs (*Lehrstühle*)[3] in Islamic theology at Frankfurt's Goethe University (the first such positions in Germany) in the Protestant Theology department.[4] The aim is to transform this center to a degree program for Islamic theology.[5]

2003: Ridvan Çakir, Religious Affairs and Education Attaché at Turkish Embassy, becomes Germany DİTİB President for three-year appointment; he earlier served as advisor to DİB president in Ankara for 15 years.[6]

2003: Former advisor to *Diyanet* president for 15 years is named Religious Affairs and Education Attaché at Turkish Embassy in Germany and Chairman of DİTİB-Germany.

2005: Religion attaché of the Turkish Consulate signs contract with a Berlin police precinct organizes "crash course" on Islam, and invites the police into the local DİTİB mosque to speak about petty crime in the neighborhood.[7]

2006: The International Theology Program is established for German high school graduates (Abitur/Fachabitur)—25 in 2006; First class to graduate in 2010—are given lodging and 200TL/month to attend institute of theology at the University of Ankara. Turkish citizens follow coursework in Ankara, while German citizens go to Istanbul.

2006: DİTİB helped train teachers for religious education courses in Baden-Württemberg and in discussions with NRW, Niedersachsen, Hessen, Bavaria, and Berlin. Similarly, the directorate assumes the annual cost for (Turkish-trained) teachers' salaries in specific *Länder*, where it is entrusted with Islamic education in public schools, e.g., Bavaria, Lower Saxony, and Baden Württemburg.

2006: First class of 50 imams participates in program formed between DİB and the Konrad Adenauer Stiftung with up to 100 participants per year, a week-long (37.5 hours) national orientation for imams, "to learn German language and culture, constitution, health social and educational customs, Christian churches, and live in a multi-religious society";[8] the first class of 50 entered Germany in 2006.[9]

(continued)

TABLE 7.4. *cont.*

Recent Examples of Support for Islam in Europe by Turkey

2006: The Minister Counselor for Religious Affairs from Turkish embassy in Sweden brought in as new chairman of DİTİB-Germany: "to achieve the unity of the Turkish citizens living in Germany."[10]

2007: DİTİB Germany's "dialogue commissioner" Bekir Alboğa is invited to EU's European Values Summit in Brussels to meet with EU Commission President Barroso, current EU president and German Chancellor Angela Merkel, and European Parliament president Hans-Gert Pöttering.

2008: German Interior Minister Schäuble met with DİB President Bardakoğlu and "requested [DİB] send educated imams to Germany to provide religious services to Turks and Muslims in the country."[11] Turkey announced it would send 110 imams to Germany, Austria, Belgium, Switzerland and the Netherlands and other European countries; receive six-month language courses in German, and 20 are taking Dutch courses four days a week onsite in the Netherlands.

2008: DİB restructures "its subordinate bodies in European countries" and announces plans to open "various training centers in countries with significant Turkish and Muslim populations."[12]

2008: DİTİB France (CCMTF) meeting with 47 board members, chaired by *Diyanet* president. The Religion Counselor to Turkish embassy in Paris, is reelected as president of DİTİB-France.

2008: Turkey announces it will send 110 additional imams to Germany, Austria, Belgium, Switzerland, and the Netherlands.

2008: French government ministers visit *Diyanet* in Ankara and invite Turkey's cooperation in establishing Islamic theology program. Department of theology would be co-established together with a Turkish theology department in Strasbourg modeled on Frankfurt's Goethe University.

2008: Diyanet sends 20 imams to civic education courses organized at the Institut Catholique de Paris by the French Interior ministry.

2008: German interior minister meets with *Diyanet* President Bardakoğlu and "requested [DİB] send educated imams to Germany to provide religious services to Turks and Muslims in the country."

2008: Dutch government organizes Dutch-language courses four days/week onsite in the Netherlands for 20 *Diyanet* Imams in 2008.

2008: 17 participants graduate from German integration course run by DİTİB's Education and Culture Administration with the cooperation of Bundesamtes für Migration und Flüchtlinge.

(continued)

Table 7.4. *cont.*
Recent Examples of Support for Islam in Europe by Turkey

2008: Diyanet announces restructuring of "its subordinate bodies in European countries . . . planning to open various training centers in countries with significant Turkish and Muslim populations.

2008: Turkey's Ambassador to Germany met with the attachés from 13 consular regions at DİTİB's Berlin offices. The ambassador stated: "We have to adopt to changing times. It is important for the Turkish citizens to speak German along with their mother tongue in order to protect their interests."

2009: 121 DİTİB imams reportedly active in France, up from (71 in 2005).[13]

2009: Turkey's Religious Affairs Directorate opens an office in Brussels with five secretaries and 30 theologians "to educate Europe about Islam, to block efforts to sow misunderstandings about Islam." This office, "primarily targeting Turks living in Europe," was conceived at a meeting with Pope Benedict XVI during his 2005 visit to Turkey.[14]

2009: Duisberg: DİTİB assumes circa €3 million of costs of €7.5 million project, thus coining the "Duisberger model": DİTİB was joined by representatives of political parties, churches, and civil society organizations.[15] The Cologne mosque, largest in Germany and one of Europe's grandest, began construction in 2010; it was "primarily funded by private donations from more than 800 families to the Cologne-based DİTİB.[16]

2009: Mannheim Kindergarten sponsored by DİTİB, "to bring children into kindergarten earlier"— approved by youth ministry of local government; 40 students per year.[17]

2009: DİB co-sponsors "Turks Abroad: Symposium on Migration and Integration in its 50th year" in Ankara.

2009: Hessen's Minister of Justice and Integration in Hessen announces that Islam Theology Department to educate teachers of Islam Religion courses in Frankfurt's Goethe University will be financed by state of Hessen. *Diyanet* and Frankfurt University concluded an agreement on initiating this program; DİB President Ali Bardakoğlu signed the agreement.[18]

2009: DİTİB is training honorary "mosque guides" in Germany under a new program called "ProDialog." As an initial step, in Berlin 30 voluntary mosque guides received their certificates. This project is also supported by European Investment Fund and the Bundesamt für Migration und Flüchtlinge (BAMF). The goal is to have three guides working in each of the 900 mosques managed by DİTİB by the end of 2010.[19]

2009: In the city of Dortmund seventeen DİTİB imams began a year-long German language course that will meet for 768 contact hours. The Turkish general consul in the area said that "it is our wish that our countrymen get much

(continued)

TABLE 7.4. *cont.*
Recent Examples of Support for Islam in Europe by Turkey

closer to German society." Roughly 77 imams will take the course in the coming year.[20]

2009: In Nuremberg's city hall, fifteen DİTİB imams began a 500-hour course in state, society, migration and religious diversity. Officials expect 130 to take the course over the coming year.[21]

2009: DİTİB encourages current employees to attend German courses and follows up on their progress. Sadi Arslan, DİTİB-Germany President and Religious Services Secretary of the Turkish Embassy in Berlin, organized a meeting to highlight these efforts.

2009: Director of *Diyanet* international relations department (Dr. Ali Dere) named new Chairman of DİTİB-Germany.

2009: İsmail Ertuğ, SPD member and local DİTİB spokesman, elected in 2009 European Parliament elections.

2010: "DİTİB State Union" in Munster Region in the state of North Rhine Westphalia organized a consultation meeting with the presidents and managers of regional branches. Munster Consulate Gürsel Evren, DİTİB President Sadi Arslan, Educational Attaché Ali Çevik, Religious Services Attaché Reşat Üstün, DİTİB General Manager V. Reşat Üstün, Munster State Union President Veli Fırtına, and other branch representatives attended. Educational Attaché Çevik gave a briefing about the Turkish-language classes, noting that the courses will be henceforth be referred to as "language of origin" courses instead of "mother tongue."[22]

2010: Creation of Presidency for Turks Abroad in Ankara; Gala Inaugural Event for 1500 religion and civil society leaders from Europe and elsewhere.

2010: DİTİB-Munster Region (NRW) meeting with presidents and managers of regional branches including Turkish Consul, DİTİB President, Educational Attaché, Religious Services Attaché, DİTİB General Manager, DİTİB-Munster President Veli Fırtına, and other branch representatives attended. The Turkish-language will be henceforth be referred to as "language of origin" courses instead of "mother tongue."

2010: Prime Minister Erdoğan proposes a major expansion of Turkish-language high schools in Germany.

2010: More than 800 DİTİB imams reportedly active in Germany.

[1] Spiewak, "Vorbeter aus der Fremde," *Die Zeit*, 2006.
[2] Mirza, "Interview with Hasan Karaca," 2007.
[3] Acikgöz, "College Launches Disputed Islamic Program," 2005.
[4] Ibid.

(continued)

Table 7.4. *cont.*
Recent Examples of Support for Islam in Europe by Turkey

[5] Cakir and Bozan, *Sivil, Seffaf ve Demokratik Bir Diyanet Isleri Baskanligi Mumkun Mu?* [Is a Civil, Transparent, and Democratic 'Presidency of Religious Affairs' Possible?], 2005, 91.

[6] Gibbons, "Diyanet, Bardakoğlu and more," 2006.

[7] Wutschke, "Crash-Kurs im Islam," 2007.

[8] Teschner, "Imame sind wichtige Vermittler," 2006.

[9] Nohl, "Evaluation der Landeskunde für Imame," 2006.

[10] *Hürriyet*, "Amtsperiode von Sadi Arslan bei DİTİB," 2006.

[11] Yavuz, "German Culture Center trains Turkish Imams for Europe," 2008.

[12] Ibid.

[13] Saphir News, "100 mosquées attendent encore leurs imams," 2009.

[14] Dunya Gazetesi, "New Religious Affairs Directorate office to work to dispel misunderstanding of Islam in Europe," 2009.

[15] Taxacher, "Miteinander in Duisburg-Marxloh: Deutschlands größte Moschee," Goethe Institute, March 2, 2009.

[16] Canadian Broadcasting Corporation, "Largest mosque in Germany to be ready by 2010," CBC News, 2008.

[17] Vorhaben eines türkischen Vereins in Mannheim stößt auf Bedenken—Goll befürwortet Projekt," DDP, March 3, 2009.

[18] Ismail Kul, State of Hessen will finance the Islam Theology College, *Euro Zaman*, 09 Nov 2009.

[19] Fahri cami rehberleri İslam'ı ve Türk kültürünü anlatacak (Honorary mosque guides will explain Islam and Turkish Culture), *Cihan News Agency (CNA)*, 14 December 2009.

[20] http://www.derwesten.de/nachrichten/wr/2009/11/13/news-140656111/detail.html.

[21] http://www.welt.de/die-welt/politik/article5494936/Imame-sollen-Vorbilder-fuer-ihre-Gemeinden-sein.html.

[22] Özcan Yüceer, Having unified state branches will allow DİTİB to use its powers more efficiently, *Euro Zaman*, 21 January 2010.

in 2010 a wealthy private foundation announced funding to support the training of Islamic theologians—a cooperative project involving six public universities that did not invite official Turkish participation.[87]

In 2010, Ankara signaled its intention to tighten its hold on religious and other diaspora affairs among emigrants by establishing a new government ministry which is expected to eventually also encompass the foreign activities of Diyanet. The government introduced a new "Presidency for Turks Living Abroad" in early 2010. With approximately one hundred employees, this new department in the prime minister's office will "address to follow up on the problems of our citizens living abroad, to improve our relations with consanguineous and related communities, to cooperate with civil society organizations." The minister Faruk Çelik summarized his duties: "Five million Turks live in Europe and they have different problems . . . Now we are creating a body which can address all the problems."[88] In March 2010, the new ministry for Turks abroad hosted 1,500 Turkish civil society leaders living in Europe at a conference in Istanbul.[89] Çelik has also pursued legislation to restructure the DİB and limit the terms of its president to five years.[90]

A Changed Playing Field

In the year 2010, most adult Muslims in contemporary Europe are still third country nationals, and thus a degree of foreign government involvement in their religious lives is to be expected. This is especially foreseeable when the foreign governments in question have an "official" religion in place at home. The gradual transformation and adaptation of Embassy Islam, however, is a significant element of what this book has referred to as "the partial emancipation"—in contrast to "full emancipation"—of Europe's Muslims.

Even as the integration of second, third, and fourth generations progresses, European governments will still need the cooperation, expertise, and support of the former sending states. This practice of relying on Embassy Islam does not necessarily have the same adverse integration effects of earlier outsourcing. The willingness of foreign governments to adapt to the use of European languages and imam training programs, in concert with host states, will pose fewer integration issues. And indeed, Embassy Islam has its advantages: They are uniquely placed to contribute to Islam's "normalization" in many European cities in several ways. Foreign governments can afford the construction of visible and dignified prayer spaces, and they can help coordinate the training of imams who are versed in European languages and cultures. Their cooperation with European authorities can build up a transparent religious infrastructure that earns greater acceptance from host societies.

Embassy Islam's hierarchical structure and law-abiding nature has also had a net positive effect on Islam Councils' stability. The notable exception is in the United Kingdom, where the absence of a strong state Islam in Pakistan, for example, has led to a more chaotic organizational environment in British state-mosque relations. The reliance on Embassy Islam is a logical short- and medium-term solution to the lack of prayer spaces and imams in Europe, but this practice could lead to complacency by European governments and the entrenchment of new drawbacks. In particular, the persistent involvement of Embassy Islam constitutes an attempted usurpation of Europeans' efforts to build "national Islams" by way of state-mosque consultations.

The homeland governments' *droit d'ingérence* (right of intervention) will become more legally and politically tenuous over time as their outreach targets mostly European citizens and not their own nationals. Future generations of European Muslims have fewer direct ties to their ancestral homelands (and hold only a European citizenship). Another exception to this is the civil liberties implications: the continued oversight of Muslim communities by the consulates and embassies of sending states can often surpass straightforward security concerns, and nonviolent reformists can get caught up in this net of surveillance and, occasionally, persecution. Foreign intervention by former "sending states" delays the true "domestication" of European Islam, and thus retards the integration of Muslims in Europe. It may also interfere with the development of the independent, reformed practice of Islam in a European context.

Conclusion

Both Embassy-Islam and Political-Islam federations have adapted and competed in the new political opportunity structure of state-mosque relations. Despite homeland governments' increased activism, they have an incentive to couch their activities within the broad framework of Islam Councils that European governments have established. Embassy-Islam and Political-Islam leaders have come to realize that their fortunes may wax and wane over time and that to participate in state-mosque relations requires an investment of resources. But to withdraw totally would be to forego manifold opportunities for control and influence over the practice of Islam in Europe.

The preliminary evidence suggests that Political-Islam federations have been changed through their participation in Islam Councils. As they have been brought into state-led consultations, they have mellowed. They are now on familiar terms with the administrators whom they negotiate with as well as with their once bitter rivals from the sphere of Embassy Islam (see figure 7.7). Their leaders have been received in the style of government ministers, their organizations' membership ranks have been strengthened, and they have gained more access to decision-making and resources. Before Political-Islam federations were granted equal footing in state-Islam consultations, European administrators characterized them as confrontational and unrealistically demanding. Now, they are more oriented toward institutions and domestic politics. To the extent that Political-Islam federations have engaged in the "public defense of Islam"—promoting religious practices, objecting to the perceived defamation of the Prophet or their religion, etc.— their repertoire of collective action is close to that used by Catholic and Jewish representatives.[91]

Figure 7.7. A Visit of the Turkish State Minister for Citizens Abroad to *Millî Görüş* headquarters in Germany, 2010. Source: IGMG, e.V.; www.igmg.de.

Political-Islam federations across Europe gained tangible advantages from their strategy of participation. In Germany, the IGMG was provisionally invited as a working group member (though not as one of the fifteen official delegates) of the *Deutsche Islam Konferenz* in 2006.[92] The Muslim-Brotherhood affiliated UOIF and UCOII federations have similarly been rewarded for their cooperative behavior with powerful institutional positions: respectively, the vice presidency of the CFCM in France, and briefly, a seat on the Consulta in Italy.

Sometimes, the transformation has been a personal one. Upon the knighting of Salman Rushdie in 2007, the former Muslim Council of Britain leader, Inayat Bunglawala, wrote wistfully of his hotheaded days nearly two decades earlier: "I used to be a book burner, but now I think the freedom to offend is a necessary freedom."[93] In an interview in 2007 with Lhaj Thami Brèze— the French Islamist leader who had been quoted as saying that "the Qur'ân is our constitution" four years earlier—he cited twentieth-century British and French statesmen in a demonstration of his European political acumen: "We do not want to be manipulated by either the French government or by foreign governments. Otherwise 'this thing isn't worth anything,' as Charles de Gaulle once said [about the UN]." Speaking of the internal regulations and voting rules of the CFCM, Brèze alluded to Winston Churchill's aphorism on democracy: "We need to find the least worst system."[94]

Some French Muslim leaders who opted out of government consultations offer more cynical explanations for their colleagues' personal transformations. Dhao Meskine, a French leader of an independent imam federation and the founder of a privately funded Muslim primary school, suggested in an interview that politicians were manipulating the mosque federations. "CFCM leaders received an informal order from the Interior Ministry saying 'do not participate in the demonstrations against the caricatures,' and the CFCM federations obeyed," he said.[95] Abdelaziz Chaambi, the founder of a youth group in Lyon, argued in an interview that federation leaders were quietly and personally rewarded for their cooperative attitude: "all the so-called 'privileged interlocutors' of the state got their papers and citizenship from one day to the next."[96]

Another criticism commonly leveled against the Islam Councils is that authorities are naïve to believe that Political-Islam leadership has sincerely changed its tune. A 2007 report by Dutch authorities, for example, argues that any behavioral modification by Islamists is inherently disingenuous.[97] Beneath these organizations' apparent calm and moderation, the report says, they aim for "Islamization through cohabitation," while secretly building a well-organized and strongly religious Islamic national infrastructure. The warning not to be fooled by these organizations' renunciation of terrorism is common to skeptics of Islamist moderation, who see feigned moderation or the practice of *taqiyya* (i.e., dissimulation masking their true designs). These movements' avoidance of violence, they say, only demonstrates a cynical awareness "that the use of violence can shock potential members and trigger repressive action from above."[98] Muslim Brotherhood organizations may not "resort to or advocate violence to achieve these goals" and they may have "chosen to work within the system and the legal framework"—but for critics, it is this subversive quality that allows them to pass under democratic society's weak radars.[99]

While the achievement of political moderation among Political-Islam leaders is not a foregone conclusion, significant evidence weighs in favor of neo-corporatism's transformative powers through institutional incentives. The effects of a neo-corporatist opportunity structure are visible in the form of behavioral modification that took place within everyday negotiations of the consultations themselves. As the director of an Islamic cultural center in Bologna put it, "I realize the comparison could seem inappropriate but for us the UCOII is like a trade union— there are no terrorists in there. . . . We simply want to be an association recognized by the local Prefecture, with access to the church-tax [enjoyed by other religious groups]."[100] The striking change in organizational behavior has been such that the French director of the *Bureau central des cultes* could refer in an interview to the UOIF as an "Islamic equivalent" to the institutionalized French Communist trade union, the *Confédération générale du travail* (CGT).[101] This same official made an argument suggesting the process of institutionalization was well under way: "The Muslim Brotherhood in general, and the UOIF in particular, are developing a strategy of taking over the institutional apparatus—in order to access power—which dominates all else. For them, it is less important to resolve problems or propose solutions than to put their men in the right places." [102] Even the CFCM president elected in 2008, Mohamed Moussaoui—who has close ties to the Moroccan government and could thus be expected to consider the UOIF as fundamentalist—said in an interview with the author, "It's better to have all the tendencies together in the CFCM than outside. The UOIF is not so different from other federations, their claims, their declarations, respect the broad orientations of the organization."[103] "The more Islam is 'officialized,'" French security officials told a journalist, "the more moderate it has been."[104]

The use of corporatism has engendered more "responsible" political behavior from participating mosque federations. The question of whether the findings are endogenous to the model is worth asking—i.e., those who participate in state consultations by definition must accept government rules and norms—but it should also be recalled that participation in a state-sanctioned Islam Council is no guarantee of docility. Indeed, there are ample incentives for political entrepreneurs to buck the system to earn street credibility and gain an advantage over competing federations. This is a key insight from the literature on neo-corporatism and government relations with trade unions and agricultural groups; when the latter were displeased with their councils, they would storm away from the round table, hold street demonstrations, or even spill their wares on the highway to slow traffic.

The influence of state-Islam consultations—or, indeed, even the *possibility* of being chosen for government consultation—has had a moderating effect on Political-Islam federations and thus contributed to the overall transition of "partial emancipation." This adaptation can be partly explained by religious leaders' new position as stakeholders in an institutional process: they now have something tangible to lose, i.e., the patina of respectability that undergirds their privileged partnership with the state. Islamists should be judged by their actions, Olivier Roy has argued, not their intentions: "wondering about these actors' sincerity is naïve because they are essentially politicians and politics has nothing in common with sincerity."[105] Political-Islam leaders have repeatedly declined to engage in inflammatory or ambiguous rhetoric and instead have demonstrated an interest in keeping hold over administrative gains in the anodyne realm of technical state-mosque relations. Governments would have far less leverage over any of these organizations in the absence of this incentive structure for political moderation.

CHAPTER EIGHT

Muslim Integration and European Islam in the Next Generation

THIS BOOK HAS PROVIDED a comparative study in the management of religious—and especially Islamic—conflict by exploring the policies that European governments have adopted in response to the presence of growing numbers of Muslims in their territories. The resulting portrait in the preceding chapters offers a model for understanding the development of state-mosque relations in Belgium France, Germany, Italy, Netherlands, Spain and the UK, and develops a typology of Islam's institutionalization, politicization, and exportation in Algeria, Morocco, Pakistan, Saudi Arabia, and Turkey. The evidence supports a cautiously optimistic view regarding the successful incorporation of Muslim minorities, but also shows how the presence of Islamic communities is affecting the long-standing relationship between state and society in Europe. The ways in which these relationships are negotiated reveals both the multifaceted goals of governments and the dilemmas they confront when they seek to integrate new groups into policymaking. European states are engaged in a complicated minuet both with the foreign "homeland" governments, on whom they once depended for help with these matters, and with domestic Islamic communities, whose fragmentation and intransigent demands initially stood in the way of simple solutions. Tracing the process whereby successive governments in Western European nations stumbled toward institutional solutions to these challenges illuminates the complexity of the issues. This book has sought to untangle this narrative and convey the significance of state-mosque relations in Europe for Muslims' emancipation.

In the years 1990–2010, European governments began in earnest to confront the responsibility of integrating the sixteen million Muslims who now call the continent home. State-mosque relations are of vital importance because these institutional links with religious communities prepare the ground for long-term political integration. Transnational religious networks left unattended, as they were in the first period of "outsourcing," have the potential to threaten the state and its maintenance of social order. By taking the initiative to incorporate and nationalize Islam in their respective institutional orders, European states have attempted to influence what kind of Islam the next generation of

Muslims will encounter —whether they search out religion for spiritual reasons, as a reaction against European societies, or to satisfy curiosity about their heritage, or to carry on family traditions. Governments considered the unintended consequences of their previous laissez-faire strategies in state-mosque relations and took stock of unanticipated developments among the immigrant populations. Of course, these populations did not "go home" and the networks of embassies and NGOs whose religious activities and proselytism European governments had uncritically tolerated for fifteen years turned out to be more tenacious than expected. But the strategy in the first period of keeping Islam out of the public sphere, and of using international diplomacy to manage the religion of immigrants, was clearly a hindrance to Muslims' overall integration. The national governments assumed an active posture in state-religion affairs after Islam emerged as a major factor of individual and group identity among the descendants of labor migrants.

After two decades of intense debate over headscarves, Islamic radicalism, and terrorism, a preliminary equilibrium of state-mosque relations has been reached. Much basic religious equality has been achieved and the contours of the outer limits of religious toleration have been drawn, even if they are occasionally contested. By several measures, integration has increased. European Muslims participate in intermarriage, experience social mobility and increasing access to higher education, share the public opinion views of the overall population, and "combine" their religious and national identities without great difficulty.[1] Tensions over issues like mosque construction and Muslim cemeteries have been eased through the improved channels of communication between governments and Muslim communities. To be certain, discrimination in host societies persists, as does social anomie and religious fundamentalism among some Muslims. But many of the basic socioeconomic inequalities endured by Muslim-origin young people reflect the familiar dynamic of relative newcomers in host societies, and do not appear to be religion-specific.

Organized Islam in Europe is still largely a foreign-run enterprise. There are increasing numbers of naturalized citizens among their deputies, but first-generation religious leaders and de facto or actual foreign diplomats predominate. The baton of organizational leadership has not yet been passed to the native-born generations. This is a central factor behind Muslims' *partial* emancipation, and it is one that reinforces European publics' views of Islam as a foreign religion and undercuts the progress made in other domains by effectively ascribing any and all unresolved religious-cultural issues to Muslims as a group. The process of state-mosque relations and domestication of Islamic organizations assuages doubts of Muslims' loyalty and motivations.

A de facto clergy from the homeland countries has stood by in Europe to elaborate the principles of religious adaptation, but new Europe-based religious authorities have joined them. The new institutions have given breathing room for the evolution of modernizing strands that seek to establish a legitimate Islamic practice within novel theories of a minority jurisprudence (*fiqh al'aqillayat*); European fatwas have begun to modify Western Muslims' notions of religious obligation and their practical implications. Their adaptation of Islamic laws to local circumstances navigates a new social and political landscape and has granted Islamic approval to otherwise uncustomary practices, from adjusting prayer times to industrial work schedules, to giving to charity instead of actually slaughtering animals, to taking mortgages, down to the necessity of wearing a headscarf at all times outside of the home.

Pragmatic adaptation need not mean theological reform, of course, but each dispensation chips away at the universal practices of an Islamic *ummah*. Despite frequent disclaimers that European fatwas are intended to apply *to Muslim minorities only*, these changes have fundamentally altered the relationship of Muslim diaspora groups with their respective holy authorities who each offered an encompassing worldview—from the Moroccan commander of the faithful, to the Turkish directorate for religious affairs, to Saudi religious authorities. Each act of acclimatization in Europe contributes to the weakening of ties between the centers of religious authority and their peripheries. Muslim religious leaders have also demonstrated that they are more than happy to engage in give and take of negotiations with local governments, in order to improve conditions for religious freedom. Together, these forces can disarm nativist reactions in Europe by illustrating the real tendencies of adaptation and domestication that are under way, such as locally trained imams, native-born leadership, and locally funded mosques. The resolution of practical local problems associated with the sudden appearance of Muslim communities helps reduce the very tensions created by Islam's inadequate religious infrastructure, such as prayer-goers lying prone on sidewalks or blocking traffic because of shortages of prayer spaces (or parking near mosques), slaughtering lambs in the bathtub because of a lack of public slaughterhouses, proselytism in prisons because of insufficient trained Islamic chaplains, etc. Even the creation of Islamic cemeteries is a clear sign that community leaders believe Muslims' "real" home is not elsewhere.

An opinion piece published in the German daily *Die Welt* in 2004 denounced a "particularly grotesque form of appeasement" by the government, undertaken in the midst of "escalating violence by Islamic fundamentalists in Holland and elsewhere."[2] What was the naïve and "cowardly" mistake that the author compared to Neville Chamberlain's vain attempts to ward off Nazi aggression? "A substantial fraction of our Government actually believes that creating an official state 'Muslim holiday' will somehow spare us from the wrath of the fanatical Islamists," Mathias Döpfner wrote in reference to a proposal to place Eid al-Adha on the official German calendar. He is not alone in his negative assessment of granting Islam institutional recognition; others have expressed concern that the state-Islam consultation process risks aggravating the politicization of the Muslim identity. This critique has been leveled by those who think that Islam Councils—and the institutionalization of the religion they entail—are a misguided attempt to create an official "Muslim church."[3] The Washington-based think tank RAND issued a report in which it cited the risks of the French strategy: "Upgrading such organizations into the official institutions of the minority is negative because it undermines the prospects of integration [. . .] if state efforts to create a national Muslim church go awry, and instead of the moderate church the state has in mind, it gets fundamentalist leadership. This second risk is not unlikely."[4] Christopher Caldwell belittles the establishment of state-mosque relations as "the elevation [of] Muslim pressure groups to pseudo-governmental status and declaring that doing so will produce an Islam that reflects the values of Europe rather than vice versa."[5] The French right-wing leader Jean-Marie Le Pen issued a similar denunciation of the "legitimating of radical Islam through the installation of the CFCM";[6] the Front National's newspaper included headlines to the effect that "Sarkozy is preparing the Islamic Republic of France [by] imposing a French Islam."[7]

The evidence gathered in this book weighs heavily against the notion that the official recognition of Islam is the equivalent of appeasement or that accommodation amounts to conceding ground to religious radicals. Rather, the second phase of accommodation and institutionalization forms a contract between community leaders and the state which entails *mutual recognition*. I have argued that state-Islam consultations during the second stage of "incorporation" are an affirmation of European governments' political traditions of integration—and not evidence that they have lost track of the same.

This book's account of European governments' policies toward the Muslim religion since 1989 suggests that policymakers believe the recognition of Muslim religious requirements and Muslim representatives will reduce tensions between community and the state. But these improved relations are not achieved at the cost of unilateral concessions. If better state-mosque relations will not "spare [Western governments] from the wrath of fanatical Islamists," then they will at least provide an open channel for dialogue with a broad set of religious community leaders during times of conflict or crisis. It neutralizes accusations of unequal treatment that are used as proof of Western society's refusal of Muslims. Indeed, it could be argued that *ignoring* Muslims' holidays would be more welcomed by the "fanatics" Döpfner has in mind, who rely on an antagonistic relationship between Islam and the West in order to stimulate recruitment to their cause.

By welcoming formal religious community structures, governments encourage the development of Islam "in the light of day": whether training imams locally rather than importing them from the homeland, overseeing the flow of money around the halal meat industry, or the business of mosque construction.[8] The success of this approach is predicated on an assumption that if governments can manage to achieve consensus among Muslim representatives for settling practical questions of state-religion affairs—regulating prison chaplains, or appointing religion teachers, for example— then they will succeed in "domesticating" Islam. Of course, the prayer spaces and federations from which the Muslim leadership is drawn will never be fully representative of most observant Muslims, let alone most people of Muslim background. But the key question of granting official recognition has several merits in favor of de-problematizing Islam as an object of public policy and political debate. By integrating Islam into national institutions, authorities encourage the "westernization" of religious practice.[9]

The first phase of "outsourcing" effectively placed state-mosque relations out of the reach of European interior ministries. The state-Islam consultations of the second phase, however, have initiated the ambitious process of reining in Embassy Islam in addition to inviting Political-Islam activists to "play the game" of national politics. European governments are not just trying to initiate a dialogue with Muslim representatives—let alone to simply appease their demands. Rather, they are trying to reconfigure the Muslim religious organizational field with explicit reference to the centrality of the national state. The offer of official recognition of Islam is conditional upon participating organizations' recognition of the state (and its constitutional framework) in return.

Neo-Corporatism and State-Mosque Relations

European governments have gone about this "domestication" process through a tripartite arrangement (State–Political Islam–Embassy Islam) characteristic of neo-corporatist style negotiations that aim to instill unity, cohesion, and moderation in state-society relations. But this is not "your grandfather's corporatism," as Suzanne Berger wrote of economic neo-corporatism; visions of Azpiazu's Supreme Corporation

Council or Mussolini's Ministry of Corporations are misplaced.[10] Muslim councils are not general governing bodies, but religious intermediaries with clearly delimited jurisdiction: government policies and administrative practice relating to religion require an interlocutor for those aspects of church-state law that touch upon public order: chaplains in prisons, armies, and hospitals; burial rites; construction of prayer space; animal slaughter, etc.

Offering Muslims some form of representation within state institutions furthers the government's broader agenda of immigrant integration. From the vantage point of a secular state, state-Islam consultations are undertaken in the interest of avoiding a development it would consider to be far less appealing. Tariq Modood, a scholar of Muslim communities in Britain, has argued that there is no reason to be a democratic purist when it comes to organizing Islam in Western democracies: "There are certainly advantages to allowing organized religion corporatist influence rather than encouraging it, or obliging it, to become an electoral player."[11] He continues, "reformed establishment [is] a form of corporatist representation and therefore open to the charge of being undemocratic [in that] special consultative committees are [a] constraint on an electoral process. But [there] is no reason to be a purist: we are after all talking about bodies with very little power."[12]

Modood's evocation of avoiding the "electoralization" of issues recalls the experience of twentieth-century Christian Democratic parties. Christian Democracy has been portrayed by one of its most prominent scholars as an unintended consequence of too-strict separation. The danger of repressive actions by the state is that it may awaken constituents around a theme and inspire political backlash. Defeated in one policy arena—e.g., national education—by officeholders, Catholics decided to simply become the officeholders. Christian Democratic parties, in this view, were a "by-product of the strategic steps taken by the Catholic Church in response to Liberal anticlerical attacks."[13] Kalyvas cites Heinrich Rommen, who observed that the growth of political Catholicism was necessary wherever the political groups that controlled the 'neutral' state showed an outspoken enmity against the church.[14] Carolyn Warner, another scholar of Christian Democracy, has found that "when religious organizations perceive that their goals require access to political resources of some sort, [their] leadership will search for the closest policy match with a political party [. . . .] If no suitable party can be found, the religion may try to create its own party.[15] The alternative to institutionalizing Islam, by comparison, would be that Muslim leaders might set a goal of Islamizing of state institutions. When it comes to Islam, European governments do not make the same mistake twice, in a sense; if removing the church from the public policy process led to thriving Christian Democratic parties, then today's "stick" of domestication is accompanied by the "carrot" of institutionalized access in the form of Islam Councils.

TWENTY-FIRST-CENTURY ISLAM

The advent of the twenty-first century was heralded with dark predictions from Ivy League historians, investigative journalists, and internet populists that, in Europe, the new century would be Islamic.[16] Some argued simply that demography is destiny—that the combination of Muslims' runaway birthrates and European natives' "suicidal" fertility rates would lead to a Western set of Islamic republics by mid-century. Moreover, politically correct governments had done little to combat "the dangerous Islamic extremism and culture of death being preached from the mosques of Europe's major cities."[17] In 2009, the futuristic novel *La Mosquée Notre-Dame* predicted the transformation of Paris's grandest cathedral into a mosque within four decades, and an Italian newspaper crowned Rotterdam the future capital of Eurabia.[18]

Some of that science fiction is based on fact. European women's fertility rates fell in the post–World War II period, and European labor migration and family reunification policies in the late twentieth century led to the exponential growth of a new Muslim minority. But this book has tried to show that the European landscape will be etched in less stark relief than the apocalyptic scenarios suggest. For the near future, Islam will continue to be the fastest-growing religion in many parts of Europe—although evangelical Protestants will likely give Muslims a run for their money in some areas. But today there is just one prayer space for every 1,000 to 2,000 or so Muslims, and the rapid increase in mosque construction will do nothing more than adjust that ratio to match more closely the proportion of Jews and Catholics to existing synagogues and churches.[19] Moreover, in retrospect, it will become clear that many of the manifestations of Muslim radicalism and cultural dislocation are not permanent features of society but the result of a combination of persistent first-generation immigrant issues and the lagging adaptation of European political institutions to second- and third-generation issues.

It does not occur to many critics that Muslims are not always deliberately trying to offend their hosts' sensibilities: that men pray outdoors due to the shortage of mosques; that some slaughter lambs in bathtubs because there are not enough halal abbatoirs; that imams are imported because Islamic theological seminaries have not yet taken root in Europe; that some Muslims took their grievances to the streets because most did not yet have the right to vote or access appropriate administrative channels. The critics instead seize on the periodic actions of unreformed Islamists to support a catch-22 logic that only delays integration of the Muslim community. The institutional accommodation of Muslims and Islam on an equal basis with other religions, they suggest, would hand a victory to the extremists. Despite their outward endorsement of the diffusion of democracy in the Muslim world, skeptics of Muslims' integration in Europe fail to consider the ways in which internal democratization might strengthen religious moderates in Europe itself.

A number of the social, cultural, and political adjustments that will characterize Europe in coming generations are already under way, although often the results are not visible to the naked eye. The most serious threats—violent extremism among Muslims and right-wing nativism among "host societies"—will ultimately be weakened by a confluence of old-fashioned integration processes in society and demographic trends. The key development will be that as the proportion of Muslims of foreign nationality residing in Europe decreases (because the number of native-born Muslims will increase), Europe's democratic political institutions increasingly will kick in. The normalization of Muslims' participation in political life will give a small voice in government to Muslim advocates of all partisan stripes. And the routinization of Islamic religious observance will diminish the significance of religious inequality as a mobilizing issue in Muslim identity politics. National Islam Councils will slowly domesticate the religious leadership, rooting it in a European context, and Muslim politicians will gradually be brought into institutional life. Whenever terrorist threats materialize, a plethora of men and women of the European Muslim establishment will stand clearly on the side of democratic societies.

As Muslim-origin citizens begin voting and joining civil society groups in larger numbers, their everyday acts of political participation will provide concrete evidence of an Islamic and Western democratic synthesis. This may not completely erode the political niches occupied by nativist politicians or their Islamist counterparts. But exclusionary or self-segregating rhetoric will come to seem more hollow and irrelevant. A longer record of successful coexistence—and a growing pool of Muslim-European role models—will strengthen a competing narrative. The practical resolution of numerous impasses of previous generations—mosque debates, insufficient imams, animal—will free up other topics for discussion, setting a new tone in media and political debate. Some substantive tensions will remain, but there is reason to believe local political culture and institutions will continue to temper views "imported" from the Middle East.

In the course of the next several decades, a small number of European cities will be on the verge of becoming "Muslim majority"—Amsterdam, Bradford, Malmø, Marseille—and as many as one of every four residents in London, Brussels, Paris, and Berlin will have a Muslim background. But as the demographer David Coleman wrote perceptively in 2006:

> The significance would obviously depend on the continued distinctiveness and self-identification of the populations concerned, and on the integration of minorities to native norms, or conversely the mutual adaptation and convergence of all groups. But even on the assumptions presented above, the countries concerned would not become "majority foreign origin". . . until the twenty-second century.[20]

As with the advent of "majority-minority" cities in the late-twentieth-century United States, the new demographic configuration in Europe will not have overtly separatist overtones: by 2008, the percentage of the non-Hispanic white population fell below 60 percent in six U.S. states (including New York), and below 50 percent in four others (including California) without major political disruptions.

Nonetheless, a small number of hardcore anti-integrationist communitarians will persist, and their obstinacy and maximalist demands will likely provide consistent fodder for political leaders with a clash-oriented worldview. The Muslim minority will gamely participate in public and political life, although it will still be underrepresented in national electoral institutions. Yet despite—or because of—the increasing equality of Islam's status as a religion and Muslims' political representation, European countries will witness the rise of nativist challenges. In each country, millions of voters will be receptive to conservative appeals to turn back the clock on Muslim integration into European society. That in turn will lead to low-grade confrontation but not to large-scale social conflict.

DEMOGRAPHY IS DESTINY

A good deal of European anxiety has been kindled in recent years by provocateurs in the Islamic world who have claimed that "We will conquer Europe . . . not through the sword but through Da'wa (proselytism)";[21] or that "the wombs of Muslim women will ultimately grant us victory in Europe";[22] or, more recently, that "You [Muslims] are a minority in Europe. Allah willing, you will become a majority one day, and you will gain the upper hand . . . You will be the imams and the heirs of

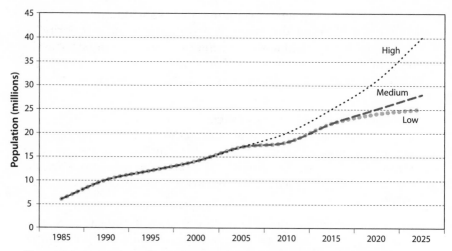

Figure 8.1. EU Estimated and Projected Muslim Population, 1985–2025.
Source: compiled from National Intelligence Council, *Global Trends 2025*,
Washington, DC: DNI, 2008 and National Intelligence Council, Mapping
the Global Future 2020, Washington, DC: DNI, 2005.

the European continent."[23] Yet the European future will come to mark a demographic turning point in a different direction.

The overall EU-25 population will grow slightly until 2025, due to immigration, before starting to drop: from 458 million in 2005 to 469.5 million in 2025 and then to 468.7 million in 2030.[24] The population of Muslim background in the EU-25, meanwhile, will increase from around 16 million in 2008 to 27 million in 2030, increasing the percentage of Muslims in European countries to more 7–8 percent (from 3.7 percent in 2008)—and to as high as 15–16 percent in France and Germany (see figure 8.1).[25] In 2030 Britain, all minorities (including non-Muslims) will make up 27 percent of the total population and 36 percent of those less than fourteen years of age.[26]

Women of Muslim background in Europe will still have higher fertility rates than the overall population, but the gap will narrow considerably. In fact, in 2008, signs already appeared that demographic change, while irreversible, would occur less abruptly than feared. The proportion of Muslims will continue to grow, but more slowly as their annual population growth rates decrease.[27] In 2008, women of North African, West African, or Turkish background in Europe still had higher rates than "native" women—2.3 to 3.3 births per woman—but the fertility rates of foreign-born women were already well below rates of women in their countries of origin. For example, the fertility rate of Moroccan-born women in the Netherlands dropped from 4.9 births in

1990 to 2.9 in 2005; that of Turkish-born women fell from 3.2 to 1.9 births in the same period.[28] In Germany in 1990, Muslim women gave birth to two more children, on average, than their native German counterparts; in 1996, the difference was down to 1; and in 2008, it dropped to 0.5. Meanwhile, overall fertility in some western European societies has risen: it rose in the United Kingdom from 1.6 births in 2001 to 1.9 in 2007, and in France, from 1.7 in 1993 to the magic replacement number of 2.1 in 2007. There will continue to be lively debate over the influence of family policies on such figures and over whether Muslim women are simply "artificially" propping up Swedish or French fertility rates (both of which increased between 2001 and 2009).[29] Muslim women's total fertility rates are predicted to settle between 1.75 and 2.25 by 2030.[30]

EU Enlargement and Demography

Because of the European pensioner bulge—the tens of millions of over-sixty-year-olds who were not there a generation earlier—Europe will remain dependent on immigration to help finance what remains of its welfare state and publicly funded retirement plans. Muslim immigration will therefore continue in various guises—high-skilled workers from India, family reunification from Turkey and North Africa, and assorted refugees from those areas—but all new arrivals will be subject to a new regime of stringent and controversial screening that aims to ensure their smooth cultural integration and their economic success: required courses in the official language of their destination country and mandatory curriculum on social mores and European history, from the Enlightenment through the latest EU treaty.

In the next generation, the latest countries likely to have acceded to the EU—Croatia, Serbia, Montenegro, and Macedonia—will increase the EU's base population but will not alter its basic trajectory toward demographic shrinkage. The annual level of net immigration would have to increase two- to threefold to reverse the downward trend in the working-age population.[31] The European Union, therefore, would accomplish several goals by admitting Turkey. (The French president and leaders of several other national governments could agree to forego a referendum if the Turks accept a smaller contingent in the European parliament and access to a single rotating commissioner.)

EU enlargement to include Turkey could be used as partial compensation for the continent's gradually shrinking population, allowing it to maintain its share of 6–7 percent of the world's population and thus ensuring that it preserves its weight as a "global player."[32] It would also allow chronic labor shortages to continue to be filled by citizens of a country committed to fulfilling the EU *acquis communautaire*. Therefore, even as governments increasingly lean away from Muslim-majority countries for immigration, Turkey eventually could provide EU states with their own "internal" source of migration. Moreover, Turkish membership could become a point of pride and a symbol of inclusiveness to the approximately 4 million residents of Turkish descent living throughout the EU, massaging a sore spot that has developed during divisive accession talks and plans to hold national referendums on the matter. In its EU accession talks, the Turkish government might agree informally to coordinate its reformed Turkish Directorate for Religious Affairs (DİTİB) with the activities of a cultures and religions bureaucracy within the European Commission.

Adding Turkey, of course, would also dramatically change the overall Muslim population in the European Union. With a population increase of 25 percent between 2008 and 2030, Turkey will expand to 85–90 million, which would make it the largest single member state—moreover, one with a higher fertility rate and lower age structure than the EU.[33] The share of Muslims in the EU as a whole—including Turkey—would be closer to 20 percent, but studies have projected that net immigration from Turkey to the rest of Europe will not exceed three million by 2030.[34]

Electoral Politics

There have been several obstacles to the integration of Muslims into political parties. Half of Europe's roughly sixteen million Muslims are still foreign nationals, and only half of those who are citizens of European states are of majority age and thus able to vote. In fact, political parties across Europe have been actively seeking the support of minority voters—during the 2007 French presidential campaign, all major candidates made stops in the *banlieues*. But very few individuals of Muslim background have gained access to elite leadership positions in political parties or eligible positions on party ballots. This situation is in part the legacy of earlier obstacles to naturalization that have led a high percentage of adult Muslims to retain their original nationality; as resident aliens they are disenfranchised. But it is also the simple reflection of a youthful population. If one excludes minors from the European Muslim population, a relatively small number of majority-age citizens (approximately one-third) remains. The number of elected and appointed political representatives and members of government hailing from these milieus is not trivial, but it is quite modest. Roughly one generation after the permanent settlement of immigrant laborers, the children of migrant workers of Muslim background have reached elected office at all levels of government. In the past decade, elections where candidates of Muslim origin were present produced, roughly:

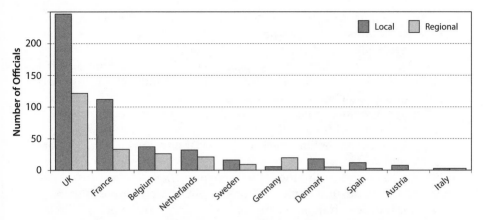

Figure 8.2. Local and Regional Elected Officials of Muslim Background (1989–2007). Source: author's compilation.

three hundred local councilors in the UK; ten to fifteen national legislators apiece in Belgium, Germany, Netherlands, the UK; and a handful of cabinet members in France, the Netherlands, and the UK (see figures 8.2 and 8.3). Islam Councils offer Muslim religious leaders some other form of interest representation within state institutions; for now, they are practically the only game in town.

How might Europe escape the political alienation of Muslims predicted by many outside observers? The central difference between the Muslim populations of 2009 and 2030 will be that most adult Muslims in Europe will be citizens, not third-country nationals. That means that they will no longer simply be the object of policy debates but will increasingly

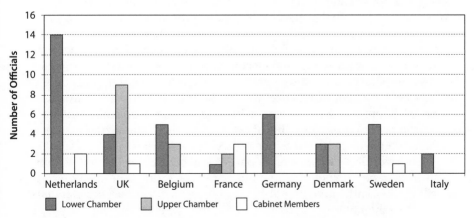

Figure 8.3. National Elected Officials and Cabinet Members of Muslim Background (1989–2007). Source: author's compilation.

participate in them as full members of society. The vast majority of European Muslims will be enfranchised, they will speak the local language with native proficiency, and their practice of Islam will be set on a course of Europeanization. European political debates about Muslims in 2030 will center mostly on the socioeconomic concerns of an emancipated and enfranchised minority group.

The most striking political development will be the emergence of a small Muslim electorate. Although today's opinion polls show Muslim respondents firmly within the socialist or labor camps in France, Germany, and the United Kingdom, Muslims' political views will evolve to include all stripes, including those who are socially conservative, economically liberal, and dovish on foreign policy. Germany will witness perhaps the most dramatic change, although it is worth noting the relative success of Turkish-origin Germans in the *Bundestag*: they account for at most 1 percent of German citizens, and held five seats (0.8 percent) between 2005 and 2013.[35] In the 2005 elections, fewer than one in five Muslims enjoyed the right to vote, but the 1999 citizenship law reform—which grants citizenship rights to children born to foreigners as long as one parent is a legal resident—has begun adding 50,000 to 100,000 newborn German citizens of Muslim background a year. The first full generation of native-born German Muslims will begin voting in 2017. Similar trends are under way in France, where 1.5–2 million voters of Muslim background voted in the 2007 national election. By 2030, the number will double to 3–4 million, accounting for just under one of every ten French voters.

The major novelty reflecting the electoral and demographic changes of coming decades will be the rise of a handful of openly religious Muslim politicians on nearly every national political scene. The number of single-issue Muslim voters in each constituency will not be able to support a viable "Muslim party," but political parties may begin to open their ranks in earnest to the growing minority after realizing it to be in their own self-interest. For this to take place, mechanisms for political recruitment from within the electorate of Muslim background would need to be expanded and nurtured, and spots at the top of candidate lists be set aside, in practice, for candidates with Muslim surnames. Socially conservative Muslims, who tend to be economically better off and supportive of the political establishment in their grandparents' home countries, will join center-right political parties.

The overtures of mainstream parties will be facilitated also by a pioneering generation of Muslim politicians who speak candidly of reconciling their faith and national citizenship and whose discourses are tailored to the national context in which they operate. In Germany and Italy, they could appeal to the tradition of politician-priests in the period between the First and Second World Wars and the advent of Christian Democracy in the wake of the church's expulsion from an official role in public policy. In France and Britain, Muslims politicians could evoke the precedent set by Jewish statesmen, nineteenth-century figures like French interior minister (and *Alliance Israëlite Universelle* president) Adolphe Crémieux, or British MP Lionel Rothschild. The victory of President Barack Hussein Obama in U.S. elections will also be cited widely, though it means different things to different people: the limitless possibilities of integration for some, the dulling constraints of western political systems for others.

Nonetheless, Muslims' transition to full political participation will continue to be a delicate affair, as Muslims seeking public office will still face an uphill battle. This partly reflects structural obstacles to all newcomers and political outsiders, but in many political contexts, it could also indicate a problem with Islam itself: will the best Muslim be an ex-Muslim? The most prominent Muslim in Italian politics—Magdi Allam—has written fierce anti-Islamist tracts and was personally baptized by Pope Benedict; the most prominent Muslim in Dutch politics— Ayaan Hirsi Ali, author of *Infidel*— rejected her religious upbringing (and eventually her adoptive nationality as well) and warned of the threat Islam posed to Western societal norms. Still, the fall of 2008 may be seen as a turning point in the political integration of European Muslims—when Ahmed Aboutaleb was elected mayor of Rotterdam and Cem Özdemir became chairman of the German Green Party.

The initiatives to enlarge political coalitions—and voter rolls—will eventually encompass several major factions within Muslim populations. The majority of Muslim voters will align themselves with Socialist and ecological parties, but two other groups could form important minorities. An alliance between remnants of the leftist "antiglobalization" movement and Political-Islam leaders will mature, leading to electoral agreements; their foreign policy agenda will seek to reduce the U.S.-European hegemony in the Arab-Muslim world, and they will oppose the terms of Turkish accession and Palestinian statehood. By 2030, the United States and its allies will have long departed from Afghanistan and Iraq, and the Islamists who once railed against blasphemous cartoons and neo-imperialist designs may seem as quaint and harmless as the middle-aged Baader Meinhof and Red Brigades who shuffled from their cells in the early 2000s.

POLITICAL VIEWS OF THE NEW GENERATION

What will Muslim politics look like in the next generation? Will European Muslims be interested in local and national issues or in international affairs and foreign policy affecting Muslims elsewhere? Cross-cutting divisions

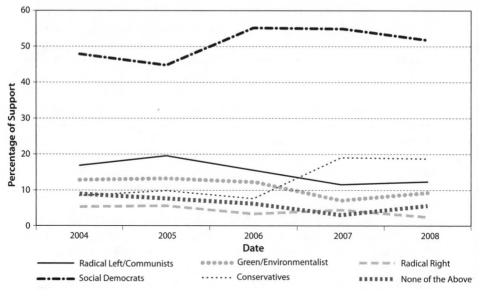

Figure 8.4. Muslims' Party Preferences in France. Source: Compiled from IFOP and Kaya, Ayhan and Kentel, Ferhat. "Euro-Turks: A bridge or a breach between Turkey and the European Union?" Centre for European Policy Studies: Brussels, January 2005.

will certainly expand across the Muslim populations of Europe. The "assimilationists" will argue that European host societies have dropped their most offensive anti-Muslim practices and have begun to open their arms and institutions to Muslims. "Separatists" will contend that Europeans' combination of latent Islamophobia and deep-seated Zionism requires Muslims to withdraw from daily social, political, and economic life and attempt to go it alone by creating enclaves. The separatists will be a small minority, and their ranks will be diminished each electoral cycle by the practical accommodations that national governments offer as incentives for political participation, including—where administrative practices permit—experimentation with voluntary shari'a courts to resolve some categories of civil disputes.

There is no evidence of a "Muslim vote," although politicians in these countries do make conscious appeals to these voters. Just because an electoral bloc does not exist does not mean that politicians have not tried to conjure it. Far from espousing the views of a conservative religious minority, it is, rather, a population that tends to lean leftward, although a small number also appear attracted by large, mainstream conservative parties (see figures 8.4 and 8.5).

Nonetheless, the fears that some Muslims have divided loyalties— that they place faith before nation—will not have completely disap-

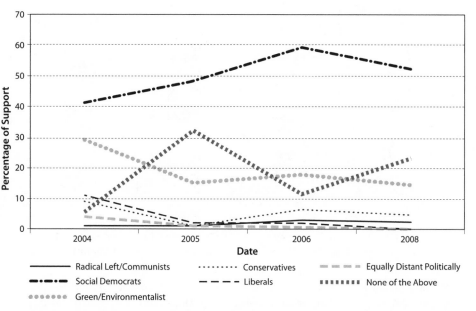

Figure 8.5: Muslims' Party Preferences in Germany. Source: Kaya, Ayhan and Kentel, Ferhat. "Euro-Turks: A bridge or a breach between Turkey and the European Union?" Centre for European Policy Studies: Brussels, January 2005.

peared in the coming generation. Poll results, like those from a 2004 *Guardian* poll, will continue to be cited as proof that a sizable minority of Muslims wants to be governed by shari'a law and supports domestic terrorism. Will Muslims grow inexorably apart from majority societies in 2030? Will they form a "distinct, cohesive and bitter" group?[36]

Polls conducted by Gallup and the Open Society Institute in 2009–2010 found that Muslims were more likely to identify with their European homelands than previously thought and that they have slightly more confidence than the overall population in the judiciary and other national institutions (see figures 8.6, 8.7, and 8.8).[37] The Gallup survey also showed that 96–98 percent of Muslims shared a lack of support for honor killings or crimes of passion (i.e., the same as the general population). These European Muslims were also revealed to be far more socially conservative by nearly every measure—from the viewing of pornography to the issue of premarital sex.

The 2009 Gallup poll's most thought-provoking section dealt indirectly with the question of tolerance for political violence and terrorism—which is a decent gauge for measuring the gap in political values between Muslims and their "host societies" in future generations. The survey showed that Muslim attitudes toward civilian deaths were far more nuanced than has sometimes been argued, especially by critics in

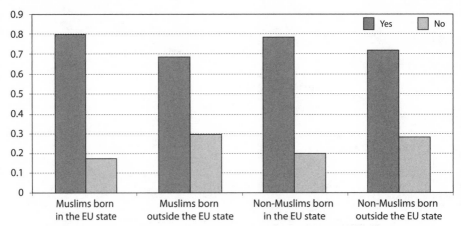

Figure 8.6. Do you feel you belong to the city? Source: Compiled from "Muslims in Europe, a report on 11 EU cities." Source: Open Society Institute, 2010.

the United Kingdom. Rather than looking for a yes or no answer, the poll provided a subtler four-point scale measuring degrees of agreement or disagreement and found that between 82 percent and 91 percent of Muslims in Britain, France, and Germany thought that civilian deaths cannot be justified at all. Muslims in these countries also said they were slightly more confident in judiciary and national institutions than the general populations.

Using data from the World Values Survey (1981–2007), Ronald Inglehart and Pippa Norris find that the basic social values of Muslims living

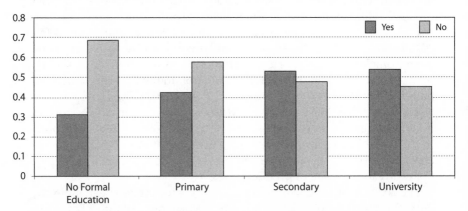

Figure 8.7. Do you see yourself as [British, French, etc.]? Muslim respondents by highest level of education completed. Source: Compiled from "Muslims in Europe, a report on 11 EU cities." Source: Open Society Institute, 2010.

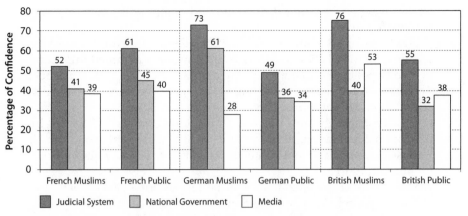

Figure 8.8. French, German, and British Muslims' Views of Institutions.
Source: Compiled from "The Gallup Coexist Index 2009: A Global Study of
Interfaith Relations." Gallup Inc., Washington, DC, 2009, pp. 22–23.

in Western societies fall approximately "half-way between the dominant
values prevailing within their countries of destination and origin."[38]
For example, they score Muslim immigrants on measures of religiosity:
76 (between 60 in the homeland and 83 in the host society); sexual liberalization: 37 (between 24 and 50); gender equality: 75 (between 57 and
82); and democratic values: 75 (between 71 and 81). They conclude that
"Muslims are not exceptionally resistant in levels of integration."[39]

With regard to the nurturing of a distinct political identity, a dynamic
set of membership-based Islamic organizations that cultivate community identification and religious practice will also begin to thrive. Federated at the European, national, regional, and local levels, these organizations will serve as social and political action networks and act as
feeders for political and religious associations. Such networks in Europe will owe much, indirectly, to the transnational proselytism of the
Muslim World League (MWL) and the twentieth-century exile of various branches of the Muslim Brotherhood (MB), whose envoys and dissidents from Egypt, Syria, Saudi Arabia, and other Gulf states encountered a combination of inviting refugee policies and undefined policies
toward Islam in 1960s and 1970s Europe. The dissidents clearing out of
Nasserist Egypt, Baathist Syria, and Kemalist Turkey came to pursue
advanced degrees and frequently created "Muslim student associations" to campaign for religious rights. But in the next generation, the
foreign-student cohort of the 1980s and 1990s will have passed the
baton to native-born Muslim leaders trained in the youth groups of existing federations, who are likely to demonstrate their independence by

freely engaging in political dialogue and compromise more actively than their parents' generation.

The transnational and pan-European federations with the most direct links to the MWL and MB will still have only a limited impact on everyday policy discussions and the daily lives of Muslims in Europe. The relevant political space for religious rights, legal recourse for discrimination, electoral influence, and so forth will remain the national stage. European Muslims will still be most affected and influenced by the national federations active in their local and regional areas, since it is those organizations that will be in a position to set the policy agenda for authorities to meet.

Many Muslim organizations will be largely irrelevant as actors in state-mosque relations because they are not associated with networks of mosques. Consequently, they will still be excluded for the most part from state-Islam consultations (for example, *Conseil français du culte musulman*, *Deutsche Islam Konferenz*, MINAB), which limit official ministerial contacts to mosque administrators and federations of prayer spaces. But the growth of lay Muslim councils to rival religious councils' influence—and often, to overcome the paralysis of the former—will reflect the growing political consciousness of a small but rising Muslim middle class.

Those who participate in activities or occupy leadership positions in Muslim organizations will experience a distinct type of political socialization that will influence their views on national and international debates. They will have been born and raised in Europe and less likely to have lived at great length abroad. They will be less connected to the politics of their ancestral homelands and far less likely to have personal ties to donors in the Gulf and other areas. In the future, therefore, their political affinities will be open to transnational and international influences. Their forums will likely continue to be critical of U.S. foreign policy, to express continuing solidarity with the Palestinian cause and opposition to Zionism, and to remain vigilant against the rise of Islamophobia in the West. Thus, even when acknowledging the misdeeds of Muslims—in terms of terrorism or anti-Semitism, for example—leaders will tend to be even more worried about the vulnerability of the Muslim world to external attack—from Afghanistan to Iran to Palestine, as well as the still-to-be consolidated political status of the Muslim minority in Europe. That tendency will fit in with a broader "victimization" narrative (also observable in published materials) and increased publicity of "Islamophobic" incidents when they occur. It will be seen in the context of minority politics, where organizations will have learned from the example of non-Muslim advocacy groups that the best offense is defense. Beyond promoting prayer and Muslim identity, many of the new generation of leadership will be acutely attuned to issues relating to discrimination and prejudice because of their own experiences as university students or young jobseekers, or even as just fellow passengers on the metro. Religious leaders will denounce incidences of blasphemy toward Islam, but they will also publicly renounce violence and suggest using the opportunity "to teach someone about Islam" as part of a broader public relations effort or an agenda of proselytism or "re-Islamization."

Social Indicators

Despite concrete instances of progress in the political realm, social integration will encounter some limitations. In order to reduce the influence of confrontational community leaders who claim Western cards are stacked against Muslims, Europeans will need to address the domestic factors of social and political alienation.

The likely welfare state reforms of the coming decades will hit Muslim-origin families hardest at first, but will have a net beneficial impact on Muslims' employment rates overall.[40] Still, fears of a developing Muslim-origin "underclass" will turn out to be well founded—higher than average proportions may continue be unemployed and collecting meager benefits. Although prison populations will still be miniscule compared with those in the United States, Muslim prisoners will make up a majority of the incarcerated and their absolute numbers will have likely increased considerably.

Disproportionate incarceration and unemployment rates will reflect the continued socioeconomic marginalization of many Muslims in Europe. On that score, the pessimists will be proven right. In the next generation, many young people of Muslim background will still fall through the cracks of education reform and affirmative action programs and will, unfortunately, be persistently involved in petty criminality and occasional urban unrest, alongside other economically marginalized subpopulations. They will not be the central thread of the tapestry, but they will be used as an example by skeptics who will continue to argue that Muslims will never fit in or successfully adjust to European society.

Progress on early education opportunities will steadily improve the basic literacy and linguistic skills of the grandchildren and great-grandchildren of North African and Turkish labor migrants from the mid-twentieth century. Outside of France, English will be increasingly accepted as a second language for Turkish and Arabic speakers. In general, the longtime linguistic "mismatch" between Germans and German immigrants, for example, will begin to resemble the better match enjoyed by people from Belgium, France, Spain, and Portugal and immigrants from the former colonies of those countries, who exhibited greater linguistic homogeneity in their ranks because immigrants from, for example, former French colonies in Africa were likely to speak French.[41]

Language, however, will increasingly be considered a superficial commonality, insufficient to ensure that the cultural values of migrant groups and host societies overlap. Several countries will continue to restrict the migration of spouses ("import brides"), a constant source of worry for authorities, not simply because many such marriages are forcibly arranged but also because the practice repeatedly renews a first-generation situation in which tens of thousands of children are born annually into households without proficient speakers of the host country language. Spouses will have to fulfill age requirements and attend linguistic and cultural training courses.

Terrorism and Nativism

The most serious challenge to integration in the next generation will still come in the forms of terrorism and nativism. Together, their periodic emergence will threaten to roll back positive social and political developments, especially with more recently settled Muslim populations. For the first time, both the leaders of the terrorist cells and those providing material support will be entirely native born. The shift of European Muslims from "foreigners" to "natives" will carry new risks that require the overhauling of counterterrorism and counter-radicalization approaches. The inspiring ideology will still come from abroad, but most terrorism incidents and arrests will be "homegrown." Suspects will be entirely the problem of European governments, which cannot simply deport them. The lasting implication of Islam's Europeanization is that many terrorism suspects will enjoy the full rights of citizenship instead of the limited rights of foreign nationals on European soil. A greater burden of proof—and controversial legislative reforms—will be required for them to be spied upon, interrogated, or deported. The radicalization threat will not have completely disappeared from the margins of organized religious groups, but the usual policy tools and techniques available for monitoring and countering radicalism among the previously foreign national adult Muslim population will not be available for use on EU citizens.

This development will throw a serious spanner in the works of the much-vaunted counterterrorism practices of Britain, France, and Germany and create new threats to the civil liberties of Muslim-origin citizens. Human rights associations and governments will exchange court cases and victories: a new generation of lawyers will manage to undercut the widespread practice of identity spot checks while governments will gain new detention powers. Caught between the two will be the thousands of new domestic law enforcement professionals of Muslim origin across Europe. Like the Italian American FBI investigators and district attorneys who helped cripple the mafia in twentieth-century U.S. cities, Muslim European agents will be key to the infiltration and dismantling of violent extremist networks. Police forces and Muslim communities will become increasingly interdependent, and the first Muslim prefects and commissioners will be appointed in a number of European cities. Security agencies in Germany and elsewhere will drop their objections to the formation of Muslim political parties, concentrating instead on providing funding to ensure that they remain well informed on the party leadership's aims and ambitions.

RELIGIOUS PRACTICES AND ORGANIZED ISLAM IN 2030

The number of mosques will continue to increase across the continent, so that the ratio of Muslims to prayer spaces will be more in line with the ratio of Jews and Catholics to synagogues and churches. Most of the prayer spaces will not be leased facilities but new construction—proper mosques with dome and minaret, built from the ground up.

Europe will still be a generation away from a fully native-born and locally trained imam corps, but for the first time, a slight majority of imams will have received supplemental "civic training" courses offered under the aegis of national integration programs. Hundreds of nationally certified chaplains will serve in European prisons to offer spiritual guidance to Muslim prisoners. Both the funding and personnel for the new prayer spaces will still come largely from abroad, but they will be increasingly channeled through national oversight institutions. Morocco and Turkey will have dramatically increased the number of prayer leaders exported for service in Europe each year, mostly to combat the growing threat of radical imams who collect donations from European congregations to support regime change on the home front.

The overwhelming majority of fourth- and fifth-generation Muslims in France, Germany, Britain, the Netherlands, and elsewhere will settle into a minority group identity, referring to themselves as "European Muslims" and socializing and engaging in organized political activities with one another across borders. Relations will be tense between the older, established, institutionalized Muslim community and the steady stream of newly arrived first-generation labor migrants from Turkey and North Africa, some of whom will establish their own prayer spaces where they can freely speak their native tongue. The old-country customs of the latter and their inferior knowledge of their host country's language will lead to community rifts, and some native Muslim leaders will look upon them with some condescension and suspicion.

The greatest commonality among national Muslim populations will be their entrenched divisions. National origin will remain a good predictor of piety and politics, although increasing intermarriage between ethnicities (Turkish/Kurdish, Arab/Berber) and nationalities (Turkish/German, Moroccan/Algerian) in addition to intermarriage between Muslims and non-Muslims will confound the simplistic categories of the turn of the twenty-first century. The biggest internal community conflict will be over the role of religion in public life, pitting adherents of Political Islam against those who remain loyal to the Embassy Islam of their ancestral countries. The two strains, once predicted to give way to a synthetic "Euro-Islam," will persist in their influence and indeed grow stronger. The internal divisions will harden into lasting cleavages. In most cities, there will be the "Turkish mosque," the "Pakistani mosque," the "Moroccan mosque," and the "Islamist" mosque, and rarely if ever will the twain meet. Such Embassy-Islam representatives will generally be the most respectful of host country norms and the separation of state and religion, whereas Political-Islam activists will continue to use institutional means to try to carve out a greater public role for religious expression.

In opinion polls, nearly all European Muslims will say that they fast during Ramadan and that they will make a pilgrimage to Mecca in their lifetime. Mosques on Fridays will not be quite as empty as Catholic and Protestant pews on Sundays—but, like churches, Islamic houses of worship will do their briskest trade on the holiest days of the year. But beyond such superficial religious shared traits, there will be nothing resembling a European ummah.

CONCLUSION

As Western democratic institutions—government ministries, but also courts, city councils, parliaments—have slowly addressed the new issues raised by the new religious diversity, the integration and institutionalization of Islam has begun to take place. The once intimidating behavior, and the sense some Muslim groups gave that public disorder could erupt in Europe after the Iranian fatwa against Salman Rushdie or the first expulsion of girls wearing headscarves in French schools, has receded. There is no "wildcat" feel to major religious demonstrations, when they occur. Even more than street protests, Islamic activism increasingly takes the form of institutional consultation, lobbying, and lawsuits. Many of these leaders have become responsible actors in an institutional setting, and they now have something to lose. This under-lying reality reminds us of another defining difference dividing Euro-pean Muslim communities from the mobilizing themes of Middle East politics. It may be in the interest of Yusuf al-Qaradawi to downplay the Holocaust for his own constituency; but European Muslim organiza-tions have quickly learned that it is not in theirs to do so.

To speak with officials in the religion offices of European interior ministries—the only ones who have day-to-day contact with Islamist leaders—one gets the impression that the present challenge is analo-gous not to the communist international but rather to an Islamic CGT or CGIL, the leftist trade unions in France and Italy whose leadership bought into negotiations with the state and abandoned their flirtations with revolutionary ideology. In other words, Islamist federation leaders may talk like they want the whole pie, but in reality they have demon-strated a willingness to settle for a piece of it.

The series of confrontations between the sensibilities of some Muslim leaders and majority societies in the last several years has afforded ob-servers several chances to test the thesis of a "clash of civilization"—and moreover, to test the institutions that were born of the shift from "outsourcing" to state-led strategies of "incorporation." When the head-scarf was banned in primary and secondary schools in France in 2004, there was no spillover onto the streets—although Islamist leaders have indeed lobbied politicians for a change in the law. When the Danish cartoon affair of 2006 led to the firebombing of embassies in parts of the Islamic world, European Islamist leaders in Europe filed suit in court.[42] On the one hand, this was indeed a story of "failure" in Europe: the failure of local dialogue in Denmark led Muslim leaders to appeal for support abroad, with consequences clear to all.

But the incidents have also been accompanied by a measure of success: during the caricatures controversy, Europe's Muslim populations en-gaged in nothing like what took place in cities across the Arab-Muslim world, from Lebanon to Libya, Nigeria to Pakistan. Instead, Muslims in Europe expressed their outrage and offense lawfully, through the new and old institutions created to govern state-mosque relations. Members of the CFCM in France, the Consulta in Italy, and the future German DIK, for example, all condemned the cartoons *and* the violence. In other words, they have behaved a lot like their Catholic and Jewish counter-parts: speaking up for their religion and its people when they feel dis-respected or threatened, and pursuing legal and political protection through institutional means. When riots broke out in French suburbs in 2005, Political-Islam leaders called the disorder "un-Islamic." That their appeals went wholly unheeded by rioters did as much to debunk their mythical influence as it did to reveal the nature of their intentions. Islamist federations have responded positively to government outreach, modifying their behavior as well as some of their most controversial stances (e.g., in intra-Muslim relations, Islamic-Jewish relations, and ambiguity regarding political violence) in order to gain influence in state-Islam consultations under way in a host of countries.

But until the "citoyennisation" of European Islam is complete, when sufficient numbers of imams are trained in Europe and local communities can afford to pay them—and mosque construction bills—not all Muslim politics will be local. Whether the councils will arrive at a stable equilibrium—and comfortably fade into daily invisibility as their non-Muslim counterparts have mostly done—is in some ways a challenge to the nation-state's relevance and its strength to filter the transnational forces exerted on its citizens. At present, the prevailing solution looks like a band-aid approach: There are still de facto diplomatic agreements—to import mosques and personnel—between Europeans and governments in the Muslim world that take place over the heads of European Muslims. European governments continue to "outsource" many of the details of Islamic religious observance to the indirect representatives of Algeria, Turkey, Saudi Arabia, and Morocco. This allows all governments involved to filter out some of the unwanted elements from the religious landscape, but it also delays the process of bottom-up integration and the creation of "European Islams."

Nonetheless, the councils have already borne some fruit regarding the "domestication" of Islam: from the nomination of national chaplains for armed forces and the penitentiary system, to the creation of training programs for religious teachers who can teach about Islam in public schools, to the signing of "values charters." While local imam training facilities are still insufficient, pre-departure training in Rabat and Ankara for imams heading to Europe is increasingly common, as are required acclimatization seminars for imams arriving in France, the Netherlands, and United Kingdom.

However, councils' impotence and the inherently limited nature of their influence and mandate has also been made clear. The French CFCM could not prevent the restrictive laws passed against headscarves (2004) and burkas (2009), for example, just as Swiss confederations could not roll back the anti-minaret ballot initiative (2009). What does this say about the institutional voice of Muslims in Europe, and what Islam Councils have to show for themselves vis-à-vis their constituencies? Are they condemned to occupying the unenviable spot between the "hammer" of the state and the "anvil" of the community, to playing the role of "fireman" to the "pyromaniacs" in their community, as some critics have written? Were skeptics of neo-corporatism in the 1970s correct to describe the arrangement as having "simultaneously the substance of state control and the appearance of democracy?"[43] Or, appearances notwithstanding, are Islam Councils the only safe bubbles in which Islamic leaders can still "be themselves" in the context of an increasingly poisonous atmosphere of rampant anti-Muslim populism?

Few U.S. policymakers surveying the burning rubble in Chicago, Los Angeles, New York, and Washington, DC, in the late 1960s could imagine that two African Americans would run the State Department from 2001 to 2009 or that a black family would move into the White House shortly thereafter. The worst tensions in U.S. inner cities were defused by way of an incoherent but effective mix of affirmative action, antidiscrimination policies, interventionist courts, electoral redistricting and reform of party nomination procedures, drug laws, and prison construction. Similarly, by 2030, Europeans will have settled into an acceptance of expanding participation in society and politics, letting democratic institutions do their work and hoping that the economy can support Muslims' entry into the labor market. As long as they make sure that there are good government protections against discrimination and policies promoting participation and educational achievement, they figure that they can hope for the best.

Looking at the skyline of small-town Europe in mid-century, it may be hard to recall the virulence with which so many citizen activist groups—patchwork coalitions of secularists made up of prominent ex-Muslims and anticlerical figures—fought mosque construction just decades earlier. Islamist terrorism will likely have faded as the driving force of policymaking on Muslim issues and as a result, the issue of Muslim integration will be put on a back burner, where it will benefit from being talked about less. Muslim leaders in 2030 will pay tribute to the trailblazers of the earlier generation—politicians, civil servants and community leaders—who went out on a limb to assert that Muslims were a permanent component of European societies at a time when it was politically costly to do so.

In 2030, it will have been decades since a great minaret went up over Oxford, fulfilling the eighteenth-century historian Edward Gibbon's prophesy.[44] In fact, every capital city will have its own showcase mosque up and running or in the planning stages. However, those domes and towers may no longer be perceived as the threat to European civilization and its Christian roots that dominated debate at the turn of the twenty-first century. To offer definitive judgment on the success or failure of the emancipation of Europe's Muslims would require perspective that the molten landscape does not yet afford. The process of emancipation and domestication will likely span generations, and it has only just begun. Nonetheless, European nation-states have established a routine of contacts with Muslim leaders, leading to a new level of mutual acquaintance and a slow but steady process of nationalization of religious authority. As the twentieth-century French scholar Jacques Berque foretold, just as a distinctive Islam of the Maghreb and an Indonesian Islam developed over time, so too have states created the spaces in which an Islam of Europe can germinate and begin to grow.

Notes

PREFACE

1. Weinryb, *Jewish Emancipation Under Attack*, 1942, 5.

CHAPTER 1. A LEAP IN THE DARK: MUSLIMS AND
THE STATE IN TWENTY-FIRST-CENTURY EUROPE

1. On the verge of an earlier age of state formation, prior to the Second Reform Act that extended suffrage to part of the working classes, British Prime Minister Benjamin Disraeli was said to have discerned the "Conservative working man as the sculptor perceives the angel prisoned in a block of marble," *The Times* (London), 1883. His contemporary Lord Derby wrote, "No doubt we are making a great experiment and taking 'a leap in the dark' but I have the greatest confidence in the sound sense of my fellow-countrymen, and I entertain a strong hope that the extended franchise which we are now conferring upon them will be the means of placing the institutions of this country on a firmer basis, and that the passing of this measure will tend to increase the loyalty and contentment of a great proportion of Her Majesty's subjects," 1867. Source for demographic projection: Pew Forum, "The Future of the Global Muslim Population," 2011.

2. Wendehorst, "Emancipation as Path to National Integration," 1999, 192–94.

3. The precise ratios of emigrants in Europe versus total nationals abroad are difficult to obtain but approximately as follows: Turkey: 4 million / 5.5 million; Algeria: 4 million / 5 million; Morocco: 2.7 million / 3.4 million; Pakistan: 1.75 million / 4 million.

4. Pollack, "Wahrnehmung und Akzeptanz religiöser Vielfalt," Münster: Religion und Politik, 2010; European Union Minorities and Discrimination Survey, "Data in Focus Report: Muslims," EU Agency for Fundamental Rights, 2009.

5. Cf. The political philosopher Patchen Markell's (2003) concept of a "double bind" and the political economist Karl Polanyi's (1944) description of the simultaneous emergence of market economies and the expansion of social protections from the market.

6. Liedtke and Wendehorst, *The Emancipation of Catholics, Jews and Protestants*, 1999; Markell, *Bound by Recognition*, 2003.

7. Judah Leib Gordon (1862) in Stanislavski, *For Whom do I Toil? Judah Leib Gordon and the Critique of Russian Jewry*, 1988.

8. Cf. Shadid and Koningsveld, *The Integration of Islam and Hinduism in Western Europe*, 1991, pp. 8–9.

9. Allievi, *Conflict over Mosques in Europe*, 2009, p. 23.

10. Brown in Markell, *Bound by Recognition*, pp. 127, 145; and Wendy Brown, *Regulating Aversion*, 2008.

11. Mandaville, "Muslim Networks and Movements in Western Europe," 2010, p. 5.

12. Sala, "Fremde Stimmen im Äther," 2009.

13. Frisch, 1989 in A. J. Seiler, *Siamo Italiani*, 1965, p. 7.

14. Gresh and Ramadan, *L'Islam en Questions*, 2000.

15. Quoted in Wright, "The Terror Web," 2004.

16. Dassetto, *Paroles d'islam: individus, sociétés et discours dans l'islam européen contemporain*, 2000; Ferrari and Bradney, eds., *Islam and European Legal Systems*, 2000; Rath et al., *Western Europe and its Islam*, 2001; Allufi and Zincone, eds., *The Legal Treatment of Islamic Minorities in Europe*, 2004; Fetzer and Soper, *Muslims and the State in Britain, France and Germany*, 2005; Maussen, "The governance of Islam in Western Europe: A state of the art report," 2007.

17. The approximately two million Jews in 1930s Western Europe formed between 0.05 percent and 1.8 percent of their respective national societies, but most Jews lived in big cities. United States Holocaust Memorial Museum, "Jewish Population of Europe in 1933: Population Data by Country," *Holocaust Encyclopedia*, 2011.

18. The Jesuits suffered suppression in eighteenth-century French, Portuguese, Italian and Spanish territories, and bans in nineteenth-century Germany and Switzerland. Cf. Casanova, "Globalizing Catholicism and the Return to a 'Universal' Church," 1997.

19. Cf. Bertrand, *Revolutionary Situations in Europe, 1917–1922*, 1977.

20. Beer, *Modern British Politics: Parties and Pressure Groups in the Collectivist Age*, 1982, p. 329.

21. Roy, *L'islam mondialisé*, 2003, 20.

22. See Fetzer and Soper, *Muslims and the State.*

23. For an excellent discussion of this, see Koopmans and Michalowski, "Citizenship Rights for Immigrants," 2010; see also Joppke, ed., *Challenge to the Nation-State: Immigration in Western Europe and the United States*, 1998.

24. Freeman, "The Decline of Sovereignty? Politics and Immigration Restriction in Liberal States," 1998; Hansen and Weil, *Towards a European Nationality. Citizenship, Immigration and Nationality Law in the EU*, 2000.

25. Krasner, *Sovereignty: Organized Hypocrisy*, 1999, 223.

26. Bentley, *The Process of Government: A Study of Social Pressures*, 1949; Skocpol, ed., *Bringing the State Back In*, 1985.

27. Koopmans et al., *Contested Citizenship*, 2005; Thomson, "State sovereignty in international relations," 1995; Thomson and Krasner, "Global transactions and the consolidation of sovereignty," 1989; Mann, "Has globalization ended the rise and rise of the nation-state?" 1997.

28. Koslowski, ed., *International Migration and the Globalization of Domestic Politics*, 2005; Tager, "Expatriates and Elections," 2006; Mullins, "The Life-Cycle of Ethnic Churches in Sociological Perspective," 1987; Stevens, "Spreading the Word: Religious Beliefs and the Evolution of Immigrant Congregations," 2004.

29. For example, Interior Minister Wolfgang Schäuble met with then-DİB President Ali Bardakoğlu and "requested [DİB] send educated imams to Ger-

many to provide religious services to Turks and Muslims in the country. Yavuz, "German Culture Center trains Turkish Imams for Europe," 2008.

30. Brubaker, *Citizenship and Nationhood in France and Germany*, 1992.

31. Philip Jenkins, *God's Continent: Christianity, Islam, and Europe's Religious Crisis*, 2007.

32. International Crisis Goup, "Understanding Islamism," 2005, 13.

33. Kepel, *Fitna*, 2007; Parekh, *Rethinking Multiculturalism*, 2002.

34. This includes approximately thirty months in France, Germany, and Italy, and brief research stays in Belgium, Ireland, Morocco, Netherlands, Turkey, and the United Kingdom. Each interview lasted approximately 1–2 hours and was conducted in English, French, German, or Italian, with a fixed outline containing both closed-ended and open-ended items. The respondents were selected as government officials responsible for Islam-related issues and as Muslims who hold leadership positions in national, regional, or local Islamic cultural or religious associations. In addition to the formal interviews, I also convened and participated in academic/policy conferences with officials and community leaders from Western Europe at Sciences Po - Paris (November 2003), during the German presidency of the Council of the EU (Spring 2007), at the Woodrow Wilson International Center for Scholars (March 2008), and at the Transatlantic Academy/Friedrich Ebert Stiftung (December 2008); conference programs can be consulted at www.jonathanlaurence.net.

35. Vidino, *The New Muslim Brotherhood in the West*, 2010.

36. Cf. Klausen, *The Islamic Challenge*, 2005.

37. Lipset and Rokkan, "Cleavage Structures, Party Systems, and Voter Alignments," 1967.

CHAPTER 2. EUROPEAN OUTSOURCING AND EMBASSY ISLAM: *L'ISLAM, C'EST MOI*

1. Langer, *Europe Leaves the Middle East, 1936–1954*, 1972.

2. Heisler and Heisler, "Transnational Migration and the Modern Democratic State: Familiar Problems in New Form or a New Problem?" 1986.

3. Shadid and Koningsveld, *The Integration of Islam and Hinduism in Western Europe*, 1991, 9.

4. In the 1980s, official incentives for return migration equaling several thousand dollars were put in place in the decade after borders were closed to labor migrants: the French promised "a million centimes" (FF10,000) to Algerian returnees, Germany offered DM10,500 checks (*Rückkehrgeld*) to Turkish return migrants (plus DM1,500 per child) through the 1983 Voluntary Repatriation Act, the Dutch *Vertrekpremie* was worth NLG5,000, and the Belgian government pursued a similar policy. Césari, *When Islam Meets Democracy*, 2004; Ireland, *The Policy Challenge of Ethnic Diversity: Immigrant Politics in France and Switzerland*, 1994, 52; Koopmans, "Germany and its immigrants: an ambivalent relationship," 1999, 627–47; Refflinghaus, *Deutsche Türkeipolitik in der Regierungszeit Helmut Kohls, 1982 bis 1998*, 2002, 264; Maussen, *Constructing mosques*, 129.

5. Cf. Galembert, "La régulation étatique du religeux à l'épreuve de la globalisation," 2001.

6. Interview by the author with Thierry Tuot in Paris, Fonds d'Action Sociale, August 2000. See Convention entre la République Française et le Royaume du Maroc relative au statut des personnes et de la famille et à la coopération judiciaire. Décret n° 83-435 DU May 27, 1983; J.O du June 1, 1983, 1643. See also Convention entre la France et l'Algérie relative aux enfants issus de couples mixtes séparés franco-algériens. Signée à Alger, June 21, 1988, Décret no. 88-879 August 17, 1988; J.O du August 19, 1988, 10505.

7. Cour d'Appel de Paris—02.02.1978; Cour de Cassation—01.03.1980: "a polygamous marriage properly concluded abroad does result in some civil rights for the second and following co-wives, not a prima facie violation of French public order." In 1980, the Conseil d'Etat ruling "l'arrêt Mondcho" granted permanent residency status to the second wife of an Algerian man; this was reversed by a 1993 law which, however, preserved "civil protection of some effects of polygamous marriages." Maier, "Multicultural Jurisprudence: Muslim Immigrants, Justice and the Law in France and Germany," 2004; Sehimi, "Sarko et la Moudawana," 2003, 15.

8. As one official said in an interview, "Whenever there is the need to take certain steps with the Algerian or Moroccan embassies, to clarify certain points, it is the role of counselor for religious affairs." Interview by the author with Jacques Nizard in Paris, religious affairs counselor at the French Foreign Ministry, July 2000.

9. Interviews by the author with Gabriela Guellil, Office for Dialogue with the Islamic World, German Foreign Ministry, July 2004 and January 2006.

10. Gibbons, "Religion, Immigration and the Turkish Government in Germany: Reexamining the Turkish-Islamic Union for Religious Affairs (DİTİB)," unpublished paper, 2009; Østergaard-Nielsen, ed., *International Migration and Sending Countries: Perceptions, Policies and Transnational Relations*, 2003.

11. Sayari, "Migration Policies of Sending Countries: Reflections on the Turkish Experience," 1986, 87–98.

12. Dassetto, *La construction de l'Islam européen: approche socio-anthropologique*, 1996.

13. Blaschke, "Islam und Politik unter türkischen Arbeitsmigranten," 1989; Feindt-Riggers and Steinbach, *Islamische Organisationen in Deutschland*, 1997; Kepel, *Die Rache Gottes: radikale Moslems, Christen und Juden auf dem Vormarsch*, 1991.

14. Maussen, *Constructing mosques: the governance of Islam in France and the Netherlands*, 2009.

15. Boyer, *L'islam en France*, 1998.

16. Blaschke, "Islam und Politik unter türkischen Arbeitsmigranten," 1989, 332.

17. Ögelman, "Immigrant organizations and the globalization of Turkey's domestic politics," 2005, 37.

18. Boyer, *L'islam en France*, 1998.

19. Joxe, *L'édit de Nantes: Une histoire pour aujourd'hui*, 1998, 338.

20. Interview by the author with Abdallah Redouane in Rome, Centro Islamico Culturale d'Italia, September 2003.

21. Interview by the author with Mehmet Yildirim in Cologne, Türkische-Islamische Union der Anstalt für Religion (DİTİB), January 2006.

22. Interview by the author with Alan Boyer in Paris, Prefecture of the Auvergne, June 2002.

23. Interview by the author with Giulio Andreotti in Rome, Senator and Former Prime Minister , October 2003.

24. Brohi, "Problems of Minorities," 1980, 31–42, 32.

25. Ibid., 31–42.

26. Kettani, "The Problems of Muslim Minorities and Their Solutions," 1980, 91–107, 103.

27. Gauhar, "Islam and the Secular Thrust of Western Capitalism," 1982, 213–29, 229.

28. Islamic Council of Europe, "Universal Islamic Declaration," 1982, 213–29 and 253–66, 265.

29. Beschluss der *Kultusministerkonferenz* vom 8 April 1976.

30. Morel, *Ecoles, territoires et identités. Les politiques publiques françaises à l'épreuve de l'ethnicité*, 2002, 65.

31. Maussen, *Constructing mosques*, 127.

32. Interviews by the author with Jacques Nizard in Paris, French Foreign Ministry, July 2000; and with Hubert de Canson in Paris, French Foreign Ministry, June 2002.

33. Gonzales, "La France," 1998, 210. The numbers would decrease somewhat in the course of the 1990s. It is worth noting that such courses also existed for Italians, Greeks, Portuguese, Spaniards, and Yugoslavs.

34. Interview by the author with Thierry Tuot in Paris, Fonds d'Action Sociale, August 2000.

35. Evangelische Kirche in Deutschland, "Religionsunterricht für muslimische Schülerinnen und Schüler," 1999.

36. Ibid., pp. 68, 70, and 140.

37. Baran, "Denkanstöße zum islamischen Religionsunterricht Säkularismus als Grundprinzip,"1999.

38. In Baden-Württemberg, 28,551 (80%); in Bavaria, 60% (circa 10,000); in Berlin, circa 3,000; in Hessen, circa 27,000 (60%); in North Rhine Westphalia, 86,000 (80%). Sources: Yildiz, "Muttersprachliche Türkischunterricht in Deutschland," 2002; and Gogolin, Neumann, and Reuter, *Schulbildung für Kinder aus Minderheiten in Deutschland, 1989–1999*, 2001, 37.

39. de Louw, "Les Pays Bas," 1998, 279.

40. Secrétaire general à l'intégration, "Immigrés: réussir l'intégration," 1990.

41. Maussen, *Constructing mosques*, 126.

42. Sala, "Gastarbeitersendungen und Gastarbeiterzeitschriften (1960–1975), Ein Spiegel internationaler Spannungen," 366–87.

43. In some cases, the promotion of minority culture was not always done with return migration in mind. Between 1975 and 1983, the Dutch government subsidized mosques for migrant workers up to approximately 30 percent of total costs, up to $75,000 (today's value). The 1983 *Minderhedennota* (Minorities Memorandum) in the Netherlands, noted that "religion fulfills a function in developing and enforcing the self-respect and emancipation of many members of ethnic groups." Shadid and Koningsveld, *The Integration of Islam and Hinduism in Western Europe*, 1991, 107–10.

44. Aşkoğlu, *Almanya'da temel eğitimdeki Türk çocuklarının din eğitimi*, 1993, 52.

45. Interview by the author with Raoul Weexsteen in Paris, French Interior Ministry, June 2002.

46. Landau, *The Politics of Pan-Islam*, 1990, 248.

47. Eickelman, "Trans-state Islam and Security," 1997, 33.

48. Landau, *The Politics of Pan-Islam*, 1990.

49. Pirrone, "Dalla colonizzazione all 'islamismo radicale,'" 2000, 67–97.

50. Sakallioglu, "Parameters and Strategies of Islam-State Interaction in Republican Turkey," 1996, 231–51.

51. Mohamed Arkoun, *Penser L'Espace Méditerranéen*, pp. 64–65; Blaschke, "Islam und Politik unter türkischen Arbeitsmigranten," 1989, 303.

52. Abedin, "The Study of Muslim Minority Problems: A Conceptual Approach," 1980, 20, 26.

53. Eickelman, "Trans-state Islam and Security," 1997; Hubel, *Frankreichs Rolle im Nahen Osten*, 1985; Rudolph, "Introduction: Religion, States, and Transnational Civil Society,"1997.

54. The Organization of Petrol-Exporting Countries (OPEC) was created in 1960 and includes Saudi Arabia, Iraq, Iran, Kuwait, and Venezuela. The Organization of Petrol-Exporting Arab Countries (OPEAC: Saudi Arabia, Libya, Kuwait) was created in 1968 as an instrument of inter-Arab economic integration; Benchenane, *Pour un dialogue euro-arabe*, 1983, 79; Hunter, *The Future of Islam and the West: Clash of Civilizations or Peaceful Coexistence?* 1998, 125.

55. Schulze, *Islamischer Internationalismus im 20. Jahrhundert: Untersuchungen zur Geschichte der Islamischen Weltliga*, 1990, 277; Islamic Council of Europe, ed. Appendix III, *Muslim Communities in non-Muslim States*, 1980, 168; Rex, "Islam in the United Kingdom," 2002, 64. In the mid-1980s, the Muslim World League also helped establish the Council of Mosques in the UK and Ireland as well as the National Federation of French Muslims (FNMF), and the Libyan Islamic Call Society sponsored the creation of the Council of Imams in the UK.

56. Gaye, "Muslim Minorities: A Framework," 1980, 1–6, 1.

57. Kettani, "The Problems of Muslim Minorities and Their Solutions," 1980, 91–107, 106.

58. Ibid., 107.

59. Bilgrami, "Educational Needs of Muslim Minorities: Nature and Extent of the Problem," 1980, 125–152, 144. Bilgrami was director, World Federation of Islamic Missions, Karachi.

60. Eickelman, "Trans-state Islam and Security," 1997.

61. Fallaci, *The Rage and the Pride*, 2002; Ye'or, *Eurabia: the Euro-Arab Axis*, 2005.

62. Ye'or, *Eurabia: the Euro-Arab Axis*, 2005.

63. Artner, "The Middle East: A Chance for Europe?" 1980.

64. Aarts, Meertens, and Van Duijne, "Kingdom with borders: the political economy of Saudi-European relations," 2008, 135–56, 136.

65. Artner, "The Middle East: A Chance for Europe?" 1980.

66. E.g., Organization of Islamic States (1969), headquartered in Jeddah. Landau, *The Politics of Pan-Islam*, 1990, 287–91; Klausen, *The Cartoons That Shook the World*, 2009.

67. *Khadim al-haramayn* means "servant of the holy places," a role previously held by the Hashemite Kingdom during the Ottoman Empire. Donini, "I rapporti fra Italia e Arabia Saudita," 2000, 47; Nonneman, "Le relazioni tra l'Arabia Saudita e l'Europa," 2000, 31; Landau, *The Politics of Pan-Islam*, 1990, 254.

68. Landau, *The Politics of Pan-Islam*, 1990, 287.

69. Hunter, *The Future of Islam and the West: Clash of Civilizations or Peaceful Co-existence?* 1998, 156; Landau, *The Politics of Pan-Islam*, 1990, 283: Muslim World League (MWL) co-opted political activists such as al-Maududi; also, Saïd Ramadan, who authored the MWL charter (see Laurence and Vaisse, *Integrating Islam: Political and Religious Challenges in Contemporary France*, 2006). Post-1972 strategy set Wahhabi against Salafi trends; Schulze, *Islamischer Internationalismus im 20. Jahrhundert: Untersuchungen zur Geschichte der Islamischen Weltliga*, 1990, 452.

70. Leveau, "De l'islam comme communauté imaginaire transnationale," 2003, 146.

71. Fraser, "In Defense of Allah," 1997, p. 221.

72. Hunter, *The Future of Islam and the West*, 1998, 159.

73. Schulze, *Islamischer Internationalismus im 20, Jahrhundert*, 1990 260.

74. Landau, *The Politics of Pan-Islam*, 1990, 284.

75. Schulze, *Islamischer Internationalismus im 20.Jahrhundert*, 1990

76. Landau, *The Politics of Pan-Islam*, 1990, 285.

77. Six branches of this Saudi-based organization are located in the Arab world, eight in Africa, five in Europe, and four in Asia. Bilgrami, "Educational Needs of Muslim Minorities: Nature and Extent of the Problem," 1980, 125–52, 146.

78. The MWL has fifty-three international board members who meet annually.

79. Hunter, *The Future of Islam and the West*, 222; See also Fraser, "In Defense of Allah," 1997, p. 221; and Hubel, *Frankreichs Rolle im Nahen Osten*, 1985.

80. Aarts, Meertens, and Van Duijne, "Kingdom with borders: the political economy of Saudi-European relations," 135–56, 140.

81. Benchenane, *Pour un dialogue euro-arabe*, 14.

82. Nonneman, "Le relazioni tra l'Arabia Saudita e l'Europa," 2000, 32.

83. "Les Véritables dialogues," in *La Pensée Nationale*, no. 25-6, Feb. 1980, cited in Benchenane, *Pour un dialogue euro-arabe*, 1983, 15; Jobert, "Préface," 1983, is apparently referring to the creation of Aramco.

84. Jobert, "Préface," 1983, 10; "Les Véritables dialogues," 1983, 15.

85. Cited in Mortimer, *The Third World Coalition*, 1980, 50.

86. Al-Mani', *The Euro-Arab Dialogue: A Study in Associative Diplomacy*, 1983; Benchenane, *Pour un dialogue euro-arabe*, 1983, 55; Hubel, *Frankreichs Rolle im Nahen Osten*, 1985, 62.

87. Hunter, *The Future of Islam and the West*, 1998, 159.

88. Fraser, "In Defense of Allah," 1997, p. 221.

89. Hunter, *The Future of Islam and the West*, 1998, 158.

90. Frémeaux, *Le Monde Arabe et la Sécurité de la France depuis 1958*, 1995, 144.

91. Hubel, *Frankreichs Rolle im Nahen Osten*, 1985.

92. Leveau, "De l'islam comme communauté imaginaire transnationale," 2001, 149; Strika, "Italia e Arabia Saudita dopo il secondo conflitto mondiale," 2000, 58.

93. Interview by the author with Abdellah Redouane in Rome, Centro Islamico Culturale d'Italia, September 2003.

94. ICC created the first Islamic school in Belgium in 1989, Al Ghazali. MWL also helped fund the Munich Islamic Center (1960)—see chapter 3: Pargeter, *The New Frontiers of Jihad: Radical Islam in Europe*, 2008; Landman, "Islam in the Benelux Countries," 2002, 106; Hallet, "The Status of the Muslim Minority in Belgium," 2004, 113.

95. Hopwood, *Euro-Arab Dialogue: The Relations between the Two Cultures, Acts of the Hamburg Symposium*, 1985, 309.

96. Minutes of Meetings with Secretary of State Henry Kissinger: "Discussion with Michel Jobert in Paris," May 22, 1973; "Memorandum on US-European Relations," November 28, 1973; "Meeting with West German Foreign Minister Scheel," March 3, 1974; "Meeting with West German Chancellor Brandt," March 4, 1974. Consulted in the Digital National Security Archives.

97. Romeo, *La politica estera italiana nell'era Andreotti, 1972–1992*, 2000.

98. Interview by the author with Giulio Andreotti in Rome, Senator and former Prime Minister, October 2003; Interview by the author with Abdellah Redouane in Rome, Islamic Cultural Center of Italy, September 2003.

99. Interview by the author with Giulio Andreotti in Rome, Senator and former Prime Minister, October 2003.

100. Interview by the author with Abdellah Redouane in Rome, Islamic Cultural Center of Italy, September 2003.

101. Beau, *Paris, capitale arabe*, 1995, 144.

102. Ibid., 142–49.

103. Dassetto, *La construction de l'Islam européen*, 1996, 154.

104. Hussein, "Alliance Behavior and the Foreign Policy of the Kingdom of Saudi Arabia, 1979–1991," 1995, p. 62; Milcent, "Interview exclusive du Cheikh Abdallah Turki," 2004; Lahouri and Thiolay, "L'argent de l'islam," 2002; Muslim World League, "Islamic Centre in Vienna: Beginning of a new era for Islam in Europe," 2000; See also Laurence and Vaisse, *Integrating Islam: Political and Religious Challenges in Contemporary France*, 2006, 116.

105. Eade, "Nationalism, Community and the Islamization of Space in London," 1996.

106. Shehabi, "The role of religious ideology in the expansionist policies of Saudi Arabia," 2008, 183–97.

107. Interview by the author with Mario Scialoja in Rome, Muslim World League, July 2001.

108. James Woolsey, former director of central intelligence, "The Global Spread of Wahhabi Islam: How Great a Threat?" Pew Forum on Religion & Public Life, May 3, 2005.

109. Pargeter, *The New Frontiers of Jihad*, 21; See also Shehabi, "The role of religious ideology in the expansionist policies of Saudi Arabia," 2008, 183–97.

110. Interview by the author with Giulio Andreotti in Rome, Senator and former Prime Minister, October 2003.

111. Aarts, Meertens, and Van Duijne, "Kingdom with borders: the political economy of Saudi-European relations," 137.

112. Ibid.

113. Sayari, "Migration Policies of Sending Countries: Reflections on the Turkish Experience," 1986, 87–98.

114. Russell, "Remittances from International Migration: A Review in Perspective," 1986, 677–96, 687, 693.

115. Ibid., 681.

116. Mouhieddine, "MRE/législatives : Choc des maux et soif des urnes," 2007.

117. "Progression de 8.2% des transferts des MREs en 2005," www.bladi.net, February 3, 2006.

118. "De villepin attendu demain au Maroc," Le Matin, October 12, 2005.

119. Miller, Foreign Workers in Europe, 1981, 39.

120. Interview by the author with Aziz Mekouar in Washington, DC, Moroccan Ambassador to the United States, May 2005; interview by the author with Moulay Abbès Kadiri in Paris, Moroccan Embassy in France, June 2002; Frégosi, Réflexions sur les contours évolutifs d'une régulation étatique de l'islam en régime de laïcité," 2000.

121. Brand, Citizens Abroad: Emigration and the State in the Middle East and North Africa, 2006, 14.

122. Miller, Foreign Workers in Europe, 35.

123. Organized in a pyramid along mass-party lines; 15- to 30-member cells were organized at the local or neighborhood level; five cells made up a section, and several sections together made up each of 12 regional AAE units, which were present in all large French cities.

124. Miller, Foreign Workers in Europe, 36.

125. Hargreaves, Immigration, 'race' and ethnicity in contemporary France, 1995, 301.

126. Schlötze, "Die Türkei zwischen Islam und westlicher Moderne," 2001.

127. Spiewak, "Vorbeter aus der Fremde," 2006.

128. Dere, "The PRA of Turkey: The Emergence, Evolution and Perception of its religious services outside of Turkey," 2008, pp. 292–93.

129. The Diyanet's foundation, Türkiye Diyanet Vakfi, was founded in 1975 to facilitate mosque construction and charitable organizations. Zuhal Kavacik, "Soziale Integration und religiös-ideologische Ansprüche in der BRD," unpublished paper, 2007.

130. Landman, "Islam in the Benelux Countries," 2002, 105.

131. Kastoryano, "Le nationalisme transnational turc, ou la redéfinition du nationalisme par les 'Turcs de l'extérieur," 2002; Lemmen, Islamische Organisationen in Deutschland, 2000.

132. Spiewak, "Vorbeter aus der Fremde," 2006; however, an internal poll found that less than half of imams in Turkey regularly used the prepared text, and DİB representatives insist the texts are meant only to serve as guidelines. See Tröndle, Die Freitagspredigten (hutbe) des Präsidiums für Religiöse Angelegenheiten (DİB) in der Türkei," p. 77.

133. Interview by the author with Bekir Alboğa in Cologne, DİTİB, January 2006; Spiewak, "Vorbeter aus der Fremde," 2006.

134. Interview by the author with Mehmet Yildirim in Cologne, DİTİB, January 2006.

135. Cakir and Bozan, *Sivil, Seffaf ve Demokratik Bir Diyanet Isleri Baskanligi Mumkun Mu? [Is a Civil, Transparent, and Democratic 'Presidency of Religious Affairs' Possible?]*, 2005.

136. Maussen, "Making Muslim Presence Meaningful," 2005, 13.

137. Zenit, "International Conference on religious life in Turkey," 2000.

138. Amiraux, *Acteurs de l'islam entre Allemagne et Turquie*, 2001, 103.

139. Tröndle, "Die Freitagspredigten (hutbe) des Präsidiums für Religiöse Angelegenheiten (DİB) in der Türkei," 52–78.

140. Annual costs in Baden-Württemburg are estimated to be as high as €3.6 million. Sources: Amiraux, *Acteurs de l'islam entre Allemagne et Turquie*, 2001; Lemmen, *Islamische Organisationen in Deutschland*, 2000; Maréchal, "Mosquées, organisations et leadership," 2001, 32.

141. Germany: Berlin, Dusseldorf, Essen, Frankfurt, Hamburg, Hannover, Köln, Karlsruhe, Munich, Nürnberg, Stuttgart, Münster, Mainz; The Netherlands: Deventer; France: Lyon. Cakir and Bozan, *Sivil, Seffaf ve Demokratik Bir Diyanet Isleri Baskanligi Mumkun Mu?* 69.

142. Interview by the author with Alain Boyer in Reims, French Interior Ministry, June 2002.

143. Miller, *Foreign Workers in Europe*, 1981.

144. Alan Boyer, CFCM Conference, 11.24.2003.

145. Interview by the author with Alan Boyer in Reims, French Interior Ministry, June 2002.

146. Interview by the author with Raoul Weexsteen in Paris, French Interior Ministry, June 2002.

147. Interview by the author with Alan Boyer in Reims, French Interior Ministry, June 2002.

148. Confidential interview by the author with a member of the CFCM in Paris, November 2003.

149. Landman, "Islam in the Benelux Countries," 2002, 106.

150. Shadid and Koningsveld, *The Integration of Islam and Hinduism in Western Europe*, 1991, 103.

151. Geisser, "L'islam consulaire (1ère partie)," Oumma.com, June 24, 2004.

152. Belguendouz, *Les marocains à l'étranger: citoyens et partenaires*, 1999, 56–57: cited in Maroshegyi, *Exporting Citizens*, 2009.

153. Zeghal and Holoch, *Islamism in Morocco: Religion, Authoritarianism, and Electoral Politics*, 2008, 172; see also Maroshegyi, *Exporting Citizens*.

154. Kaltenbach and Kaltenbach, *La France, une chance pour l'Islam*, 1991, 115.

155. See Laurence, "Managing Transnational Islam," 2006; and Brand, *Citizens Abroad: Emigration and the State in the Middle East and North Africa*, 2006.

156. Royaume du Maroc, Ministére des Habous et des Affaires Islamiques, www.islam-maroc.ma/fr/index.aspx, accessed August 4, 2006.

157. Shadid and Koningsveld, *The Integration of Islam and Hinduism in Western Europe*, 1991, 18

158. Leichtman, "Transforming Brain Drain into Capital Gain: Morocco's Changing Relationship with Migration and Remittances," 2002, 109–37, p. 117;

Schüttler, *Die marokkanische Diaspora in Deutschland. Ihr Beitrag zur Entwicklung Marokkos*, 2007, 19–20.

159. Ibid., 104.

160. La Fondation Hassan II pour les marocains résidents à l'étranger, http://www.alwatan.ma/html/FHII/presentation.html (access date February 2, 2008).

161. La Fondation Hassan II pour les marocains résidents à l'étranger, "Discours de Sa Majesté le Roi Hassan II à Paris," May 7, 1996, http://www.alwatan.ma/html/FHII/presentation.html (access date February 2, 2008).

162. Chatou and Belbah, *La double nationalité en question: enjeux et motivations de la double appartenance*, 2002.

163. Ibid.; Brand, *Citizens Abroad: Emigration and the State in the Middle East and North Africa*, 2006.

164. Landau, *The Politics of Pan-Islam*, 1990, 253.

165. Ibid., 254.

166. Lewis, *Islamic Britain: Religion, Politics, and Identity among British Muslims: Bradford in the 1990s*, 1994.

167. Pakistan Facts, 2004.

168. Interview by the author with Abdellah Redouane in Rome, CICI, September 2003.

169. Interview by the author with Bekir Alboğa in Cologne, DİTİB, January 4, 2006. In a newspaper interview, Alboğa denied that DİTİB was under the control of the Turkish government: "We do not represent Diyanet in Ankara, but we work very closely together with it. Only one of our board members is a Diyanet employee. We request imams from Diyanet, who stay here for 3–4 years." Source: Kükrekol, "DİTİB: wir sind bereit, alle Muslime zu vertreten," 2005.

170. Hallet, "The Status of the Muslim Minority in Belgium," 2004, 44.

171. Laurence and Vaisse, *Integrating Islam*, 117.

172. Pargeter, *The New Frontiers of Jihad*, 22.

CHAPTER 3. A POLITICIZED MINORITY: *THE QUR'ÂN IS OUR CONSTITUTION*

1. See Pargeter, *The New Frontiers of Jihad: Radical Islam in Europe*, 2008, 50; Melanie Philips, *Londonistan*, New York: Encounter Books, 2006, 50.

2. Vidino, "The Muslim Brotherhood Conquest of Europe," 2005, 3.

3. Amghar, "Europe puts Islamists to the Test: The Muslim Brotherhood (France, Belgium and Switzerland)," 2008, 63–77.

4. Kepel, *Die Rache Gottes: radikale Moslems, Christen und Juden auf dem Vormarsch*, 1991; Bouzar, "Etude de 12 associations à référence musulmane: l'islam entre mythe et religion: le nouveau discours religieux dans les associations socioculturelles musulmanes," 2004.

5. Vidino, "The Muslim Brotherhood's Conquest of Europe," 1; it was used as a slogan of the Moroccan movement *Al Adl wa al Ihsan* in 2002.

6. Maréchal, *The Strength of the Brothers—Roots and Discourses of the Muslim Brotherhood in Europe*, 2008, 30.

7. Klausen, "Europe's uneasy marriage of secularism and Christianity and the challenge of pluralism after 1960," 2009.

8. Confidential interview with CFCM executive board member in Paris, October 2003.

9. Mustafa Yoldas quoted in Wilms, "Ausbildung für Muslime," 2001.

10. Shadid and Koningsveld, *The Integration of Islam and Hinduism in Western Europe*, 1991, 17–18.

11. Langer, *Europe Leaves the Middle East, 1936–1954*, 1972.

12. Interview by the author with Bernd Knopf in Berlin, Federal Commissioner for Migrants, Refugees and Integration, June 2000.

13. Interview by the author with Raoul Weexsteen in Paris, French Interior Ministry, June 2002.

14. Mandaville, *Global Political Islam*, 2007, 4.

15. Roy, *L'islam mondialisé*, 2002, 29.

16. Landau, *The Politics of Pan-Islam*, 1990, 253.

17. Haqqānī, *Pakistan: between mosque and military*, Carnegie Endowment for International Peace, 2005, 25; Global Security, "Jamaat-e-Islami," http://www.globalsecurity.org/military/world/pakistan/ji.htm (accessed April 5, 2005).

18. Haqqānī, *Pakistan: between mosque and military*, 137.

19. Ibid., 141.

20. Karasik and Benard, "Muslim Diasporas and Networks," 2004, 470; Eickelman, "Trans-state Islam and Security," 1997.

21. Eickelman, "Trans-state Islam and Security," 1997, 31.

22. Maréchal, *The Strength of the Brothers—Roots and Discourses of the Muslim Brotherhood in Europe*, 2008, 28.

23. Bernard Lewis, *Islamic Awakening*.

24. Maréchal, *The Strength of the Brothers*, 46.

25. Kristiansen, "Muslim Brotherhood Divided," 2000, 19.

26. Maréchal, *The Strength of the Brothers*, 38–41.

27. Ibid., 50.

28. Ibid., 46.

29. Mandaville, *Global Political Islam*, 2007, 334.

30. Hugh Roberts, *Understanding Islamism*, International Crisis Group report, 2005, 7.

31. Boubekeur, "Political Islam in Algeria," 2007.

32. Maulion, *L'organisation des frères musulmans*, 2004, 284–301.

33. Haqqānī, *Pakistan: between Mosque and Military*, 2005.

34. Tank, "Political Islam in Turkey: A State of Controlled Secularity," 2005, 9; see also Topraki, "Islam and Democracy in Turkey," 2005, 167–86.

35. Lewis, "Free at Last? The Arab World in the Twenty-first Century," 2009, 77–88, 87.

36. Pirrone, "Dalla colonizzazione all'"islamismo radicale,'" *Studi Emigrazione/Migration Studies*, 2000, 67–97, 86.

37. Karasik and Benard, "Muslim Diasporas and Networks," 2004, 451–461.

38. Shain, *The Frontier of Loyalty*, 1989, 52.

39. Ternisien, *Les frères musulmans*, 2005.

40. Maréchal, *The Strength of the Brothers*, 57.

41. Ibid.

42. Boubekeur and Amghar, "Islamist Parties in the Maghreb and their Links with the EU," 2006, 15; Pargeter, The New Frontiers of Jihad, 50.

43. Boubekeur, "Political Islam in Algeria," 2007.

44. Maulion, L'organisation des frères musulmans, 2004, 198; See also Boubekeur and Amghar, "Islamist Parties in the Maghreb and their Links with the EU," 2006, 55.

45. Maréchal, "Universal Aspirations: The Muslim Brotherhood in Europe," 2008, 36–37.

46. Ibid.

47. Boubekeur and Amghar, "Islamist Parties in the Maghreb and their Links with the EU," 2007, 55.

48. Boubekeur, "Political Islam in Algeria," 2007.

49. Vidino, "Islam, Islamism and Jihad in Italy," 2008, 85.

50. Geisser, "L'islam consulaire (2ème partie)," 2004.

51. Ramadan, "Les musulmans d'Europe pris en tenaille," 2000, 12–13.

52. Geisser, "L'islam consulaire (2ème partie)," 2004.

53. Ibid.

54. Koopmans and Statham, "'Challenging the Liberal Nation-State? Postnationalism, Multiculturalism, and the Collective Claims Making of Migrants and Ethnic Minorities in Britain and Germany," 1999, pp.652–96.

55. Interview by the author with Fabrizio Spinetti in Rome, Italian Interior Ministry, January 2003.

56. The Dutch IGMG versus the German IGMG, for example. See Tol 2009.

57. Yukleyen, "State Policies and Islam in Europe: Millî Görüş in Germany and the Netherlands," 2008.

58. Interview by the author with Mustafa Yeneroğlu in Kerpen, IGMG, December 2005.

59. Lipset, "Radicalism or Reformism: The Sources of Working-class Politics," 1983.

60. Ibid., 1–18.

61. Bilgrami, "Educational Needs of Muslim Minorities: The Nature and Extent of the Problem," 1980, 147.

62. From Mohamed Nour Dachan (UCOII) to Lhaj Thami Brèze and Fouad Alaoui (UOIF) to the heirs of Necmettin Erbakan (IGMG).

63. Some indicative statistics are available: There are roughly 1.5 million children of Muslim background under age eighteen in France, and 800,000 school-age children of Muslim background in Germany. One-third of British Muslims are under sixteen, compared to one-fifth for Britain's population as a whole. Source: "The census in England and Wales, 2001," http://www.statistics.gov.uk/census2001.

64. Except in Germany, where this will be true in approximately 6 years, i.e., 18 years after 1999 Staatsbürgerschaftsgesetz.

65. Shain, The Frontier of Loyalty, 1989, 154.

66. Ibid., 146.

67. Kramer, "Fundamentalist Islam: The Drive for Power," 1996, pp. 37–49.

68. Fourest, Brother Tariq: The Doublespeak of Tariq Ramadan, 2008.

69. Vidino, "Islam, Islamism and Jihad in Italy," 86.

70. Ibid.

71. Johnson, "Muslim Brotherhood in Europe," US Congressional Testimony, 2006.

72. Interview by the author with Raoul Weexsteen in Paris, French Interior Ministry, June 2002.

73. Frisch and Inbar, eds., *Radical Islam and International Security: Challenges and Responses*, 2008, 13.

74. ICG, "Understanding Islamism," 2005.

75. ICG, "Understanding Islamism," 2005, 12.

76. Maréchal, *The Strength of the Brothers*, 7.

77. Valérie Amiraux 2001, 100; Ewing, "Living Islam in the Diaspora: between Turkey and Germany," 2003.

78. Interview by the author with Eberhard Schenck in Berlin, Kreuzberg/Steglitz, January 2006.

79. Hamburg Verfassungsschutz 2005.

80. Ewing, "Living Islam in the Diaspora: between Turkey and Germany," 2003; interview by the author with security officials in Düsseldorf, December 2005.

81. Interview by the author with security officials in Düsseldorf, December 2005.

82. Interview by the author with Johannes Kandel in Berlin, Friedrich Ebert Stiftung, December 2006.

CHAPTER 4. CITIZENS, GROUPS, AND THE STATES

1. A paradigm shift refers to the "framework of ideas and standards that specifies goals of policy and the kind of instruments that can be used to attain them." The accumulation of failures of one paradigm led to a breakdown in its underlying belief system, leading to the adoption of a new one, which changed how a policy problem is viewed and the policy instruments used to address it. Hall, "Policy Paradigms Social Learning and the State: The Case of Economic Policy-Making in Britain," 1993, 275–96.

2. Rex, "Islam in the United Kingdom," 2002, 70.

3. The other two countries with more than one million Muslims—Spain and Italy—had not yet reached this mark by 2010 because labor migration started later.

4. Favell, *Philosophies of Integration. Immigration and the idea of citizenship in France and Britain*, 1998; Bleich, *Race Politics in Britain and France: Ideas and Policymaking since the 1960s*, 2003; Weil, "Access to Citizenship: A Comparison of Twenty-Five Nationality Laws," 2001, 17–35.

5. Spiegel Online, "Thierses Traum vom Euro-Islam," *Der Spiegel*, 2001.

6. Albert, *The Modernization of French Jewry: Consistory and Community in the 19th Century*, 1977; Schwarzfuchs, *Napoleon, The Jews and the Sanhedrin*, 1979; Hervieu-Léger, "Faces of Catholic Transnationalism: In and Beyond France,"

1997; Long, *Le confessioni religiose "diverse dalla cattolica" : ordinamenti interni e rapporti con lo Stato*, 1991.

7. Caldwell, *Reflections on the Revolution in Europe*, 2009, 25.

8. Berger, *Organizing Interests in Western Europe: Pluralism, Corporatism, and the Transformation of Politics*, 1981; Casanova, "Globalizing Catholicism and the Return to a 'Universal' Church," 1997; Norris & Inglehart, "God, Guns and Gays: The Supply and Demand for Religion in the U.S. and Western Europe," 2006.

9. Deltombe, *L'islam imaginaire: la construction médiatique de l'islamophobie en France, 1975–2005*, 2006.

10. Caldwell, *Reflections on the Revolution in Europe*, 286.

11. Rosenblum, *Obligations of Citizenship and Demands of Faith: Religious Accommodation in Pluralist Democracies*, 2000.

12. Parekh, *Rethinking Multiculturalism*, 2002; Mendes-Flores and Reinharz, *The Jew in the Modern World: A Documentary History*, 1995.

13. McConnell, "Believers as Equal Citizens," 2000, 92.

14. Rosenblum, *Obligations of Citizenship and Demands of Faith*, 9.

15. Caldwell, *Reflections on the Revolution in Europe*, 2009; Tribalat and Kaltenbach, *La république et l'islam: entre crainte et aveuglement*, 2002; Sartori 2000; Fallaci, *The Rage and the Pride*, 2002; Ulfkotte, *Der Krieg in unseren Städten: wie radikale Islamisten Deutschland unterwandern*, 2003.

16. Hagendoorn and Sniderman, *When Ways of Life Collide: Multiculturalism and Its Discontents in the Netherlands*, 2007, 9.

17. Ibid., 21.

18. Modood, "Multiculturalism, Secularism and the State," 1998.

19. Rémond, *Religion and Society in Modern Europe*, 1999; Tribalat and Kaltenbach, *La république et l'islam: entre crainte et aveuglement*, 2002; Fallaci, *The Rage and the Pride*, 2002, Ulfkotte, *Der Krieg in unseren Städten*, 2002.

20. Debré, *En mon for intérieur*, 1997: 89.

21. Rémond, *Religion and Society in Modern Europe*, 1999.

22. Kalyvas, "Religion and Democratization: Algeria and Belgium," 1997.

23. Rémond, *Religion and Society in Modern Europe*, 1999.

24. Interview by author with Manfred Beckman in Berlin, Berlin Culture Ministry, December 1998.

25. Interview by the author with Eric Raoult in Paris, Rassemblement pour la République, July 2000.

26. Warner and Wenner, "Religion and the Political Organization of Muslims in Europe," 2006.

27. Warner, *Confessions of an Interest Group: The Catholic Church and Political Parties in Europe*, 2000: 203.

28. Sartori, *Pluralismo, multiculturalismo e estranei. Saggio sulla società multietnica*, 2003.

29. Sartori, "Gli islamici e noi Italiani," 2000.

30. Casanova, "Catholic and Muslim Politics in Comparative Perspective," 2005, 95.

31. Warner, *Confessions of an Interest Group*, 203.

32. Champion, "Entre Laïcisation et sécularisation: Des rapports Église-État dans l'Europe communautaire," 1993, 47, 64.

33. Motchane, "L'Islam de France sera-t-il républicain?" 2000.

34. See, for example: Debergé, "Bible et Laïcité," 2005.

35. Book IV, chapter VIII.

36. Rousseau, *On the Social Contract: With Geneva Manuscript and Political Economy*, 1978, 126.

37. Ibid., 128.

38. Ibid., 130.

39. Ibid.

40. Champion, "Entre Laïcisation et sécularisation: Des rapports Église-État dans l'Europe communautaire," 1993.

41. Wendehorst, "Emancipation as Path to National Integration," 1999, 197.

42. Debidour, *Histoires de Rapports de L'Eglise et L'Etat en France de 1789 à 1870*, 1898, 151.

43. Ibid., 42.

44. Casanova "Globalizing Catholicism and the Return to a 'Universal' Church," 1997, 205.

45. Runciman, *Pluralism and the Personality of the State*, 1997, 130.

46. Barker, *Political Thought in England from Herbert Spencer to the Present Day*, 1915, 249.

47. Dyson, *The State Tradition in Western Europe: A Study of an Idea and Institution*, 1980, 50.

48. Hobbes, *Leviathan*, 1996, 230; Hume, "Essay VIII 'Of Parties in General,'" 1985, 55.

49. Runciman, *Pluralism and the Personality of the State*, 1997, 113.

50. Kaplan, *La fin des corporations*, 2001.

51. Runciman, *Pluralism and the Personality of the State*, 1997. Since the state knows only individuals, individual citizens should articulate their interests as members of the *national* community by way of parliament, other elected office, or the judiciary.

52. Beer, *Modern British Politics: Parties and Pressure Groups in the Collectivist Age*, 1982.

53. Even with the advent of mass parties, the franchise has often been imperfectly extended; issues of universal suffrage or the ineligibility of early immigrant generations for naturalization, or simply the lack of their integration into political parties. Source: Maier, "'Fictitious bonds . . . of wealth and law': on the theory and practice of interest representation," 1981; Pizzorno points to the limitations of the political parties, whose function of social integration has been weakened. Source: Pizzorno, "Interests and parties in pluralism," 1981, 272; Parties who claim to defend general interests actually "represent only a fraction of the population . . . thus the need for structures that defend special interests is again bound to rise." Source: Pizzorno, "Interests and parties in pluralism," 1981, 256; The corporatization of these groups, he argues, would lead effectively to extra-parliamentary assemblies of specialists.

54. Durkheim, *Professional Ethics and Civic Morals*, 1958, 45.

55. Beer, *Modern British Politics*, 408.

56. Keynes, "The End of Laissez-Faire," 1926.

57. Beer, *Modern British Politics*, 45.

58. Epstein, *Political Parties in Western Democracies*, 1980.

59. Schmitt, *Crisis of Parliamentary Democracy*, 1926.

60. Powell, *British Politics, 1910–1935: The Crisis of the Party System*, 2004, 13.

61. Epstein, *Political Parties in Western Democracies*, chap. 8.

62. Maier, "'Fictitious bonds . . . of wealth and law': on the theory and practice of interest representation," 1981, 41; Maier, *Recasting Bourgeois Europe*, 1988, chap. xii.

63. Pizzorno, "Interests and parties in pluralism," 1981.

64. Schmitter, "Interest intermediation and regime governability in contemporary Western Europe and North Americaa," 1981, 288.

65. Maier, "'Fictitious bonds . . . of wealth and law': on the theory and practice of interest representation," 1981, 41.

66. Ibid., 44.

67. Dyson, *The State Tradition in Western Europe*, 58 Dynastic loyalties on the one hand and nation-building on the other.

68. Weber, *Peasants into Frenchmen: The Modernization of Rural France, 1870–1914*, 1979, 485.

69. Scott, *Seeing Like a State: How Certain Schemes to Improve the Human Condition Have Failed*, 2000.

70. Foucault, *Dits et Écrits (1954–1988)*, 1994, 654; Scott, *Seeing Like a State*, 11.

71. Foucault, *Discipline and Punish: The Birth of the Prison*, 1975, 189.

72. Ibid., 197–201.

73. Foucault, *Dits et Écrits (1954–1988)*, 655.

74. Scott, *Seeing Like a State*, 6.

75. Baron, *The Jewish Community: Its History and Structure to the American Revolution*, 1942.

76. Foucault, *Discipline and Punish: The Birth of the Prison*, 213.

77. Ibid., 212.

78. Offe, "The attribution of public status to interest groups: Observations on the West German case," 1981; Bendix, *Nation-building and Citizenship: Studies of Our Changing Social Order*, 1996, 170.

79. Weber, *On Law in Economy and Society*, 1967, 181.

80. Figgis, *Churches in the modern state*, 1914, 191; Figgis is a contemporary of Barker's, who is rehabilitated by Runciman; Runciman, *Pluralism and the Personality of the State*, 1997, 32.

81. With the introduction of legislation in Britain tolerating minority churches, Runciman argues alongside Figgis, the government finally recognized that the "legal version of events had been the wrong one," Runciman, *Pluralism and the Personality of the State*, 1997, 137.

82. Locke, "A Letter Concerning Toleration," 1983, 52.

83. Interview with Nicolas Sarkozy in *Nouvel observateur* 14 October 2003.

84. Schwarzfuchs, *Napoleon, The Jews and the Sanhedrin*, 1979, 47, 50.

85. Bendix, *Nation-building and Citizenship*; Maier, *Recasting Bourgeois Europe*, 1988; Dyson, *The State Tradition in Western Europe*, 1980.

86. Vital, *A People Apart: The Jews in Europe, 1789–1933*, 1999; Mendes-Flohr, *The Jew in the Modern World: A Documentary History*, 1995.

87. Schwarzfuchs, *The Jews and the Sanhedrin*, 1979.

88. Wendy Brown, "Tolerance in the Age of Identity and Empire," *Regulating Aversion*, 2006, 67.

89. Markell, *Bound by Recognition*, 2003, 137.

90. Barkai, *Der Centralverein deutscher Staatsbürger jüdischen Glaubens: 1893–1938*, 2002, 37.

91. Sorkin, *The Transformation of German Jewry, 1780–1840*, 1987, 23.

92. Schwarzfuchs, *The Jews and the Sanhedrin*, 1979; Markell, *Bound by Recognition*, 2003.

93. Trigano, *La démission de la République: Juifs et musulmans en France*, 2003.

94. Markell, *Bound by Recognition*, 141.

95. Wessels, "Interest Groups and Political Representation in Europe," 1997, 6.

96. Sorkin, *The Transformation of German Jewry*, 24, 27.

97. Markell, *Bound by Recognition*, 2003, 187.

98. Penslar, *Shylock's Children: Economics and Jewish Identity in Modern Europe*, 2001, 176.

99. Brown in Markell, *Bound by Recognition*, 127, 145.

100. Vital, *A People Apart: The Jews in Europe, 1789–1933*, 1999, 58.

101. Markell, *Bound by Recognition*, 146.

102. Wendehorst, "Emancipation as Path to National Integration," 1999, 195.

103. Schwarzfuchs, *Napoleon, The Jews and the Sanhedrin*, 1979, 20.

104. Markell, *Bound by Recognition*, 31.

105. Ibid., 141.

106. Ibid., 135.

107. Schwarzfuchs, *Napoleon, The Jews and the Sanhedrin*, 1979, 55.

108. Ibid., 54.

109. Ibid., 57; Albert, *The Modernization of French Jewry: Consistory and Community in the 19th Century*, 1978.

110. Trigano, 2003.

111. Schwarzfuchs, *Napoleon, The Jews and the Sanhedrin*, 1979, 179–182.

112. A classic legibility tool, according to Scott: "permanent inherited patronyms" in Austria, France, Prussia. Scott, *Seeing Like a State: How Certain Schemes to Improve the Human Condition Have Failed*, 2000, 71.

113. The civil constitution of rabbis in France, which entitled them to receive a state salary like Catholic clergy, happened later, in 1831.

114. Jarach, *Il Nuovo Ordinamento delle Comunità Israelitiche in Italia*, 1931, 72.

115. De Felice, *The Jews in Fascist Italy: A History*, 2001, 612.

116. Sibalis, "Corporatism after the Corporations; The Debate on Restoring the Guilds under Napoleon I and the Restoration," 1988, 730; cf. Schwarzfuchs, *Napoleon, The Jews and the Sanhedrin*, 1979.

117. Baron, *The Jewish Community: Its History and Structure to the American Revolution*, 1942, 22.

118. Ibid.

119. Barkai, *Der Centralverein deutscher Staatsbürger jüdischen Glaubens: 1893–1938*, 2002, 27.

120. Quotation from Martin-Saint-Léon, *Les deux C.G.T. Syndicalisme et communisme*, 1923, 15.

121. Caldwell, *Reflections on the Revolution in Europe*, 2009, 162.

122. Baillet, *Militantisme politique et intégration des jeunes d'origine maghrébine*, 2001, 355.

123. Coolsaet, "Au temps du terrorisme anarchiste," 2004, 26–27.

124. Mucchieli, *Le scandale des 'tournantes.' Dérives médiatiques et contre-enquête sociologique*, 2005.

125. Bendix, *Nation-building and Citizenship*; Dyson, *The State Tradition in Western Europe*, 1980; Jacobs,"Black Minority Participation in the USA and Britain," 1982; Skerry, "The Affirmative Action Paradox," 1998.

126. Martin-St-Léon, *Les deux C.G.T. Syndicalisme et communisme*, 17.

127. Roy, *La laïcité face à l'Islam*, 2005; Coolsaet, "Au temps du terrorisme anarchiste," 2004.

128. Keeler, *The Politics of Neocorporatism in France*, 1987, 7; Wilson, *Interest Group Politics in France*, 1987.

129. Jobert and Muller, *L'Etat en Action*, 1989.

130. Schmitter, "Modes of Interest Intermediation and Societal Change in Western Europe," 1977, 9.

131. Heisler, and Heisler, "Transnational Migration and the Modern Democratic State: Familiar Problems in New Form or a New Problem?" 1986, 12–22; Williamson, *Varieties of Corporatism: A Conceptual Discussion*, 1985, 131.

132. Safran, "France," 1983, 315–43.

133. Berger, *Organizing Interests in Western Europe*, 1981.

134. Dyson, *The State Tradition in Western Europe*," 1980, 68–69.

135. Keeler, *The Politics of Neocorporatism in France*, 17.

136. Dyson, *The State Tradition in Western Europe*.

137. Schmitter and Lehmbruch, *Trends Toward Corporatist Intermediation*, 1979; Boismenu, "Systèmes de représentation des intérêts et configurations politiques: les sociétés occidentales en perspective comparée," 1994; Williamson, *Varieties of Corporatism: A Conceptual Discussion*, 1985; Beer, *Modern British Politics*.

138. Williamson, *Corporatism in Perspective: An Introductory Guide to Corporatist Theory*, 1989.

139. Olson, "A theory of the incentives facing political organizations. Neocorporatism and the Hegemonic State,"1986.

140. Offe, "The attribution of public status to interest groups: Observations on the West German case," 1981.

141. Touraine, Wieviorka, and Dubet, *Le mouvement ouvrier*, 1984; Alaluf, "Syndicalisme, syndicalisme révolutionnaire et renardisme," *Changer la société sans prendre le pouvoir*, 2005.

142. Leroy, *Les Techniques nouvelles du Syndicalisme*, 1921, 10.

143. The 47 members were split into three groups representing capital, labor, and consumers; see: www.conseil-economique-et-social.fr.

144. Leroy, *Les Techniques nouvelles du Syndicalisme*, 1921, 43.

145. "Un islam compatible avec les valeurs de la République," *Le Figaro*, 30 April 2003. Sarkozy, Interview in *Le Figaro*, April 30, 2003.

146. Keeler, *The Politics of Neocorporatism in France*, 32.

147. Wilson, *Interest Group Politics in France*, 1987, 34.

148. Offe, "The attribution of public status to interest groups: Observations on the West German case," 1981, 135.

149. Interview by the author with Michel Rocard in Paris, Member of the European Parliament and Former Prime Minister, June 2000.

150. Owen, "The Task of Liberal Theory after September 11," 2004, 325.

151. Baker, "World Religions and National States in E. Asia," 1997, 154.

152. Ibid., 156.

Chapter 5. The Domestication of State-Mosque Relations

1. Heclo, *Modern Social Politics in Britain and Sweden: From Relief to Income Maintenance*, 1974, 306.

2. Eickelman,"Trans-state Islam and Security," 1997, 31.

3. Favell, *Philosophies of Integration. Immigration and the Idea of Citizenship in France and Britain*, 1998; Bleich, *Race Politics in Britain and France: Ideas and Policymaking since the 1960s*, 2001.

4. Senoçak, "Den Islam übersetzen," 2003.

5. De Galembert, "La régulation étatique du religieux à l'épreuve de la globalisation," 2001; Grillo, "Islam and Transnationalism," 2004.

6. Allocution de Jean-Pierre Chevènement, ministre de l'Intérieur à la suite de l'ordination épiscopale de Mgr Joseph Doré, nouvel évêque de Strasbourg, Strasbourg, le 23 novembre 1997; This formulation was inspired by the historian Maurice Agulhon, who wrote, "S'il y a place pour trois, il doit bien y avoir place pour quatre, à la table de la République."

7. Crul and Vermeulen, eds., "The Future of the Second Generation: The Integration of Migrant Youth in Six European Countries," 2003, 966.

8. Andolfatto, *L'état de la France 2002*, 2001.

9. Interview with Mouloud Aounit, president of the anti-racist association and a member of the French Communist Party, *Le Nouvel Observateur*, October 15, 2003.

10. Roy, *L'islam mondialisé*, 2002, 117.

11. Bouzar, "Etude de 12 associations à référence musulmane: l'islam entre mythe et religion: le nouveau discours religieux dans les associations socioculturelles musulmanes," 2004; Finan and Geisser, *L'islam à l'école: Une analyse sociologique des pratiques et des représentations du fait islamique dans la population scolaire de Marseille*, 2000–2001.

12. Lubeck, "The Challenge of Islamic Networks and Citizenship Claims: Europe's Painful Adjustment to Globalization," 2002.

13. Interview by author with Jean-Pierre Chevènement in Paris, Former Minister of the Interior, November 2003.

14. Finan and Geisser, *L'islam à l'école.*

15. Bouzar, "Etude de 12 associations à référence musulmane: l'islam entre mythe et religion: le nouveau discours religieux dans les associations socioculturelles musulmanes," 2004.

16. Baier, Dirk, Christian Pfeiffer et al., "Kinder und Jugendliche in Deutschland, Gewalterfahrungen, Integration und Medienkonsum," Bundesministerium des Innern/Kriminologisches Forschungsinstitut Niedersachsen, Forschungsbericht 109, Hannover: 2010.

17. Shadid and Koningsveld, *The Integration of Islam and Hinduism in Western Europe*, 1991, 99.

18. Interview by the author with Heidrun Tempel in Berlin, German Chancellery, January 2006.

19. Interview by the author with Alan Boyer in Reims, French Interior Ministry June 2002.

20. Interview by the author with Mario Scialoja in Rome, Centro Islamico Culturale d'Italia, November 2004.

21. Interview by the author with Fouad Alaoui in Seine-Saint-Denis, Union des Organisations Islamiques de France, June 2002.

22. Allievi, *Conflict over Mosques in Europe*, 2009, 23.

23. Interview by the author with Thierry Tuot in Paris, Fonds d'Action Sociale, June 2000.

24. Idriss Elouanali, *Libération*, December 8, 2004.

25. Chevènement, "Allocution," 1997.

26. *Le Monde*, May 4, 2004.

27. 30 percent are Moroccan; 20 percent are Algerian; 13.5 percent are Turkish; and 5 percent are Tunisian.

28. 84 percent have Pakistani or Indian citizenship; source: Gest and Norfolk, "British imams 'failing young Muslims,'" January 7, 2008.

29. See Laurence and Vaisse, *Integrating Islam: Political and Religious Challenges in Contemporary France*, 2006.

30. Al-Azhar University (Egypt), Al-Qarawiyyin (Morocco), or Al-Zaytûna (Tunisia), Source: Klausen, *The Islamic Challenge*, 2005.

31. Interview with Nicolas Sarkozy in *Le Figaro*, 04.30.2003.

32. Shadid and Koningsveld, *The Integration of Islam and Hinduism in Western Europe*, 1991, 196.

33. Ibid.

34. Berque and Sur, *Il reste un avenir*, 1993, 203.

35. Allievi, "Immagini di un Islam plurale," 2000, 858–73; Maréchal, "Mosquées, organisations et leadership," 2001.

36. Ramadan, *Being a European Muslim*, 2000; Koopmans, Statham, Giugni, and Passy, *Contested Citizenship: Immigration and Cultural Diversity in Europe*, 2005.

37. Kepel, *Jihad, expansion et déclin de l'Islamisme*, 2000.

38. Jospin initially ordered the girls to be reinstated. Jospin's disappointment was that he thought conseil d'etat would be more strict (see: interview with Lionel Jospin by the author, Cambridge, MA, December 2003); Jospin, however, was denounced as a "latter-day Chamberlain" in an open letter by prominent leftist intellectuals: "the future will tell if the year of the Bicentennial will have been the Munich of Republican education" (Badinter et al., "Profs, ne capitulons pas!" *Nouvel Observateur*, November 1989; Maier, "Multicultural Jurisprudence: Muslim Immigrants, Justice and the Law in France and Germany," 2004.

39. Interview by the author with Alan Boyer in Reims, French Interior Ministry, June 2002.

40. Activists of Maghrebin origin divided over the first Iraq war, Baillet, *Militantisme politique et intégration des jeunes d'origine maghrébine*, 2001, 260–65: "Integrationnistes"—find Chevenement's resignation courageous, find Saddam a tyrant, and disapprove of military action; whereas "Francais musulmans/classe moyennes"—approve of military action.

41. Interview by the author with Hakim el Ghissassi in Seine-Saint-Denis, *La Médina*, June 2000.

42. Amiraux, "Les Musulmans dans l'espace politique européen: la délicate expérience du pluralisme confessionnel," 2004, 126.

43. Klausen, *The Cartoons that Shook the World*, 2009.

44. Interview by the author with Thomas Lemmen in Berlin, Interior Ministry, February 2003.

45. Interview by the author with Alain Billon in Paris, Former Advisor to the Minister of the Interior, October 2003; emphasis mine.

46. Wintour, "Muslim groups draft rulebook for mosques to drive out extremists," *The Guardian*, 2007; *Daily Mail*, "Muslim advisors publish 'constitution' to help combat extremism," 2007.

47. A poll in 2008 found that 47 percent of French Muslim respondents felt "well represented" by the CFCM—including a majority of those under 30 (54 percent); by contrast, 31 percent said it "badly represented"; L'institut CSA, "Islam et citoyenneté, Le Monde des religions," sondage de l'institut CSA 2008. A study by the German Interior Ministry in 2009 (*Muslimisches Leben in Deutschland*) found that 20 percent of Muslims were members of Islamic prayer organizations.

48. Staff writer, "Nominati i membri della consulta islamica," *Inform*, 2005.

49. Wolfgang Schäuble, "Deutsche Islam Konferenz—Perspektiven für eine gemeinsame Zukunft: Regierungserklärung zur DIK am 27. September," www .cducsu.de 28 September 2006.

50. German Interior Ministry, "Aims of the DIK," Powerpoint Presentation, Feb. 29, 2008.

51. Dassetto, La construction de l'Islam européen: approche socio-anthropologique, 1996, 257–8.

52. Césari, 2002.

53. Ferrari, "Etats, Religion, Islam," 2001; Minkenburg, "The Policy Impact of Church-State Relations: Family Policy and Abortion in Britain, France, and Germany," 2003; Offe, "The attribution of public status to interest groups: Observations on the West German case," 1981, 123–58.

54. Soysal, *Limits of Citizenship: Migrants and Postnational Membership in Europe*, 1994, 5.

55. Fetzer and Soper, "Explaining the Accommodation of Muslim Religious Practices in France, Britain and Germany," 2003.

56. Soysal, *Limits of Citizenship*, 1994; Koopmans and Statham, 1999.

57. Minkenberg, "The Policy Impact of Church-State Relations," 197; Soysal, *Limits of Citizenship*, , 25.

58. Soysal, *Limits of Citizenship*:, 37–38.

59. Ferrari, "Etats, Religion, Islam," 2001; Ferrari, "Islam and the Western European Model of Church and State Relations," 2002.

60. Messner, "Les relations état-religions dans les pays membres de l'Union Européenne," 2000; Messner, *Archives de Sciences sociales des Religions*, 1998.

61. Messner, *Archives de Sciences Sociales des Religions*, 1998, 29.

62. Cf. Frégosi, "L'islam en Europe," 1999.

63. Ferrari, "Islam and the Western European Model of Church and State Relations," 2002.

64. Messner, "Les relations état-religions dans les pays membres de l'Union Européenne," 2000; Woehrling, "Réflexions sur le principe de la neutralité de l'Etat en matière religieuse et sa mise en oeuvre en droit français," 1998.

65. Fetzer and Soper, *Muslims and the State in Britain, France and Germany*, 2005, 126.

66. Zolberg and Long, "Why Islam is Like Spanish," 1999.

67. Frégosi, "L'Islam en Europe," 1999, 97.

68. Fetzer and Soper, "Explaining the Accommodation of Muslim Religious Practices in France, Britain and Germany," 2003.

69. Minkenburg, "The Policy Impact of Church-State Relations," 196.

70. Amiraux, "Les Musulmans dans l'espace politique européen: la délicate expérience du pluralisme confessionnel," in Daniel Rivet, ed., Islam et politique en Méditerranée au 20e siècle, Vingtième Siècle, No. spécial, 82, April—June 2004, 128.

71. Ferrari 2000.

72. Ferrari, *Consortium européen pour l'étude des relations Églises-État*, 1998. Messner, ed., Archives de Sciences sociales des Religions; Woehrling, "Réflexions sur le principe de la neutralité de l'Etat en matière religieuse et sa mise en oeuvre en droit français."

73. Hollerbach, "Quelques remarques sur la neutralité de l'Etat en matière religeuse en RFA," 1998.

74. Ferrari, *Consortium européen pour l'étude des relations Églises-État*, 54.

75. Freeman, "The Decline of Sovereignty? Politics and Immigration Restriction in Liberal States," in Christian Joppke, ed., *Challenge to the Nation-State: Immigration in Western Europe and the United States*, 1998.

76. Freeman, "The Decline of Sovereignty? Politics and Immigration Restriction in Liberal States," 1998; Hollifield, *L'immigration et l'état-nation: à la recherche d'un modèle national*, 1997; Joppke, ed., *Challenge to the Nation-State: Immigration in Western Europe and the United States*, 1998; Lubeck, "The Challenge of Islamic Networks and Citizenship Claims: Europe's Painful Adjustment to Globalization," 2002.

77. Soysal, *Limits of Citizenship*, 1994.

78. Sassen, "The *de facto* Transnationalizing of Immigration Policy," 1998.

79. Guiraudon, *Les politiques d'immigration en Europe*, 2000.

80. Geddes, "Lobbying for migrant inclusion in the EU," 2000, 633.

81. Koopmans and Statham, "Challenging the Liberal Nation-State?" 1999.

82. Statham, Koopmans et al., "Resilient or adaptable Islam?" 2005.

83. Stepan, "The Multiple Secularisms of Modern Democratic and Non-Democratic Regimes," 2010, p. 7.

84. Bleich, *Race Politics in Britain and France: Ideas and Policymaking since the 1960s*, 2003.

85. Joxe, *L'Édit de Nantes: une histoire pour aujourd'hui*, 1998, 10–11.

86. Interview by the author with Thomas Lemmen in Berlin, Bundesministerium des Innern, February 2003.

87. Interview by the author with Fabrizio Spinetti in Rome, Italian Interior Ministry, January 2003.

88. Ibid.

89. The account of the CORIF creation is reconstructed from interviews conducted by the author with former Interior Minister Pierre Joxe and his advisor Raoul Weexsteen, June 2002.

90. Joxe, *L'Édit de Nantes*, 10–11, 338.

91. For a full account of the CORIF, see Laurence, "The French Council for the Muslim Religion," 2005.

92. Schily, "Soziale Integration in der deutschen Gesellschaft als politische Aufgabe," 2002.

93. This process is reconstructed based on ten interviews conducted by the author with two Interior Ministry officials, one official from the Prime Minister's office, and representatives of three of the four Muslim organizations involved. For a full account of this period, see Laurence, "Managing Transnational Islam," 2006.

94. UCOII, CICI/MWL, and COREIS, the three organizations mentioned in preceding note.

95. The council began with President Scialoja and Vice President Mohamed Dachan Nour (who switched roles from 1998 to 2000) and expanded to 14 members. The council's appointment of Yahya Pallavicini as Imam of Milan infuriated Moroccans, who had not been informed in advance. The Moroccan ambassador even asked Italian President Oscar Luigi Scalfaro not to meet with CII; Allam, "I Musulmani in Italia," 2001.

96. Interview by the author with Magdi Allam in Rome, La Repubblica, October 2003.

97. Interview by the author with Anna Nardini in Rome, Presidenza del Consiglio dei Ministri, July 2001.

98. Shadid, "The Integration of Muslim Minorities in the Netherlands," 1991, 355–74.

99. Richard M. Anderiesse, Pieter Bol, et al., "Migration and major cities policy in Rotterdam," 2nd International Metropolis Conference, Copenhagen, September 1997.

100. Klausen, *The Islamic Challenge: Politics and Religion in Western Europe*, 2005, 41.

101. Pędziwiatr, "Creating New Discursive Arenas and Influencing the Policies of the State: Case of the Muslim Council of Britain," 2005.

102. Following publication of Salman Rushdie's novel *The Satanic Verses*, Iran's Ayatollah Ruhollah Khomeini called for Rushdie's execution in a *fatwa* of February 14, 1989, on grounds of blasphemy, as a result of which Britain broke off diplomatic relations with Iran and Rushdie was forced into hiding for many years.

103. Policy Exchange memos, cited in annex to Bright, *When progressives treat with reactionaries: the British state's flirtation with radical islamism*, 2006.

104. *Economist*, "The kiss of death: British Muslims," 2004.

105. *Economist*, "Who speaks for British Muslims?" 2006.

106. Rahman, "Communities Research—Race Relations," November 2003/ Updated March 2004; Home Office, Foreign and Commonwealth Office, April 2004.

CHAPTER 6. IMPERFECT INSTITUTIONALIZATION: ISLAM COUNCILS IN EUROPE

1. Schmitter and Lehmbruch, *Trends Toward Corporatist Intermediation*, 1979; Berger, *Organizing Interests in Western Europe: Pluralism, Corporatism, and the Transformation of Politics*, 1981; Williamson, *Varieties of Corporatism: A Conceptual Discussion*, 1985; Swidler, "Culture in Action: Symbols and Strategies," 1986, 273–86.

2. Offe, "The attribution of public status to interest groups: Observations on the West German case," 1981, 123–58; Lehmbruch, "Liberal Corporatism and Party Government," 1977, 3.

3. In the interest of typological simplicity, the treatment here of Islam councils omits one comparative aspect, namely, that there are *degrees* of neo-corporatist (and "structured pluralist") variants of state-mosque relations.

4. Coleman and Chasson, "State Power, Transformative Capacity and Adapting to Globalization: An Analysis of French Agricultural Policy, 1960–2000," 2002, 173.

5. Schmitter and Lehmbruch, *Trends Toward Corporatist Intermediation*.

6. Wessels, "Interest Groups and Political Representation in Europe," 1997, 6.

7. Schmitter, "Still the Century of Corporatism?" 1974.

8. Interview by the author with Thomas Lemmen in Berlin, Federal Ministry of the Interior, February 2003; ultimately, the IGMG was invited to participate in a DIK working group, though not as an official participant in the conference.

9. See Alain Billon in *France-Pays Arabes*, No. 274, Oct. 2001: "On ne se préoccupé que des fidèles, et l'on ne compte pas les musulmans, dits sociologiques, sans doute les plus nombreux, qui se trouvaient dans une anarchie totale . . . parce que'ils avaient besoin de dialoguer avec les pouvoirs publics, et prejudiciable aux pouvoirs public qui ont besoin d'interlocuteurs pour dialoguer"; and Bernard Godard in *France-Pays Arabes*, No. 274, Oct. 2001 : "on ne s'intéresse pas à la communauté musulmane, on s'intéresse à ceux qui pratiquent le culte musulman. Alors, il est vrai que cela ne concerne que 10 à 20% de ceux que l'on appelle pratiquants musulmans, c'est à dire qui fréquentent assidûment les lieux de culte. Notre rôle, c'est de savoir comment les gens qui veulent pratiquer leur religion, dans le champ public, et non pas dans le privé peuvent le faire."

10. Pisanu, "La sfida delle religioni alla democrazia," 2004.

11. Ibid.

12. MCB, BMF, Al-Khoei Foundation (A Shi'a organization in its consultations for the first time), and MAB, *The Muslim News*, "Tentative start for mosques advisory body," 2006.

13. Garcia and Contreras, "Islam in Spain," 2002, 168; Mantecon, "Islam in Spain," 2004, 215.

14. Spanish Federation of Religious Entities (FEERI, 1989) and the Union of Islamic Communities in Spain (UCIDE, est. 1991); Arigita, "Representing Islam in Spain," 2006, 563–84. Six members sit on the Permanent Commission, three from FEERI and three from UCIDE. But FEERI is itself inclusive of "convert Islam" and "free of foreign influence," in contrast with UCIDE, which is associated with the Muslim Brotherhood; Moreras, "Muslims in Spain," 2002.

15. Contact Body of Muslims and the Government (Contactorgaan Moslims en Overheid—CMO) includes seven sunni (Turkish, Moroccan, and Surinamese) organizations and one shia group (Iraqi); the Contact Group Islam (Contactgroep Islam—CGI) includes several Sunni movements and smaller groups such as the Alevis and the Amhadiyya.

16. See Laurence and Vaisse, *Integrating Islam: Political and Religious Challenges in Contemporary France*, 2006, chap. 5.

17. Interview by the author with Raoul Weexsteen in Paris, Former Advisor to the Minister of the Interior, June 2002.

18. Interview by the author with Alain Billon in Paris, Former Advisor to the Minister of the Interior, November 2003.

19. Capoccia, *Defending Democracy: Reactions to Extremism in Interwar Europe*, 2005, 451.

20. Lambert, "Empowering Salafis and Islamists against Al Qaeda," 2008, 31–35.

21. *Libertà*, "La Consulta islamica condanna," 2006.

22. Interview by the author with Vianney Sevaistre in Paris, Chef du Bureau central des cultes, June 2002.

23. Islamrat, ZMD, DİTİB, VIKZ, and the Alevis.

24. "The choice of using the square footage of prayer spaces and not the number of members of prayer attendees allowed us to reinforce the so-called 'regional' grand mosques that had more than 1,000 square meters of prayer space, which each received 15 delegates, plus a 'bonus' for the Grand mosque of Paris, which was assigned 18 delegates." Interview by the author with Alain Boyer, French Ministry of the Interior, October 2003.

25. In France, 992 of the 1,200 prayer spaces registered as 1901-law associations joined, with low abstention rates (between 1 percent and 12 percent) in the first round of votes in April 2003. Two-thirds of elected members of the CFCM's governing board and the council's general assembly are selected by an electoral college of 4,000 delegates appointed by the 1,200 or so participating prayer spaces, in bi-annual two-round elections. A third round was held in 2008 for the presidencies of the twenty-five regional councils (CRCM). Since 1999, 80 percent of eligible prayer spaces voluntarily participated in the government consultation and the CFCM/CRCM elections.

26. Up to 100m2: 1 delegate; Up to 200m2: 2 delegates; Up to 300m2: 3 delegates, etc.; More than 800m2: 15 delegates.

27. Interview by the author with Vianney Sevaistre in Paris, Chef du bureau central des cultes, June 2002.

28. "Ideally, we would have had each mosque elect representatives, but we need to be realistic. All of the decisions were dictated by the reality on the

ground. The only electoral college that the State could recognize was based on prayer spaces—French laïcité forbids the creation of ad hominem lists on a confessional basis." Interview by the author with Alain Billon in Paris, Former Advisor to the Minister of the Interior, November 2003.

29. Interview by the author with Heidrun Tempel in Berlin, German Chancellery, January 2006.

30. January 10, 2007, Commissione hearings, author's personal notes.

31. el-Ghissassi, "Entretien avec Nicolas Sarkozy," *La Medina*, 2002.

32. The total number of members was eventually twenty; the CORIF had fifteen members.

33. Seyran Ates, Necla Kelek, and Feridun Zaimoğlu.

34. Kepel, *The War for Muslim Minds: Islam and the West*, 2004; Tribalat and Kaltenbach, *La République et l'Islam. Entre crainte et aveuglement*, 2002; Necla Kelek, "Die Suspekte Freiheit," 2010.

35. Berman, "Islamism, Revolution and Civil Society," 2003, 257–72.

36. Caldwell, *Reflections on the Revolution in Europe*, 2009.

37. Loyalty to and acquaintance with the constitutional order is something that has been pursued by host governments at the level of individual migrants as well. On citizenship and integration tests, see Michalowski, "Liberal States—Privatised Integration Policies?" 2008; Laurence, *Islam and Identity in Germany*, 2007.

38. Some were excluded; Interview by the author with Vianney Sevaistre in Paris, Chef du Bureau central des cultes, Paris, June 2002—although he had arrived only in September 2001.

39. Interview by the author with Alain Billon in Paris, Former Advisor to the Minister of the Interior, November 2003.

40. Al Istîchara, *Le Journal de la Consultation*, no. 1, Mars 2000.

41. Interview by the author with Vianney Sevaistre in Paris, Bureau Central des Cultes, June 2002.

42. Rübel, "Sind die Muslime ein Stück Deutschland, Herr Schäuble?" 2006.

43. Berlin, den 25. April 2007 Deutsche Islam Konferenz (DIK) AG 2, "Religionsfragen im deutschen Verfassungsverständnis," *Die Arbeitsgruppe* 2 hat sich auf folgende Zusammenfassung verständigt.

44. Butt, "Preachers from overseas 'may bring problems,'" 2008.

45. Casciani, "Mosques body to target extremism," 2009; Mignot, "L'islam de Grande-Bretagne adopte un code de conduite," 2007.

46. Interview by the author with Luca Mantovani, Italian Ministry of the Interior, September 2004.

47. *La Repubblica*, April 29, 2006; in an interview with the author in October 2008, former Prime Minister Giuliano Amato said that Interior Ministry consultant Carlo Cardia was "more than an advisor. He told me what to do! Starting with writing the Carta dei valori," a commission of four other consulting professors who wrote the charter.

48. Collectif des jeunes musulmans de France; étudiants musulmans de France; jeunes musulmans de France; l'union des jeunes musulmans.

49. Confidential interview with the author, September 2008.

50. Federations have signed alternative charters, e.g., the FIOE charter of Muslims in Europe.

51. Private correspondence with Didier Leschi, former head of the Bureau Central des Cultes, June 2008.

52. E.g., a corporation of public law in Germany (*Körperschaft des öffentlichen Rechts*), a 1905-Law association (*loi 1905*) in France, or signatory of an *Intesa* in Italy.

53. German Bundestag Document, Bundesdrucksache 14/4530, Berlin, 2000.

54. This status is described in Article 137, paragraph 5, sentence 2 of the Weimar Constitution and in Article 140 of Basic Law (German Constitution).

55. Interview by the author with an advisor to the chancellor in Berlin, Federal Chancellery, January 2006.

56. Interview by the author with Heidrun Tempel, Federal Chancellery, December 2006.

57. Bundesministerium des innern, "Struktur der Deutschen Islam Konferenz in der zweiten Phase," March 2011.

58. Rübel, "Sind die Muslime ein Stück Deutschland, Herr Schäuble?" 2006.

59. Wintour, "Muslim groups draft rulebook for mosques to drive out extremists," 2007; *Daily Mail*, "Muslim advisors publish 'constitution' to help combat extremism," 2007.

60. The saga of the Home Office Working Groups & its projects; Salam: Muslims in Britain, "Sane Voices & Responses," 2005–2006.

61. Gledhill, "Code of practice for mosques aims to stamp out extremism," 2007.

62. el-Ghissassi, " Réflexions sur le Conseil Français du Culte Musulman," 2004.

63. Interview by the author with Didier Leschi in Paris, Chef du Bureau central des cultes, April 2007.

64. Schmitter, "Interest intermediation and regime governablity in contemporary Western Europe and North Americaa," 1981, 295; Schmitter and Lehmbruch, *Trends Toward Corporatist Intermediation*, 1979.

65. Lutz, "Schäuble startet Islam-Konferenz im September," 2006.

66. Interview by the author with Luca Mantovani in Rome, Italian Ministry of the Interior, September 2004.

67. Muslim Council of Britain (MCB), British Muslim Forum (BMF), the al-Khoei Foundation (AKF) and the Muslim Association of Britain (MAB).

68. Spalek and Imtoual, "Muslim Communities and Counter-Terror Responses: 'Hard' Approaches to Community Engagement in the UK and Australia," 2007, 185–202.

69. "Schlussfolgerungen des Plenums vom 17. Mai 2010 und Künftiges Arbeitsprogramm," Deutsche Islam Konferenz (DIK).

70. Peter Carstens, "Islamkonferenz: Der Dialog soll weitergehen, aber wie?" 2010.

71. Tuncay Yildirim, "We decided not to attend," *Hurriyet Avrupa*, 3 June 2010.

72. Rasche, "Integration: Einen großen Schritt weiter," 2009.

73. Sachverständigenrat deutscher Stiftungen für Integration und Migration, *Einwanderungsgesellschaft 2010*, Berlin 2010.

74. CFCM participating federations rotate the chairmanship of the foundation, and five government ministers sit on its executive board.

75. Gabizon, "Enquête sur le financement des nouvelles mosquées," 2008.

76. The responsibility of certifying slaughterhouses and overseeing halal production . . . —if a consensus is reached . . . of course, this would not exclude other steps to promote halal products, etc." Inspection Générale de l'Agriculture, "Le champ du Halal," 2005, 66–67. Currently monopoly held by GMs of Paris, Lyon, Evry.

77. Bahri, "Les nouveautés du pélérinage 2006," 2006.

78. Interview by the author with Okacha ben Ahmed in Seine-Saint-Denis, Union des Organisations Islamiques de France (UOIF), March 2007.

79. Le Bars, "La création des mosquées se banalise en France," Le Monde, December 4, 2008.

80. Ibid.

81. ben Rhouma, "L'Islam de France, Une affaire de maires: entretien avec Françoise Duthu," 2009.

82. Interview by the author with Bertrand Gaume in Paris, Chef du Bureau central des cultes, March 2009.

83. Le bars, "Une deuxième promotion d'imams à l'institut catholique," Le Monde, December 9, 2008.

84. Agreed to initial 375,000 investment, along with Switzerland and Austria.

85. Mantecon, "Islam in Spain," 2004, 228.

86. Special representative for relations with Muslim Communities, Ferré de la Peña, "Spain's Relations with the Muslim Communities," 2008.

87. Many of the CIE's press releases and other descriptions of its activities can be found on http://islamhispania.blogspot.com.

88. Arigita, "Muslim Organisations and State Interaction in Spain: Towards a More Pluralistic Representation?" 2010, 73–91.

89. Of 791 mosques participating in the Commission, 58% belong to UCIDE; 9% to FEERI; and 32% are made up by assorted other associations. Source: Ana del Barrio, "el gobierno impula una reforma," 2010.

90. UCIDE, "The creation of the Spanish Islamic Council," 2011.

91. MP Marco Boato in Commission Hearing on Religious Freedom, 10 January 2007, personal notes.

92. Ministero dell'Interno, "Costituito al Viminale il Comitato per l'Islam italiano," Rome, 10 February 2010.

93. Il Velino, "Nuovo Comitato per l'Islam italiano, dalla rappresentanza alle idee, Il Velino," 11 February 2010.

94. Khaled Fouad Allam, "Un think tank aperto a tutti per integrare l'Islam italiano," Il Sole 24 Ore, 12 February 2010.

95. Editorial, "Islam and the Pluralist State," Independent Online in English 19 July 2008.

96. Adding context to the context—as the early Muslims (Salaf) in Abyssinia; cf. Laurence and Strum (2008), pp. 49–56; Laurence (2007) in Foreign Affairs.

97. Butt, "Smith invites moderate imams into UK to help Muslim communities fight extremism," The Guardian, April 17, 2008.

98. Blair, Kelly, and Blears are members of religious minorities. Ruth Kelly is a Catholic, member of Opus Dei; and Hazel Blears is married to a Catholic and

attends mass; Tony Blair attended mass with his wife for many years and converted to Catholicism shortly after leaving office. For an informative account of of this period, see Vidino, "The New Muslim Brotherhood in the West," 2010, 114.

99. Quotations in this and the subsequent paragraph are the words of two anonymous senior officials in the Race, Cohesion and Faiths Directorate, Communities and Local Government, 3 March 2010, London.

100. Mosques and Imams National Advisory Board, "Internal Consultations on MINAB," 2009.

101. HM Treasury, *Spending Review*, http://www.hm-treasury.gov.uk/spend_index.htm, October 2010.

102. Luke Heighton, "A Jihadist Census," Opendemocracy.net, 5 October 2010.

103. Cf. Altay Manço, "Dialoguer avec les communautés musulmanes d'Europe: propositions pratiques pour résoudre et prévenir des problèmes de cohabitation interculturelle," 2009.

104. CFCM Vice President Fouad Alaoui cited in Stéphanie Le Bars, "Les instances de l'islam de France présentent un maigre bilan," Le Monde, 2008.

105. Interview by the author with Azzedine Gaci in Washington, DC, Conseil regional du culte musulman–Rhône Alpes March 2008.

106. Interview by the author with Bernard Godard in Paris, Ministère de l'Intérieur, April 2009.

107. Gehrmann, "Interview mit Islam-Vertreter Nihat Sorgec," *Frankfurter Rundschau* online, 2009.

CHAPTER 7. THE PARTIAL EMANCIPATION: MUSLIM RESPONSES TO STATE-ISLAM CONSULTATIONS

1. Interview by the author with Didier Leschi in Paris, Chef du Bureau central des cultes, March 2009.

2. Levy, "Radical Reform," 2003.

3. Del Valle and Kaci, "Pourquoi traiter avec les intégristes," 2002.

4. Olson, "A theory of the incentives facing political organizations. Neocorporatism and the hegemonic state," 1986, 165–89.

5. Offe, "The attribution of public status to interest groups: Observations on the West German case," 1981.

6. Berger, *Organizing Interests in Western Europe*, 1981.

7. Jacobs "Black Minority Participation in the USA and Britain,"1982, 238.

8. Jacobs, "Black Minority Participation in the USA and Britain,"1982.

9. This is what neo-corporatist theory refers to as cooperation amongst civil society organizations; see Lehmbruch, "Liberal corporatism and party government," 1977; cf. L. Panitch, "The Development of Corporatism in Liberal Democracies," *Comparative Political Studies* 10, no. 1 (1977): 61–90.

10. The IGMG via the Islamrat; the MCB had already been an interlocutor from 1997 to 2005.

11. Interview by the author with Renate Eichenhorn in Berlin, Berlin State Ministry of Education, June 2000; interview by the author with Fabrizio Spinetti, January 2000.

12. Nouripour, *Mein Job, Meine Sprache, Mein Land*, 2007.

13. Interview by the author with Raoul Weexsteen in Paris, Former Advisor to the French Interior Minister, June 2002, "c'est ça ou je m'en vais, ou je quitte la table."

14. Interview by the author with Raoul Weexsteen in Paris, Former Advisor to the French Interior Minister, June 2002.

15. Interview by the author with staff of the Berliner Senatverwaltung für Schulen in Berlin, 2002.

16. Interview by the author with Magdi Allam in Rome, *Corriere della Sera*, July 2001; interviews by the author with Mario Scialoja in Rome, Muslim World League, July 2001, January 2003.

17. Tincq, Le débat sur "les foulards" et la laïcité : Les boutefeux de l'Islam, 1989.

18. Pedersen, *Newer Islamic Movements in Europe*, 1999, 93.

19. Tincq and Lesnes, "L'affaire des 'Versets sataniques' La communauté musulmane sous le choc," 1989.

20. Tincq, "Des organisations musulmanes réclament la saisie du livre," 1989.

21. "L'affaire des "Versets sataniques" et les suites du défilé de musulmans intégristes à Paris," *Le Monde*, 02.03.1989.

22. L'affaire des "Versets sataniques," *Le Monde*, 02.03.1989.

23. Tincq, Le débat sur "les foulards" et la laïcité : Les boutefeux de l'Islam, 1989.

24. *Le Monde*, "Un entretien avec le cheikh Tedjini Haddam recteur de la Mosquée de Paris. Je lance un appel à la dédramatisation et au dialogue," 1989.

25. See: Laurence and Vaisse, *Integrating Islam: Political and Religious Challenges in Contemporary France*, 2006; also, a Norwegian affiliate of the ECFR condemned the remarks of Yusuf al-Qaradawi in which he said the Holocaust was "divine punishment."

26. A CFCM Communiqué stated, in part, "The CFCM joins the whole of the nation to give homage to the French soldiers who died in Afghanistan while accomplishing their mission of peace and protection of civilian populations." it also "deplored" the death of civilians, but ended by expressing its "respect for the French army for its acts on behalf of world peace." Paris, August 23, 2008.

27. Ücüncü continued, "At the Friday prayer I talk to about 100,000 people and they are listening to me. I would not be able to get 100,000 people out on the street," in "Muslims in Germany: instead of protest, raising awareness in mosques," Deutsche Welle.de, April 12, 2004.

28. See: Laurence and Vaisse, *Integrating Islam*, chap. 6: "Intolerance or Integration? The ban on religious symbols in public schools."

29. Interview of Mohamed Nour Dachan with *l'Unita*, September 13, 2004.

30. Interview of Mohamed Nour Dachan by Magdi Allam, *La Repubblica*, January 29, 2003. See also the Allam interviews in *La Repubblica*, January and February 2003.

31. Published in *Corriere della Sera*, September 2, 2004.

32. Interview with Mohamed Nour Dachan, *L'Unita*, September 13, 2004.

33. In November 2004, the UCOII organized a "Conference on Institutional Relations" and managed to attract the attendance of some local administrators;

participants in the "giornata di studio" included ACEII, GMI, and local administrators.

34. Vita.it, "I musulmani d'Italia: Chiuso l'incidente di Ratisbona," 2009.

35. ADN Kronos, "Italy: Muslim leader visits former Nazi camp," 2009.

36. Carratù, "L'islam a scuola non si introduce dall'oggi al domani . . ." 2009.

37. "Papa e Islam: l'UCOII consegna una lettera al Papa," Passi Nel Deserto, 2006.

38. Vita.it, "I musulmani d'Italia: Chiuso l'incidente di Ratisbona," 2009.

39. *Le Monde*, March 21, 2003.

40. *Le Monde*, September 16, 2003.

41. Gabizon, "La circulaire sur la laïcité finalisée, " *Le Figaro*, 2004.

42. Baverel, "L'enigmatique patron des fondamentalistes," *Le Parisien*, 2003.

43. July 24, 2008 France24.com; leparisien.fr July 16, 2008.

44. Le Bars, "Tarek Oubrou: Les musulmans doivent s'adapter à la société française," *Le Monde*, 2009.

45. Although individual arrests have been made in two countries of those who allegedly plotted to kill editors or cartoonists.

46. The lawsuit was filed in the 7th correctional chamber in Paris, which specializes in press and libel affairs (the suit was dismissed on appeal).

47. Quoted in Klausen, *The Cartoons that Shook the World*, 2009, see: 120–24.

48. Interview with Madame Nadia Chekrouni, *la Gazette du Maroc*, 2003.

49. Dalil Boubakeur for the CORIF and Haydar Demiryurek for the CFCM.

50. Interview by the author with Bekir Alboğa in Cologne, DİTİB, January 2006.

51. Interview by the author with Abdallah Redouane in Rome, Centro Islamico Culturale d'Italia, October 2003.

52. "Bayerische Muslime kooperieren bei Unterricht," Islamische Zeitung, 27 May 2001.

53. Interview by the author with Bekir Alboğa in Cologne, DİTİB, January 2006.

54. Interview by the author with Bekir Alboğa in Cologne, DİTİB, January 2006.

55. Confidential interview by the author in Rome, January 2003.

56. Ibid.

57. Adnkronos, "Islam: Redouane, Moschea Roma Punto Riferimento Per Musulmani Italiani," 2009.

58. Moual, "Nasce l'organo di rappresentanza dell'Islam italiano," 2009.

59. Interview by the author with Alain Boyer in Reims, French Ministry of the Interior, June 2002.

60. Interview by the author with Raoul Weexsteen in Paris, Former Advisor to the French Interior Minister, June 2002.

61. Cherfaoui and Alliot-Marie, "Nous sommes demandeurs de l'expertise algérienne, "*El Watan*, 2008.

62. Arigita, "Representing Islam in Spain," 2006, 563–84, 573.

63. Javier Pagola, "Rabat Toma El Control Del Órgano Que Representa A Los Musulmanes En España," Abc.es, 11 July 2007; Jesus Bastante, "Los "Agentes" De Rabat Gestionarán Más De 1,6 Millones De Euros Del Estado," Abc.es, 11 August 2008.

64. Interview by the author with Raoul Weexsteen in Paris, Former Advisor to the French Interior Minister , June 2002.

65. Interview by the author with Jean-Pierre Chevènement in Paris, Former Interior Minister of France, November 2003.

66. Interview by the author with Fabrizio Spinetti in Rome, Italian Interior Ministry, November 2004.

67. Xavier Ternisien, *Le Monde*, 30 November 2001.

68. Interview by the author with Fouad Alaoui in Seine-Saint-Denis, Union des Organisations Islamiques de France (UOIF), June 2002.

69. Interview by the author with Mustafa Yeneroğlu in Cologne, Islamische Gemeinschaft Millî Görüş (IGMG), October 2003.

70. Mouslim, "Vive l'Islam de France?!" 2005.

71. Interview by the author with Dhao Meskine in Aubervillier, Conseil des Imams de France, April 2007.

72. Interview by the author with Raoul Weexsteen in Paris, Former Advisor to the French Interior Minister , June 2002.

73. Brandt, "'Weltliche' Kompetenz für Imame," 2009.

74. Interview by the author with Mohamed Moussaoui in Paris, CFCM, September 2008.

75. Butt, "Smith invites moderate imams into UK to help Muslim communities fight extremism," *The Guardian*, 2008; federazione per l'Islam italiano; fondation pour les oeuvres de l'Islam de France; DİTİB in DIK; Foreign and Commonwealth Office's outreach.

76. La Fondation Hassan II, "La Fondation Hassan II pour les marocains résidents à l'étranger. "

77. El-Ghisassi, "A quoi sert le Conseil du culte musulman?" *L'économiste*, 2004.

78. La Fondation Hassan II, "La Fondation Hassan II pour les marocains résidents à l'étranger. "

79. Aşıkoğlu, *Almanya'da temel eğitimdeki Türk çocuklarının din eğitimi [Religious Education of Turkish Children in Germany*, 1993, 142–48.

80. Zaptcioğlu, "Setting Guidelines for Islam and Politics," 2004.

81. Ibid.

82. Name withheld, Pol 320.15, HR: -119, "Vermerk, Betrifft: Das Türkische Präsidium für Religiöse Angelegenheiten," Ankara, Germany Embassy, August 24, 2006.

83. Ibid.

84. Deutsche Islam Konferenz, *Fortbildungen von Imamen*, www.deutsche-islam-konferenz.de, 8 December 2010.

85. Thelen, "Ein deutscher Islam," *Stuttgarter Zeitung*, 15 October 2010.

86. Mehmet Görmez was the official interviewed; he was named President of Diyanet two weeks later. Welt-Online, "Religionsbeamter sieht Deutschland in Niedergang," *Welt-Online*, 3 November 2010.

87. Münster, Erlangen-Nürnberg, Frankfurt, Hamburg, Osnabrück, and Paderborn; Pro Christliches Medienmagazin, "Forschungsstellen für islamische Studien an deutschen Hochschulen, 12 October 2010.

88. "Devlet Bakani Celik," *Ikinci Vatan* 22 February 2009.

89. Temel Elcivan, "Yurt dışında yaşayan Türkler Başkanlığı' kuruluyor," *Hurriyet*, 21 March 2010.

90. "Diyanet İşleri Başkanlığı'nda Yeni Dönem," *Güncel Haber*, 01.25.2010.

91. Alexander, "Illiberal Europe," *AEI Online*, 2006.

92. Lehnart will keinen Dialog mit Milli Görüş," http://www.echo-online .de"www.echo-online.de, June 24, 2006.

93. Bunglawala, *The Guardian*, June 19, 2007.

94. Interview by the author with Lhaj Thami Brèze in Seine-Saint-Denis, Union des Organisations Islamiques de France (UOIF), April 2007.

95. Interview by the author with Dhao Meskine in Aubervilliers, Conseil des Imams de France, April 2007.

96. Interview by the author with Abdelaziz Chaambi in Lyon, Jeunes Musulmans de France, April 2007.

97. AIVD, "Radicale dawa in verandering: De opkomst van islamitisch neoradicalisme in Nederland," The Hague: Algemene Inlichtingen- en Veiligheidsdienst, 2007.

98. AIVD, 2007.

99. Vidino, "Islam, Islamism and Jihad in Italy," 2008, 86.

100. "Islam/Vicepresidente Moschea: 'UCOII come un sindacato,'" APCOM. net, April 29, 2008.

101. Interview by the author with Didier Leschi in Paris, Chef du Bureau central des cultes, , April 2007.

102. Hamel, "Bernard Godard, co-auteur des 'Musulmans en France,'" 2007. "I consider myself to be a personal consultant to the Minister"—Mohamed Nour Dachan.

103. Interview by the author with Mohamed Moussaoui in Paris, CFCM, September 2008.

104. Gabizon, "Enquête sur le financement des nouvelles mosquées," *Le Figaro*, 2008.

105. Roy, *La Laïcité face à l'Islam*, 2005, 161; Zekri, "God's Counterculture," 2008.

Chapter 8. Muslim Integration and European Islam in the Next Generation

1. Note: See 2005 Pew poll (see Laurence and Vaisse, *Integrating Islam: Political and Religious Challenges in Contemporary France*, 2006).

2. Döpfner, "Europa, dein Name ist Feigheit," 2004.

3. Rabasa et al., *The Muslim World After 9/11*, 2004.

4. Ibid., 444.

5. Caldwell, *Reflections on the Revolution in Europe*, 2009, 23.

6. *Le Monde*, 17 March, 2003.

7. *National Hebdo*, 9 January, 2003.

8. Klaussen, *The Islamic Challenge*, 2005.

9. Roy, *L'islam mondialisé*, 2002.

10. Berger, *Organizing Interests in Western Europe: Pluralism, Corporatism, and the Transformation of Politics*, 1981; Williamson, *Varieties of Corporatism: A Conceptual Discussion*, 1985.

11. Modood, "Multiculturalism, Secularism and the State," 1998, 114.

12. Ibid., 115.

13. Kalyvas, *The Rise of Christian Democracy in Europe*, 1996, 6.

14. Ibid., 124.

15. Warner, *Confessions of an Interest Group: The Catholic Church and Political Parties in Europe*, 2000, 220.

16. Fallaci, *The Rage and the Pride*, 2002; Bernard Lewis, *Europe and Islam* (Washington: AEI Press, 2007); Niall Ferguson, "The End of Europe," Bradley Lecture Series, AEI, Washington, March 1, 2004.

17. Quotation from Richard Trank and Marvin Hier, *Ever Again* (Beverly Hills, CA: Starz/Anchor Bay, 2006); on white flight, see Caldwell, *Reflections on the Revolution in Europe: Immigration, Islam, and the West*, 2009.

18. Elena Tchoudinova, *La Mosquée Notre-Dame de Paris: année 2048* [The Notre-Dame Mosque of Paris], 2009; Giulio Meotti, "Nella casbah di Rotterdam [In the Casbah of Rotterdam]" *Il Foglio*, May 14, 2009, p. 1.

19. Gabizon, "Enquête sur le financement des nouvelles mosquées," 2008.

20. Coleman, "Immigration and Ethnic Change in Low-Fertility Countries: A Third Demographic Transition," 2006, pp. 401–46, 422.

21. Phrase attributed to a Muslim Brotherhood spiritual guide, Yusuf Al-Qaradawi; source: Blog entry, "Islam and American Politics: Deepening the Dialogue," http://newsweek.washingtonpost.com/onfaith/georgetown/2008/04/west_islam_dialogue.html.

22. Phrase attributed to former Algerian president Houari Boumédiène, source: "Houari Boumédiène," http://fr.myafrica.allafrica.com/view/people/main/id/07QTlFAnWKbUCoym.html.

23. Muammar Qaddafi's remarks, *Al-Shams* (Libya), June 8, 2010. Translated by MEMRI, http://www.memri.org/report/en/0/0/0/0/0/0/4349.htm.

24. Green Paper, "Confronting Demographic Change: A New Solidarity between Generations," European Commission, Brussels, March 16, 2005.

25. Projections of the overall Muslim population in Europe for 2005 range from 13.8—17 million, and for 2025 range from 25 million to 40 million, although they obviously do not take into account the possibility of Turkish accession to the European Union. In its 2025 report, released in 2008, the National Intelligence Council sided with the low to medium estimates, saying that if current fertility and immigration rates remain stable, Europe will have a Muslim population of 25–30 million. See Pew Forum, "The Future of the Global Muslim Population," January 2011; DNI, *Global Trends 2025*; European Parliament, *Islam in der Europäischen Union: Was steht für die Zukunft auf dem Spiel?* 2007).

26. Among those aged sixty-five and older, the minority proportion would be just 11 percent. See Coleman, "Immigration and Ethnic Change in Low-Fertility Countries," 422.

27. Pew Forum, "The Future of the Global Muslim Population," January 2011.

28. Martin Walker, "The World's New Numbers," *Wilson Quarterly*, May 2009.

29. See Richard Jackson et al., *The Graying of the Great Powers: Demography and Geopolitics in the 21st Century*, 2008, versus Kröhnert, Hoßmann and others, *Europe's Demographic Future. Growing Regional Imbalances* (pp. 31 and 131) for different viewpoints.

30. Ulrich, "Migration und zukünftige Bevölkerungsentwicklung in Deutschland," 2001; Coleman, "Immigration and Ethnic Change in Low-Fertility Countries," 2006; and Jackson et al., *The Graying of the Great Powers*, 2008.

31. DNI, 2008.

32. Kröhnert, Hoßmann, and Klingholz, *Europe's Demographic Future*, p. 60.

33. MEMO/05/96, Brussels, 17 March 2005, "Europe's Changing Population Structure and Its Impact on Relations between the Generations," MEMO/05/96, Brussels, March 17, 2005 (http://europa.eu/rapid/pressReleasesAction.do?ref erence=MEMO/05/96&format=DOC&aged=1&language=EN&guiLanguage =en).

34. Immigration from Turkey to the rest of the European Union is expected to total between 2.1 and 2.7 million new migrants between 2004 and 2030; Germany will receive roughly half of the new migrants (the higher scenario actually assumes failed accession). See Erzan, Kuzubaş, and Yıldız, "Growth and Migration Scenarios: Turkey-EU," December 2004.

35. Akturk, "The Turkish Minority in German Politics," 2010.

36. Leiken, "Europe's Angry Muslims," 2005.

37. See "The Gallup Coexist Index 2009: A Global Study of Interfaith Relations" (www.muslimwestfacts.com/mwf/118249/Gallup-Coexist-Index-2009 .aspx).

38. Inglehart and Norris, *Cosmopolitan Communications*, 2009.

39. Ibid., 2009; see also Maxwell, "Evaluating Integration: Political Attitudes Across Migrant Generations in Europe," 2010.

40. Kröhner, Hoßmann et al., *Europe's Demographic Future*, p. 46.

41. Alicia Adserà and Barry R. Chiswick, "Divergent Patterns in Immigrant Earnings across European Destinations," in *Immigration and the Transformation of Europe*, edited by Craig A. Parsons and Timothy M. Smeeding New York: Cambridge University Press, 2006), p. 110.

42. See Jytte Klausen's definitive account of the cartoon crisis, *The Cartoons that Shook the World*, 2009.

43. Winkler, "Law, State and Society," 1979, 11.

44. Niall Ferguson, "The End of Europe?" 2004.

Interviews

In addition to consultation with journalists, academics, and other experts, the author conducted interviews with individuals and staff from the following offices (1998–2011)

Belgium

Associations

Éxecutif Musulman de Belgique

Officeholders

Director, Centre pour l'égalité des chances et de lutte contre le racisme
Secretary General, Parliament of Belgium

European Union

Associations

EU Migrant Forum

Officeholders

President of the European Commission
Commissioner for Justice and Home Affairs
Principal Administrator, Employment and Social Affairs, European Commission
Member, European Parliament (5)

Offices

DG-Justice and Home Affairs, European Commission
Forward Studies Unit, Presidency of the European Commission
DG-Enlargement, European Commission
Mission of Turkey to the EU
Mission of the United States to the EU

France

Associations

Alliance Israélite Universelle
Association Islamique de France
Association musulmane de Grigny

Association Sepharadite
Collège Lycée Réussite
Comité de Coordination des Musulmans Turcs de France
Comité National de Soutien aux Harkis
Conseil des Imams de France
Conseil français du culte musulman
Conseil régional du culte musulman– Rhône Alpes
Conseil représentatif des institutions juives de France
Étudiants musulmans de France
Fonds social juif unifié
Forum culturel musulman français
Grand Rabbinat de France
Grande Mosquée de Paris
Grande Mosquée de Lyon
Institut Catholique de Paris
Institut des hautes études islamiques
Jeunes musulmans de France
La Médina
Le Monde
Librairie Tawhid
Ligue des Droits de l'Homme
Mouvement Europe et Laïcité
New York Times-Paris Bureau
Rassemblement des musulmans de France
Rassemblement pour la République
SOS-Racisme; Fonds Sociales Juifs Union
Union des organisations islamiques de France

Officeholders

Ambassadeur
Chef de Cabinet, Président de la République
Chef du Bureau Central des Cultes (3)
Chef du bureau des étrangers, Ministère de l'intérieur
Conseiller Constitutionnel (3)
Conseiller municipal de Seine St-Denis
Conseiller pour la vie musulmane, Mairie de Paris
Conseiller pour les affaires religieuses, Ministère des affaires étrangères (2)
Conseiller Technique, Ministère de l'Intérieur (6)
Maire adjointe, Paris
Ministre de l'intérieur (2)
Premier Ministre (2)
Président de l'Assemblée Nationale
Secrétaire d'état aux rapatriés
Secrétaire Générale adjoint de l'Elysée

Offices

Ambassade du Royaume de Maroc
Bureau central des cultes

Cabinet du ministère de l'intérieur
Commission Droits de l'Homme, Loge du Grand Orient
Conseil d'Etat
Conseil Supérieur de la Magistrature
Cour des Comptes
Direction de la Police Générale
Fonds d'Action Sociale
Haut Conseil a l'Intégration
Mairie de Paris
Ministère de l'immigration, de l'intégration et de l'identité nationale
Ministère de l'Intérieur
Ministère des affaires étrangères
Mission Mattéoli
Préfecture de la région Auvergne
Préfecture de Paris
Service pour l'administration des étrangers, Ministère de l'intérieur

GERMANY

Associations

Anti-Defamation Forum/B'nai Brith Youth Organisation
Arab-Sozialdemokratische Partei Deutschlands
Arab-Western Summit of the Skills
Begegnungs- und Fortbildungszentrum muslimischer Frauen
Böll Stiftung; Islamische Gemeinschaft Deutschland
Bundesvorstand, Freie Demokratische Partei
Bündnis 90/Die Grünen
Christlich Demokratische Union Deutschlands
Der Spiegel
Deutschsprächiger Muslimenkreis
European Forum for Migration Studies
Freie Demokratische Partei
Friedrich Ebert Stiftung
German Marshall Fund-Berlin Office
Günes e.V.
Hauptschule Kreuzberg/Steglitz
Inssan e.V.
Islamische Föderation-Berlin
Islamische Gemeinschaft Milli Görüs
Islamische Zeitung
Jüdische Gemeinde zu Berlin
Jüdische Gemeinde zu Brandenburg
Jüdischer Kulturverein e.V.
New York Times-Berlin Bureau
Referat für Kirchen, Religions- und Weltanschauungsverbände, Senatsverwaltung für Wissenschaft, Forschung und Kultur
Sozialdemokratische Partei Deutschlands

Ronald Lauder Foundation
Survivors of the Shoah GmbH
Die Tagesszeitung
Türkische Gemeinde zu Deutschland
Türkische-Islamische Union der Anstalt für Religion
Türkischer Bund-Berlin-Brandenburg
Türkischer Elternverein
Wall Street Journal-Berlin Bureau
Zentralrat der Juden in Deutschland
Zentralrat der Muslime in Deutschland
Zentralwohlfahrtstelle der Juden in Deutschland

Officeholders

Beauftragte der Bundesregierung für Ausländerfragen
Beauftragter der Bundesregierung für Angelegenheiten der Kultur und der
Medien,
Bundesminister des Innern
Innenminister des Landes Brandenburg
Ministerialrätin, Bundeskanzleramt
Mitglied des Abgeordnetenhauses, Berlin (3)
Mitglied des Bundestages (6)
Parlamentarische Staatssekretärin, Bundesministerium des Innern
Regierungsdirektor für Ausländerfragen, Senatsverwaltung für Innere, Berlin

Offices

Abteilung IV, Staatsangehörigkeit, Ausländer Senatsverwaltung für Inneres
Allgemeine Grundsatzangelegenheiten der Familienpolitik
Angelegenheiten des Religionsunterrichts, der Schulpsychologie, Begabungs-
förderung, Senatsverwaltung für Bildung, Jugend und Sport
Arbeitsgruppe Inneres, Fraktion im Deutschen Bundestag
Ausländerbeauftragte des Senats von Berlin
Baden-Württemberg Landesamt für Verfassungsschütz
Bundeskanzleramt
Bundesministerium für Inneres
Bundesministerium für Familie, Senioren, Frauen und Jugend
Bundespräsidialamt
Bundesamt für Migranten und Flüchtlinge
Büro der Ausländerbeauftragte des Senats von Berlin
Büro der Beauftragte der Bundesregierung für Migranten, Flüchtlinge und
Integration
Büro Stellvertretender Fraktionsvorsitzender, Bundestag
Deutsche Islam Konferenz
Dialog mit der Islamischen Welt, Auswärtiges Amt
Fachhochschule für Verwaltung und Rechtspflege
Grundsatzangelegenheiten der Innenpolitik und Planung, Senatsverwaltung
für Inneres

Islam analysis unit, Bundesministerium des Innern
Kirchenangelegenheiten, Bundesministerium des Innern
Muncipality of Stuttgart
Nordrhein Westfalen Landesamt für Verfassungsschütz
Office of the Chancellor
Referat für Ausländerrecht, Senatsverwaltung für Inneres
Senatsverwaltung für Inneres

IRELAND

Associations

European Council for Fatwa and Research
Irish Council of Imams
Islamic Cultural Center of Ireland

Offices

Ministry of Immigration
Ministry of Justice

ITALY

Associations

Agenzia Nazionale Stampa Associata
American Joint Committee
ArabRoma
Aspen Institute
Caritas
Centro Islamico Culturale d'Italia
Comunità ebraica di Roma
Confronti
Consiglio per gli stati uniti e l'Italia
Consiglio Religioso Islamico Italiano
Corriere della Sera
Federazione Evangelica d'Italia
Fondazione Magna Carta
Forza Italia
La Repubblica
Lega Musulmana Mondiale
Lega Nord
Pontificio Istituto Studi Arabi e Islamistica
Unione dei Democratici Cristiani e di Centro
Unione delle Comunità e Organizzazioni Islamiche in Italia
Unione delle Comunità Ebraiche d'Italia

Officeholders

Consigliere Comunale di Roma
Consigliere per la Multietnicità, Comune di Roma
Deputato, Camera dei Deputati (6)
Ministro della gioventù
Presidente del consiglio dei ministri (2)
Presidente, Commissione per le politiche d'integrazione
Senatore della Repubblica (2)

Offices

Area degli Affari dei Culti diversi da quello Cattolico, Ministero dell'Interno
Consiglio Comunale di Roma
Embassy of the United States
Ministero degli Affari Esteri
Ministero del Lavoro
Ministero Dell'Interno
Organizzazione Internazionale per le Migrazioni
Presidenza del Consiglio dei Ministri
Presidenza del Senato
Ufficio Speciale Immigrazione, Comune di Roma

MOROCCO

Associations

Fondation Hassan 2
Fondation Mohamed VI
Université de Casablanca
Université de Rabat-Agdal

Officeholders

Advisor to the King
Advisor to the Minister for Islamic Affairs
Ambassador of the Netherlands
Chargée d'Affaires for Ministère pour la Communauté marocaine à l'étranger
Deputy Chief of Mission, French Embassy
Advisor to the Interior Minister
General Secretary, Conseil consultatif des marocains de l'étranger

Offices

Ambassade de France
Ambassade des Etats-Unis
Ambassade des Pays-Bas
Conseil consultatif des marocains de l'étranger
Ministère pour la Communauté Marocaine à l'étranger

NETHERLANDS

Associations

de Volkskrant
Islamic Elementary School Yunus Emre
Polder Mosque
Wijblijvenhier!

Officeholders

Chairman, Slotervaart Neighborhood Council
Minister for European Affairs
Member of Parliament (4)

Offices

Amsterdam Police
Ministerie van Binnenlandse Zaken
Ministerie van buitelandse Zaken
Ministerie van Justitie
Ministry of Housing
Municipality of Oss

SWITZERLAND

Associations

Schweizerischer Rat der Religionen

Officeholders

Conseiller Fédéral

TURKEY

Associations

Armenian Patriarchy
Böll Stiftung
Greek Orthodox Patriarchy
Jewish Community of Turkey
Türkiye Ekonomik ve Sosyal Etüdler Vakfi
Yeni Şafak
Zaman

Officeholders

President, Diyanet İşleri Başkanlığı

Offices

German Consulate, Istanbul

UNITED KINGDOM

Associations

Birmingham Citizens
Quilliam Foundation
United Kingdom Islamic Mission

Officeholders

Minister for Security

Offices

London City Police
Department of Communities and Local Government
West Midlands Police Authority

UNITED STATES

Officeholders

Ambassador, Kingdom of Morocco

Offices

Consulate of Turkey, New York
Embassy of Egypt
Embassy of France
Embassy of Italy

Bibliography

Aarts, Paul, Roos Meertens, and Joris Van Duijne. "Kingdom with borders: the political economy of Saudi-European relations," in Madawi Al-Rasheed, *Kingdom without Borders: Saudi Political, Religious and Media Frontiers.* New York: Columbia University Press, 2008.

Abbas, Tahir. "Muslim Council of Britain," *The Oxford Encyclopedia of the Islamic World,* http://www.oxfordislamicstudies.com/article/opr/t236/e0371?_hi=46&_pos=1 (August 11, 2009).

Abedin, Syed. "The Study of Muslim Minority Problems: A Conceptual Approach," in Islamic Council of Europe, ed., *Muslim Communities in non-Muslim States.* London: Islamic Council of Europe, 1980.

Acikgöz, Vedat. "College Launches Disputed Islamic Program," Deutsche Welle, http://www.dw-world.de/dw/article/0,,1529661,00.html (accessed April 6, 2005).

Adams, Jr., Richard H. "Migration, Remittances and Development: The Critical Nexus in the Middle East and North Africa," United Nations Expert Group Meeting on International Migration and Development in the Arab Region, Beirut, May 15–17, 2006.

Adnkronos. "Italy: Muslim leader visits former Nazi camp," http://www.adnkronos.com/AKI/English/Religion/?id=3.0.3020791707, February 16, 2009.

———. Islam: Redouane, Moschea Roma Punto Riferimento Per Musulmani Italiani, Roma, http://www.libero-news.it/adnkronos/view/68558, Febuary 28, 2009.

Ahmad, Mujeeb. "Political role of the Sunnis (Barelwis) and their Factions in Pakistan," in *Political Role of Religious Communities in Pakistan,* Institute for Security and Development Policy and Islamabad Policy Research Institute, 2008, 28. www.isdp.eu/files/publications/ap/08/pc08politicalrole.pdf (accessed July 14, 2009).

Akturk, Sener. "The Turkish minority in German politics," *Insight Turkey* 12, no. 1 (2010), 65–81.

Alaluf, Mateo. "Syndicalisme, syndicalisme révolutionnaire et renardisme," *Changer la société sans prendre le pouvoir,* Bruxelles: Labor, 2005.

Albert, Phyllis Cohen. *The Modernization of French Jewry: Consistory and Community in the 19th Century.* Boston: Brandeis University Press, 1977.

Alexander, Gerard. "Illiberal Europe," *AEI Online,* 2006.

Al Istîchara. *Le Journal de la Consultation,* no. 1. Paris: Ministère de l'Intérieur. March 2000.

Allam, Khaled Fouad. "Un think tank aperto a tutti per integrare l'islam italiano," *Il Sole 24 Ore,* 12 February 2010.

Allam, Magdi. "I Musulmani in Italia," Dipartimento di Sociologia, Universita la sapienza Roma, June 12, 2001.

————. "Il Ramadan Italiano, apelli e sospetti," *Corriere della Sera*, October 26, 2003.

Allam, Magdi, and Roberto Gritti. *Islam, Italia*. Milano: Guerini, 2001.

Allievi, Stefano. "Immagini di un Islam plurale," *Humanitas* 55, June 2000, 858–73.

————. *Conflict over Mosques in Europe*, NEF Initiative on Religion and Democracy in Europe. London: NEF, 2009.

Allufi, B.-P.R., and G. Zincone. *The Legal Treatment of Islamic Minorities in Europe*. Leuven, Belgium: Peeters, 2004.

Al-Mani'. Saleh A. *The Euro-Arab Dialogue: A Study in Associative Diplomacy*. New York: St. Martin's Press, 1983.

Almond, Gabriel, and G. B. Powell. *Comparative Politics: System, Process, and Policy*. Boston: Little, Brown, 1978.

AlSayyad, Nezar, and Manuel Castells, eds. *Muslim Europe or Euro-Islam: Politics, Culture and Citizenship in the Age of Globalization*. Lanham: Lexington Books, 2002.

American Open University. "Fundamentals of Iman and Tauhid," 2000.

Amghar, Samir. "Les mutations de l'islamisme en France: Portrait de l'UOIF, porte-parole de l' 'Islamisme de minorité," January 10, 2007 http://www.la viedesidees.fr/Les-mutations-de-l-islamisme-en.html (accessed June 20, 2009).

————. "Europe puts Islamists to the Test: The Muslim Brotherhood (France, Belgium and Switzerland)," *Mediterranean Politics* 13, no. 1 (2008), 63–77.

Amghar, Samir, and Amel Boubekeur, in Amghar, Boubekeur and Michael Emerson, *European Islam: Challenges for Society and Public Policy*. Brussels, Belgium: Centre for European Policy Studies, 2007.

Amiraux, Valerie. *Acteurs de l'islam entre Allemagne et Turquie*, Paris: L'Harmattan, 2001.

————. "Turkish Political Islam and Europe: Story of an Opportunistic Intimacy," Stefano Allievi and Jørgen Nielsen, eds., *Muslim Networks and Transnational Communities in and Across Europe*. Boston: Brill, 2003.

————. "Les Musulmans dans l'espace politique européen: la délicate expérience du pluralisme confessionnel," Daniel Rivet, ed., Islam et politique en Méditerranée au 20e siècle, *Vingtième Siècle*, No. spécial, 82, April–June 2004.

Andolfatto, Dominique et al., in Serge Cordelier and Elisabeth Lau, *L'etat de la France 2001–2002: un panorama unique complet de la France*. Paris: Decouverte, 2001.

"Antwort der Bundesregierung auf die grosse Anfrage Islam in Deutschland." Berlin: Bundestag-Drucksache 14/4530, 2000.

Apcom.net. "Islam/Vicepresidente Moschea: 'UCOII come un sindacato,'" APCOM.it, April 29, 2008.

Arigita, Elena. "Representing Islam in Spain," *The Muslim World* 96, Oct. 2006, 563–84.

————. "Muslim Organisations and State Interaction in Spain: Towards a More Pluralistic Representation?" in Mark Bodenstein and Axel Kreienbrink, eds., *Muslim Organisations and the State: European Perspectives*. Nürnberg: BAMF, 2010, 73–91.

Arkoun, Mohamed. *Penser L'Espace Méditerranéen*. Paris: PUF, 2004.

Artner, Stephen J. "The Middle East: A Chance for Europe?" *International Affairs* 56, no. 3 (Summer 1980), 420–42.

Artoni, Anna Maria. "L'Islam in Italia, Libertà religiosa, diritti, doveri," Intervento della Presidente Giovani Imprenditori Confindustria al Convegno organizzato da A Buon Diritto e Open Society Institute, February 11, 2003.

Aşıkoğlu, Nevzat Yaşar. *Almanya'da temel eğitimdeki Türk çocuklarının din eğitimi* [Religious Education of Turkish Children in Germany]. Ankara: Türkiye Diyanet Vakfı, 1993.

Atacan, Fulya. "Explaining Religious Politics at the Crossroad: AKP-SP," *Turkish Studies* 6, no. 2 (2005), 187–99.

Bahri, Fouad. "Les nouveautés du pélérinage 2006," December 19, 2006, http://www.saphirnews.com/Les-nouveautes-du-pelerinage-2006_a5371.html (accessed September 29, 2009).

Baillet, G. Dominique. *Militantisme politique et intégration des jeunes d'origine maghrébine*. Paris: L'Harmattan, 2001.

Bajoria, Jayshree. "Pakistan's Institutions and Civil Society," Council on Foreign Relations: Backgrounder, August 25, 2008, http://www.cfr.org/publication/14731/ (accessed June 15, 2009).

Baker, Don. "World Religions and National states in E. Asia," in Susanne Hoeber Rudolph and James Piscatori, eds., *Transnational Religion and Fading States*. Boulder, CO: Westview Press, 1997.

Baran, Rizan. "Denkanstöße zum islamischen Religionsunterricht-Säkularismus als Grundprinzip," 1999, www.Migrationsrat.de (accessed July 28, 2009).

Barkai, Avraham. *Der Centralverein deutscher Staatsbürger jüdischen Glaubens: 1893–1938*. Munich: Beck, 2002.

Barker, Ernest. *Political Thought in England from Herbert Spencer to the Present Day*. New York: H. Holt and Company, 1915.

Baron, Salo Wittmayer. *The Jewish Community: Its History and Structure to the American Revolution*, Vol. 1–3. Westport, CT: Greenwood Press, 1942.

Barreau, Jean-Claude. *De l'Islam en général et du monde moderne en particulier*. Paris: Le Pré aux clercs, 1991.

Del Barrio, Ana. "El gobierno impula una reforma de la Comisión Islámica para que sea más democrática," *El Mundo*, June 4, 2010.

Le Bars, Stéphanie. "La création des mosquées se banalise en France," *Le Monde*, December 4, 2008.

———. "Les instances de l'islam de France présentent un maigre bilan," *Le Monde*, May 27, 2008.

———. "Tarek Oubrou: Les musulmans doivent s'adapter à la société française," *Le Monde*, October 15, 2009.

———. "Le Maroc a envoyé 150 religieux en France pour assurer le Ramadan," *Le Monde*, September 5, 2008, http://www.lemonde.fr/cgi-bin/ACHATS/acheter.cgi?offre=ARCHIVES&type_item=ART_ARCH_30J&objet_id=1049837 (accessed November 23, 2009).

Bauman, Zygmunt. *Modernity and the Holocaust*. Ithaca, NY: Cornell University Press, 1989.

Baverel, Philippe. "L'enigmatique patron des fondamentalistes," *Le Parisien*, June 23, 2003.

BBC. "Profile: Iqbal Sacranie," http://news.bbc.co.uk/2/hi/uk_news/4081208.stm (accessed August 11, 2009).

———. "Profile: Dr Muhammad Abdul Bari," http://news.bbc.co.uk/2/hi/uk_news/5046970.stm (accessed August 11, 2009).

Beau, Nicolas. *Paris, capitale arabe.*Paris: Editions du Seuil, 1995.

Beauftragte der Bundesregierung für Ausländerfragen, *Bericht über die Lage der Auslaender in Deutschland*, Berlin: Bundesministerium für Familie, 2002, 2003, 2004.

Beer, Samuel. *Modern British Politics: Parties and Pressure Groups in the Collectivist Age*. New York: Norton, 1982.

Belga press agency, "176 marokkaanse Predikanten naar Europa," Belga press agency, July 16, 2008, http://www.telegraaf.nl/binnenland/1504341/__Pre dikanten_Marokko_naar_Europa__.html?p=17,1 (accessed November 23, 2009).

Belguendouz, Abdelkrim. *Les marocains à l'étranger: citoyens et partenaires*. Kénitra, Maroc: Boukili impression, 1999.

Benchenane, Mustapha. *Pour un dialogue euro-arabe*. Paris: Berger-Levrault, 1983.

Bendix, Reinhard. *Nation-building and Citizenship: Studies of Our Changing Social Order*. New Brunswick, NJ: Transaction Publishers, 1996.

Bentley, Arthur. *The Process of Government: A Study of Social Pressures*. Evanston, IL: Principia, 1949.

Berezin, Mabel. "Introduction: Territory, Emotion, and Identity," in Mabel Berezin and Martin Schain, eds., *Europe without Borders: Remapping Territory, Citizenship, and Identity in a Transnational Age*. Baltimore: Johns Hopkins University Press, 2003.

Berger, John, and Jean Mohr. *A Seventh Man*. London: Writers and Readers Publishing Cooperative, 1982.

Berger, Suzanne, ed. *Organizing Interests in Western Europe: Pluralism, Corporatism, and the Transformation of Politics*. New York: Cambridge University Press, 1981.

Bertrand, Charles L. *Revolutionary Situations in Europe, 1917–1922*. Montréal: Interuniversity Center for European Studies, 1977.

Berkley Center for Religion, Peace, and World Affairs. "Italy: Organizations" http://gdc.georgetown.edu:3000/resources/countries/database?country=IT&record_type=Organization&region=4 (accessed June 29, 2009).

Berlusconi, Silvio. "Attacco mirato senza vittime fra i civili," *La Repubblica*, September 26, 2001.

Berman, Sheri. "Islamism, Revolution and Civil Society," *Perspectives on Politics* 1, no. 2 (June 2003), 257–72.

Berque, Jacques, and Jean Sur. *Il reste un Avenir*. Paris: Arléa, 1993.

Biffi, Giacomo Cardinale. "Sulla Immigrazione," speech at a *Migrantes Foundation* seminar, September 30, 2000.

Bilgrami, Hamid Hassan. "Educational Needs of Muslim Minorities: Nature and Extent of the Problem," in Islamic Council of Europe, ed., *Muslim Communities in Non-Muslim States*. London: Islamic Council of Europe, 1980.

Birnir, Johanna. *Ethnicity and Electoral Politics*. Cambridge: Cambridge University Press, 2007.

Blaschke, Jochen. "Islam und Politik unter türkischen Arbeitsmigranten," Jochen Blaschke and Martin van Bruinessen, eds., *Islam und Politik in der Türkei*. Berlin: Parabolis, 1989.

Bleich, Erik. *Race Politics in Britain and France: Ideas and Policymaking since the 1960s*. Cambridge: Cambridge University Press, 2003.

———. "Religion, Violence, and the State in 21st Century Europe," paper prepared for Paris conference on Laïcité, 2005.

Boismenu, Gérard. "Systèmes de représentation des intérêts et configurations politiques: les sociétés occidentales en perspective comparée," *Canadian Journal of Political Science* 27, no. 2 (1994), 309–43.

Boubekeur, Amel. "Political Islam in Algeria," Working Document No. 268, Brussels: Center for European Policy Studies, May 2007.

Boubekeur, Amel, and Samir Amghar. "Islamist Parties in the Maghreb and their Links with EU: Mutual Influences and the Dynamics of Democratization," EuroMeSCo Exchange Facility, 2006. http://www.euromesco.net/images/55_eng.pdf (accessed July 14, 2009).

Bouzar, Dounia. "Etude de 12 associations à référence musulmane: l'islam entre mythe et religion: le nouveau discours religieux dans les associations socio-culturelles musulmanes," IHESI, *Les Cahiers de la Sécurité Intérieure*, no. 54, 2004.

Bowen, John. *Why the French Don't Like Headscarves*. Princeton, NJ: Princeton University Press, 2005.

———. "France's Revolt," *Boston Review*, January/February, 2006.

———. *Can Islam Be French?* Princeton, NJ: Princeton University Press, 2010.

Boyer, Alain. *L'islam en France*, PUF collection"Politique d'aujourd'hui," Paris: Presses Universitaires de France, 1998.

"Bozza di Intesa fra la Repubblica Italiana e l'Associazione Musulmani Italiani."

Brand, Laurie A. *Citzens Abroad: Emigration and the State in the Middle East and North Africa*. New York: Cambridge University Press, 2006.

Brandt, Silke. "Weltliche" Kompetenz für Imame," German Islam Conference website, http://www.deutsche-islam-konferenz.de/cln_117/nn_1319566/SubSites/DIK/DE/Themen/Imame/BerlinMuenchenKompetenz/berlin-muenchen-kompetenz-node.html?__nnn=true.

Bright, Maritin. *When Progressives Treat with Reactionaries: the British State's Flirtation with Radical islamism*. London: Policy Exchange, 2006.

Brohi, A. K. "Problems of Minorities," in Islamic Council of Europe, ed., *Muslim Communities in non-Muslim States*. London: Islamic Council of Europe, 1980.

Brown, L. Carl. *Religion and State: The Muslim Approach to Politics*. New York: Columbia University Press, 2000.

Brown, Wendy. *Regulating Aversion. Tolerance in the Age of Identity and Empire*. Princeton, NJ: Princeton University Press, 2008.

Brubaker, Rogers. *Citizenship and Nationhood in France and Germany*. Cambridge, MA: Harvard University Press, 1992.

Bruce, Benjamin. "Promoting Belonging through Religious Institutionalisation? The CFCM and the German Islamkonferenz," *Political Perspectives* 4, no. 2 (2010), 49–69.

Bundesministerium des innern, "Struktur der Deutschen Islam Konferenz in der zweiten Phase," March 2011, www.deutsche-islam-konferenz.de.

Bunglawala, Inayat. *The Guardian*, June 19, 2007.

Buruma, Ian. *Murder in Amsterdam: The Death of Theo van Gogh and the Limits of Tolerance*. New York: Penguin Press, 2006.

Butt, Riazat. "Preachers from overseas 'may bring problems,'" *The Guardian*, http://www.guardian.co.uk/world/2008/apr/17/islam.religion1 April 17, 2008.

———. "Smith invites moderate imams into UK to help Muslim communities fight extremism," *The Guardian*, April 17, 2008. www.guardian.co.uk/world/2008/apr/17/islam.religion.

Caffé Europa, 249, 20 March 2004.

Cakir, Ruhsen, and Irfan Bozan. *Sivil, Seffaf ve Demokratik Bir Diyanet Isleri Baskanligi Mumkun Mu?* [Is a Civil, Transparent, and Democratic 'Presidency of Religious Affairs' Possible?]. Istanbul: Tesev Yayinlari, 2005.

Caldwell, Christopher. "Islamic Europe? When Bernard Lewis Speaks," *The Weekly Standard* 10, no. 4, October 4, 2004.

———. *Reflections on the Revolution in Europe*. New York: Doubleday, 2009.

Canadian Broadcasting Company. "Dutch officials report calm following release of anti-Islamic film," http://www.cbc.ca/world/story/2008/03/28/film-dutch.html (accessed March 28, 2009).

———. "Largest mosque in Germany to be ready by 2010," CBC News, November 6, 2008, http://www.cbc.ca/world/story/2008/11/06/cologne-mosque.html (accessed November 23, 2009).

Capoccia, Giovanni. *Defending Democracy: Reactions to Extremism in Interwar Europ*. Baltimore: Johns Hopkins University Press, 2005.

"Il cardinale Sodano: libertà di culto per tutti," *Corriere della Sera*, 19 October 2000.

Caritas-Migrantes. Caritas-Migrantes. *Dossier Statistico: 2002, 2004*.

Carratù, Maria Cristina. "L'islam a scuola non si introduce dall'oggi al domani . . ." http://espresso.repubblica.it/dettaglio-local/lislam-a-scuola-non-si-introduce-dalloggi-al-domani/2113057, October 22, 2009.

Carstens, Peter. "Islamkonferenz: Der Dialog soll weitergehen, aber wie?" *Frankfurter Allgemeine Zeitung*, 31 January 2010.

Casa Arabe. *Musulmanes en Espana. Guia de* referencia. Madrid: ODIHR/OSCE, April 2009.

Casanova, Jose. "Globalizing Catholicism and the Return to a 'Universal' Church," in Susanne Rudolph and James Piscatori, eds., *Transnational Religion and Fading States*. Boulder, CO: Westview Press, 1997.

———. "Catholic and Muslim Politics in Comparative Perspective," *Taiwan Journal of Democracy* 1, no. 2 (2005), 89–108.

Casciani, Dominic. "Mosques body to target extremism," *BBC News* http://news.bbc.co.uk/2/hi/uk_news/7117630.stm (accessed September 27, 2009).

Castelfranco, Sabina. "Italian Officials Unveil Plan to Establish Italian-Islamic Federation," Rome, April 23, 2008. http://www.voanews.com/english/archive/2008-04/2008-04-23-voa56.cfm?moddate=2008-04-23 (accessed June 29, 2008).

Casuscelli, Giuseppe. "Le proposte d'intesa e l'ordinamento giuridico italiano," in Silvio Ferrari, ed., *Musulmani in Italia. La condizione giuridica delle comunità islamiche*. Bologna: il Mulino, 2000.

Centre d'Etudes et de prospective du ministère de l'intérieur (CEP). *1905: La séparation des églises et de l'Etat, les textes fondateurs*. Paris: Perrin, 2004.

Centre Islamique de Genève. "Historique Les Frères Musulmans Politique de "rabbaniyya," les prières avant le pouvoir Dr Saïd Ramadan, 1926–1995," http://www.cige.org/cige/historique.html (accessed June 20, 2009).

Césari, Jocelyne. *Être Musulman en France*. Paris: Karthala-Ireman, 1994.

———. "Islam in France: The Shaping of a Religious Minority," in Yvonne Yazbeck Haddad, *Muslims in the West: From Sojourners to Citizens*. New York: Oxford University Press, 2002.

———. *When Islam Meets Democracy*. Hampshire, UK: Palgrave Macmillan, 2004.

———. "Ethnicity, Islam, and *les banlieues*: Confusing the Issues," November 30, 2005. http://riotsfrance.ssrc.org/Cesari/, (accessed July 15, 2009).

Césari, Jocelyne, and Sean McLoughlin. *European Muslims and the Secular State*. Aldershot: Ashgate Publishers, 2005.

Champion, Françoise. "Entre Laïcisation et sécularisation: Des rapports Église-État dans l'Europe communautaire," *Le Débat*, no. 77, 1993.

Chapin, Wesley. *Germany for the Germans? The Political Effects of International Migration*. Westport: Greenwood Press, 1997.

Chartier, Claire. "Du rififi au Conseil français du culte musulman," *l'Express*, March 20, 2009.

Chattou, Zoubir, and Mustapha Belbah. *La double nationalité en question: enjeux et motivations de la double appartenance*. Paris: Editions Karthala, 2002.

Chekrouni, Nadia. Ministre deleguee chargee des Affaires des MRE mene, *la Gazette du Maroc*, July 21, 2003.

Cherfaoui, Zine, and Michèle Alliot-Marie. "Nous sommes demandeurs de l'expertise algérienne, " *El Watan* (Algeria), May 5, 2008.

Chevènement, Jean-Pierre. "Allocution à l'occasion de l'ordination épiscopale de Mgr Joseph Doré, nouvel Archevêque de la ville," speech given by the minister of the interior in Strasbourg, November 23, 1997.

Çitak, Zana. "Between Turkish Islam' and 'French Islam': The Role of the Diyanet in the Conseil français du culte musulman," *Journal of Ethnic and Migration Studies* 36, no. 4 (2010), 619–34.

"Clandestino & criminale: pregiudizi e realtà," *GNOSIS* No.1, October–December 2004.

Coleman, David. "Immigration and Ethnic Change in Low-Fertility Countries: A Third Demographic Transition," *Population and Development Review* 32, no. 3 (2006), 401–46.

Coleman, William, and Christine Chasson. "State Power, Transformative Capacity and Adapting to Globalization: An Analysis of French Agricultural Policy, 1960–2000," *Journal of European Public Policy* 9, no. 2, April 2002.

Collier, Ruth Berins, and David Collier. "Inducements versus Constraints: Disaggregating Corporatism," *American Political Science Review* 73, no. 4 (December 1979), 967–86.

Coolsaet, Rick. "Au temps du terrorisme anarchiste," *Le monde diplomatique*, September 2004.

COREIS. "La rappresentanza dei musulmani italiani," La conferenza stampa della CO.RE.IS.e dell'UIO alla Provincia di Roma, May 10, 2001.

Coroller, Catherine. "Clash au sein du futur Conseil du culte musulman," *Libération*, February 7, 2003.

Cour des Comptes. "L'accueil des immigrants et l'intégration des populations issues de l'immigration," Rapport au Président de la République, Cour des Comptes, November 2004, 427.

Couvreur, Gilles. *Musulmans de France. Diversité, mutations et perspectives de l'islam français.* Paris: Les Éditions de l'Atelier, 1998.

Crul, Maurice, and Hans Vermeulen, eds. "The Future of the Second Generation: The Integration of Migrant Youth in Six European Countries," *International Migration Review*, vol. 37, Winter 2003.

Cuvillier, Élian. *L'Evangile de Marc.* Bayard: Paris, 2002.

Dachan, Mohamed Nour. Interview with *l'Unita*, September 13, 2004.

———. Interview with Magdi Allam, *La Repubblica*, January 29, 2003.

Dahl, Robert. *Who Governs? Democracy and Power in an American City.* New Haven CT: Yale University Press, 1961.

———. *Dilemmas of Pluralist Democracy: Autonomy and Control.* New Haven, CT: Yale University Press, 1982.

Daily Mail. "Muslim advisors publish 'constitution' to help combat extremism." MailOnline, Oct. 29, 2007, http://www.dailymail.co.uk/news/article-490522/Muslim-advisors-publish-constitution-help-combat-extremism.html (accessed September 24, 2009).

Dassetto, Felice. *La construction de l'Islam européen: approche socio-anthropologique.* Paris: L'Harmattan, 1996.

———. *Paroles d'islam: individus, sociétés et discours dans l'islam européen contemporain.* Paris: Maisonneuve et Larose, 2000.

Dassetto, Felice, Brigitte Maréchal, and Jørgen Nielsen, eds. *Convergences Musulmanes: aspects contemporains de l'islam dans l'Europe élargie,* Paris: L'Harmattan, 2001.

Davie, Grace, and Danielle Hervieu-Léger. *Identités religieuses en Europe.* Paris: La découverte, 1996.

Debergé, Père Pierre. "Bible et Laïcité," *Documents épiscopat*, 2005, No. 8, http://www.eglise.catholique.fr/download/1-2637/de-n-8-de-2005-bible-et-laicite.pdf (accessed September 14, 2009).

Debidour, Antonin. *Histoires de Rapports de L'Eglise et L'Etat en France de 1789 à 1870.* Paris: Félix Alcan, 1898.

Debré, Jean-Louis. *En mon for intérieur.* Paris: Jean-Claude Lattès, 1997.

De Felice, Renzo. *The Jews in Fascist Italy: A History.* New York: Enigma Books, 2001.

De Galembert, Claire. "État, Nation et religion dans l'Allemagne réunifiée," *Vingtième siècle*, 66, April–June 2000, 37–51.

———. "La régulation étatique du religeux à l'épreuve de la globalisation" in Jean Pierre Bastian, Françoise Champion, and Kathy Rousselet, eds., *La globalisation du religieux.* Paris: L'Harmattan, 2001.

———. "France et Allemagne: L'islam à l'épreuve de la derégulation étatique du religieux" in Rémy Leveau, Khadija Mohsen-Finan and Catherine Wihtol de Wenden eds., *L'Islam en France et en Allemagne*, Paris: La Doc Française, 2001.

Deltombe, Thomas. *L'islam imaginaire: la construction médiatique de l'islamophobie en France, 1975–2005*. Paris: Découverte, 2006.

del Valle, Alexandre, and Rachid Kaci. "Pourquoi traiter avec les intégristes," *Le Figaro*, 21 August 2002.

Dere, Ali. "The PRA of Turkey: The Emergence, Evolution and Perception of its religious services outside of Turkey," *The Muslim World* 98 no. 2 (2008), 292–93.

Der Spiegel. "Thierses Traum vom Euro-Islam," *Der Spiegel*, December 2001, http://www.spiegel.de/politik/debatte/0,1518,174243,00.html (accessed August 24, 2009).

Deutsche Islam Konferenz, *Fortbildungen von Imamen*, 8 December 2010, URL: http://www.deutsche-islam-konferenz.de/cln_117/SharedDocs/Anlagen/DE/DIK/Downloads/Sonstiges/20101208-imamfortbildungen,templateId=raw, property=publicationFile.pdf/20101208-imamfortbildungen.pdf (accessed December 14, 2010).

Deutsche Welle, Oguz Üçüncü Speech, www.dw-world.de/, April 12, 2004.

Diner, Dan. "Die Moschee muss sich unterordnen," *Die Welt*, 30 June 2007.

Directorate of National Intelligence. *Mapping the Global Future, Report of the National Intelligence Council's 2020 Project*, Washington, DC: DNI, 2004.

———. *Global Trends 2025: A Transformed World*, Washington, DC: DNI, 2010.

Donini, Pier Giovanni. "I rapporti fra Italia e Arabia Saudita," in Roberto Aliboni and Daniela Pioppi, eds., *Arabia Saudita Cent'Anni: cooperazione, sicurezza, identità*. Roma: FrancoAngeli, 2000.

Donovan, Mark. "The Italian State: No Longer Catholic, No Longer Christian," *West European Politics* 26, no. 1, January 2003.

Döpfner, Mathias. "Europa, dein Name ist Feigheit," *Die Welt*, 20 November, 2004.

Dunya Gazetesi. "New Religious Affairs Directorate office to work to dispel misunderstanding of Islam in Europe," 05.14.2009, http://www.dunyagazetesi.com.tr/haber.asp?id=47582&cDate= (accessed November 23, 2009).

Durkheim, Emile. *Professional Ethics and Civic Morals*. Glencoe IL: Free Press, 1958.

Dyson, Kenneth. *The State Tradition in Western Europe: A Study of an Idea and Institution*. New York: Oxford University Press, 1980.

Eade, John. "Nationalism, Community and the Islamization of Space in London," in Barbara Metcalf, ed., *Making Muslim Space in Europe and North America*. Berkeley: University of California Press, 1996.

Earnest, David C. "Neither Citizen nor Stranger: Why States Enfranchise Resident Aliens," *World Politics* 58, no. 2, January 2006, 242–75.

Editorial, "Islam and the Pluralist State," *Independent Online* in English, 19 July 2008.

The Economist. "The kiss of death: British Muslims," August 14, 2004.

———. "Who speaks for British Muslims?" June 17, 2006.

L'Economiste. *"MRE: Enseignement de la langue arabe et de la culture marocaine,"* *l'Economiste* and MAP (Maghreb Arab Press), 2004, http://www.yabiladi.com/societe-mre-enseignement-langue-arabe-culture,20.html (accessed November 23, 2009).

El-Ghali, Mohamed. "The Cold Embrace: U.S. & Islamists in North Africa," *Arab Insight* 1, no. 1 (Spring 2007), 52. www.worldsecurityinstitute.org/temp/ArabInsightVol1No1.pdf (accessed July 6, 2009).

Eickelman, Dale. "Trans-state Islam and Security," in Susanne Hoeber Rudolph and James Piscatori, eds., *Transnational Religion and Fading States*. Boulder, CO: Westview Press, 1997.

Encyclopædia Britannica. "Necmettin Erbakan," Encyclopædia Britannica Online, 2009. http://www.britannica.com/EBchecked/topic/191078/Necmet tinErbakan (accessed July 1, 2009).

Entelis, John P. *Algeria: The Revolution Institutionalized*. Boulder, CO: Westview Press, 1986.

Epstein, Leon D. *Political Parties in Western Democracies*. New Brunswick, NJ: Transaction Publishers, 1980.

Erzan, Refik, Umut Kuzubaş, and Nilüfer Yıldız. "Growth and Migration Scenarios: Turkey-EU," EU-Turkey Working Paper 13, Center for European Policy Studies, December 2004.

Escobar Stemmann, Juan José. "Activismo islámico en España," *Política Exterior* m\no. 124, July/August, 2008. http://www.revistasculturales.com/articulos/25/politica-exterior/930/1/activismo-islamico-en-espana.html (accessed June 29, 2009).

Euro Islam. "Country Profile: Italy," Euro Islam, http://www.euro-islam.info/country-profiles/italy/ (accessed June 30, 2009).

———. "Country Profile: The Netherlands," Euro-Islam, http://www.euro islam.info/country-profiles/the-netherlands/ (accessed June 30, 2009).

European Commission. "Confronting Demographic Change: A New Solidarity between Generations," Green Paper, Brussels, March 16, 2005 (http://ec.europa .eu/employment_social/news/2005/mar/comm2005-94_de.pdf).

European Court of Human Rights. "Chamber Hearing Kavakçi v. Turkey, Fazilet Partisi and Kutan v. Turkey, Silay v. Turkey and Ilicak v. Turkey," October 13, 2005. http://www.echr.coe.int/Eng/Press/2005/Oct/Hearing Kavakci-FaziletPartsisandKutan-Silay-IlicakvTurkey131005.htm (accessed June 16, 2009).

European Muslim Network. "Profile of Belgium," http://www.euromuslim.net/index.php/islam-in-europe/country-profile/profile-of-belgium/, May 2007 (accessed December 16, 2010).

European Parliament. *Islam in the European Union: What's at Stake in the Future?* Study IP/B/CULT/IC/2006_061, May 2007.

European Union Minorities and Discrimination Survey, "Data in Focus Report: Muslims," Vienna: EU Agency for Fundamental Rights, 2009.

Evangelische Kirche in Deutschland. "Religionsunterricht für muslimische Schülerinnen und Schüler," Eine Stellungnahme, Hannover, den 16. February 1999, http://www.ekd.de/EKD-Texte/religionsunterricht_muslimisch_ 1999.html (accessed July 28, 2009).

Ewing, Katherine Pratt. "Living Islam in the Diaspora: between Turkey and Germany," *South Atlantic Quarterly* 102: 2/3 Spring/Summer 2003.

Fallaci, Oriana. *The Rage and the Pride*, New York: Rizzoli, 2002.

Faust, Elke. "Close Ties and New Boundaries: Tablighi Jama'at in Britain and Germany," in Muhammad Khalid Masud, ed., *Travelers in Faith: Studies of the Tablighi Jama'at as a Transnational Islamic Movement for Faith Renewal*. Leiden: Brill, 2000.

Favaro, Graziella. "I minori musulmani in Italia," in Stefano Allievi, ed., *I Bambini dell'Islam.* OpenSociety, 2002.

Favell, Adrian. *Philosophies of Integration. Immigration and the Idea of Citizenship in France and Britain.* Houndsmills: MacMillan, 1998.

———. *Philosophies of Integration: Immigration and the Idea of Citizenship in France and Britain,* second edition. New York: Palgrave, 2001.

Federation of Student Islamic Societies. "About FOSIS," http://www.fosis.org.uk/index.php?option=com_content&view=article&id=248&Itemid=19 (accessed June 26, 2009).

Feindt-Riggers, Nils, and Udo Steinbach. *Islamische Organisationen in Deutschland: eine aktuelle Bestandsaufnahme und Analyse; Pilotuntersuchung.* Hamburg: Deutsches Orient-Institut, 1997.

Ferguson, Niall. "The End of Europe," Bradley Lecture Series, AEI, Washington, March 1, 2004.

———. "Eurabia," *The New York Times,* April 4, 2004. http://www.nytimes.com/2004/04/04/magazine/04WWLN.html (accessed July 17, 2008).

Ferrari, Alessandro, and Cristina Chinni. "Sinossi delle bozze di Intesa—AMI, UCOII, COREIS)," Osservatorio delle liberta' ed istituzioni religiose, 2000.

Ferrari, Silvio. Consortium européen pour l'étude des relations Églises-État. Milan: A. Giuffré, No. 6, 1998.

———. ed. *Musulmani in Italia: la codizione giuridica delle comunità islamiche.* Bologna: Il Mulino, 2000.

———. "Etats, Religion, Islam," in Felice Dassetto, Brigitte Maréchal, Jørgen S. Nielsen, and Stefano Allievi, eds., *Convergences musulmanes: aspects contemporains de l'islam dans l'Europe.* Paris: Harmattan, 2001.

———. "Islam and the Western European Model of Church and State Relations," in W.A.R. Shadid and P. S. van Koningsveld, eds., *Religious Freedom and Neutrality of the State: the Position of Islam in the European Union.* Leuven: Peeters, 2002.

Ferrari, Silvio, and Anthony Bradney, eds. *Islam and European Legal Systems.* Farnham, UK: Ashgate, 2000.

Ferré de la Peña, José María. "Spain's Relations with the Muslim Communities," Al-Arab Online, June 8, 2008.

Fetzer, Joel, and J. C. Soper. "Accommodating the Religious Practices of Muslim Immigrants in England, France and Germany," APSA paper, 2001.

———. "Explaining the Accommodation of Muslim Religious Practices in France, Britain and Germany," *French Politics* 1, no. 1, 2003.

———. *Muslims and the State in Britain, France and Germany.* Cambridge: Cambridge University Press, 2005.

Figgis, John Neville. *Churches in the Modern State.* London, 1914.

Figueras, Amanda. "La España que reza a Alá," *El Mundo,* May 20, 2004, http://www.elmundo.es/elmundo/2004/05/04/espana/1083623510.html, (accessed June 28, 2009).

Finan, Khadija, and Vincent Geisser. *L'islam à l'école: Une analyse sociologique des pratiques et des représentations du fait islamique dans la population scolaire de Marseille.* Monbéliard et Lille, Rapport Final de l'Étude. Paris: l'Institut national des hautes études de sécurité, 2000–2001.

Fondazione ISMU/Universita' Bicocca. *Il Giornale*, June 26, 2005.

Foucault, Michel. *Discipline and Punish: The Birth of the Prison*. New York: Vintage, 1975.

———. *Dits et Écrits (1954–1988)*, vols. 3 and 4. Paris: Gallimard, 1994.

La Fondation Hassan II. "La Fondation Hassan II pour les marocains résidents à l'étranger." http://www.alwatan.ma/html/FHII/presentation.html (November 22, 2009).

———. Discours de Sa Majesté le Roi Hassan II à Paris, le 7 Mai 1996, http://www.alwatan.ma/html/FHII/presentation.html (November 22, 2009).

Fourest, Caroline. "The War for Eurabia," *Wall Street Journal*, February 2, 2005. http://online.wsj.com/article/SB110729559310242790.html (accessed July 17, 2009).

———. *Brother Tariq: The Doublespeak of Tariq Ramadan*. New York: Encounter Books, 2008.

Frankel, Jonathan. "Assimilation and the Jews in Nineteenth-century Europe," in Frankel and Steven J. Zipperstein, eds., *Assimilation and Community: The Jews in Nineteenth-century Europe*, Cambridge: Cambridge University Press, 1992, 1–37.

Fraser, Cary. "In Defense of Allah's Realm: Religion and Statecraft in Saudi Foreign Policy Strategy," in Susanne Hoeber Rudolph and James Piscatori, eds., *Transnational Religion and Fading States*. Boulder, CO: Westview Press, 1997.

Freeman, Gary. "The Decline of Sovereignty? Politics and Immigration Restriction in Liberal States," in Christian Joppke, ed., *Challenge to the Nation-State: Immigration in Western Europe and the United States*. Oxford: Oxford University Press, 1998.

Frégosi, Franck. "L'Islam en Europe, Entre Dynamiques d'Institutionnalisation, de Reconnaissance et Difficultés Objectives d'Organisation," in *Religions, Droits, Sociétés en Europe Communautaire*. Aix: Presses de l'Université Aix-en-Provence, 1999.

———. "Réflexions sur les contours évolutifs d'une régulation étatique de l'islam en régime de laïcité," L'islam dans un espace laïque, colloque June 22–23, 2000. Département des actions internationales, l'Institut national des hautes études de sécurité, 2000.

———. *La problématique de l'institutionnalisation du culte musulman en France et en Europe: Réflexions sur l'organisation d'un Islam minoritaire dans un espace sécularisé*, IEP/Univ. Robert Schuman Strasbourg III, Habilitation à diriger les recherches sciences politiques, 2003.

Frémeaux, Jacques. *Le Monde Arabe et la Sécurité de la France depuis 1958*. Paris: Presses Universitaires de France, 1995.

Frisch, Hillel, and Efraim Inbar, eds. *Radical Islam and International Security: Challenges and Responses*. New York: Routledge, 2008.

Fukuyama, Francis. "Voile et contrôle sexuel," *Le Monde*, February 3, 2004.

Gabizon, Cecilia. "La circulairesur la laicite finalisee," *Le Figaro*, May 1, 2004.

———. "Enquête sur le financement des nouvelles mosquées," *Le Figaro*, December 22, 2008.

Gaborieau, Marc. "The Transformation of Tablighi Jama'at into a Transnational Movement," in M. K. Masud, ed., *Travelers in Faith: Studies of the Tablighi*

Jam'at as a Transnational Islamic Movement for Faith Revival. Boston: Brill, 2000, 121–38.

Gadi, Abdelhadi. "100 prédicateurs," *Le Matin* (Casablanca), October 10, 2006.

de Galembert, Claire, and Nikola Tietze. "Institutionalisierung des Islam in Deutschland," *Mittelweg* 36, January 2002.

Galli della Loggia, Ernesto. Untitled editorial, *Corriere della Sera*, July 17, 2000.

Garcia, Bernabe Lopez, and Ana I. Planet Contreras. "Islam in Spain," in Shireen Hunter, ed., *Islam, Europe's Second Religion: The New Social, Cultural, and Political Landscape*. Washington, DC: Center for Strategic and International Studies, 2002.

Gauchet, Marcel. *Le désenchantement du monde*. Paris: Gallimard, 1985.

Gauhar, Altaf. "Islam and the Secular Thrust of Western Capitalism," in Islamic Council of Europe, ed., *Islam and Contemporary Society*. New York: Longman, 1982.

Gaye, Amadou Karim. "Muslim Minorities: A Framework," Islamic Council of Europe, ed., *Muslim Communities in non-Muslim States*. London: Islamic Council of Europe, 1980.

Geddes, Andrew. "Lobbying for migrant inclusion in the EU: new opportunities for transnational advocacy?' *Journal of European Public Policy* 7, no. 4, pp. 632–49, 2000.

Gehrmann, Sebastian. "Interview mit Islam-Vertreter Nihat Sorgec," *Frankfurter Rundschau* online, June 29, 2009, http://www.fr-online.de/in_und_ausland/politik/aktuell/1812026_Interview-mit-Islam-Vertreter-Nihat-Sorgec-Blackbox-Islam-wurde-transparenter.html (accessed September 29, 2009).

Geisser, Vincent. *Ethnicité républicaine*. Paris: Presses de Sciences Po, 1997.

———. "L'islam consulaire (1ère & 2eme partie) Le rôle des États d'origine dans la gestion de l'islam de France." http://oumma com/L-islam-consulaire-2eme-partie-et, June 24, 2004.

Geisser, Vincent, and Scherhazade Kelfaoui. "Trois générations de militantisme politique sous la Vème république: l'activiste immigre, le beur civique, et l'électeur musulman," *La Médina*, December 2001.

German Bundestag. "German Bundestag Document," Bundesdrucksache 14/4530, Berlin, 2000.

German Interior Ministry. "Aims of the DIK," Powerpoint Presentation from the German Interior Ministry, February 29, 2008.

Gest, Justin, and Andrew Norfolk. "British imams 'failing young Muslims,'" *The Times* (London), January 7, 2008.

El Ghissassi, Hakim. "Entretien avec Nicolas Sarkozy," *La Medina*, no. 16, October 2002.

———. "A quoi sert le Conseil du culte musulman?" *L'économiste* (Casablanca), January 24, 2004.

——— *Regard sur le Maroc de Mohammed VI*, Neuilly-sur-seine: Michel Lafon, 2006.

———. "Réflexions sur le Conseil Français du Culte Musulman," July 9, 2004, http://www.communautarisme.net/Reflexions-sur-le-Conseil-Francais-du-Culte-Musulman_a255.html (accessed September 29, 2009).

———. "La restructuration du champ religieux marocain, entretien avec Mohamed Tozy," January 16, 2007, http://www.sezamemag.net/La-restructuration-du-champ-religieux-marocain,-entretien-avec-Mohamed-Tozy_a702.htmlt (accessed July 27, 2009).

———. "Le gouvernement marocain pour la création de centres culturels en Europe," Sezamemag.net, May 11, 2008, http://www.sezamemag.net/Le-gouvernement-marocain-pour-la-creation-de-centres-culturels-en-Europe_a1805.html, (accessed November 23, 2009).

———. "Première Assemblée plénière du Conseil de la comunauté Marocaine à l'étranger," June 4, 2008 http://www.sezamemag.net/Premiere-Assemblee-pleniere-du-Conseil-de-la-comunaute-Marocaine-a-l-etranger_a1893.html (accessed November 23, 2009).

———. "Principaux axes du programme 2009 du Conseil marocain des ouléma pour l'Europe," www.sezamemag.net, January 30, 2009.

Gibbon, James. "Diyanet, Bardakoğlu and more," August 19, 2006 http://jimgibbon.com/2006/08/19/diyanet-bardakoglu-and-more/ (accessed November 23, 2009).

———. "Religion, Immigration and the Turkish Government in Germany: Re-examining the Turkish-Islamic Union for Religious Affairs (DİTİB)," in *Living Islam in Europe*, ed. Dietrich Reetz. Boston, MA: Brill Academic Publishers, forthcoming.

Gledhill, Ruth. "Code of practice for mosques aims to stamp out extremism," TimesOnline, Nov. 28, 2007, http://www.timesonline.co.uk/tol/comment/faith/article2957492.ece (accessed September 29, 2009).

Global Security. "Jamiat Ulema-e-Islam," Globalsecurity.org, http://www.globalsecurity.org/military/world/pakistan/jui.htm (accessed June 15, 2008).

———. "Muttahida Majlis-e-Amal (MMA)," Globalsecurity.org, http://www.globalsecurity.org/military/world/pakistan/mma.htm (accessed June 15, 2009).

Gogolin, Ingrid, Ursula Neumann, and Lutz Reuter. *Schulbildung für Kinder aus Minderheiten in Deutschland, 1989–1999*. Münster: Waxmann Verlag, 2001.

Goldberg, Jonah. *National Review*, December 16, 2004. http://article.nationalreview.com/?q=NTgwNDAwNjYyNGI3MTJjNTgyMjMzYTRjZDI5NGIzYjg= (accessed July 20, 2009).

Gonzales, Manuel Cabezas. "La France," in José Carlos Herreras, ed., *L'enseignement des langues étrangères dans les pays de l'Union européenne*. Louvain: Peeters, 1998.

Gresh, Alain, and Tariq Ramadan. *L'Islam en Questions*. Sindbad: Actes Sud, 2000.

Grillo, Ralph. "Islam and Transnationalism," *Journal of Ethnic and Migration Studies* 30, no. 5 (2004), 861–78.

Gritti, Roberto, and Magdi Allam. "Percorsi identitari: essere musulmani in Italia," *Islam, Italia*. Milan: Guerini, 2001.

Guiraudon, Virginie. "Citizenship Rights for Non-Citizens: France, Germany and the Netherlands," in Christian Joppke, ed., *Challenge to the Nation-State: Immigration in Western Europe and the United States*. Oxford: Oxford University Press, 1998.

———. *Les politiques d'immigration en Europe: Allemagne, France, Pays-Bas*. Paris: L'Harmattan, 2000.

Guolo, Renzo. *Xenofobi e Xenofili: Gli Italiani e l'Islam*. Rome: editori Laterza, 2004.

Haddad, Yvonne Yazbeck, and Michael J. Balz. "The October Riots in France: A Failed Immigration Policy or the Empire Strikes Back?" *International Migration* 44, no. 2 (June 2006), 23–34.

Haddad, Yvonne Yazbeck, and Tyler Golson. "Overhauling Islam: representation, construction, and co-option of 'moderate Islam' in Western Europe," *Journal of Church and State* 49, no. 3, 2007.

Hagendoorn, A., and Paul M. Sniderman. *When Ways of Life Collide: Multiculturalism and Its Discontents in the Netherlands*. Princeton, NJ: Princeton University Press, 2007.

Hall, Peter. "Policy Paradigms Social Learning and the State: The Case of Economic Policy-Making in Britain," *Comparative Politics* 25, no. 3 (1993), 275–96.

Hall, Peter, and John Keeler. "Interest Representation and the Politics of Protest," in *Developments in French Politics*, vol. 2, Alain Guyomarch, Howard Machin, Peter A. Hall, and Jack Hayward, eds., London: Palgrave, 2001, 50–67.

Hallet, Jean. "The Status of the Muslim Minority in Belgium," in Roberta Aluffi Beck-Peccoz, *The Legal Treatment of Islamic Minorities in Europe*. Leuven: Peeters, 2004.

Hamel, Ian. "Bernard Godard, co-auteur des 'Musulmans en France,'" Oumma. com, May 3, 2007.

Hammar, Thomas. *Democracy and the Nation State: Aliens, Denizens, and Citizens in a World of International Migration*. Aldershot: Avebury/Gower, 1990.

Hansen, Randall, and Patrick Weil/ *Towards a European Nationality. Citizenship, Immigration and Nationality Law in the EU*. Houndmills: Macmillan, 2000.

Haqqānī, Husain. *Pakistan: Between Mosque and Military*. Carnegie Endowment for International Peace, 2005.

Haug, Sonja, Stephanie Müssig, and Anja Stichs. *Muslimisches Leben in Deutschland*, im Auftrag der Deutschen Islam Konferenz, Forschungsbericht 6, Nürnberg: BAMF, 2009.

Heclo, Hugh. *Modern Social Politics in Britain and Sweden: From Relief to Income Maintenance*. New Haven, CT: Yale University Press, 1974.

Heighton, Luke. "A Jihadist Census," Opendemocracy.net, 5 October 2010.

Heisler, Barbara Schmitter, and M. O. Heisler. "Transnational Migration and the Modern Democratic State: Familiar Problems in New Form or a New Problem?" *Annals of the American Academy of Political and Social Science* 485, no. 1 (1986), 12–22.

Herbert, Ulrich. *Geschichte der Ausländerbeschäftigung in Deutschland, 1880–1990*. Berlin-Bonn: Dietz, 1986.

HM Treasury. *Spending Review*, http://www.hm-treasury.gov.uk/spend_index .htm, October 2010.

Hervieu-Lèger, Danièle. "Faces of Catholic Transnationalism: In and Beyond France," in Susanne Rudolph and James Piscatori, eds., *Transnational Religion and Fading States*. Boulder, CO: Westview Press, 1997.

Hes, Georg Schreuder. "Morocco invites at least 40 imams for visit," *Expatica .com*, Oct. 29, 2008, http://www.expatica.com/nl/news/local_news/Mo rocco-invites-at-least-40-imams-for-visit-.html (accessed April 3, 2009).

Hobbes, Thomas. *Leviathan*. Cambridge: Cambridge University Press, 1996.

Hofhansel, Claus. "Accommodating Islam and the Utility of National Models: The German Case," *West European Politics* 33, no. 2 (2010), 191–207.

Hoffmann, Stanley. *In Search of France*. New York: Harper & Row, 1963.

Hollerbach, Alexander."Quelques remarques sur la neutralité de l'Etat en matière religeuse en RFA," *Archives de sciences sociales des religions*, no. 101, January– March, 1998, 61–66.

Hollifield, James. *L'immigration et l'état-nation: à la recherche d'un modèle national*. Paris: L'Harmattan, 1997.

———. "The Politics of International Migration: How Can We 'Bring the State Back In,'" in Caroline Brettell and James F. Hollifield, eds., *Talking Across Disciplines: Migration Theory in Social Science and Law*. New York: Routledge, 1999.

Hopwood, Derek, ed. *Euro-Arab Dialogue: The Relations between the Two Cultures, Acts of the Hamburg symposium*, April 11–15, 1983. London: Croom Helm, 1985.

Hourani, Albert. *History of the Arab Peoples*. Warner Books: Clayton, 1992.

Hubel, Helmut. *Frankreichs Rolle im Nahen Osten*, Arbeitspapiere zur internationalen Politik No. 37, Forschungsinstitut der Deutschen Gesellschaft für Auswärtige Politik, Bonn: Europa Union Verlag, 1985.

Hudnell, Kevin. "Democratization and Reform in Tunisia," Roosevelt Institution, http://rooseveltinstitution.org/policy/defensediplomacy/_file/_democra tization_and_reform_in_tunisia.pdf (accessed June 13, 2009).

Hume, David. "Essay VIII 'Of Parties in General,'" in Eugene F. Miller, ed., in *Essays, Moral, Political, and Literary*. Indianapolis, IN: Liberty Classics, 1985.

Hunter, Shireen. *The Future of Islam and the West: Clash of Civilizations or Peaceful Coexistence?* Westport, CT: Praeger, 1998.

———, ed. *Islam, Europe's Second Religion: The New Social, Cultural, and Political Landscape*. Washington, DC: Center for Strategic and International Studies, 2002.

Hürriyet. "Amtsperiode von Sadi Arslan bei DİTİB," *Hürriyet*, December 7, 2006.

Hussein, Abdulrahman A. "Alliance Behavior and the Foreign Policy of the Kingdom of Saudi Arabia, 1979–1991." Ph.D. Dissertation, George Washington University, January 1995.

Il Velino, "Nuovo Comitato per l'Islam italiano, dalla rappresentanza alle idee," *Il Velino*, 11 February 2010.

"Immigrazione tra i banchi," *Il sole 24 ore*, April 17, 2000, 18.

Inglehart, Ronald, and Pippa Norris. *Cosmopolitan Communications: Cultural Diversity in a Globalized World*. New York: Cambridge University Press, 2009.

Internationale Muslimische Studenten Union e. V.- Aachen. "Historischer Überblick," http://www.imsu.rwth-aachen.de/Verein/geschichte.html (accessed June 22, 2009).

Inform staff writer. "Nominati i membri della consulta islamica," *Inform* (Rome), no. 247, December 5, 2005.

Innenministerium des Landes Nordhein-Westfalen. "Islamische Gemeinschaft Milli Gorus," innenministerium Nordrhein-Westfalen, http://www.im.nrw.de/sch/582.htm (accessed August 10, 2009).

Inspection Générale de l'Agriculture, "Le champ du Halal," Rapport d'activité 2005, 66–67.

L' institut CSA. "Islam et citoyenneté, Le Monde des religions," sondage de l'institut CSA, 0800679, August 2008, http://www.csa-fr.com/dataset/data2008/opi20080730-islam-et-citoyennete.htm (accessed September 29, 2009).

Institut Européen des Sciences Humaines. "Teachers of the IESH," http://www.iesh.org/index.php?option=com_content&task=section&id=10&Itemid=113&lang=en (accessed June 22, 2009).

International Crisis Group. "Understanding Islamism," Middle East/North Africa Report, No. 37, March 2005.

International Foundation for Electoral Systems. "Election Profile: Algeria 2002," Election Guide, http://www.electionguide.org/election.php?ID=442 (accessed June 30, 2009).

———. "Election Profile: Algeria 2007," Election Guide, http://www.electionguide.org/election.php?ID=1107.

———. "Election Profile: Morocco," Election Guide, http://www.electionguide.org/election.php?ID=1137 (accessed June 30, 2009).

———. "Election Guide: Morocco 2002," Election Guide, http://www.electionguide.org/election.php?ID=463 (accessed July 6, 2009).

———. "Election Profile: Pakistan," Election Guide, http://www.electionguide.org/election.php?ID=1368 (accessed July 1, 2009).

———. "Election Profile: Tunisia," Election Guide, http://www.electionguide.org/election.php?ID=265 (accessed July 6, 2009).

———. "Election Profile: Turkey," Election Guide, http://www.electionguide.org/election.php?ID=481 (accessed July 6, 2009).

———. "Election Profile: Turkey 1999," Election Guide, http://www.electionguide.org/election.php?ID=742 (accessed June 30, 2009).

———. "Election Profile: Turkey 2007," Election Guide, http://www.electionguide.org/election.php?ID=1147 (accessed June 30, 2009).

Ippolito, Nelly. "Uno sguardo sull'Islam," *Amministrazione Pubblica, rivista di cultura istituzionale dei funzionari dell'amministrazzione civile dell'interno* 3, no. 16, November–December 2000.

Ireland, Patrick. *The Policy Challenge of Ethnic Diversity: Immigrant Politics in France and Switzerland.* Cambridge: Harvard University Press, 1994.

———. "Reaping What They Sow: Institutions and Immigrant Political Participation in Western Europe," in Koopmans and Statham, eds., *Challenging Immigration and Ethnic Relations Politics.* Oxford: Oxford University Press, 2000.

Islamic Council of Europe. "Universal Islamic Declaration," in Islamic Council of Europe, ed., *Islam and Contemporary Society.* New York: Longman, 1982.

Islamonline.net. "Ask a Scholar: Faysal Mawlawi," http://www.islamonline.net/servlet/Satellite?cid=1119503615017&pagename=IslamOnline-English-Ask_Scholar%2FFatwaCounselorE%2FFatwaCounselorE (accessed June 22, 2009).

IslamOnline.net. "Ahmed JABALLAH," http://www.islamonline.net/live dialogue/english/Guestcv.asp?hGuestID=N1OJ92 (accessed June 22, 2009).

"L'islam è ancora un pericolo per i cristiani," *La Stampa*, 10 December 2000.

"Islam in Bayern—Entschliessung des Vorstands der CSU-Fraktion im Bayerischen Landtag." March 11, 2003.

"L'Islam in Italia: libertà religiosa, diritti, doveri," Intervento pronunciato dal Presidente del Senato Marcello Pera in occasione del convegno organizzato dall'Open Society Institute nella Sala dei Presidenti di Palazzo Giustiniani, February 11, 2003.

Islamische Gemeinschaft Milli Görüş. "Organizational Structure," http://www.igmg.de/verband/islamic-community-milli-goerues/organisational-structure.html (acessed June 30, 2009).

Islamischen Zentrums Aachen (Bilal-Moschee), "Historischer Überblick" http://izaachen.de/index.php?site=geschichte (accessed June 22, 2009).

Islamrat and the Föderation der Aleviten-Gemeinden. "Bayerische Muslime kooperieren bei Unterricht," IZ, 05.27.2001.

Italian Muslim Assembly. "History," http://www.amislam.com/history.htm (accessed June 30, 2009).

Jackson, Richard et al., *The Graying of the Great Powers: Demography and Geopolitics in the 21st Century*. Washington, DC: Center for Strategic and International Studies, 2008.

Jacobs, Brian. "Black Minority Participation in the USA and Britain," *Journal of Public Policy* 2, no. 3 (1982), 237–62.

Jansen, Klaus. "Fighting Terror in Germany," *Bundeskriminalamt*, American Institute for Contemporary German Studies, 2001. www.aicgs.org/documents / jansen.pdf (accessed July 20, 2009).

Jarach, Renato. *Il Nuovo Ordinamento delle Comunità Israelitiche in Italia*, R. Università degli Studi di Milano, Facoltà di Giurisprudenza, Tesi di Laurea, Anno Accademico 1930–1931.

Jobert, Michel. "Préface" in Mustapha Benchenane, *Pour un dialogue euro-arabe*. Paris: Berger-Levrault, 1983.

Jobert, Michel, and Stéphane Muller. *L'Etat en Action*. Paris: Presses Universitaires de France, 1989.

Johnson, Ian. "Muslim Brotherhood in Europe," Congressional Testimony, February 9, 2006, http://www.aifdemocracy.org/policy-issues.php?id=1727 (accessed June 29, 2009).

———. *A Mosque in Munich*. New York: Houghton Mifflin, 2010.

Joly, Daniele. *Britannia's crescent: making a place for Muslims in British Society*. Brookfield, VT: Avebury, 1995.

Joppke, Christian, ed. *Challenge to the Nation-State: Immigration in Western Europe and the United States*. Oxford: Oxford University Press, 1998.

Joxe, Pierre. *L'edit de Nantes: Une histoire pour aujourd'hui*. Paris, 1998.

Kaci, Rachid. Discours au congrès UMP de Bourget, May 2003

Kalin, Ibrahim. «Islam in Turkey," *Oxford Islamic Studies Online* (accessed May 12, 2011).

Kaiser, Joseph H. *Die Repräsentation organisierter Interessen*. Berlin: Duncker & Humblot, 1956.

Kaltenbach, Jeanne-Hélène, and Pierre-Patrick Kaltenbach. *La France, une chance pour l'Islam*. Paris: Félin, 1991.

Kalyvas, Stathis. *The Rise of Christian Democracy in Europe*. Ithaca: Cornell University Press, 1996.

———. "Religion and Democratization: Algeria and Belgium," working paper 107, Madrid: Instituto Juan March de Estudios e Investigaciones, 1997.

Kandel, Johannes. "Islamischer Religionsunterricht in Berlin: kontroversen um religöse Bildung und Islamismus," *Fazetten der Islamismus*, August 2002.

Kant, Immanuel. *Die Metaphysik der Sitten*. 1797.

Kaplan, Steven L. *La fin des corporations*. Paris: Fayard, 2001.

———. "Un laboratoire de la doctrine corporatiste sous le régime de Vichy: l'Institut d'études corporatives et sociales," *Le Mouvement Social*, No. 195, April–June 2001.

Karasik, Theodore, and Cheryl Benard. "Muslim Diasporas and Networks," in Angel Rabasa et al., *The Muslim World after 9/11*. Santa Monica, CA: RAND, 2004.

Kastoryano, Riva. "Transnational Participation and Citizenship: Immigrants in the EU," unpublished manuscript, 2001.

———. *Negotiating Identities: States and Immigrants in France and Germany*. Princeton, NJ: Princeton University Press, 2002.

———. "Le nationalisme transnational turc, ou la redéfinition du nationalisme par les 'Turcs de l'extérieur," in Alain Dieckhoff and Riva Kastoryano, eds., *Nationalismes en mutation en Méditerranée orientale*. Paris: Editions du Centre national de la recherche scientifique, 2002.

———. "Transnational Networks and Political Participation: The Place of Immigrants in the European Union," in Martin Schain and Mabel Berezin, eds., *Europe without Borders: Remapping Territory, Citizenship and Identity in a Transnational Age*. Baltimore: Johns Hopkins University Press, 2003.

———. "Groupement Islamique En France," *The Oxford Encyclopedia of the Islamic World*, http://www.oxfordislamicstudies.com/article/opr/t236/e0279?_hi=4&_pos=1, (accessed August 11, 2009).

Kavacik, Zuhal. "Soziale Integration und religiös-ideologische Ansprüche in der BRD," unpublished paper, 2007.

Keats, Anthony. "In the spotlight: Al-Gam'a al Islamiyya- Islamic," Center for Defense Information, December 2, 2002, http://www.cdi.org/terrorism/algamaa.cfm (accessed June 12, 2009).

Keeler, John. *The Politics of Neocorporatism in France: Farmers, the State, and Agricultural Policy-Making in the Fifth Republic*. New York: Oxford University Press, 1987.

Kelek, Necla. "Die Suspekte Freiheit," *Der Tagesspiegel*, 20 June 2010.

Kepel, Gilles. *Les banlieues de l'Islam: naissance d'une religion en France*. Paris: Seuil, 1987.

———. *Die Rache Gottes: radikale Moslems, Christen und Juden auf dem Vormarsch*. München: u.a. Piper, 1991.

———. *Jihad, expansion et déclin de l'Islamisme*. Paris: Gallimard, 2000.

———. *The War for Muslim Minds: Islam and the West*. Cambridge: Harvard University Press, 2004.

———. *Fitna: Guerre au coeur de l'islam*. Paris: Folio, 2007.

Kerba, Richard. "Muslim Population 'rising 10 times faster than rest of society,'" *The Times* (London), January 30, 2009.

Kettani, Ali. "The Problems of Muslim Minorities and Their Solutions," in Islamic Council of Europe, ed., *Muslim Communities in Non-Muslim States*. London: Islamic Council of Europe, 1980.

Keynes, John Maynard. "The End of Laissez-Faire," London: Hogarth Press, 1926.

Khosrokhavar, Farhad. *L'Islam dans les prisons*. Paris: Balland, 2004.

Kingdom of Jordan. "Biographical Information: Sharif Hussein bin Ali (1853–1931) http://www.kinghussein.gov.jo/sharif_hussein.html (accessed July 28, 2009).

Kissinger, Henry. Minutes of Meetings with Secretary of State: "Discussion with Michel Jobert in Paris," May 22, 1973; "Memorandum on US-European Relations," November 28, 1973; "Meeting with West German Foreign Minister Scheel," March 3, 1974; "Meeting with West German Chancellor Brandt," March 4, 1974, Consulted in the Digital National Security Archives.

Klausen, Jytte. *The Islamic Challenge: Politics and Religion in Western Europe*. Oxford: Oxford University Press, 2005.

———. *The Cartoons That Shook the World*. New Haven, CT: Yale University Press, 2009.

———. "From Left to Right: Religion and the Political Integration of German Muslims," in *Religion, Politics, and Policy in the US and Germany*. Washington, DC: American Institute for Contemporary for German Studies, 2005.

———. *The Islamic Challenge: Politics and Religion in Western Europe*. Oxford: Oxford University Press, 2005.

———. "Europe's Uneasy Marriage of Secularism and Christianity Since the 1960s and the Challenge of Religious Pluralism," in Gareth Stedman-Jones and Ira Katznelson, eds., *Religion and the Political Imagination*. Cambridge: Cambridge University Press, 2010.

KMK. Neufassung der Empfehlungen der Kultusministerkonferenz: Unterricht für Kinder ausländischer Arbeitnehmer. Beschluß der Kultusministerkonferenz vom 10.25.1996 In: KMK, Nr. 671.1.

Koenig, Mathias. "Europeanising the governance of religious diversity. An institutionalist account of Muslim struggles for public recognition," *Journal of Ethnic and Migration Studies* 33, no. 6, 2007.

Koopmans, Ruud. "Germany and its immigrants: an ambivalent relationship," *Journal of Ethnic and Migration Studies* 25, no. 4, 1999, 627–47.

Koopmans, Ruud, Ines Michalowski, and Stine Waibel. "Citizenship Rights for Immigrants: National Paths and Cross-National Convergence in Western Europe, 1980–2008," Wissenschaftszentrum Berlin für Sozialforschung, Spring 2010.

Koopmans, Ruud, and Paul Statham. "Challenging the Liberal Nation-State? Postnationalism, Multiculturalism, and the Collective Claims Making of Migrants and Ethnic Minorities in Britain and Germany," *American Journal of Sociology* 105, no. 3 (1999), 652–96.

———. "Muslim and Islamic Claims-making in 5 European Nation-States: the Challenge of Multiculturalism," Draft manuscript, October 2002.

Koopmans, Ruud, Paul Statham, Marco Giugni, and Florence Passy. *Contested Citizenship: Immigration and Cultural Diversity in Europe*. Minneapolis, MN: University of Minnesota Press, 2005.

Kramer, Martin. "Fundamentalist Islam: The Drive for Power." *Middle East Quarterly* 3, no. 2 (June 1996), pp. 37–49.

Krasner, Steven. *Sovereignty: Organized Hypocrisy*. Princeton, NJ: Princeton University Press, 1999.

Krieger-Krynicki, Annie, and Laurent Bonnefoy. "Fédération Nationale des Musulmans de France," *The Oxford Encyclopedia of the Islamic World*, http://www.oxfordislamicstudies.com/article/opr/t236/e0244?_hi=10&_pos=1 (accessed August 11, 2009).

Kristiansen, Wendy. "Muslim Brotherhood Divided," *Le Monde Diplomatique*, April 2000, 19.

Kröhnert, Steffen, Iris Hoßmann, and Reiner Klingholz. *Europe's Demographic Future. Growing Regional Imbalances*. dtv, München, 2008.

Kükrekol, Filiz. "The Divided Muslim Community has problems asserting its interests," Deutsche Welle/Qantara.de, March 24, 2005. http://www.qantara.de/webcom/show_article.php/_c-478/_nr-256/i.html (accessed July 20, 2009).

———. "DİTİB: wir sind bereit, alle Muslime zu vertreten," Frankfurter Allgemeine Zeitung, February 8, 2005.

Kuru, Ahmet T. "Passive and Assertive Secularism: Historical Conditions, Ideological Struggles, and State Policies towards Religion," *World Politics* 59, no. 4, 2007.

———. *Secularism and State Policies Towards Religion: The United States, France and Turkey*. Cambridge: Cambridge University Press, 2009.

Lahouri, Besma, and Boris Thiolay. "L'argent de l'islam," *L'Express*, November 21, 2002.

Lal, Rollie. "The Maghreb," in *The Muslim World After 9/11*, Santa Monica, CA: RAND Corporation, 2004, 158. http://www.rand.org/pubs/monographs/2004/RAND_MG246.pdf (accessed June 15, 2009).

Lambert, Robert. "Empowering Salafis and Islamists against Al Qaeda," PS, January 2008, 31–35.

Landau, Jacob. *The Politics of Pan-Islam*. Oxford: Oxford University Press, 1990.

Landman, Nico. "Islam in the Benelux Countries," in Shireen Hunter, ed., *Islam, Europe's Second Religion: The New Social, Cultural, and Political Landscape*. Washington, DC: Center for Strategic and International Studies, 2002.

Langer, William L. *Europe Leaves the Middle East, 1936–1954*. New York: Alfred A. Knopf, 1972.

Laurence, Jonathan. "(Re)constructing Community in Berlin: Turks, Jews and German Responsibility," *German Politics and Society* 19, no. 2 (2001), 22–61.

———, ed. "The French Council for the Muslim Religion," *French Politics, Culture and Society* 23, no. 1, 2005.

———. "Managing Transnational Islam," in Parsons and Smeeding, eds., *Immigration and the Transformation of Europe*. Cambridge: Cambridge University Press, 2006.

———. *Islam and Identity in Germany*. Europe Report No. 181, Brussels: International Crisis Group, 2007.

———. "The Prophet of Moderation: Tariq Ramadan's Quest to Reclaim Islam," *Foreign Affairs. May/June 2007.*

———. "Muslims and the State in Western Europe," in Simon Reich and Ariane Chebel d'Appollonia, eds., *Immigration, Integration and Security.* Pittsburgh, PA: University of Pittsburgh Press, 2008.

Laurence, Jonathan, and Philippa Strum, eds. *Governments and Muslim Communities in the United States, United Kingdom, France and Germany.* Division of United States Studies, Woodrow Wilson International Center for Scholars. March 3–5, 2008.

Laurence, Jonathan, and Justin Vaïsse. *Integrating Islam: Political and Religious Challenges in Contemporary France.* Washington, DC: Brookings Press, 2006.

———. "The Dis-Integration of Europe," *Foreign Policy,* March 2011.

Lavau, Georges. "Political Pressures by Interest Groups in France," in Henry Walter Ehrmann, ed., *Interest Groups on Four Continents.* Pittsburgh, PA: University of Pittsburgh Press, 1958.

Le Bars, Stephanie. "Une deuxième promotion d'imams à l'institut catholique," *Le Monde,* December 9, 2008.

Leggewie, Claus. "Turcs, Kurdes et Allemands. Histoire d'une migration: de la stratification sociale à la différenciation culturelle, 1961–1990," *Le Mouvement Social,* no. 188, 1999, 103–18.

Lehmbruch, Gerhard. "Liberal Corporatism and Party Government," *Comparative Political Studies* 10, no. 1, 1977.

Leichtman, M. A. "Transforming Brain Drain into Capital Gain: Morocco's Changing Relationship with Migration and Remittances," *Journal of North African Studies,* 7, Part 1, 2002, 109–37.

Leiken, Robert. "Europe's Angry Muslims," *Foreign Affairs* 84, no. 4, July/August 2005.

Lemmen, Thomas. *Islamische Organisationen in Deutschland.* Bonn: Friedrich Ebert Stiftung, 2000.

Lenzi, Enrico. "La scuola italiana si scopre multietnica," *Avvenire,* September 19, 2000.

Leroy, Maxime. *Les Techniques nouvelles du Syndicalisme.* Paris: Marcel Rivière, 1921.

Leveau, Rémy. "Islam and the Reconstruction of Europe," in *Arab Immigrants and Muslims in Europe: Issues and Prospects,* Proceedings of the Euro-Arab Dialogue V Amman, 1–2 September 1993. Amman: Arab Thought Forum, 1994.

———. "De l'islam comme communauté imaginaire transnationale" in Michel Wieviorka, ed., *l'avenir de l'islam en France et en Europe,* Paris: Balland, 2003.

Leveau, Rémy, Khadija Finan, and Catherine Wihtol de Wenden, eds. *L'Islam en France et en Allemagne. Identités et citoyennetés.* Paris: IFRI/La Doc Française, 2001.

Léveau, Rémy, and Catherine Wihtol de Wenden. *La Beurgeoisie: Les trois âges de la vie associative issue de l'immigration.* Paris: Centre National de la Recherche Scientifique, 2001.

Levitt, Peggy. "Local-Level Global Religion: The Case of US-Dominican Migration," in Peter Beyer, ed., *Religion und Globalisierung.* Wurzburg: Ergon Verlag, 2001.

Levy, Jacob T. "Radical Reform," *The New Republic*, April 30, 2003.

Levy, Jonah D. *Tocqueville's Revenge: State, Society, and Economy in Contemporary France*. Cambridge: Harvard University Press, 1999.

Lewis, Bernard. "Free at Last? The Arab World in the Twenty-first Century," *Foreign Affairs*, March/April 2009, 77–88.

Lewis, Philip. *Islamic Britain: Religion, Politics, and Identity among British Muslims: Bradford in the 1990s*. New York: I. B. Tauris, 1994.

Libertà. "La Consulta islamica condanna," *Libertà*, February 10, 2006.

Liberté, Rédaction, "29 imams algériens à pied d'oeuvre," Liberté (Algiers), April 6, 2005.

Library of Congress. "Jamaat-e-Islami," Country Study: Pakistan, Library of Congress 1994, http://lcweb2.loc.gov/frd/cs/pktoc.html (accessed June 15, 2009).

Liedtke, Rainer. "Introduction" in Liedtke and Stephan Wendehorst, eds., *The Emancipation of Catholics, Jews and Protestants: Minorities and the Nation-State in 19th Century Europe*. Manchester: Manchester University Press, 1999, 1–10.

Lijphart, Arend. *Democracy in Plural Societies: A Comparative Exploration*. New Haven, CT: Yale University Press, 1977.

Lipset, Seymour Martin. "Radicalism or Reformism: The Sources of Working-class Politics," *American Political Science Review* 77, no. 1 (March 1983), 1–18.

Lipset, Seymour Martin, and Stein Rokkan. "Cleavage Structures, Party Systems, and Voter Alignments," in Lipset and Rokkan, eds., *Party Systems and Voter Alignments: Cross-National Perspectives*. New York: Free Press, 1967.

Locke, John. "A Letter Concerning Toleration," Indianapolis, IN: Hackett, 1983.

Long, Gianni. *Le confessioni religiose "diverse dalla cattolica": ordinamenti interni e rapporti con lo Stato*. Bologna: Il Mulino, 1991.

de Louw, Gilbert van. "Les Pays Bas," in José Carlos Herreras, ed., *L'enseignement des langues étrangères dans les pays de l'Union européenne*. Louvain: Peeters, 1998.

Lowenstein, Steven M. *The Berlin Jewish Community: Enlightenment, Family, and Crisis, 1770–1830*. Oxford: Oxford University Press, 2004.

Lowi, Theodore. *At the Pleasure of the Mayor: Patronage and Politics in New York City, 1896–1956*. New York: Free Press, 1964.

Lubeck, Paul. "The Challenge of Islamic Networks and Citizenship Claims: Europe's Painful Adjustment to Globalization," in Nezar AlSayyad and Manuel Castells, eds., *Muslim Europe or Euro-Islam: Politics, Culture and Citizenship in the Age of Globalization*. Lanham, MD: Lexington Books, 2002.

Luizard, Pierre-Jean. *Laïcités autoritaires en terres d'Islam*. Paris: Fayard, 2008.

Lutz, Martin. "Schäuble startet Islam-Konferenz im September," *Die Welt*, May 24, 2006.

Lycée Averroès. "Le Lycée Averroès Premier établissement privé musulman," http://www.lycee-averroes.com/institution.php?page=historique (accessed June 22, 2009).

Maddy-Weitzman, Bruce. "The Islamic Challenge in North Africa," *Middle East Review of International Affairs* 1, no. 2, July 1997. http://meria.idc.ac.il/journal/1997/issue2/jv1n2a7.html (accessed June 30, 2009).

el Madkoury, Halim. "How a film which spreads hate had a healing effect on relations between Muslims and non-Muslims in the Netherlands," Conference on "Violent extremism in Europe," organized by the U.S. Department of State and The George C. Marshall European center for Security Studies, Garmisch-Partenkirchen, Germany, November 5–7, 2008.

Magnus, Shulamit. *Jewish Emancipation in a German City: Cologne 1798–1871.* Stanford, CA: Stanford University Press, 1997.

Maier, Charles. "'Fictitious bonds . . . of wealth and law': on the theory and practice of interest representation," in Suzanne Berger, ed., *Organizing Interests in Western Europe.* Cambridge: Cambridge University Press, 1981.

———. *Recasting Bourgeois Europe.* Princeton, NJ: Princeton University Press, 1988.

Maier, Sylvia. "Multicultural Jurisprudence: Muslim Immigrants, Justice and the Law in France and Germany," Paper prepared for presentation at the Council for European Studies Conference, Chicago, IL, March 11–13, 2004.

Malik, Mustafa. "Islam in Europe: Quest for a Paradigm," *Middle East Policy* 8, no. 2, June 2001.

Mammeri, Achira. "Algeria's Islamist parties opt out of presidential elections," Feb. 10, 2009, http://www.magharebia.com/cocoon/awi/xhtml1/en_GB/features/awi/features/2009/02/10/feature-01 (accessed July 5, 2009).

Manço, Altay. "Dialoguer avec les communautés musulmanes d'Europe: propositions pratiques pour résoudre et prévenir des problèmes de cohabitation interculturelle," Brussels: Fondation Roi Baudouin, 2009.

Mandaville, Peter. *Global Political Islam.* London: Routledge, 2007.

———. "Muslim Networks and Movements in Western Europe," Pew Forum on Religion and Public Life, Washington, DC, 2010.

Mann, Michael. "Has globalization ended the rise and rise of the nation-state?" *Review of International Political Economy* 4, no. 3 (1997), 472–96.

Mantecon, Joaquin. "Islam in Spain," in Roberta B. Aluffi, Giovanni Zincone, and Giovanni, eds., *The Legal Treatment of Islamic Minorities in Europe.* Louvain: Peeters, 2004.

Maréchal, Brigitte. "Mosquées, organisations et leadership," in Felice Dassetto and Stefano Allievi, eds., *Convergences Musulmanes: aspects contemporains de l'islam dans l'Europe élargie.* Louvain-la-Nueve: Bruylant Academia, 2001.

———. "Courants Fondamentalistes en Belgique," *Journal d'etude des relations internationales au Moyen-Orient* 3, no. 1, article 4/6, March 2008. http://meria.idc.ac.il/journal_fr/2008/issue1/jv3no1a5.html (accessed July 6, 2009).

———. *The Strength of the Brothers—Roots and Discourses of the Muslim Brotherhood in Europe.* Brill: Leiden, 2008.

———. "Universal Aspirations: The Muslim Brotherhood in Europe," *ISIM Review* 22 (Autumn 2008), 36–37.

Markell, Patchen. *Bound by Recognition.* Princeton, NJ: Princeton University Press, 2003.

Maroshegyi, Christopher. *Exporting Citizens: The Power Politics and Economic Behind Moroccan Emigration Policy,* Senior Thesis, Boston College, 2009.

Martin-Saint-Léon, Etienne. *Les deux C.G.T. Syndicalisme et communisme.* Paris: Plon, 1923.

Masood, Aluddin. "PML Perpetually Multiplying Leagues," *Weekly Pulse Islamabad,* January 25, 2008. http://www.weeklypulse.org/pulse/article/1228.html (accessed June 15, 2009).

Le Matin. "De villepin attendu demain au Maroc," *Le Matin*, October 12, 2005.

Marx, Karl. "On the Jewish Problem (1844)," in Paul Mendes-Flores, and Yehuda Reinharz, eds., *The Jew in the Modern World: A Documentary History*. Oxford: Oxford University Press, 1995, 324–27.

Maulion, Fabrice. *L'organisation des frères musulmans*, Diplôme universitaire de 3è cycle, Université Panthéon-Assas, December 2004.

Maussen, Marcel. "Making Muslim Presence Meaningful," Amsterdam School for Social Science Research, May 2005.

———. "The governance of Islam in Western Europe: A state of the art report," Working Paper No. 16, IMISCOE Working Paper, 2007.

———. *Constructing Mosques: The Governance of Islam in France and the Netherlands*. Amsterdam: Amsterdam School for Social Science Research, 2009.

Maxwell, Rahsaan. "Evaluating Integration: Political Attitudes Across Migrant Generations in Europe." *International Migration Review* 44, no. 1 (2010), 25–52.

Mayer, Michael, ed. *Deutsch-jüdische Geschichte in der Neuzeit*. Munich: Beck, 1997.

McConnell, Michael W. "Believers as Equal Citizens" in Nancy Rosenblum, ed., *Obligations of Citizenship and Demands of Faith: Religious Accommodation in Pluralist Democracies*. Princeton, NJ: Princeton University Press, 2000.

McMahon, Colin, and Catherine Collins. "State comes first, mosque second in Turkey's system," *Chicago Tribune*, October 24, 2004.

Memorandum. "Scheda 11: L'Islam non è integrabile," Ministero per gli affari sociali.

Mendes-Flores, Paul, and Yehuda Reinharz, eds. *The Jew in the Modern World: A Documentary History*. Oxford: Oxford University Press, 1995.

Meotti, Giulio. "Nella casbah di Rotterdam [In the Casbah of Rotterdam]" *Il Foglio*, May 14, 2009, p. 1.

Messner, Francis, ed. *Archives de Sciences sociales des Religions*, no. 101 January–March 1998.

———. "Les relations état-religions dans les pays membres de l'Union Européenne," in Blandine Chelini-Pont, ed., *Religion, Droit et Société en Europe Communautaire*. Aix: Aix-en-Provence, 2000.

Michalowski, Ines. "Liberal states—privatised integration policies?" in Elspeth Guild and Kees Groenendijk, eds., *Illiberal Liberal States. Immigration, Citizenship and Integration in the EU*. Surren: Ashgate, 82–98.

Migazin, "Islamophobie 2010—Deutschland ist Europameister," Migazin.de 3 December 2010.

Mignot, Elisa. "L'islam de Grande-Bretagne adopte un code de conduite," 10/12/2007, http://www.rue89.com/2007/12/10/lislam-de-grande-bretagne-adopte-un-code-de-conduite (accessed September 27, 2009).

Milcent, Thomas. "Interview exclusive du Cheikh Abdallah Turki," January 1, 2004, http://oumma.com/Interview-exclusive-du-Cheikh (accessed July 30, 2009).

Miller, M. *Foreign Workers in Europe*. New York: Praeger Press, 1981.

Ministère des Affaires Etrangères. "La France a la loupe: Le culte musulman en France, " March 2007, http://www.botschaft-frankreich.de/IMG/culte_musulman (accessed June 26, 2009).

Ministero dell'Interno."Memorandum," *Dialogo Interreligioso N.5185/M (1),* Gabinetto del Ministro, Ministero dell'Interno, September 23, 2004.

———. "Costituito al Viminale il Comitato per l'Islam italiano," Rome, 10 February 2010.

Ministero Evangelico *tra* Arabi (Met*A*), 2002, www.meta.it.

Minkenberg, Michael. "The Policy Impact of Church-State Relations: Family Policy and Abortion in Britain, France, and Germany," *West European Politics* 26, no. 1, January 2003.

Mirza, Ariana. "Interview with Hasan Karaca," April 23, 2007, http://www.qantara .de/webcom/show_article.php/_c-478/_nr-600/i.html (accessed November 23, 2009).

Modood, Tariq. "Multiculturalism, Secularism and the State," *Critical Review of International Social and Political Philosophy* 1, no. 3 (1998), 114.

Moe, Christian. "Refah Partisi (The Welfare Party) and Others v. Turkey," *The International Journal of Not-for-Profit Law* 6, No. 1, September 2003 http:// www.icnl.org/KNOWLEDGE/ijnl/vol6iss1/special_5.htm (accessed July 1, 2009).

Le Monde. "Un entretien avec le cheikh Tedjini Haddam recteur de la Mosquée de Paris "Je lance un appel à la dédramatisation et au dialogue," *Le Monde,* October 24, 1989.

———. "Les Grandes Mosquées de France" *Le Monde,* October 13, 2001.

———. "La plupart des salles de prière n'ont pas été construites pour cet usage," *Le Monde,* January 26, 2002.

Morel, Stéphanie. *Ecoles, territoires et identités. Les politiques publiques françaises à l'épreuve de l'ethnicité,* Paris: L'Harmattan, 2002.

Moreras, Jordi. "Muslims in Spain," *Muslim World* 92, no. 1–2, April 2002.

Mortimer, Robert. *The Third World Coalition.* New York: Praeger, 1980.

Mosques and Imams National Advisory Board (MINAB). "About us," http:// www.minab.org.uk/about-us/about-us (accessed June 29, 2009).

——— "Internal Consultations on MINAB," http://www.minab.org.uk/about -us/61-founders/97-internal-consulations-on-minab (accessed June 29, 2009).

Motadel, David. "Germany Profile," Euro-Islam, http://www.euro-islam.info/ country-profiles/germany/ (accessed June 30, 2009).

Motchane, Didier. "L'Islam de France sera-t-il républicain?" Unpublished manuscript, 2000.

Moual, Karima. "Nasce l'organo di rappresentanza dell'islam italiano," http://temi .repubblica.it/metropoli-online/nasce-lorgano-di-rappresentanza-dellislam -italiano/, March 3, 2009.

Mouhieddine, Abdessamad. "MRE/législatives: Choc des maux et soif des urnes," *Gazette du Maroc,* June 29, 2007.

Mouhoud, El Mouhoub, Joël Oudinet, and Elif Unan. "'Macroeconomic Determinants of Migrants' Remittances in the Southern and Eastern Mediterranean Countries," Séminaire Démographie, emploi et migrations entre les rives de la Méditerranée, CEPN– CNRS– Université Paris nord et GDRI DREEM– CNRS, Paris, January 25, 2008.

Mouslim, Charafeddine. "Vive l'Islam de France?!" CRCM President Aquitaine, Summer 2005.

Mucchieli, Laurent. *Le scandale des 'tournantes.' Dérives médiatiques et contre-en-quête sociologique.* Paris: La Découverte, 2005.

Mullins, Mark. "The Life-Cycle of Ethnic Churches in Sociological Perspective," *Journal of Religious Studies* 14, no. 4 (1987), 321–34.

Mumtaz, Ashraf. "Parties to inform EC about merger with PML," *Dawn*, May 20, 2004, http://www.dawn.com/2004/05/20/nat1.htm (accessed July 5, 2009).

Muslim Association of Britain (MAB). "About," http://mabonline.net/?page_id=2 (accessed June 26, 2009).

Muslim Council of Britain (MCB). "The Muslim Council of Britain—its history, structure and working," http://www.mcb.org.uk/downloads/MCB_achievments.pdf (accessed June 26, 2009).

The Muslim News. "Tentative start for mosques advisory body," *The Muslim News*, March 10, 2006, http://www.muslimnews.co.uk/index/press.php?pr=223 (accessed September 25, 2009).

Muslim World League. "Islamic Centre in Vienna: Beginning of a new era for Islam in Europe," *Muslim World League Journal* 27, no. 10, January 2000.

Name withheld, Pol 320.15, HR: -119, "Vermerk, Betrifft: Das Türkische Präsidium für Religiöse Angelegenheiten," Ankara, Germany Embassy, August 24, 2006.

Narli, Nilufer. "The Rise of the Islamist Movement in Turkey," *Middle East Review of International Affairs*. 3, no. 3, September 1999, http://www.biu.ac.il/SOC/besa/meria/journal/1999/issue3/jv3n3a4.html (accessed June 15, 2009).

Naso, Paolo. "Intese fatte, quasi fatte e da fare," *Confronti*, November 2000.

Naylor, Phillip C. *Historical Dictionary of Algeria*, 3rd edition. Lanham, MD: Scarecrow Press, September 28, 2006, 362–63.

Nielsen, Jørgen. "Transnational Islam and the Integration of Islam in Europe," in Stefano Allievi and Jørgen Nielsen, eds., *Muslim Networks and Transnational Communities in and Across Europe*. Boston, MA: Brill, 2003.

Nohl, Arnd-Michael. "Evaluation der Landeskunde für Imame," Veranstaltung der Konrad Adenauer Stiftung vom 15.-20.5.2006 in Ankara, http://www.kas.de/wf/de/33.9355/ (accessed November 23, 2009).

Noiriel, Gérard. *Le Creuset Français: Histoire de l'immigration, XIXe—XXe siècles.* Paris: Le seuil, 1988.

Nonneman, Gerd. "Le relazioni tra l'Arabia Saudita e l'Europa," in Roberto Aliboni and Daniela Pioppi, eds., *Arabia Saudita Cent'Anni: cooperazione, sicurezza, identità.* Roma: FrancoAngeli, 2000.

Norell, Magnus. "The Taliban and the Muttahida Majlis-e- Amal (MMA)," *China and Eurasia Forum Quarterly* 5, no. 3 (2007), 69.

Norris, Pippa, and Ronald Inglehart. "God, Guns and Gays: The Supply and Demand for Religion in the U.S. and Western Europe," *Public Policy Research* 12, no. 4 (2006), 224–33.

Nouripour, Omid. *Mein Job, Meine Sprache, Mein Land.* Freiburg: Herder Verlag, 2007.

Le Nouvel Observateur. Interview with Mouloud Aounit, president of the anti-racist association and a member of the French Communist Party, *Le Nouvel Observateur*, October 15, 2003.

Offe, Claus. "The attribution of public status to interest groups: Observations on the West German case," in Suzanne Berger ed., *Organizing Interests in Western Europe*. Cambridge: Cambridge University Press, 1981, 123–58.

———. "Societal Preconditions of Corporatism and Some Current Dilemmas of Democratic Theory," Working Paper 14, Kellogg Institute, 1984.

Ögelman, Nedim. "Immigrant organizations and the globalization of Turkey's domestic politics," in Rey Koslowski, ed., *International Migration and Globalization in Domestic Politics*. Verlag: Routledge, 2005.

Olson, Mancur. "A theory of the incentives facing political organizations. Neo-corporatism and the Hegemonic State," *International Political Science Review*. 7, no. 2 (1986), 165–89.

Open Society Institute. "Monitoraggio della protezione delle minoranze nell'Unione Europea: La situazione dei Musulmani in Italia," 2002.

Østergaard-Nielsen, Eva, ed., *International Migration and Sending Countries: Perceptions, Policies and Transnational Relations*. New York: Palgrave Macmillan, 2003.

Owen, J. Judd. "The Task of Liberal Theory after September 11," *Perspectives* 2, no. 2, June 2004.

Pakistan Facts. "Not so good news about British Pakistanis," September 21, 2004, http://www.pakistan-facts.com/article.php?story=20040921223003761.

Panafit, Lionel. "Les relations religions-état en Europe au prisme de l'économique," in Blandine Pont-Chelini, ed., *Religions, Droits, Sociétés en Europe Communautaire*. Aix: Presses de l'Université Aix-en-Provence, 2000.

Parekh, Bikhu. *Rethinking Multiculturalism*. Cambridge: Harvard University Press, 2002.

Pargeter, Alison. *The New Frontiers of Jihad: Radical Islam in Europe*. London: I. B. Tauris, 2008.

Le Parisien. "Enfin une mosquée à Clichy," *Le Parisien*, *Marocain du Monde*, May 26, 2004, http://www.bladi.net/enfin-une-mosquee-a-clichy.html (accessed November 23, 2009).

———. Islam de France: La mosquée de Créteil prête pour accueillir les fidèles dès le mois du Ramadan, http://www.yawatani.com/pdf/actualite/islam-de-france-la-mosquee-de-creteil-prete-pour-accueillir-les-fideles-des-le-mois-du-ramadan.pdf (accessed August 16, 2009).

Passi Nel Deserto. "Papa e Islam: l'UCOII consegna una lettera al Papa," http://passineldeserto.blogosfere.it/2006/09/papa-e-islam-lucoii-consegna-una-lettera-al-papa.html, 2006.

Pedersen, Lars. *Newer Islamic Movements in Europe*. Surrey, UK: Ashgate, 1999.

Pędziwiatr, Konrad. "Creating New Discursive Arenas and Influencing the Policies of the State: Case of the Muslim Council of Britain," paper for the ISSR Conference in Zagreb, 18–22 July 2005.

Penslar, Derek J. *Shylock's Children: Economics and Jewish Identity in Modern Europe*. Berkeley: University of Califonia Press, 2001.

Pew Forum on Religion and Public Life. "The Global Spread of Wahhabi Islam: How Great a Threat?" Washington, DC: Pew Research Center, May 2005.

———. "The Future of the Global Muslim Population," Washington, DC: Pew Research Center, January 2011.

Pfaff, Steven, and Anthony Gill. "Will a million Muslims march? Muslim interest organizations and political integration in Europe," *Comparative Political Studies*. 39, no. 7 (2006), 803–28.

Piacentini, M. *I culti ammessi nello stato italiano*. Milano: Hoepli, 1934.

Pirrone, Marco Antonio. "Dalla Colonizzazione all' 'islamismo radicale,'" *Studi Emigrazione-Migration Studies* 37, no. 137, 2000.

Pisanu, Giuseppe. "La sfida delle religioni alla democrazia," ACLI Convegno nazionale di studi, Orvieto, September 11, 2004.

Pizzorno, Alessandro. "Interests and parties in pluralism," in Suzanne Berger ed., *Organizing Interests in Western Europe*. Cambridge: Cambridge University Press, 1981.

Polanyi, Karl. *The Great Transformation*, Boston: Beacon Press, 1957 (copyright 1944).

Pollack, Detlef. "Wahrnehmung und Akzeptanz religiöser Vielfalt," Münster: Religion und Politik, 2010

Poulter, Sebastian. *Ethnicity, Law and Human Rights*. Oxford: Clarendon Press, 1998.

Powell, David. *British Politics, 1910–1935: The Crisis of the Party System*, Florence, KY: Routledge, 2004.

Prélot, Pierre-Henri. "Les Religions et l'égalité en droit français," *Revue du Droit Public*, no. 3, 2001.

Pro Christliches Medienmagazin. "Forschungsstellen für islamische Studien an deutschen Hochschulen, *Pro Christliches Medienmagazin*, 12 October 2010.

Pucciarini, Marco. "A colloquio con il presidente del Centro islamico italiano Mujahed Badaoul," www.LaVoce.it, September 20, 2002.

Muammar Qaddafi's remarks, *Al-Shams* (Libya), June 8, 2010. Translated by MEMRI, http://www.memri.org/report/en/0/0/0/0/0/0/4349.htm.

Qattab, Tariq. "L'Islam en France: Le Maroc et l'Algérie à couteaux tirés," *Le Soir Échos* (Algiers), February 18, 2009.

Rabasa, Angel, Cheryl Benard, Peter Chalk, C. Christine Fair, Theodore Karasik, Rollie Lal, Ian Lesser, and David Thaler. *The Muslim World After 9/11*. Santa Monica, CA: RAND Corporation, 2004.

Rahman, Mohibur. Communities Research—Race Relations, RDS, Home Office. November 2003/Updated March 2004; Home Office, Foreign and Commonwealth Office, April 2004, http://www.globalsecurity.org/security/library/report/2004/muslimext-uk.htm (accessed September 25, 2009).

Ramadan, Tariq. *Being a European Muslim*. Lyon: Tawhid, 2000.

———. "Les musulmans d'Europe pris en tenaille," *Le monde diplomatique*, June 2000, 12–13.

Rasche, Uta. "Integration: Einen großen Schritt weiter," *Frankfurter Allgemeine Zeitung*, August 9, 2009.

Rath, Jan et al. *Western Europe and its Islam*. Leiden: Brill, 2001.

La Razón. "La población africana aumenta un 800% en España desde 1996," *La Razón* (Madrid), May 15, 2009, http://www.larazon.es/noticia/la-poblacion-africana-aumenta-un-800-en-espana-desde-1996 (accessed November 24, 2009).

Refflinghaus, Alexander. *Deutsche Türkeipolitik in der Regierungszeit Helmut Kohls, 1982 bis 1998*. Berlin: Verlag Dr.Köster, 2002.

Rémond, René. *Religion and Society in Modern Europe*. Cornwall: Blackwell, 1999.

la République Française et le Royaume du Maroc. "Convention entre la République Française et le Royaume du Maroc relative au statut des personnes et de la famille et à la coopération judiciaire," Décret n° 83-435 DU May 27, 1983 ; J.O. June 1, 1983, 1643.

la République Française et République algérienne démocratique et populaire. "Convention entre la France et l'Algérie relative aux enfants issus de couples mixtes séparés franco-algériens," Signée à Alger, June 21, 1988, Décret n° 88-879 August 17, 1988; J.O. August 19, 1988, 10505.

Rex, John. "Islam in the United Kingdom," in Shireen Hunter, ed., *Islam, Europe's Second Religion: The New Social, Cultural, and Political Landscape*. Washington, DC: Center for Strategic and International Studies, 2002.

ben Rhouma, Hanan. "L'Islam de France, Une affaire de maires: entretien avec Françoise Duthu," Saphirnews.net, March 3, 2009.

Romeo, Giuseppe. *La politica estera italiana nell'era Andreotti, 1972–1992*. Milan: Rubettino, 2000.

Rosenblum, Nancy, ed. *Obligations of Citizenship and Demands of Faith: Religious Accommodation in Pluralist Democracies*. Princeton, NJ: Princeton University Press, 2000.

Rousseau, Jean-Jacques. *On the Social Contract: With Geneva Manuscript and Political Economy*, Roger D. Masters, ed., translated Judith R. Masters, Bedford: St. Martins, 1978.

Roy, Olivier. *L'islam mondialisé*. Paris: Seuil, 2002.

———. *La laïcité face à l'Islam*. Paris: Stock, 2005.

———. "The nature of the French riots," 2005, www.riotsfrance.ssrc.org (accessed March 6, 2006).

Roy, Olivier, Antoine Sfeir, and John King. "Al-Jama'a al-Islamiya (JI) (Islamic Association) (Lebanon)," *The Columbia World Dictionary of Islamism*. New York: Columbia University Press, 2007, 209.

Royaume du Maroc, Ministère des Habous et des Affaires Islamiques, www.islam-maroc.ma/fr/index.aspx (accessed July 2006).

Rübel, Jann. "Sind die Muslime ein Stück Deutschland, Herr Schäuble?" *Welt am Sonntag*, May 28, 2006.

Rudolph, Susanne Hoeber. "Introduction: Religion, States, and Transnational Civil Society," in Rudolph and Piscatori, *Transnational Religion and Fading States*. Boulder, CO: Westview Press, 1997.

Runciman, David. *Pluralism and the Personality of the State*. Cambridge: University of Cambridge Press, 1997.

Russell, Sharon Stanton. "Remittances from International Migration: A Review in Perspective," *World Development* 14, no. 6 (1986), 677–96, 687, 693.

Saadet Partisi (Felicity), Blog entry, May 9, 2008, http://felicityparty.blogspot.com/2008_05_01_archive.html (accessed June 16, 2009).

Sachverständigenrat deutscher Stiftungen für Integration und Migration, *Einwanderungsgesellschaft 2010*, Berlin 2010.

Safran, William. "France and Her Jews: From '*culte israëlite*' to '*lobby* juif,'" *Tocqueville Review* 5, no. 1, Summer 1983.

————. "France," in F. Eidlin, ed., *Constitutional Democracy: Essays in Comparative Politics*. Boulder, CO: Westview Press, 1983, 315–43.

————. *The French Polity*, 6th ed. New York: Longman, 2002, 166.

————. "Ethnic Lobbying in France: Maghrebis and Jews." The American Political Science Association, 2003.

Saint-Blancat, Chantal. "Immigrati di origine musulmana, una indagine" *Humanitas* 55 (June 2000), 874–81.

Sakallioğlu , Ümit Cizre. "Parameters and Strategies of Islam-State Interaction in Republican Turkey," *International Journal Middle East Studies* no. 28, 1996, 231–51.

Sala, Roberto. "Gastarbeitersendungen und Gastarbeiterzeitschriften (1960-1975), Ein Spiegel internationaler Spannungen," in *Zeithistorische Forschungen* 2, no. 3 (2005), 366–87.

————. "Fremde Stimmen im Äther. Wie das "Gastarbeiterradio" zum demokratischen Problemfall wurde," WZB Mitteilungen - Nr. 126/Dezember 2009, Wissenschaftszentrum Berlin für Sozialforschung.

Salam: Muslims in Britain. "Sane Voices & Responses," http://www.salaam.co.uk/themeofthemonth/september03_index.php?l=60 (accessed September 29, 2009).

Salih, Ruba. "Islam in Italy," *Journal of Ethnic and Migration Studies* 30, no. 5 (September 2004), 995–1011.

Saphir News. "100 mosquées attendent encore leurs imams," September 30, 2009, http://www.saphirnews.com/100-mosquees-attendent-encore-leurs-imams_a10565.html (accessed November 23, 2009).

Sarkozy, Nicolas. Interview in *Le Figaro*, April 30, 2003.

————. Interview in *Nouvel Obervateur*, October 14, 2003.

————."Dieu peut-il se passer de la République?" Discours prononcé à la Synagogue de Neuilly, June 20, 2005.

Sartori, Giovanni. "Gli islamici e noi Italiani," *Corriere della Sera*, October 25, 2000.

————. *Pluralismo, multiculturalismo e estranei. Saggio sulla società multietnica*. BUR Biblioteca University Rizzoli, 2003.

Sassen, Saskia. "The *de facto* Transnationalizing of Immigration Policy," in Christian Joppke, ed., *Challenge to the Nation-State: Immigration in Western Europe and the United States*. Oxford: Oxford University Press, 1998.

Savage, Timothy. "Europe and Islam: Crescent Waxing, Cultures Clashing," *Washington Quarterly* 27, no. 3 (2004), 25–50.

Sayari, Sabri. Migration Policies of Sending Countries: Reflections on the Turkish Experience," *Annals of the American Academy of Political and Social Science* 485, 1986, 87–98.

Schäuble, Wolfgang. "Deutsche Islam Konferenz—Perspektiven für eine gemeinsame Zukunft: Regierungserklärung zur DIK am 27. September," www.cducsu.de 28 September 2006.

Schiffauer, Werner. "Milli Görüs: the right to be different," *Die Zeit*, June 2005.

Schily, Otto."Soziale Integration in der deutschen Gesellschaft als politische Aufgabe." Symposium, "Religion, Kirche, Islam," September 9, 2002.

Schlötze, Christiane. "Die Türkei zwischen Islam und westlicher Moderne," *Frankfurter Allgemeine Zeitung*, December 19, 2001.

Schmitt, Carl. *Crisis of Parliamentary Democracy*. Cambridge: MIT Press, 1926 (1986).

Schmitter, Philippe. "Still the Century of Corporatism?" *Review of Politics* 36, 1974, 85–131.

———. "Modes of Interest Intermediation and Models of Societal Change in Western Europe," *Comparative Political Studies* 10 no. 1 (1977), 7–36.

———. "Interest intermediation and regime governablity in contemporary Western Europe and North Americaa," in Suzanne Berger, ed., *Organizing Interests in Western Europe*. Cambridge: Cambridge University Press, 1981.

Schmitter, Philippe, and Gerhard Lehmbruch, eds. *Trends Toward Corporatist Intermediation*. London: Sage, 1979.

Schofield, Hugh. "France's Islamic heartland," *BBC*, http://news.bbc.co.uk/2/hi/europe/2959389.stm (accessed June 22, 2009).

Schulze, Reinhard. *Islamischer Internationalismus im 20. Jahrhundert: Untersuchungen zur Geschichte der Islamischen Weltliga*. Köln: Brill, 1990.

Schüttler, Kirsten. *Die marokkanische Diaspora in Deutschland. Ihr Beitrag zur Entwicklung Marokkos*. Eschborn: Deutsche Gesellschaft für Technische Zusammenarbeit, 2007.

Schwarzfuchs, Simon. *Napoleon, The Jews and the Sanhedrin*. London: Routledge, 1979.

Scott, James. *Seeing Like a State: How Certain Schemes to Improve the Human Condition Have Failed*, New Haven, CT: Yale University Press, 2000.

Secrétaire général à l'intégration, "Immigrés: réussir l'intégration," Services du Premier Ministre, June 1990.

Sehimi, Mustapha. "Sarko et la Moudawana," *Maroc Hebdo*, No. 554, Week of 18th to 25th April, 2003.

Seidel, Eberhard, Claudia Dantschke and Ali Yildirim. *Politik im Namen Allahs*. Berlin: Tageszeitung Bericht, 2000.

Senoçak, Zafer. *Atlas of a Tropical Germany: Essays on Politics and Culture, 1990–1998*, trans. and ed., Leslie A. Adelson. Lincoln: University of Nebraska Press, 2000.

———. "Den Islam übersetzen," *Die Welt*, September 26, 2003.

Shadid, W. A. "The Integration of Muslim Minorities in the Netherlands," *International Migration Review* 25, no. 2 (1991), 355–74.

Shadid, W. A., and P. S. van Koningsveld. "Structural Barriers Facing Muslims in Western Europe" and "Institutionalization and Integration of Islam in the Netherlands, in Shadid and Koningsveld, eds., *The Integration of Islam and Hinduism in Western Europe*. Kampen: KOK Pharos Publishing House, 1991.

———. *Muslims in the Margin: Political Responses to the Presence of Islam in Western Europe*. Kampen: KOK Pharos Publishing House, 1996.

Shafir, Gershon, ed. *The Citizenship Debates: A Reader*. Minneapolis: University of Minnesota Press, 1998.

Shain, Yossi. *The Frontier of Loyalty*. Middletown: Wesleyan University Press, 1989.

Shavit, Uriya. *The New Imagined Community*, Brighton: Sussex Academic, 2009.

Shehabi, Saaed. "The Role of Religious Ideology in the Expansionist Policies of Saudi Arabia," in Madawi Al-Rasheed, *Kingdom without Borders, Saudi Politi-*

cal, Religious and Media Frontiers. New York: Columbia University Press, 2008, 183–97.

Shore, Zachary. "Breeding New Bin Ladens: America's New Western Front," Foreign Policy Research Institute 5, no. 11, 2004.

Sibalis, Michael David. "Corporatism after the Corporations; The Debate on Restoring the Guilds under Napoleon I and the Restoration," *French Historical Studies* 15, no. 4 (Autumn 1988), 718–30.

Skerry, Peter. "The Affirmative Action Paradox," *SOCIETY* 35, no. 6 (September 1998), 8–16.

Skocpol, Theda, ed. *Bringing the State Back In*. Cambridge: Cambridge University Press, 1985.

Soares, Claire. "Netherlands Braced for Muslim Anger as Politician Releases 'Anti-Islam' Film," *The Independent*, http://www.independent.co.uk/news/world/europe/netherlands-braced-for-muslim-anger-as-politician-releases-antiislam-film-773882.html, January 25, 2008.

Sorkin, David. *The Transformation of German Jewry, 1780–1840*. Oxford: Oxford University Press, 1987.

———. "The Impact of Emancipation on German Jewry: A Reconsideration," in Jonathan Frankel and Steven J. Zipperstein, eds., *Assimilation and Community: The Jews in Nineteenth-century Europe*. Cambridge: Cambridge University Press, 1992, 177–98.

Soysal, Yasemin Nuhoğlu. *Limits of Citizenship: Migrants and Postnational Membership in Europe*. Chicago: University of Chicago Press, 1994.

Spalek, Basia, and Alia Imtoual. "Muslim Communities and Counter-Terror Responses: "Hard" Approaches to Community Engagement in the UK and Australia," *Journal of Muslim Minority Affairs* 17, no. 2 (August 2007), 185–202.

Spiegel Online. "Thierses Traum vom Euro-Islam," *Der Spiegel*, 23 December 2001.

Spiewak, Martin. "Vorbeter aus der Fremde," *Die Zeit*, September 21, 2006.

Stanislavski, Michael. *For Whom Do I Toil? Judah Leib Gordon and the Critique of Russian Jewry*. New York: Oxford University Press, 1988.

Stasi, Bernard. *Rapport Stasi*, Rapport au président de la république, Commission de réflexion sur l'application du principe de laïcite dans la république, December 11, 2003.

Statham, Paul. "The Need to Take Religion Seriously for Understanding Multicultural Controversies: Institution Channelling versus Cultural Identification?" in M. Giugni and F. Passy, eds., *Dialogues in Migration Policy*. Lanham, MD: Lexington, 2006, 157–68.

Statham, Paul, Ruud Koopmans, Marco Giugni, and Florence Passy. "Resilient or Adaptable Islam? Multiculturalism, Religion and Migrants' Claims-making for Group Demands in Britain, the Netherlands and France," *Ethnicities* 5, no. 4 (2005), 427–59.

Steinberg, Guido. "Der Islamismus in Niedergang? Anmerkungen zu den Thesen Gilles Kepels, Olivier Roys und zur europäsichen Islamimismusforschung" in *Islamismus*. Berlin: Bundesministerium für Inneres, 2004.

Stepan, Alfred. "The Multiple Secularisms of Modern Democratic and Non-Democratic Regimes," in Craig Calhoun and Mark Juergensmeyer, eds., *Rethinking Secularism*. New York and London: Oxford University Press, 2011.

Stevens, W. David. "Spreading the Word: Religious Beliefs and the Evolution of Immigrant Congregations," *Sociology of Religion* 65, no. 2 (2004), 121–38.

Streeck, Wolfgang."Vielfalt und Interdependenz," in *Korporatismus in Deutschland: zwischen Nationalstaat und europaeischer Union*. Frankfurt: Campus, 1999.

———. "National Diversity, Regime Competition and Institutional Deadlock: Problems in Forming a European Industrial Relations System," *Journal of Public Policy* 12, no. 4 (1992), 301–30.

Strika, Vincenzo. "Italia e Arabia Saudita dopo il secondo conflitto mondiale," in Roberto Aliboni and Daniela Pioppi, eds., *Arabia Saudita Cent'Anni: cooperazione, sicurezza, identità*. Roma: FrancoAngeli, 2000.

Swedish South Asian Studies Network. "Pakistan," Lund University, http://www.sasnet.lu.se/pakistan.html (accessed June 15, 2009).

Swidler, Ann. "Culture in Action: Symbols and Strategies," *American Sociological Review* 51, no. 2, 1986.

Tank, Pinar. "Political Islam in Turkey: A State of Controlled Secularity," *Turkish Studies* 6, no. 1 (March 2005), 3–19, 9.

Taxacher, Gregor. "Gelungenes Miteinander, in Duisburg-Marxloh: Deutschlands größte Moschee," Goethe Institute, March 2, 2009.

Tchoudinova, Elena. *La Mosquée Notre-Dame de Paris: année 2048* [The Notre-Dame Mosque of Paris]. Paris: Tatamis, 2009.

Ternisien, Xavier. "Pressés par les attentats, les musulmans se préparent à élire leurs représentants," *Le Monde*, October 13, 2001.

———. "Un budget encore très dépendant des "généreux donateurs" du Golfe," *Le Monde*, December 12, 2002.

———. "Contestations en Egypte après la visite de M. Sarkozy" *Le Monde*, January 6, 2004.

———. "Le temps des 'mosquées cathédrales' semble révolu," *Le Monde*, June 18, 2004.

———. *Les frères musulmans*, Paris: Fayard, 2005.

———. "Mille et un jours," *Le Monde*, August 8, 2005.

Teschner, Katrin. "Imame sind wichtige Vermittler," *Braunschweiger Zeitung*, October 30, 2006, http://www.newsclick.de/index.jsp/menuid/2046/artid/6037400 (accessed November 23, 2009).

Thelen, Sybille. "Ein deutscher Islam," *Stuttgarter Zeitung*, 15 October 2010.

Thomson, J. E. "State Sovereignty in International Relations," *International Studies Quarterly* 39 (1995), 213–33.

Thomson, J. E., and Stephen Krasner. "Global Transactions and the Consolidation of Sovereignty," in Ernst Otto Czempiel and James N. Rosenau, eds., *Global Changes and Theoretical Challenges*. Lanham, MD: Lexington Books, 1989.

Tincq, Henri. "Des organisations musulmanes réclament la saisie du livre," *Le Monde*, July 21, 1989.

———. Le débat sur "les foulards" et la laïcité: Les boutefeux de l'Islam, *Le Monde*, 10 August 1989.

Tincq, Henri, and Corinne Lesnes. "L'affaire des 'Versets sataniques' La communauté musulmane sous le choc," *Le Monde*, 2 March 1989.

Toepfer, Stefan. "Beim Islam-Unterricht keine Organisation ausschließen," http://www.faz.net/s/Rub8D05117E1AC946F5BB438374CCC294CC/Doc~ECB928

F7E8B1D41C9A92D70B846DAEACF~ATpl~Ecommon~Scontent.html (accessed April 13, 2009).

Topraki, Binnaz. "Islam and Democracy in Turkey," *Turkish Studies* 6, no. 2 (June 2005), 167–86.

Touraine, Alain, Michel Wieviorka, and François Dubet. *Le mouvement ouvrier.* Paris: Fayard, 1984.

Tribalat, Michèle. *Faire France: Une grande enquête sur les immigrés et leurs enfants.* Paris: La Découverte, 1985.

Tribalat, Michèle, and Jeanne-Hélène Kaltenbach. *La république et l'islam: entre crainte et aveuglement.* Paris: Gallimard, 2002.

Trigano, Shmuel. *La démission de la République: Juifs et musulmans en France.* Paris: les Presses Universitaires de France, 2003.

Tröndle, Dirk. "Die Freitagspredigten (hutbe) des Präsidiums für Religiöse Angelegenheiten (DİB) in der Türkei," KAS-Auslandsinformationen, 4/06, 52–78.

Turam, Berna. *Between Islam and the State: The Politics of Engagement.* Stanford, CA: Stanford University Press, 2007.

Türkisch-Islamische Union der Anstalt für Religion eV. "Historie," http://www.ditib.de/default1.php?id=5&sid=40&lang=de (accessed June 30, 2009).

UCIDE, "The creation of the Spanish Islamic Council," http://www.consejois lamico.es (accessed May 10, 2011).

UCOII. "Manifesto against terrorism and for life," Published in Corriere della Sera, September 2, 2004.

Ulfkotte, Udo. *Der Krieg in unseren Städten: wie radikale Islamisten Deutschland unterwandern*, 2003.

Ulrich, Ralf. "Migration und zukünftige Bevölkerungsentwicklung in Deutschland." In *Wirtschaftspolitische Herausforderungen an der Jahrhundertwende.* Hrsg. Von W. Franz. Tübingen: Mohr Siebeck, 2001, S. 181–200.

United Kingdom Islamic Mission. http://www.ukim.org/webpages/Branches_ Centres.aspx (accessed August 9, 2009).

United Kingdom Office for National Statistics. "The census in England and Wales 2001," http://www.ons.gov.uk/census/index.html.

Ventura, Marco. "Perspectives d'entente entre État et communautés islamiques. L'expérience Italienne," *PJR* 11, 1994, 101–50.

Vidino, Lorenzo. "The Muslim Brotherhood's Conquest of Europe," *Middle East Quarterly*, Winter 2005, http://www.meforum.org/687/the-muslim-brother hoods-conquest-of-europe (accessed June 9, 2009).

———. "Aims and Methods of Europe's Muslim Brotherhood," Hudson Institute, November 1, 2006, http://www.investigativeproject.org/173/aims -and-methods-of-europes-muslim-brotherhood (accessed June 22, 2009).

———. "Islam, Islamism and Jihad in Italy," *Current Trends in Islamist Ideology* 7 no. 85, 2008.

———. Vidino, Lorenzo. *The New Muslim Brotherhood in the West.* New York: Columbia University Press, 2010.

Vita.it, "I musulmani d'Italia: Chiuso l'incidente di Ratisbona," http://beta.vita .it/news/view/91867, May 13, 2009.

Vital, David. *A People Apart: The Jews in Europe, 1789–1933.* Oxford: Oxford University Press, 1999.

Waardenburg, J.D.J. "Muslim Associations and Official Bodies in some European Countries," in W. A. Shadid and P. S. van Koningsveld, eds., *The Integration of Islam and Hinduism in Western Europe*. Kampen: KOK Pharos Publishing House, 1991.

Walker, Martin. "The World's New Numbers," *Wilson Quarterly*, May 2009.

Warner, Carolyn M. *Confessions of an Interest Group: The Catholic Church and Political Parties in Europe*. Princeton, NJ: Princeton University Press, 2000.

Warner, Carolyn, and Manfred Wenner. "Religion and the Political Organization of Muslims in Europe," WCFIA Working Paper, Cambridge: Harvard University, 2000.

———. "Organizing Islam for Politics in Western Europe," WCFIA Working Paper, Cambridge: Harvard University, 2002.

———. "Religion and the Political Organization of Muslims in Europe," *Perspectives on Politics*, 2006.

Weber, Eugen. *Peasants into Frenchmen: The Modernization of Rural France, 1870–1914*. Palo Alto, CA: Stanford University Press, 1979.

Weber, Max. *On Law in Economy and Society*. Cambridge: Harvard University Press, 1967.

Weigel, George. *The Cube and the Cathedral: Europe, America, and Politics without God*. New York: Basic Books, 2005.

Weil, Patrick. "A nation in diversity: France, Muslims and the Headscarf," March 25, 2004. http://www.opendemocracy.net/faith-europe_islam/article_1811.jsp (accessed July 20, 2009).

———. "Access to Citizenship: A Comparison of Twenty-Five Nationality Laws," in T. Alexander Aleinikoff and Douglas Klusmeyer, eds., *Citizenship Today: Global Perspectives and Practices*. Washington, DC: Brookings Institution Press, 2001, 17–35.

Weiner, Myron. *The Global Migration Crisis*. New York: HarperCollins, 1995.

Weinryb, Bernhard Dov. *Jewish Emancipation under Attack*. New York: American Jewish Committee, 1942.

Welt-Online, "Religionsbeamter sieht Deutschland in Niedergang," *Welt-Online*, 3 November 2010.

Wendehorst, Stephan. "Emancipation as Path to National Integration," in Liedtke and Wendehorst, eds., *The Emancipation of Catholics, Jews and Protestants: Minorities and the Nation-State in 19th Century Europe*. Manchester: Manchester University Press, 1999, 188–206.

Wessels, Bernhard. "Interest Groups and Political Representation in Europe," Paper for presentation at the joint sessions of workshops of the ECPR Bern, February 27–March 4, 1997.

Westerlund, David, and Ingvar Svanberg. *Islam outside the Arab World*. Florence: Kentucky Routledge Curzon, 1999.

Williamson, Peter. *Varieties of Corporatism: A Conceptual Discussion*. New York: Cambridge University Press, 1985.

———. *Corporatism in Perspective: An Introductory Guide to Corporatist Theory*. London: Sage, 1989.

Wilson, Frank. *Interest Group Politics in France*. Ithaca, NY: Cornell University Press, 1987.

Winkler, J. T. "Law, State and Society: The Industry Act of 1975 in Context," *British Journal of Law and Society* 2, no. 2, 1979.

Wintour, Patrick. "Muslim groups draft rulebook for mosques to drive out extremists," *The Guardian*, October 30, 2007.

Woehrling, Jean-Marie. "Réflexions sur le principe de la neutralité de l'Etat en matière religieuse et sa mise en oeuvre en droit français," in Messner, ed., *Archives des sciences sociales des religions* 101, no. 101, 1998.

Wright, Lawrence. "The Terror Web," *The New Yorker*, July 26, 2004, 52.

Wutschke, Jürgen. "Crash-Kurs im Islam," July 5, 2007 http://www.tagesspiegel .de/berlin/Landespolitik-Integration;art124,2333810 (accessed November 23, 2009).

Yahmid, Hadi. "Brussels Mosques Neighborhood," Islam Online, http://www .islamonline.net/servlet/Satellite?c=Article_C&cid=1226471465581&page name=Zone-English-News/NWELayout (accessed June 22, 2009).

———. "Countries Fight Over French Muslims," Islam On-Line, April 27, 2008, http://www.islamonline.net/servlet/Satellite?c=Article_C&cid=1209049 708490&pagename=Zone-English-News/NWELayout.

Yavuz, Ercan. "German Culture Center Trains Turkish Imams for Europe," *Today's Zaman*, April 4, 2008.

Yavuz, Hakan. "Adalet ve Kalkinma Partisi (AKP)" The Oxford Encyclopedia of the Islamic World, Oxford: Oxford University Press, 2007–2009, http://www .oxfordislamicstudies.com/article/opr/t236/e0924 (accessed June 16, 2009).

Ye'or, Bat. *Eurabia: The Euro-Arab Axis.* Madison, NJ: Fairleigh Dickinson University Press, 2005.

Yildirim, Tuncay. "We decided not to attend," *Hurriyet Avrupa*, 3 June 2010.

Yildiz, Cemal. "Muttersprachliche Türkischunterricht in Deutschland," Istanbul: Marmara University, 2002, http://yadem.comu.edu.tr/1stELTKonf/GR_ Cem_Yildiz_Muttersprachlicher.htm (accessed July 27, 2009).

Yilmaz, Hacer, and Maxim Moussa. "Algeria," European Forum for Democracy and Solidarity, June 4, 2009, http://www.europeanforum.net/country/algeria (accessed July 5, 2009).

Yoldas, Mustafa. In Hamburg, quoted in Suleiman Wilms, "Ausbildung für Muslime," Islamische Zeitung, May 14, 2001.

Yukleyen, Ahmet. "State Policies and Islam in Europe: Milli Görüş in Germany and the Netherlands," *Journal of Ethnic and Migration Studies* 36, no. 3 (2010), 445–63.

Zaptcioğlu, Dilek. "Setting Guidelines for Islam and Politics," www.Qantara.de, October 5, 2004.

Zeghal, Malika, and George Holoch. *Islamism in Morocco: Religion, Authoritarianism, and Electoral Politics.* Princeton, NJ: Markus Wiener Publishers, 2008.

Zekri, Sonja. "God's Counterculture," 02/18/2008, http://www.qantara.de/ webcom/show_article.php/_c-476/_nr-924/i.html.

Zenit. "International Conference on religious life in Turkey," May 10, 2000, www.zenit.org, (accessed April 28, 2007), http://www.zindamagazine.com/ html/archives/2000/zn051600.htm (accessed August 3, 2009, stable URL).

Zincone, Giovanna, ed. "L'Islam contemporaneo in Europa e in Italia fra affermazione identitaria e nuova religione minoritaria," *Secondo rapporto sull'inte-*

grazione degli immigrati in Italia. Commisione per le politiche di integrazione degli immigrati, Bologna: Mulino, 2001.

Zoccatelli, Pierluigi. "La presenza islamica in Italia," *Vivere con l'Islam, Integrazione, coabitazione o conflitto?* Convegno a cura del gruppo di AN della camera dei deputati, November 22, 2000.

Zolberg, Ari, and Litt Woon Long. "Why Islam Is Like Spanish," in *Politics and Society* 27, no. 1, 1999.

Zoubir, Yahia H. "Algerian Islamists' conception of democracy," *Arab Studies Quarterly* (ASQ) 18, no. 3, Summer 1996, Academic OneFile. Gale. Boston College, June 12, 2009, http://find.galegroup.com.proxy.bc.edu/itx/infomark .do?&contentSet=IAC-Documents&type=retrieve&tabID=T002&prodId=A ONE&docId=A19129732&source=gale&srcprod=AONE&userGroupName= mlin_m_bostcoll&version=1.0. 2–3.

Index

Page numbers in **bold** type indicate illustrations.

PRINCETON STUDIES IN MUSLIM POLITICS

Series Editors: Dale F. Eickelman and Augustus Richard Norton

Diane Singerman, *Avenues of Participation: Family, Politics, and Networks in Urban Quarters of Cairo*

Tone Bringa, *Being Muslim the Bosnian Way: Identity and Community in a Central Bosnian Village*

Dale F. Eickelman and James Piscatori, *Muslim Politics*

Bruce B. Lawrence, *Shattering the Myth: Islam beyond Violence*

Ziba Mir-Hosseini, *Islam and Gender: The Religious Debate in Contemporary Iran*

Robert W. Hefner, *Civil Islam: Muslims and Democratization in Indonesia*

Muhammad Qasim Zaman, *The 'Ulama in Contemporary Islam: Custodians of Change*

Michael G. Peletz, *Islamic Modern: Religious Courts and Cultural Politics in Malaysia*

Oskar Verkaaik, *Migrants and Militants: Fun and Urban Violence in Pakistan*

Laetitia Bucaille, *Growing Up Palestinian: Israeli Occupation and the Intifada Generation*

Robert W. Hefner, ed., *Remaking Muslim Politics: Pluralism, Contestation, Democratization*

Lara Deeb, *An Enchanted Modern: Gender and Public Piety in Shi'i Lebanon*

Roxanne L. Euben, *Journeys to the Other Shore: Muslim and Western Travelers in Search of Knowledge*

Robert W. Hefner and Muhammad Qasim Zaman, eds., *Schooling Islam: The Culture and Politics of Modern Muslim Education*

Loren D. Lybarger, *Identity and Religion in Palestine: The Struggle between Islamism and Secularism in the Occupied Territories*

Augustus Norton, *Hezbollah: A Short History*

Bruce K. Rutherford, *Egypt after Mubarak: Liberalism, Islam, and Democracy in the Arab World*

Emile Nakhleh, *A Necessary Engagement: Reinventing America's Relations with the Muslim World*

Roxanne L. Euben and Muhammad Qasim Zaman, eds., *Princeton Readings in Islamist Thought: Texts and Contexts from al-Banna to Bin Laden*

Irfan Ahmad, *Islamism and Democracy in India: The Transformation of Jamaat-e-Islami*

Kristen Ghodsee, *Muslim Lives in Eastern Europe: Gender, Ethnicity, and the Transformation of Islam in Postsocialist Bulgaria*

John R. Bowen, *Can Islam Be French? Pluralism and Pragmatism in a Secularist State*

Thomas Barfield, *Afghanistan: A Cultural and Political History*

Emile Nakhleh, *A Necessary Engagement: Reinventing America's Relations with the Muslim World*

Sara Roy, *Hamas and Civil Society in Gaza: Engaging the Islamist Social Sector*

Michael Laffan, *The Makings of Indonesian Islam: Orientalism and the Narration of a Sufi Past*

Jonathan Laurence, *The Emancipation of Europe's Muslims: The State's Role in Minority Integration*